CW00850615

MAKE SOCIAL MEDIA WORK FOR YOUR BUSINESS

Alex Stearn

ISBN:
ISBN-13:978-1502911490
ISBN-10:1502911493

This book is dedicated
to Sonia, Tony and Ollie.

Table of Contents

Book Nine

Any Questions?

Thank you for your recent purchase of 'Make Social Media Work for your Business' I really hope you will enjoy the book and your business will benefit greatly.

If you have any questions about the book or about social media marketing in general, please do not hesitate to contact me by email at **alex@alexstearn.com** or on Facebook **at www.facebook.com/alexandrastearn** and I will do my best to reply as soon as possible. I also offer regular updates, ebooks and social media tips in my newsletter at www.alexstearn.com and a group on Facebook which is all about supporting each other in our social media efforts and networking. Would love you to come and join us at this link http://bit.ly/yourgroup

Looking forward to seeing you soon in the group

Why This Book?

SO YOU WANT to launch a social media marketing campaign for your business or maybe you've already done so and you're just not achieving the results you expected. Perhaps that's because you've found it difficult to build a sizeable following or your audience is simply not converting into paying customers.

Every day hundreds of businesses are setting out on their social media journey excited about the opportunities and possibilities that this relatively new type of marketing may be able to offer their business. Some are getting it right, reaping huge rewards, and managing to leverage the enormous power of the Internet through social media, but the majority are struggling to make it work at all. Those who are struggling often don't really understand exactly how social media works and launch into a campaign without any plan or strategy or without even knowing exactly what they are looking to achieve. They perhaps create a Facebook page and Twitter profile and ask their web developer to add a 'like' or 'follow' button to their website, invite their friends and customers to join their page, and then start posting updates. After a while they realize that whatever they are doing is having little or no positive effect on their sales and they are left with the same questions:

> How do I leverage the almighty power of the Internet and social media to make money for my business?
> How do I find the people who are interested in my products?
> How do I draw these people away from a social media platform and onto my website or blog?
> And the ultimate question, how do I convert all these people into

paying customers and actually profit from social media marketing?

These businesses either continue to go round in circles waiting for a miracle to happen, give up altogether, or continue to believe that there is a way they can make social media work for their business and start looking for a solution to solve their problem.

This is exactly what I did and this is where my social media journey began. I started to look for a solution but kept coming up with the same brick walls, the same fluffy vague information about engagement, and lots of very expensive courses. I read books and blogs but they never really seemed to solve my problem and get to the heart of the matter.

I then decided to make it my mission to demystify the hype surrounding social media marketing and discover everything I possibly could about how to make all the major social media platforms work for any business. I studied literally hundreds of campaigns to see what was working and what wasn't and completely immersed myself in social media marketing until all my questions were answered. My aim was to discover how to utilize the almighty power of social media to help any business achieve their marketing goals. I made it my mission to leave no stone unturned in terms of a marketing opportunity which could help any business generate leads and ultimately increase their sales.

After 18 months of immersing myself in this subject, I am now delighted to hand this information over to you. My goal is to help you save your time and your resources and provide you with a highly effective system to make social media work for your business. In this book I am going to share with you everything you need to know to take your business to the next level and leverage the power of social media so you can achieve the highest profits, the best customers, the best ambassadors for your business, and make money 24/7.

This book is perfect for anyone who is seriously committed to growing their business and achieving incredible results. Whether you are just starting out or already up and running and uncertain how to make social media work for your business then this book is to going to teach you exactly how to do just that. You will have absolutely everything you need to learn, prepare, plan, and implement a campaign which is going to help you generate leads and find new customers.

The fact is social media is a game changer, a dream come true for any business and has ·completely revolutionized the way business is being done today. However, it is still just a marketing tool and while on the face of it seems free, if not used correctly and effectively, it is simply just a waste of your time and resources.

In this book you will not only learn the skills and strategies of social media marketing but also everything you need to know about how social media works in marketing and how to plan, prepare, and execute your campaign including:

> What social media marketing is, why it is so good, why it is absolutely essential for any business today, and why so many businesses are getting it wrong
>
> The psychology behind why people make buying decisions and how you can use this knowledge to succeed in your social media campaign and other social media campaigns as well
>
> The importance of defining your business, your brand, and your target audience and how to do this
>
> How to set clear goals and objectives for your social media campaign
>
> How to prepare your website or blog for success, capture leads, and build a highly targeted list of subscribers
>
> How to plan, create, maintain, and manage your social media campaign

Detailed information about how to set up your business profile on the main social media platforms

The strategies you need to implement to attract the best prospects and build and maintain a targeted following on social media and build lasting relationships

The importance of content and how to easily find ideas to create content for your page

How to convert your followers into leads, paying customers, and ambassadors and brand advocates of your business

How to constantly measure and monitor your campaign so you can steer your campaign to achieve your goals

A great deal of love and joy has gone into writing this book. Love of the subject itself and joy at the opportunity to share with you the information and knowledge within. I have devoted 18 months to researching and writing this book, along with the others in the series, in order to uncover the truth about social media. I truly hope you will be inspired and that your business will thrive and flourish by implementing the suggested strategies.

Even within the time it has taken to write this book, certain things have changed in the social media world and so some sections have been updated to reflect those changes. The world of social media is dynamic and therefore it is my commitment to keep updating this book as those changes occur. If you wish to keep up-to-date with latest social media updates, tips, and changes, please subscribe to my newsletter at www.alexstearn.com

THE IMPORTANCE OF UNDERSTANDING SOCIAL MEDIA MARKETING

BEFORE LAUNCHING INTO your social media marketing campaign, and so that you are absolutely committed when you do start, you will need to be convinced that social media marketing does actually work for businesses and that you are going to be able to make it work for yours. In this chapter, you will learn why social media marketing has gained so much attention, why so many brands are using it, and why it is so different from other forms of marketing. The aim here is to help you truly appreciate the power and importance of this relatively new method of marketing. Once you are totally convinced that the time you will be investing will be truly worthwhile, you will be ready to launch into your social media marketing campaign with strength, confidence, and conviction.

So what is social media exactly? Social media is the place where people connect with other people using the technology we have today. It's where people engage, share, cooperate, interact, learn, enjoy, and build relationships. The number of ways in which we connect with each other has grown massively in recent years from telephone, mobiles, email, text, video, newspaper, or radio to what we have today, the social media networks.

As humans, the majority of us want to belong, be accepted, loved, respected, and heard. We are social animals and social media has provided us with new tools which allow us to be more social, even if our lives are more hectic and we are living a long way from our friends and family. It's now not unusual for family and friends to be located at opposite sides of the country or even in a different country. Our lives have become far busier and more transient than ever, and yet we still crave the same social connections as we did 100 years ago when we would probably have been living in the same village or town as our family and friends.

The impact that social media is having on our lives and on businesses is massive. Social media has completely changed the way we communicate and the way we do everything. It has made connecting with people and building relationships so much easier. Now, staying in contact with someone we may only have met once is straightforward. We can find old friends we went to school or college with, and the opportunities for making new contacts are limitless. Social media has given us the ability to quickly and easily share ideas, experiences, and information on anything we like, and we can find out about anyone, any business, or anything. With the massive growth in smartphone ownership, most people can now access the internet instantly. We are living in a virtual world and we can literally connect to anyone, from anywhere, at anytime.

Understanding the reasons why people love social media so much will help give you a really good idea about how, as a business, you need to engage so you can connect,grow and maintain that your audience. Most people are on social media to be social, to connect with other family and friends, and to have fun. However, here are a few more reasons why so many use and love social media:

To be part of a community or common interest group
To express their feelings and have a voice
To reconnect with old college or school friends
To find out where their friends are
To tell their friends where they are
To announce a piece of news
To find out if a product or service is good
To connect with thought leaders

To make business contacts

To follow brands

To keep up-to-date with current affairs, football scores etc

To connect with famous people

To find inspiration and motivation

To learn by reading blogs, watching videos, and listening to podcasts

To help other people

To launch a business

To advertise and grow a business

To make new friends

To make new contacts

To connect with others in different countries

To make a difference

To be entertained

To communicate quickly and save time

To support important causes or people

To find a job

The power and enormity of social media

Everyone is doing Social! Okay, so not everyone is, but the majority of people are! Wherever you go you will see somebody with their heads down looking at some device, and you can bet your bottom dollar that they are accessing some social site, whether it's Facebook, Twitter, Instagram, LinkedIn, YouTube, Google+, Pinterest, or Snapchat.

The growth in social media is huge, and it's no wonder that it is being called 'The Social Media Revolution.' Without going into too much statistical information, it's safe to say that your customer is probably using at least one social network, either for personal or business use, and they very likely accessing multiple sites.

All the social media platforms are growing at incredible speeds. You only have to type 'Social media statistics' into Google and you will blown away by figures in the millions and billions. Facebook now has over one billion users and 95% of those users access it at least once a day and some more than five times, a day More than one billion unique users visit YouTube per month, and Twitter has 215 monthly active users. The most popular websites are social. The world loves being on social.

WHAT IS SOCIAL MEDIA MARKETING

Not long ago promoting a business could feel very much like being alone on a desert island. You could have a great idea but unless you had vast sums of money for television, magazine or direct mail advertising then frustratingly your idea was very likely to remain a secret. Today it is totally different and social media has given businesses endless opportunities to reach their target audience, connect with new prospects and enter new markets. The playing field has been levelled out and now anyone with the right knowledge has more chance than ever of making their business a success.

Social media marketing is a relatively new form of marketing and refers to the processes, strategies and tactics used by businesses on social networking sites and blogs to gain attention and ultimately increase their revenue. Businesses and large brands are now using the fact that people love to engage and connect with other people with the other very important fact that they are very likely to find their target audience on social media so that they can do the following:

- Find, reach and connect with potential customers.
- Drive traffic to a website or blog.
- Stay connected with, and communicate with, existing customers. It is a well known fact that existing customers are far more likely to purchase and also pay more for a product than someone who has not bought before.
- To build trust, interest and loyalty by interacting with your followers (potential customers) so that ultimately they will purchase your product, continue to purchase your products and hopefully recommend your product to their friends.

- To produce content that users will share with their social network or recommend to their friends. Social media marketing strongly centres around the creation of content for a particular audience with the intention that it can be shared , liked and commented by on the user. When this happens the content is being passed to other users by word of mouth, the most powerful form of advertising.
- To listen and find out what your customers want.

THE BIG LINK, THE PSYCHOLOGY BEHIND BUYING BEHAVIOUR

Not only have successful marketeers recognised that people want to engage with people, they have also tapped into the psychology behind why people make buying decisions and incorporated this into their social media campaigns.

As a business you will need to understand a great deal about your customers in order to market your products successfully to your target audience. Understanding how and why people make the final purchase decision will go a long way in understanding how you can actually make social media marketing work for your business. There seem to be a number of common factors that influence consumers when they are making their buying decision. Leveraging and using this knowledge with your social media campaign is incredibly powerful and a recipe for success.

The Like Factor

This is a Biggie. When we look at the findings and the psychology behind buying decisions it often comes down to simply being likeable. Consumers are far more likely buy a product from someone they like, respect or trust. Word of mouth advertising has always proven to be the most powerful form of advertising and now social media has taken this to another level and managed to harness this online with the like, follow, subscribe or +1 button. Having your business name or brand reach hundreds or even thousands of people is now possible and someone only has to 'like' or interact with your business on social media and you can almost guarantee that someone else will see it. The truth is people do business with people they like and are more likely to spread the word to their network about deals and special offers from people they like, trust and respect.

Social proof

When a consumer finds themselves at a point of indecision they will look for social proof and seek advice and corroboration from others. They are far more likely to buy if they see that their friends or a similar group of people have bought or used product. People generally look to others for advice or look to see what others are buying to get over their personal insecurity when making a buying decision. This is why you see so many women shopping in pairs, the opinion of a friend about an item can often be the deciding factor when making the decision to buy or not.

A recent study revealed that Facebook is the most trusted platform when it comes to product or service recommendations. This is where the Facebook plugins come in, they actually display social proof by showing the faces of your friends or a number count of the people who 'liked' the product, article or page. The reason this is so powerful with social media marketing is simply because seeing a large number of people 'liking' a product or service can be enough to persuade someone to make a buying decision, to read something or follow a business. The truth is that people trust the opinion of others more than they trust advertising and in order to make social media marketing work then businesses need to leverage this fact.

Authority and reviews

Even before the internet was introduced people have been keen to find reviews about products they were interested in buying particularly if they were planning to make a major purchase. They would either buy a special magazine or believe an authoritative figure on a TV advertisement. Today however shoppers are far more savvy, they can smell an advert a mile off and they will go out of their way to find honest reviews about something they may want to buy. They are also spoilt for choice not only with the number of products available to them but they can find a review about literally anything just by a simple search on the internet or looking at a brand's social media pages. People always have and always will want as much evidence as possible that they are making the right buying decision. Any business who wants to succeed today needs to embrace this fact and try and gain as many reviews for their products and services as possible. Reviews could be in the form of customer blog articles, reviews on your website, on social media sites or articles in newspapers and magazines. Displaying articles, client testimonials or the logos of magazines that you have been featured in on your website will also go a long way to building authority and gaining the trust of your prospects.

Scarcity or exclusivity

Scarcity or exclusivity can play a big part in people buying decisions and social media is the perfect place to communicate and use this factor to sell your products. If a product is scarce or less available the consumer will often perceive that this product has greater value and as they become less available the consumer fears that they may lose out on a great deal or a one time offer. Giving your prospects a deadline or a specific time to purchase something or redeem an offer is an incredibly powerful way of focussing their mind to make a decision. When they know they need to make that decision by a certain time or they may lose out on a one time deal they are far more likely to make that decision. Another very effective way of using this factor is by simply suggesting to your prospects that by signing up for your email opt-in, they will be the first to hear about your new products, or your exclusive offers.

Consistency

Consumers do not like taking risks and often prefer to repeat their past purchasing behaviour by buying from a brand they have bought from before. The majority of shoppers are brand loyal and social media is another way of nurturing this type of behaviour by building up even deeper relationships with your customers through constant contact and updates.

Reciprocation

Reciprocation is a very powerful factor to take into consideration if you are looking to succeed on social media. As humans, the majority of us have a natural desire to repay favours and with social media you can really put this into practise. If you show support by either liking, sharing or commenting on other peoples content not only will it attract their attention they will, more often than not, return the favour by 'liking,' commenting and sharing your content. Also if you are sharing great content on your network or offering good, valuable and free advice you are very likely to earn a great deal of respect and this will often result in a good pay back of some sort.

WHY IS SOCIAL MEDIA MARKETING SO GOOD FOR YOUR BUSINESS?

We know that an enormous number of people are accessing the social networks to connect with each other and now we need to understand why this type of marketing is so different from other forms of marketing and why it is so important for your business. The main reason is that social media marketing is fundamentally more effective. Consumers today are smart, they are tired and suspicious of traditional forms of advertising, more often than not they will fast forward a TV commercial, switch channel or skip a printed page with an advertisement on it. Todays consumers want to hear that a product has been tried and tested, they want to see a product being demonstrated and they often need a recommendation from a trusted source to make a purchase, most probably a friend. Here are some reasons why social media marketing is more effective than other more traditional marketing methods:

Social media offers you the opportunity to find the right target audience

Never before has it been so easy to find and access your target audience. With the information that most of the social networks hold about their users you can now target and find the very people who are more likely to buy your products or services.

Social media allows you to have a direct contact with your customer

Literally you have the opportunity to communicate directly and stay in touch with your customer, unlike traditional forms of advertising. For example, with a Facebook business page , a 'places' page, A Google + page or a page on Foursquare you can stay in touch with your customers well after they have left your establishment or bought your product and you can send them offers to encourage them to return or buy again.

Social media marketing harnesses the power of peer recommendation

The majority of people trust recommendations by others. Social media marketing is the only media that can harness the most powerful form of advertising, word of mouth, by making it possible for consumers to communicate with each other and vote for products or services by pressing the 'like' or 'follow' button.

Helps builds your brand

Never has there been so much opportunity to build your brand. Your brand is simply the most valuable asset of your business. Your brand is what differentiates you from other businesses, it is the image people have of your business and it establishes loyalty. With social media you have the opportunity to engage with consumers and build positive brand associations in a way that no other media can. Consumers now have the choice and opportunity to follow your brand and if they do, this means they actually want to hear or see what you have to say.

Humanises your brand

Social media allows you to communicate with your audience in a totally unique way. Your brand is no longer a rigid logo but a personality, not only can you show your appreciation and the value you place on your audience but they can also grow to love your brand too. No other type of marketing allows this type of two way live communication.

Offers continual exposure to your product

Social media marketing allows you to be continually in contact with your followers. Once you have your audience they can hear from you and see your brand on a daily basis. Statistics prove that on average a person needs to see or connect with a brand 7 times before purchasing. This is a difficult and costly goal to achieve with traditional forms of advertising but incredibly easy with social media marketing.

The Consumer has a choice

Unlike other traditional methods of advertising the consumer has the opportunity to be exposed to your product by choice, they can opt in or out whenever they want.

Your audience is relaxed and receptive

The majority of people are accessing social accounts to be social and in their own leisure time. Social media is all about connecting with friends and relatives, meeting new people and making new contacts. People are far more receptive to hearing from a brand in their own time when they are relaxed, as long as the brand is not continually pushing their product.

You can continually engage with your audience

Social media marketing allows you to have an ongoing dialogue with your audience like no other media. Fans or followers who have interacted with a business on social media are far more likely to visit their online store than those who did not.

It's viral

Once your followers choose to interact or share your content then this interaction is seen by their network of friends who are then also exposed to your brand. This is how viral growth happens which results in audience growth and brand awareness, more prospects, more customers and increased sales.

Social media is an asset to your business

Unlike other forms of advertising where you see your marketing investment disappear your social media account becomes a valuable asset. If you are using your social media marketing correctly your network will grow, you will be building trust and your asset will increase in value. With traditional advertising once an advert is delivered the connection with the buyer is over and you see your investment literally disappear.

It is like having your own broadcasting channel

Once you have your campaign set up and your follower numbers are growing, you literally have your very own broadcasting channel which you own. You can communicate with your followers about anything 24/7. Nobody can take this away unless of course you are not running it correctly and you are losing followers. If you provide content that is so useful and interesting, your followers will keep coming back again and again to check if you have anything new to say. You then have a following of people who will associate your valuable content and their positive experience with your brand.

You can offer your customers proof of trading

Having a social media presence which is active and engaging helps to reassure customers that your business actually exists. They can easily check, by comments left by customers, whether your business is reputable and trustworthy and they are far more likely to buy from you once they see your active presence on social media.

Improve your search engine ranking

Google counts social sharing when ranking your website or blog. If people are finding your content valuable then the search engines will register that and then rank you accordingly. Social media sites are highly ranked in the search engines and having a well optimized profile is yet another way of being found on the internet.

Opens up a worldwide playing field

It used to be only the large companies who could afford to build their brand and have the opportunity to access thousands of potential customers. Now everybody with a business has the opportunity to reach thousands of people both nationally and globally, grow their business and benefit from one of the most powerful forms of marketing. Having a business no longer has to be a lonely island you literally have the opportunity to get your message heard by thousands of people through social networking.

Provides advantages for the consumer

With just a few clicks of the mouse or the tap of a smart phone, consumers can be in contact with any business very quickly. For once their opinions are important, taken seriously and valued, they can contact a brand for customer service issues or just follow a brand because they are interested. For the first time they have a voice and a very powerful one. This is showing in the continual rise in the number of people following brands. People want to remain close to the brands they are interested in.

You can listen to your customers.

You can now hear what your customers are saying about your product or service and you can use this information to improve or develop your products and improve your customer service. This will result in your business becoming more transparent and shows your customers that you care and value their opinion which ultimately leads to more trust for your brand.

You can become a thought leader.

By producing valuable and rich content for your audience you can become a thought leader. Not only will this help if you are a personal brand but will also help in building respect and reputation for any business or brand.

You can make a difference.

With social media you can actually make a positive difference to people's lives. Once you know your audience you can provide content for them which is of value to them and is actually going to help them in some way. Helping your audience like this goes a long way and will hopefully result in them remembering your business when they are ready to make that purchasing decision.

Endless opportunities.

Never has there been so much opportunity to have direct access to so many people and neither has there been so much opportunity for businesses of any size to have ongoing contact with so many of their potential customers. This is a marketeer or business owner's dream.

IS SOCIAL MEDIA ACTUALLY WORKING FOR BUSINESS?

It is evident that the majority of major brands are running successful social media marketing campaigns. These brands are investing huge amounts of money, time and resources into this type of marketing, however you don't have to go too far to see whether social media marketing is actually working for business, simply ask yourself these questions:

- Would you prefer to buy a product if you knew that a friend or somebody you know of had tried it?

- Would you prefer to buy a product from a business or person that you do know rather than a business or person that you don't

17

know?

- If you were thinking of buying a product from a business you had no history with, would you go and look to see if they had a social media site and see what other people were saying about their product?

If you answered yes to these questions then you can be pretty sure that social media marketing does actually work for businesses. It has to work doesn't it?

WHY SO MANY BUSINESSES ARE GETTING IT WRONG

Even though most business owners have heard how powerful social media marketing can be the majority are still unsure as to how to use it to benefit their business. So many social media profiles have been created with enthusiasm only to be abandoned a couple of months even weeks down the line. Others are painstakingly posting consistently every day but posting the wrong type of content without a clue how to get their fans to buy their products. Many businesses are just paying lip service and seem to think that displaying a few social media icons on their site is enough to miraculously increase their revenue and some are not even connected to any networks at all. Although on the face of it, social media marketing seems free it actually takes a sizeable investment of man hours, and if you are getting it wrong you may as well be throwing a great deal of money out of the window. Here are some common reasons why so many businesses are getting it wrong:

Not 100% committed and convinced Many businesses are not convinced that it actually works at all and therefore are not prepared to put in the time it takes to learn how to plan and implement the effective strategies it takes to build a successful campaign. As a result their campaign falls flat and they simply give up after a few months.

Little or no understanding about how social media marketing works Many still think that setting up a profile and putting an icon on their website is what it's all about. They may even post a few status updates and post some pictures of their product in the hope that their website is suddenly going to be inundated with new traffic and think that these new visitors are miraculously going to convert into customers.

They don't understand the fact that fans and followers are worthless unless they know what to do with them Just because a business has maybe 1000 or 30,000 fans or followers, does not mean this will automatically transfer to their balance sheet. Fans are just fans, and as long a business doesn't know what do with those fans they will stay as just fans and not customers.

Not understanding the psychology behind buying decisions They have absolutely no idea about the psychology behind how and why people make buying decisions and therefore, do not know how to use this knowledge to their advantage in their campaign.

Lack of clear goals Aimlessly sharing content on their network without setting specific and measurable goals is just a waste of time and resources.

Not having a system to capture and convert leads Building a following is almost useless if those followers are not visiting the business' website or subscribing to the newsletter so that they can be converted into paying customers. Many businesses are still not making lead capture one of their main goals.

Unrealistic expectations Social media is a long terms strategy, it needs to be an integral part of a business' marketing plan and today it's as important as any other daily task a business may undertake. It is not a one size fits all solution and is not a solution for overnight success. It takes careful planning and long term commitment.

The wrong audience It's no good having a huge number of fans if they are not the correct audience. There are even sites where you can buy fans, but if they are not the right audience then they are very unlikely to be interested in what that business has to offer.

Not enough followers The majority of businesses are going to need a sizeable audience to make any impact at all, and although engagement is important, unless a business has a healthy number of followers it's not going to be a great deal of benefit.

Not being proactive Many businesses seem to assume that people are just going to press the 'like' or 'follow' button on their blog or website. Unfortunately it doesn't work like that and people generally need a good reason or incentive to follow a business, unless it's a very well known brand.

Trying to push their products all the time This is not what social media marketing is about and businesses that continually push their products are just missing the whole point of how social media marketing works and will lose followers as a result.

Posting too little, posting too often, or posting the wrong content altogether
If you post too much your posts will be considered as spam. If you post too little you will just be forgotten and if you post the wrong content you will not attract the right audience which may harm your brand. In an online survey top three reasons for losing fans were:

i.) The Company posted too frequently
ii.) The business pushed their products too much
iii.) The business posted offensive content

HOW TO RUN A SUCCESSFUL SOCIAL MEDIA MARKETING CAMPAIGN, AN OVERVIEW

ONCE YOU HAVE made the decision to be 100% committed to your campaign, you fully understand the theory behind it, and you plan and implement the strategies and tactics outlined in this book your business is going to reap the benefits and you will in time develop an extremely valuable asset. One thing is for certain: if you choose to ignore social media, you can be sure that your competition will not and you'll be allowing them to steal the advantage. Social media is a powerful way to increase your revenue by driving sales, increasing customer loyalty, and building your brand while at the same time pushing down your cost of sales, marketing, customer service, and much more. Now let's get started!

So how do you leverage the power of social media and put it to work to benefit your business and produce amazing results? This chapter is designed to give you a brief overview about what is required to build a successful campaign so that as you read each chapter it will make more sense. Every aspect of this overview and everything you need to do and implement will be mapped out in more detail in the subsequent chapters.

The opportunity to reach an unlimited number of new contacts and prospects is available to every business today. You can safely say that your prospects are out there and all you need to do is know where to find them, how to connect with them, and how to capture and convert them into your customers.

Successful businesses are using social media in a totally different way from traditional methods of marketing. With social media marketing there is no need to employ pushy sales techniques. Once you put the essential work, planning, and system in place, you will find your products are practically selling themselves and your prospects are buying your products and becoming your brand advocates as a natural progression from your initial contact with them. The whole process is straightforward and as long as you carry out the necessary background work, planning, and preparation, you can make it work for your business.

Know what you want

You need to have a very good idea where you want your business to be in the next one to three years. If you don't know what you want, then it is unlikely that your business will achieve anywhere near its potential. When you have a clear vision for your business, it helps you to focus and create the necessary goals you need to put into place to achieve that vision.

Define your business, brand, and target audience

Brands establish customer loyalty, and social media offers you a huge opportunity to build your brand. In order to communicate in the right way, you need to create and consistently deliver the right message and brand experience to your prospects and customers. To do this, you need to define your business and define and understand your target audience so you can create your brand.

Choose your social media platform/platforms

Many business become overwhelmed with the number of social media platforms available to promote their business. What you decide to do, will of course depend on the size of your business and the resources available to you. If you are a large businesses or brand then you may have the resources to be able to actively and consistently post unique content to all the different platforms and engage with your followers. However, if you are a smaller business it does not need to be overwhelming and can be very straightforward, you simply need to be where your audience are. May be your audience are big fans of Pinterest or LinkedIn, if this is the case then this is where you should be concentrating your efforts. If you are concerned that you are possibly missing out then you can create a presence on all the major platforms and simply post content using a social media management system like Hootsuite or Buffer. This way you can be confident you are not missing out and if anyone visits your website or blog they can follow you on their preferred network. There is one must have, and that is Facebook, it is becoming increasingly important to have a presence on Facebook. Many consumers will search to see if a business has a page on Facebook just to see if they are active and what their fans are saying about them. Having an active presence on Facebook can help to create immediate trust with consumers when they see that you have fans and they are engaging on your page.

Whether or not to employ a social media marketing agency
There will come a time when you have to decide whether you are going to manage your social media in house or employ a specialist agency to do the job. You may even decide to launch your campaign with assistance from an agency and then take it over once it is up and running.

Whatever your decide is going to depend on the size and type of your business and the resources available to manage your campaign. Many businesses run their campaigns in house while others prefer to use an agency. If you are a solopreneur you may decide you do not have the time to consistently create and post content on a day to day basis. You may decide that you are better off paying a flat monthly fee to an agency to take care and manage your campaign.

There are advantages and disadvantages to both methods. A good agency will have the expertise and knowledge to create and manage the campaign. It can often save you money and time but also it is unlikely they will be able to offer you any guarantees. You will need to keep a constant eye on your campaign to see if it is being managed properly and also listen to what is being said. If you do decide to go with an agency then you need to make sure that you have clearly communicated your goals and that they will be able to offer you evidence that they are bringing you a return on your investment.

If you decide to manage your social media marketing in house there are many advantages. You are going to know your business, brand and product better than any agency. It's much more likely that you are going to be far more sincere, caring, transparent and engaged with your audience than any outsider which will go a long way in building lasting relationships. Managing your own campaign will guarantee that you know what is going on all the time with your fans and followers. The main advantage of keeping it in house is that nobody else is going to care and pay attention to your campaign as you will.

If you do decide to manage in house you are going to have to make sure that you or whoever you appoint has the skills and knowledge required to be the authentic voice of your brand. Many businesses give this job to the new intern which is fine as long as the intern has been fully trained and has the knowledge to be able to speak in the voice of the brand. Whoever you decide to run the campaign needs to be either given a social media plan or be involved in creation of the plan and they will need the skills, materials and resources to carry out that plan.

Plan, plan, plan

Social media is not a quick fix. The majority of businesses start a campaign and then fall by the wayside. If you want to grow your business, then careful planning is required and it will involve creating your mission statement, setting clear and measurable goals and objectives, and planning your content strategy in line with who and what your target audience wants. Without a carefully crafted plan your campaign is extremely unlikely to reach its full potential.

Prepare your business

Before launching your campaign you need to prepare your whole business so your brand and your brand message are evident throughout.

You will need to communicate your brand through everything your do or say. This includes your website or blog, all your marketing material, brochures, promotional material and your email.

Your website is one of the best sales people you can have. It works 24/7 and can help to make your business turn up in your customer's home at the click of a mouse. When your prospect arrives on your website it immediately needs to make them feel that they have arrived at the right place, that you understand their needs, and that you can either provide a solution or give them exactly what they want. If you already have a website, you need to check that it has all the necessary features it takes to grab your visitors' attention, deliver the right message, capture them, and convert them into customers. Statistics prove that unless a business has a clever method of capturing leads, the majority of visitors to a website will leave without buying anything or ever returning again. Therefore, before even starting your social media campaign, you will need to check or create your website so that it does the job it is supposed to, which is to capture leads for later sales conversion.

Set up your email campaign

Email is still one of the most effective methods of converting leads, and an up-to-date list of prospects who have given their permission for you to contact them on a regular basis has got to be one of your business' most valuable assets. Capturing email addresses on your website and through social media needs to be your most important marketing goal. Therefore, you will need to plan your opt-in campaign and set up an account with an email provider so you can continue to build a relationship with your prospects and sell your products.

Create your social media profile/profiles

Your profile on social media will in many cases be the first impression your prospects have about your business and is as important as your website or blog. The aim of your business profile is to capture your prospects so that you can continue to communicate and build a relationship with them through the chosen platform and through email. It is unlikely that the majority of your followers or fans will return to your main profile after their initial visit. Therefore your profile needs to grab your prospect's attention as quickly as possible and also needs to prompt them to take some kind of action by liking or following, and joining your opt-in list.

Create your social media posting calendar

Social media is not like traditional forms of advertising so frequently pushing your products, posting adverts and plugging your business is not going to work and is likely to lose you fans. One of the most important things you are going to have to do for a successful social media campaign is to regularly produce and post compelling content that your audience actually wants to engage with and share. Social media marketing is all about selling without selling and the aim of producing content is not to directly sell your products but to do the following:

- Boost traffic to your blog or website, generate, capture and nurture leads.
- Create brand awareness.
- Constantly remind your audience of your brand so when they are ready to buy they buy from you.
- Improve your ranking in the search engines.
- Create engagement, build relationships and encourage your audience to share your content with their friends.
- Support others by liking, commenting on and sharing their content.
- Stand out as a thought leader and build your reputation as an expert in your industry.
- Create such good content that your audience stays liking your page and continuing to read your updates which builds and encourage brand loyalty.

Your content is where you can connect with your audience through their interests and passions. Your quality of content needs to be outstanding and you need to delight your audience with the best possible fresh, new and compelling material, excellence is what you should be aiming for every time you post. The biggest thing to remember is that you need to tailor all your content to your audience's desires and needs.

Once you are absolutely clear about who your target audience is, what makes them tick, and what their values and aspirations are you can determine what subjects and topics they will be interested in. The majority of the content you post will need to be about their needs and not yours. There is nothing more off putting and likely to lose you followers than continually posting about your business and shouting about your products or services. Of course you can do this occasionally if you have new products or special offers but you need to be selective otherwise your posts just become bad noise. Remember your followers are mostly on social to be social and if your posts ruin their social experience they will associate your brand with a bad experience and it won't be long before you start losing your fans and potential customers.

When you have decided on the subjects and topics you are going to create content about, then you will need to create a social media posting calendar which will help you to consistently deliver this high quality content. You will need to incorporate everything in this calendar including any events you are planning, any special industry events, public holidays, blog posts, videos and offers or contests you may be planning. You then need to map it all out so you know exactly how you are going to promote them on social media with the functionality you have available to do so.

Build a sizeable and highly targeted following

The main aim of building your audience is to grow a community of followers who are interested in your products, will engage with your content, and become advocates for your brand. In order to have any impact at all you are going to need a sizeable number of targeted fans or

27

followers. Building your audience will be an ongoing task, and it involves many different strategies which will be covered in this book. The size of audience and time it takes will depend on the time and resources you have available.

The essential day-to-day activity

To build a strong presence, trust, relationships, and reputation, you will need to be active and nurture your fans. Social media is not a one-way street. It's an ongoing two-way communication. It's about going out and showing that you are interested in what others have to say, and it's about building community and getting your brand out there in the most positive light possible. Here are some of the things you will need to do on a day-to-day basis:

- Consistently post high-quality content
- Follow your followers and fans
- Engage, comment, share, and reply
- Show your audience you value and respect them
- Follow influencers in your niche
- Deal with negative comments

Analyzing and measuring your campaign results

This book is all about how to make social work for your business, and the only way you are going to find out if it is working or not is by constantly monitoring and analyzing your results. You will need to constantly check your results against the goals and objectives you have set. Once you know what is working and what is not then you can adjust and steer your campaign accordingly to achieve more positive results.

Make Facebook Work For Your Business

Alex Stearn

Table of Contents

Chapter One

Getting Started on Facebook

It is quite unlikely that any business today is going to limit itself to just one social media platform for marketing but there is one 'must have,' which is, of course, Facebook.

Facebook's mission is to give people the power to share and make the world more open and connected. Saying that Facebook has been successful in achieving their mission is an understatement. With over one billion users, Facebook is now the most popular social network and the largest referrer of traffic after Google. More time is spent on Facebook than any other social network.

Many businesses and most major brands now have a page on Facebook, and it's getting to the stage that not having a business presence on Facebook looks odd. Just seeing the number of fans and activity on the page will often be enough to reassure a prospective customer that the business is bona fide. It's now common practice for individuals to check to see if a business has an active Facebook page and see what other people are saying before purchasing.

Facebook offers endless marketing opportunities for both businesses and individual brands, and this book will offer you a comprehensive guide on how to harness the enormous power of Facebook to drive a successful marketing campaign and actually make Facebook work for your business.

This chapter will cover will cover getting started on Facebook, setting up your personal profile, creating your Facebook page, and getting it ready for business. To get started, here are a few basics about what a personal account is, what a Facebook page is, what a Facebook group is, and definitions of the terms that are commonly used on Facebook.

THE BASICS

Each person who sets up a Facebook account is permitted to have just one account and one login. Personal timelines are for individuals to post status updates for their friends. They are not for commercial use and must be under the individual's name.

You are allowed up to 5000 friends on Facebook and if your goal is to share your personal status updates with a broader audience than just your friends, you can allow an unlimited number of people to follow you. Your followers will see your status updates that you post publicly in their News Feed. However, if your goal is to promote your business, under Facebook's terms and conditions, you will need to create a Facebook page.

Facebook Pages

Facebook pages can be created by the official representative of a business, brand, organization , or celebrity. They are similar to personal timelines but unlike your personal profile, they are visible to everyone on the Internet and offer businesses. It gives you the chance to connect with a wider audience of Facebook users. Pages, therefore, offer numerous marketing opportunities for businesses to gain attention, build awareness of their brand, drive traffic to a website or blog, and ultimately increase sales.

Pages allow businesses to connect and share their content and updates with a fan base of customers and prospects who have voluntarily chosen to 'like' a page. People who 'like' a page will see the activity from that page in their News Feed. Businesses can then grow their target audience by either using Facebook advertising, encouraging their audience to share and engage with their content, and other marketing strategies.

Creating a page for your business allows you much more functionality than just having a follow button on your personal profile. They can be customized with the addition of apps, stores, events, and lots more, and they can be managed by the page creator. Admins have a profile on Facebook and have been appointed by the page owner.

Facebook Groups

Facebook groups are where people can share their interests and opinions with others who have similar interests. Anyone can create a group around a common interest from their personal timeline. As with pages, group status updates will appear in the group members' News Feed, and they can share and comment with other members of that group. If a group is under 5000 members you can send updates to the group which will arrive in the members' Facebook mail.

Groups are more personal in nature than pages because the administrators have more control over who can join and participate and whether the group is publicly available or by invitation only. Groups are great for organizations , clubs, fan clubs, causes, church groups, and employee groups.

Facebook groups can have a number of administrators and be set up if you want more personal interaction, as the posts come from the administrators themselves rather than the page name since they are connected to the administrator's personal profile.

As a group, you have the ability to only let certain people join and you can set joining permissions. There are three types of groups:

Closed - users need approval from an administrator of the group to join.

Open - anyone can join.

Secret - by invitation only. Businesses often use the Facebook group function to create a 'Secret Group' where only the group members can see the posts. Secret groups offer a more private work and communication area and are ideal for coaching groups, groups set up to organize an event, or groups of people working together on an idea. Posts from group members will appear in the news feed of all the group members, everyone in the group can use the chat feature; documents and photos can be shared among members.

You may want to create a group to build awareness around a certain product, but you need to think carefully about whether you have the time to manage both a group and a page. Joining a group which is already running may be a better option for you. This will obviously depend on the resources you have available.

YOUR FACEBOOK DICTIONARY

Just in case you are unfamiliar with Facebook terminology, here are the common Facebook Terms and their definitions:

Timeline: Your timeline or profile shows a history of all your status updates, photos and videos, and anything you have posted.

News Feed: This is where you see all the status updates of your friends, people you follow, and pages you have liked.

Cover Photo: This is the large picture that spans the space at the top of your page.

Profile Photo: This is the small box at the top left of your profile where you can display your photo or maybe a logo on your page.

Friend: A connection on your personal profile is called a friend.

Friend request: This is a request you send to another user, or they send to you, so you can connect and view each other's status updates.

Status Update: This is anything you post in the status update box. This could be an image, text, video, or podcast.

Like: This is the action taken that shows your approval of an update from one of your friends or an update from a page you have liked.

Comment: Users can leave a comment in the comment section of any status update from a friend or page they have liked.

Share: If you see an update that you like and you want your friends to see this update you can share it on your timeline by pressing the 'share' button. This includes anything from within Facebook and outside of Facebook on external websites which are accompanied by the share button.

Message: A message is a private message that you can send another Facebook user.

Poke: The poke is a gesture on Facebook used to get someone's attention.

Pages: Facebook pages are for businesses, organizations , celebrities, and bands.

Privacy settings: Privacy settings let users control who can see their posts.

Tagging/Tags: Users can tag other users in posts and photos. When someone is tagged, the post will appear in their timeline.

Reach: This is the number of people who see a status update.

Admin: This is a user who is given access to a business page and can make changes to it.

Chat: This is the instant messaging service that is available to all users on their personal profile.

The Ticker: The ticker is a column on the right side of your News Feed that lets you see things as they happen on Facebook in real time. If you have the subscribers' button activated on your personal profile, your public notifications will appear in the ticker of your subscribers. You can interact with any item on the ticker by hovering over any item. Every time you add a picture to either your personal profile or your business page it will appear in the ticker. Also, any comment that has been made on any post will appear in the ticker. Basically, the ticker lets you see things as they happen.

SETTING UP YOUR PERSONAL PROFILE

The first thing you need to do if you have not already done so is to set up your Facebook account. This is very straightforward and once you have created your personal profile, you will be able to create your business page or a Facebook group. If you do not already have a personal profile on Facebook you will be offered the option to create a page for a celebrity, band, or business. Do not be tempted to click this or you will set up a business account which is quite different from a Facebook page which is attached to a personal profile. A business account does not offer you the marketing opportunities that a page offers and you cannot have a personal profile and a business profile under the Facebook terms and conditions. Basically if you choose a business account over a personal profile you will be unable to utilize certain aspects of Facebook such as:

- You will have limited functionality
- You will not be found in 'search'
- You cannot send or receive friend requests because you will not have a personal profile
- You cannot build apps
- You can only build one Facebook page

NB If you do already have a personal profile and you want to use this for business, you can convert this into a business page. However, all in our slightly this is not recommended for the reasons above. It's always best to have a personal profile and then create a page for your business, and when you are completing your personal profile you will need to use your own name and not your business name. Facebook terms and conditions state that Facebook timelines are for personal use only and not commercial and they must represent an individual and be held under an individual's name.

Personal profile photo and cover photo

Many businesses use a business logo on their Facebook personal profile as they feel it is a good way to get their brand out there when they are commenting on other people's posts. However, people see through this and are put off because they see this as an individual pushing their business and not really connecting and trying to build relationships. People like to connect with people and not logos. The place for a business logo is on your Facebook page. Your personal profile photo should contain a professional and friendly looking head shot of yourself and it needs to be 180 X 180 pixels or more and Facebook will shrink your image automatically to 160 X 160 pixels. You can get really creative with the image for your cover photo and you can definitely use this to show who you are in your personal and business life if you wish. Your cover photo image needs to be 851 X 315 pixels.

Promoting your business on your personal profile

When you complete your profile information you will be asked for where you have worked. This is where you will be able to display your business page name once you have created it. If you do not want to publicize the fact that you have a business page then you can leave this blank and remain anonymous as far as your business is concerned. However, if you are planning to network, displaying your page name on your profile will be much more advantageous than if you don't display it. When you go and 'like' or comment on another page from your personal profile, the people who check back to see who you are will be able see you have a business. When anyone hovers over your page name they will be able to view a mini shot of your business page and can 'like' your page from there or send you a message.

When it comes to adding your contact information, you will find a space where you can add the link to your website or blog. When you have fully completed your Facebook profile, you can use the friend finder to start connecting with your friends and then you can start posting your status updates.

Adding the 'Follow' button to your profile

If you want to share your posts on your personal profile with more than just your friends you can do this by adding the **Follow** button to your profile. This is similar to the Twitter **Follow** button. Doing this allows you to share your posts with your subscribers as long as you have set your post to **Public**. There are advantages to doing this, particularly if you are a personal brand. It can be a much more personal way of connecting as people do like to connect with people. However, this Follower option does not offer you the marketing opportunities and analytics that a business page does so it may be a good idea to have Followers and also create a business page. This way you can invite your subscribers along with your friends to like your business page. To add the **Follow** button simply go to your settings page, click on **Followers** on the right hand side, and select **Everybody** from the drop down menu.

Controlling your privacy on your personal profile

Once you have set up your **Subscribe** button, you will probably want to make sure that your content is reaching the right people and that you are keeping the posts you want to have only your friends see marked as personal. You need to make sure that your privacy settings on things like photo albums are set to **friends** and not **public.** To make sure that your contact information is not viewed by the public, simply click on **Edit**

Profile and then **Contact Info** and then choose **Friends** in the drop down menu.

Things you can do with a personal page and not a business page
Before going on to creating your Facebook page there are a number of things that you should know about what you can do on your personal profile but not on your page, these include: wishing your friends a happy birthday, sending private messages, and all the following:

- **Participating in groups:** Participating, commenting, and posting in groups are a great way to network, but they can only be done from your personal profile.
- **Subscribe to and comment on personal profiles:** If the individual has allowed subscribers to comment on their status updates, you can do this from your personal profile. This is a great way of making new connections and starting to building relationships.
- **Create interest lists:** When you create an interest list of individuals or pages from your personal profile, your list is available for public view. You can add yourself to a list, if the subject is relevant, which gives you the opportunity to be followed by the subscribers of that list.
- **Suggest your page to your friends:** You can only invite your friends to like your Page from your personal profile.
- **Chat:** You can only use chat with your friends on your personal profile.

FACEBOOK LISTS

Facebook lists are available on your personal profile and help you organize the people you connect with and the things that you are interested in. They let you control who you post your content to and also let you choose whose content you see.

Just before you post your status update you can choose from the drop down menu next to the word **post** and select who you want to post to. It may be that you want only close friends to see certain posts or maybe just family or maybe do not mind everyone seeing it and therefore you can choose public. You can have lists for close friends, acquaintances and family and you can even put people who you do not want to see your posts on the restricted list. You will see all your lists on the left hand menu under **Friends**.

Smart Lists

Facebook also compiles what are called **Smart lists** which are lists based on your interests or things you may have in common with your friends, for example, school, college, work or maybe the area that you live in, etc. To see your smart lists simply click on **Friends** in the left hand side of your news feed. You can edit these lists if you like simply by clicking on the list name and then Clicking on **Manage List** on the top left of the page.

Custom Lists

Custom lists are lists you can create yourself and these are particularly good if you have potential customers mixed in with your friends. If you click on **More** next to **Friends** on the left of your news feed your lists appear here and then you can click **Create List** on the top right. You can name your lists whatever you like as nobody else will see this list. Custom lists allow you to post only to people you want to and also manage updates in your news feed. Here is how you do that:

- **Posting to custom lists** When you go to make a status update you can then select who you want to post to on the drop down menu beside the blue **Post** button.
- **Managing your news feed** Custom lists let you view only the updates you want to view. You simply select the list you want to see on the left and Facebook filters those particular posts for you . You can also add a list to your favorites by hovering your mouse over the list name and clicking on the pencil icon.

Interest lists

Interest lists let you add people you are subscribed to and also pages that you like, as well as your friends. This helps you to keep up to date with those who you are really interested in. You will never see every single post with Facebook Edgerank (an algorithm that Facebook uses to determine what appears in the News feed) so creating an interest list helps you to makes sure you see everything you want too see and you are not missing anything from those pages you are particularly interested in. You can also share your interest lists with everyone on Facebook.

To create an interest list simply go to www.facebook.com/addlist You can select from pages you have liked and people you have subscribed to . You can then name your list and choose who can view that list: public, friends or only you. **Top tip:** make sure to add yourself and your page to the list!

Facebook offers you suggestions of lists that you can follow which is a great way of finding pages you may be interested in.

CHAPTER TWO

CREATING AND BUILDING YOUR FACEBOOK PAGE FOR SUCCESS

IN THIS CHAPTER you will learn how you can maximize on the marketing opportunities available to you by creating a Facebook page for your business. You will learn how to best create and prepare your page so you are ready to start promoting your brand, building your audience, posting content, and converting your audience into customers.

Your page is going to be the central focus to grow your business on Facebook and is as important as your website as a source of traffic. This is where you are going to welcome your customers, introduce your business and brand to your future customers, and continue to connect with them on a daily basis. This is also where people will be going to check to see if you are a genuine and active business. In many cases your page will be the first impression your prospects receive about your business. Your page is going to be a dynamic hub of activity. It's going to be where you engage and build relationships with your target audience and it needs to scream out your brand in your page name, business description, profile picture, and cover photo.

GETTING YOUR PAGE READY

To create your Facebook Page you need to be the official representative of an organization, business, brand, or public figure. To set up your page, go to the bottom of your personal profile page and click on **Create a Page**. You will then need to select your type of business, whether it is local, company, brand or product, or artist. It is very important that you choose an accurate category for your business as it is prominently displayed alongside your profile photo. When finished, agree to the terms and conditions.

If you have a business where you actually have a physical location then the **Local Business or Place** option allows you to take advantage of Facebook's location feature and you can enter your location details here. You will then have what is called a Places Page. There are details at the end of this section about Places Pages and how to claim it if it has already been taken.

Facebook will take you through a process of setting up your page, including adding your business name, website URL, a description of your business, and profile picture. You will then be offered the opportunity to invite contacts and friends, however, it's best to skip this section until your page is properly set up. After you have agreed and ticked the terms and conditions box, your page will be public. You can change the visibility of your page until it is fully set up by simply clicking **Settings** and then check the box **Unpublish Page** under **Page Visibility**. You can view and edit everything you have entered about your page including your business type. Simply click **Settings** on the top of your page and then **Page Info.**

Once you have set up your page, this will be completely separate from your personal profile. The fans of your page will not be able to see that you are the owner of the page unless you have publicly listed yourself as admin for that page. Also, your friends will not be able to see who the owner of your page is unless you decide to add it to your 'Work and education' section on your personal profile.

Information for local businesses, claiming your places page, and the nearby places tab

There are many advantages to having this type of page, particularly with the **nearby places tab** for mobile which allows Facebook users to see which establishments are nearby to them at any time. With the nearby tab you can:

- Find a business and find directions
- Check in when you arrive
- See which of your friends have visited previously
- Like the business
- Recommend the business
- Share with your friends
- Call the business

When creating your page it is really important to complete all the sections about your location so you maximize the opportunity for your business to be found. With the introduction of Facebook's graph search it is likely that businesses which have the highest number of check-ins and recommendations will be ranked higher in a Facebook search.

Claiming your places page

Your places page may have been created if someone has already visited your business and checked in and a new places page will have been created to represent that location. You can claim your page by simply clicking on the 'gear' icon and then selecting **Is this your business?** Here you can add information about your business and verify your business by either email or other documentation. If you find that someone else is managing your places page, simply click on the 'gear' icon of that page and select **Report Page**.

Naming your Page

Your page name is what is going to appear in your fans' news feed every time you post or make a comment. It's incredibly important to get this right from the very beginning as once you reach 200 fans it cannot be changed. You need to use your business name or a name that truly represents your brand. You may find it advantageous to use your business name together with your own name, as people like to connect with people.

It may be tempting to cram your page name with lots of generic keywords to get found in a search, but this is not a good idea since people are unlikely to 'like' or share pages which look impersonal. There are lots of opportunities for adding searchable generic keywords in your description and **about** section. It is also important not to choose a generic term as in Facebook's terms it states that page names must not consist solely of generic terms. Facebook is cracking down on this and they have actually blocked publishing rights for some pages due to a violation of their terms and conditions. You are also not allowed to use or include unusual capitalizations, character symbols, numbers, professional titles, and trademark designations.

Another thing to consider is that even though you have up to 75 characters for your page name, it may be important to keep it shorter, particularly if you are going to advertise, as the Facebook ad titles only allow a maximum of 25 characters.

Uploading your profile photo

Your profile photo can be either your logo or a photo of yourself, depending on what you are promoting. This image is embedded in the cover photo so both these images need to complement each other. If you are a personal brand, a photo of yourself is often a better choice rather than a corporate logo as people tend to connect much better with faces than logos. It's worth spending time to take a really good head shot of yourself in well-lit surroundings. Once you have this you can use it on all your social platforms to keep your brand recognizable and consistent.

Whichever image you decide upon needs to be at least 180 X 180 pixels. and it will be automatically cropped and displayed at 160 X 160 pixels. If the image is smaller than this, it will be stretched to fit the space which will not look good. Once added, you can click on your image and add a description and URL

The cover photo area

Your cover photo is the most valuable area of marketing real estate on your page. This is where you can really shout-out and promote your brand and use this space to communicate, visually, exactly what your business is about and how you can help your ideal customer. Many businesses miss out on this opportunity by just uploading a fairly generic image without any message and the visitor is left feeling they have no real reason to press the 'like' button. This is not what you want. When it comes to your cover photo you have two main goals:

1. To get your visitor to 'like' your page

The action of liking a page is important not only because you get to stay in touch with your fans but also the action of liking your page is very likely to be seen in the news feed of your fan's friends. This word-of-mouth advertising is one of the most powerful forms of advertising.

In many cases, the first time your visitor arrives at your page may often be the only time they actually see your page in its entirety. After that, they may not have a reason to actually return to the page itself. It is therefore of paramount importance that whatever you put on your cover photo impacts your ideal customer enough to get them to 'like' your page. In order to do this, you need to grab their attention by choosing a compelling image and creating a message that connects with them emotionally. Your message needs to let them know immediately that they have arrived at the right place by stating clearly how you are going to help them or offer them a solution to their problem. The right image and message is a winning combination. If you are targeting the right audience, they are very likely to press the 'like' button.

2. To get your visitor to sign up to your email opt-in

One of the most important things to realize with any social media profile is that you don't actually own it. Changes are taking place all the time and although social media is incredibly powerful, there is nothing more important than building your own list of ideal customers. Your next goal is therefore to get your visitors to opt-in to your email list. This way, you have permission to communicate with them on a regular basis through their email inbox. You can do this in two ways: you can either send them to another page within Facebook using a custom application (instructions about how to do this later) or send them to a separate landing page off Facebook where you can collect their email address.

Using your cover photo to collect leads within Facebook

You can use your cover photo to direct your visitors or fans to a custom page within Facebook which houses a form where you can collect their name and email address or any other information you require.

Custom pages are created by using custom applications which allow you to add virtually any type of page to promote your business or products. These pages can also be used for a competition, an email sign-up page, a sign-up for a webinar, or contest. To create custom pages you will either need to find a web developer who can set up an application or you can use one of the many websites on the Internet, like www.heyo.com, www.shortstack.com, or www.grosocial.com, who create custom applications. Some email service providers like www.constantcontact.com and www.mailchimp.com also provide apps for social campaigns like this.

By adding the details of your offer on your cover photo with a clear call-to-action and an image of an arrow, you can direct your visitor to any page within Facebook using any of the call-to-action buttons which are available within your cover photo.

Using your cover photo to collect leads outside Facebook

The other effective way of collecting leads is to send your fans or visitors to a page on your website where you have a compelling offer and a form to capture their name and email address. You can use your cover photo to promote your offer by adding the details of your offer to your cover photo and then using any of the call-to-action buttons to direct your visitors to any URL you choose. This could be your website or blog or a specific landing page for a particular offer. Companies like www.leadpages.com or www.Instapage.com let you create landing pages for lead capture using any of their templates, and you can also publish these pages to a custom tab on Facebook.

Facebook call-to-action feature

Facebook have been rolling the call-to-action buttons since December 2014. By now most businesses will have had the opportunity to add a call-to-action button to their Facebook page.

There are seven call-to-action buttons to choose from;
Book Now (Book appointments, tables, or hotel rooms)
Contact Us (To help customers find your local business or contact you)
Shop Now (Drives people straight where you sell your products)
Sign Up (Very effective if you want to grow your email list)
Watch Video
Use App
Play Game

These buttons are great for a few reasons:
- **Calls to action work:** A call-to-action is the most effective tactic to convert random traffic into loyal customers
- **To set clear goals:** These buttons have given business owners the clarity they need to actually decide what goals they want to focus on for their Facebook page. Up until now there has been a certain vagueness about Facebook pages for businesses, but now these buttons are the icing on the cake and have made it even easier for the Facebook page visitor or 'liker' to take action and the owner to benefit from this action.
- **To Measure Results:** Now businesses can measure the success of their page with the metrics provided by Facebook. These statistics are great for testing because they let you see how effective each call-to-action is. For instance, you could try and

test the various calls-to-action one week at a time to see which one is the most effective. You never know. You may be surprised.

- **How to add your call-to-action button to your Facebook Page** Adding your call-to-action is incredibly simple. You click on the call-to-action button on your cover photo and then click 'Edit call-to-action' from the drop down list. It will offer you seven options to choose from and then you simply add the URL where you want your visitor to go to. If you want to make it more obvious then you can add an arrow to your cover photo to help draw attention to the button.

Designing your cover photo

To make your photo stand out and look as professional as possible it's important to keep it as clean and crisp by using a strong, colorful, and bold image. When you add text it's important to keep it to a minimum so you can make the message you want to deliver as clear as possible. Since Facebook lifted their rules governing what you are allowed to put on your cover photo, this area is even more valuable. You can now add your website URL, email address, pricing information, contact information, and a call to action.

There are many inventive ideas for cover photos. Just by browsing other Facebook pages you can find inspiration, and there are also many custom tools available on the internet for creating cover photos, like www.pagemodo.com . Using a graphic designer to create your image may be a good idea, and they can size it to fit all your other social profiles as well. The dimensions of the image you need for Facebook are 315 X 851. Once you have added your image you can reposition it and then if you click the image, you can add a description and URL.

You can change your cover photo whenever you wish. You could do this for a special offer which ties in with a special occasion, season, or holiday. Not only will your new fans see this when they arrive on your page but also your existing fans will see your new photo in their news feed as well, which is a great way of reminding them about your brand.

Your business descriptions

With the introduction of Facebook's graph search, never has there been a more important time to make sure you complete all the written descriptive sections on your page and make the most of every bit of space available. All Facebook pages are indexed by Google, but with the new graph search, it is even more vital for you to be found within Facebook by as many keywords relating to your niche as possible. You can edit all your descriptions by clicking **Settings** and then **Page Info.**

The About section

The 'About' section of your page can be viewed by clicking **About** under your cover photo and also on the left side of your page. Depending on the type of business you are, Facebook will pull in different types of information into your 'about' section. If you are a 'Places page' then details of your address, telephone number, opening hours, and type of business are going to be displayed here.

With other types of businesses, the 'About' information is pulled in from the short description. The information you offer about your business needs to be concise and thoughtfully put together so your audience knows exactly what your business is about after reading the first sentence. In your short description you need to include a brief summary of what your business is, how it will benefit your fans, and include your website URL. You can expand on your business in more detail in your long description. The more relevant keyword rich and search engine friendly information you include the better, but most importantly you need to make it interesting reading for your audience.

Start date

The start date does not need to be the start date of the page but can be the start date of your business. A great way of adding interest to your page is by giving a brief history or the story about your business by adding events or milestones which have already passed. You can do this as long as you have created your start date sometime in the past.

Choosing a vanity URL for your Facebook page

When you have created your page, Facebook will automatically assign a URL with a number. However you can change this to something more memorable like facebook.com/yourbusinessname, which will be much easier to direct people to. To change it you will need to have 25 fans on your page then you can choose your vanity URL or Facebook username. To create your vanity URL simply go to your 'About' page where you can change your **Facebook web address.** It is best practice to use your business name or, if that is not available, then something that is going to be easy to remember. After you have set your username you may change it only once. If your trademark name has been taken, you can notify Facebook about retrieving it.

Your message settings

You can choose whether or not users can send you a message on your Facebook page. If you do choose to allow users to send you messages then this will be clearly displayed on your Facebook page with a message box below your cover photo. To change whether you want to allow people to send you messages, click on **Settings** and then **General** and you can edit your **message** settings there.

It is definitely advisable to allow your fans to send you messages. If you do not, then you are cutting off possible communication, turning away opportunities to connect, and making your business look cold and unwelcoming.

Admin roles

If you are going to have a team of people managing your Facebook page you can set up admin roles. Facebook allows you to set up unlimited admin roles. As manager you can assign different levels of access depending on what each person is allowed to do.

To find this section simply click on **Settings** and then **Page Roles**. There are 5 admin roles: Manager, Content Creator, Moderator, Advertiser, and Insights Analyst. Each role has different permissions so you can control what each person is allowed to do as follows:

- **Admin** can manage admin roles, send messages, create posts on the page, create ads, and view insights.
- **Editor** can edit the page, send messages, create posts on the page, create ads, and view insights.
- **Moderator** can respond to and delete comments on the page, send messages on the page, create ads, and view insights.
- **Advertiser** can create ads and view insights.
- **Analyst** can see who created or commented on a post and can view insights.

CUSTOMIZING YOUR PAGE WITH APPS

Facebook allows you to customize your Facebook page. By using custom applications, you can add promotions, contests, stores, email sign-up pages, videos, and more. Once you have added your custom applications they can be viewed by your fans in two places: below your cover photo and on the left sidebar of your page. Below your cover photo you can display up to two tabs, and the rest will be listed under the **More** tab. Creating a really interesting and unique page is what is going to make your page stand out from the crowd. There are four apps which have been developed by Facebook. You will see **Photos** under your cover photo and the other three (**Video**, **Notes**, and **Events**) can be found by clicking **Settings** and then **Apps**.

Photos

The photos app is where all the photos are displayed and can be organized into albums. When you add a photo you have the opportunity to add a description and a URL, so if you are adding products, you can direct the user to the page where they can buy that product. It is extremely important to complete all details and optimize your photos so you can maximize the chance of being found in a search.

Events

Facebook can be a powerful platform for marketing any event, party, product launch, or trade show. The events app lets you create an event from your personal profile or business profile. This will be covered in depth later.

Notes

The notes app offers you your very own built-in blogging platform. Even if you have your own blog, it's a really good idea to copy your blog posts into the notes. Notes are incredibly underutilized by Facebook users, but they are incredibly straightforward to use and another way of getting found within Facebook. You can add a title, upload a photo, tag people's pages, and there is basic formatting available too. When you create a note it will appear in your News Feed, and that of your fans, with an image if you have added one.

You can also use an app to automatically syndicate your blog posts to Facebook and Twitter with an app called NetworkedBlogs, which works through your Facebook account. To do this, simply type "NetworkedBlogs" into Facebook search and add the app, register your blog, and then go through the steps to pull your blog into Facebook.

Video App

To use this you will need to actually upload videos directly to the Facebook video app. Facebook offers you the opportunity to upload a video directly from your webcam, which is great if you have updates you wish to post quickly.

Displaying and viewing your apps

You can display two custom apps under your cover photo and if you wish to add more apps, they will be displayed by clicking **More** under the cover photo and also on tabs down the left side of your page. You can choose which ones to display by clicking **More** and then **Manage Tabs,** where you will be able to drag and change the position of your app. It is obviously important to display the most important app in first position so it displays both under your cover photo and as the first tab on the left of your page.

Using Custom Apps to achieve your marketing goals

Custom apps let you create pages of your own to help you promote your products and services. These apps are created by third party developers and there are literally thousands of apps available for Facebook business pages. (These are not to be confused with the apps that you can add to your personal profile, like games, etc.)

Custom Apps offer more marketing opportunities for your business page, more functionality, and more to help increase the way you interact with your audience. However, before you start adding apps, the most important thing you need to do is think carefully about what your goals are and which apps are actually going to help you achieve those goals and objectives. There are many bells and whistles available for you to add to your page, but there is no point in adding an app which is only going to pull your audience away from your main goal and objective.

If you want to create your own iframe application, you can do this yourself by installing the Facebook Developer Application which can be found at https://developers.facebook.com/

Here are some more examples of custom apps that you can add to your page:

- A custom welcome page with opt-in to catch fans (THIS IS ABSOLUTELY ESSENTIAL. More about this in the next section.)

- A store to sell your products
- Webinar sign up
- Your YouTube Channel
- Welcome page
- Sales coupons
- Sync & display your Twitter feed or Pinterest account
- Your webpage and your products
- Display location maps
- A staff page with images of your team
- An event announcement
- A competition or contest app
- Pull in your pins from Pinterest
- Pull in your posts from Google +
- Add a SlideShare app
- If you are a restaurant, you can add reservations through Opentable
- Add an Etsy app and share your Etsy shop on Facebook
- Create polls
- Automatically stream your Flickr stream into Facebook
- Publish your blog post so they automatically display on your timeline

Creating Facebook custom pages and tabs using iframes on Facebook

Facebook allows you to create a custom tab on your page with an iframe application. This is where your index page is not actually hosted on Facebook but another server. An iframe application allows you to embed an external web page into your custom Facebook page tab and lets you build any content you want inside your tab using HTML, javascript, and CSS. You can also have forms, images, and videos. Basically anything that can be created on a website can be brought into Facebook.

The Thunderpenny static HTML iframe tabs application is a free third party application that makes it very easy to customize a Facebook page even if you have little or no technical know-how. Simply type "static HTML iframe" into the Facebook search box and it will come up with a grey star logo. You then need to follow the simple instructions to install the application. You can add images, forms, and videos. They offer online tutorials with instructions on how to do this at www.thunderpenny.com

There are also many other third party applications available which are really easy to install and use with simple drag and drop features. All the following providers offer apps like this: www.heyo.com, www.involver.com, www.shortstack.com, www.wildfireapp.com, and www.tabsite.com. They certainly take away the headache if you do not have the technical know-how to build HTML Pages. You can also find apps by searching in the Facebook search page. You need to check whether the apps use adobe flash, as apps with adobe flash cannot be displayed on an iPhone, iPod, and iPad.

How to add apps to your page
Simply visit any of the app websites, select the app you want to install, and follow the directions through a simple installation process. Once you have completed the installation process the app should appear on one of the tabs just under the cover photo. If you decide to delete the app, it is very straightforward. Simply click the cross to the right of the app and it will be removed.

If you want to create your own iframe application then you can do this yourself by installing the Facebook Developer Application. You can find it at https://developers.facebook.com/

Displaying and viewing your apps
You can display two custom apps under your cover photo and if you wish to add more apps, they will be displayed by clicking **More** under the cover photo and also on tabs down the left side of your page. You can choose which ones to display by clicking **More** and then **Manage Tabs,**

where you will be able to drag and change the position of your apps.

Changing the text on your custom tabs

To change the text on your custom tab simply click **Settings** and **Apps** and then under the custom tab image, click **Edit Settings.**

Adding images to custom tabs

Adding custom images to your tabs is a really effective way of attracting users to your custom pages. To do this, you need to create some eye catching images which fit in with your brand and add a clear call to action. You can upload a JPG, GIF or PNG file. The size of the image must be 111 x 74 pixels. To upload or change an image, click **Settings.** Go to the app listing, click on **Edit Settings,** and then **Change** where it says **Custom Tab Image.**

Changing the position of the custom tabs

You need to think carefully about which tabs are most important and which ones you wish to appear under your cover photo. You can choose up to two which will display under your cover photo. Any others you add will be features under the **More** tab. You can manage the position of your tabs by clicking **More** and then **Manage Tabs,** and you can then drag your apps into position.

Finding the URL to your custom page

If you wish to direct your users to a particular page, simply click **Settings, Apps,** and then **Link to this tab** under the App description.

CREATING CUSTOM PAGES FOR YOUR OPT-IN OR A CONTEST

Adding an opt-in form to your Facebook page is absolutely essential if you want your campaign to succeed, and transferring your fans from your page to your opt-in should be your main marketing goal. With Facebook's new algorithm, which is making it more and more difficult to reach your fans organically, it is absolutely essential to get them onto your email opt-in at the very first opportunity. Once your fans have opted into your email list and given you permission to contact them on a regular basis, this is where you are going to win. Email is where you convert your fans into your customers.

Facebook users do not generally like to leave the platform so when a new fan arrives at your page, it is really important to capture their email address on Facebook rather than sending them to an exterior landing page and then losing them. To set up your email opt-in on Facebook you will need to build a custom page with a compelling offer to encourage your audience to sign, together with a sign-up form. You can easily create this with the 'Static HTML iFrame app' or use one of the many other third party apps like: www.pagemodo.com, www.heyo.com, www.wishpond.com, or www.leadpages.com . There are also many email providers who will provide an app for this which is easily integrated with your email capture form. These providers include: www.icontact.com, www.constantcontact.com, www.aweber.com, or www.mailchimp.com .

Creating a competition or sweepstakes

A very effective way of capturing fans for your page and creating buzz is to create a competition or sweepstakes. Facebook has relaxed their rules considerably in regards to competitions so you can now run a competition on your page's timeline but not your personal timeline. You can either create your own competition or use a third party to do this for you. All this will be covered in detail later.

SETTING UP A STORE ON FACEBOOK

There are four ways that you can set up a store on Facebook:

A Storefront

You display your products with buy buttons on an app on your page which is connected to your website store. When the customer clicks the buy button they are then transferred to your website. Companies like http://storefrontsocial.com offer simple integration and sometimes a free trial.

A Facebook Store

This is when all the activity takes place on Facebook and customers do not have to leave Facebook Page to purchase an item. There are many third parties that create online stores within Facebook. Simply type in 'Facebook Store application' into Google search or use a company like www.ecwid.com

Selling directly from your news feed

You can sell products directly from your news feed by adding photos and directing customers to the URL of your external website or you can use a third party app to do this for you. You can also create an album with your Facebook products, enter the details and pricing and links to your website. www.rocxial.com is a third party app which enables you to sell products through Facebook news feed and photos.

ADDING STARTER CONTENT AND MILESTONES

As mentioned earlier, Facebook allows you to add a start date which can be any date before you actually created your page. This allows you to create interest or a story behind your business before you actually start. This is also a good way of letting your visitors to your page know how long your business has been trading for.

Milestones are key moments you decide to highlight on your page. They have a flag icon and use up the full width of the News Feed with a lovely big image. Facebook creates your first milestone for you, and you can edit this by hovering over the top right hand corner of the milestone box and add a story and a photo, if desired.

A milestone could be anything from the opening of a business, the launch of a product, the launch of a website, or participation at a meaningful event or trade show. By adding milestones to your timeline you will add interest and depth to your page. To create a milestone simply click on **Offer/Event** on the top right of your page and then select 'Milestone'. Milestone images display at 843 pixels wide 403 pixels tall. You can use your own photos or use photos from stock photo sites or free photo sites such as Flickr.

CHAPTER THREE

HOW TO BUILD YOUR AUDIENCE ON FACEBOOK

ONCE YOU HAVE created your page, added all your custom pages, a Facebook store if needed, and your opt-in page, you will be ready to publish your page and start building a highly targeted audience of fans for your page together with quality leads for your business.

Your main aim should be to use Facebook as a way to source traffic, create a relationship, and then drive them to take action either on or off your Facebook page on a Facebook store, on to your website, a landing page for an email sign up, sales page, video demonstration, or on your blog.

The more fans you have on your page the more potential you have to drive traffic to your website, especially when you crossed the 1000 fans milestone. Also with the introduction of Graph Search, fans are more important than ever. It is becoming evident that the more fans you have on your page the higher you will rank on a Facebook search.

Building an audience can seem like a very daunting process at first. However, building a sizeable audience in a short amount of time is possible and very rewarding when you see the number of fans (potential customers) growing on your page. But do not be misled into thinking it is going to be easy. As much as you may like to think that as soon as anyone sees your Facebook icon on your website they are going to like your page, it doesn't always work like that. Here are some strategies for you to use to build a highly targeted audience:

Add your page to your personal profile

When you add your page name to the **Work and Education** section of your personal profile, it lets anyone viewing your profile see the name of your page. When they hover over the page name they will be able to see a mini image of your cover photo and they can 'like' or message you. Simply start to type your page name into the **Work and Education** section and your page name will display in the drop down for you to click on.

This is incredibly useful if you are networking and 'liking' other business pages on Facebook. When the owner of that page sees you have 'liked' their page, they may very well check out your profile, see you have a page, and may reciprocate by 'liking' your page too. Reciprocating by 'liking' your fans' pages is a very good practice. Supporting your fans this way goes a long way in building relationships, especially when you start engaging with their content.

Invite your friends

Now your page and your personal profile are ready, and you can invite your Facebook friends. Simply go to your page, make sure you are using your page as yourself, and then click on **Build Audience** and then **Invite Friends**. You can select whoever you want to and send them an invitation to 'like' your page.

Invite your email contacts

What better way to build relationships with your current contacts than inviting them to your Facebook page. Simply go to your page and, by using your page as yourself, click **Build Audience** and then **Import Contacts** and invite your contacts.

Share your Page

This is another great feature within Facebook to build your audience. You can share your page on your own timeline by simply clicking **Share** on your cover photo. You can share it on your own timeline, on a friend's timeline, on another page you manage, or in a group.

Create a free offer

Offering something free like an ebook or report can help increase the number of 'likes'. You used to be able to install something called a 'Like Gate' where people had to 'like' your page to get your offer, but unfortunately Facebook has stopped this now. However, all is not lost. You can still ask users to submit their email address to obtain your offer, and this can easily be set up with an app. Often email service providers will provide an easy-to-install application to catch email addresses, and you can add an image and text to promote your offer. Using other social networks like Twitter to direct people to your Facebook page can work very well. Simply ask followers to join you on Facebook by directing them to your free offer.

Promote your page with a Facebook ad

Facebook advertising is a highly effective way of building your audience and lets you reach people who are not yet connected to your page. Because Facebook holds so much information about their users, they have made finding your target audience incredibly easy. You can target by age, gender, location, marital status, and interest. To advertise, simply click **Create Ad** from your personal profile and then select your page and the option **Page likes**. You simply design your ad by choosing your headline, text, image, and the page you want them to land on. You can then select the audience that you want to advertise to and your daily budget and you are ready to start promoting your page.

When people see your ad they can either 'like' it from the ad or click on the page link to see your page. If you have an offer on one of your pages then it would be a good idea to send them to that page and capture them with your opt-in.

When you are creating your ad you will see a tick next to the words **Sponsored Stories**. Sponsored stories help businesses promote word-of-mouth recommendations on their page by promoting the actions taken by their fans and making them more visible to their friends. For instance, if you have activated sponsored stories on your page and a Facebook user was to either check your page or 'like' your page, then their friends would see this action taken on the right side of their News Feed. This is an incredibly effective form of advertising because it creates social proof and word-of-mouth advertising, which is the most powerful.

Post really good content

If you are posting really good content and your fans are engaging with that content by 'liking', commenting, and sharing, these actions will show up in their friends' News Feed which will help to encourage others to 'like' your page and join in the conversation. You need to make sure you are regularly creating the right type and balance of content that will appeal to your target audience.

Use images in your posts

The introduction of larger images in the new News Feed design is really good news for businesses, and wherever possible you should use images to promote your posts. All the statistics show that images receive the most engagement and are far more likely to be shared than text only posts. You can either use your own photos or use stock photos or other photo sites like Flickr, as long as you first check the licenses for using these free images. For branding purposes it's always a good idea to add a small logo, Facebook page name, or watermark on your images.

Create a competition or sweepstakes

To help attract people to their Facebook pages, more and more companies are giving away prizes in Facebook sweepstakes and contests. This type of promotion can be incredibly effective, and since Facebook has relaxed their rules concerning competitions, you can now run them on your timeline without having to use a third party application. To see Facebook terms about running contests please follow this link http:// www.facebook.com/page_guidelines.php#promotionsguidelines

There are a great number of companies that can help you with your competition such as: www.woobox.com, www.pagemodo.com, www.offerpop.com, www.strutta.com, www.wildfireapp.com, www.votigo.com, and the list goes on and on.

Be Social
Being active on Facebook, commenting, and sharing other people's posts will increase visibility of your profile and your business page. Going to other pages and posting helpful comments is a sure way of getting people to come over and see what you are about. You can select whether you want to comment as yourself or your page by clicking the 'gear' icon at the top right of your page. This is particularly good for personal brands which have their own photo for their profile photo rather than a logo, as people much prefer to connect with a face.

Use embedded posts to drive engagement
Facebook now lets you actually embed public posts in your blog and website by simply adding a line of code. To find the code simply go to the relevant post and open the drop down menu by clicking the arrow on the top right of your post and then click **Embed Post**. Embedding a post which has had lots of comments and 'likes' on it, will not only help create social proof but also help encourage others, who are not fans of your page, to 'like' your page. If you have a video, uploading it to Facebook and then embedding it on your website will increase the possibility of more people commenting on your video and increasing your reach too.

Use Facebook groups to grow your audience
Finding your Facebook audience is made really easy with Facebook search and you can find all sorts of interest groups, pages, and people relating to your niche. By entering the relevant keywords into the search box at the top of your page Facebook will come up with a list of results relevant to your search and you can then filter the search information

into various categories: groups, people, places, pages, events, etc. Joining groups in your niche and then joining in the community will not only help you make new connections, but you can post links to your blog posts or your Facebook page if the content is relevant.

Leave comments on blogs, articles, and forums

If you are leaving relevant and interesting comments on other people's blogs, you can also leave an invitation to connect with you on your Facebook page. You may even get the blogger themselves.

Promote your page on your blog

Writing a blog article about your Facebook page, and giving your readers reasons and an incentive to join, is a really effective way of promoting your page.

Add your Facebook page to all your promotional and sales materials

Make sure you add your Facebook URL to any literature, business cards, brochures, shop signs, your transportation, or any other promotional material you produce. Make sure you have set up your Facebook username so it's easy for people to remember. You can also download Facebook table tents and stickers here http://fbrep.com//SMB/tent-cards-self-serve.pdf for promotion at your business place.

Make Google Adwords work for you

Google Adwords can be a very effective way of finding new fans and then directing them to a specific page for a competition or a 'like' gate with a compelling offer. With Google Adwords you can find people who are actually looking for your specific product, and your page will not only offer them social proof that your business is bona fide but also give you the opportunity to stay in contact with them. This is a really good way to get Adwords to work for you. If you offer them an incentive to like your page, you can carry on the relationship with them on Facebook and have more chance of converting them into a customer than by just sending them to your website where they will more than likely disappear.

Integrate Facebook with current advertising

Using Facebook in conjunction with magazines or newspaper advertising can really increase the effectiveness of your advertising. By adding your Facebook URL together with a good incentive for them to like your page you can continue a relationship that otherwise would have been lost.

Encourage fans to ensure your updates show up in their news feeds

Because of Facebook's algorithms, your Facebook fans probably will not get to see all your posts unless they have switched on **Get notifications**. To do this you simply hover over the arrow where it says **liked** and click on **Get Notifications**. It's a good idea to encourage your fans to select this so they don't miss out on any of your updates. You could do this by announcing that you have something really exciting coming up in the near future and if they want to make sure they hear about it then they need to switch on **Get Notifications**.

Add your Facebook handle to other social networks

Inviting your followers from Twitter or other networks to like your Facebook page is a really good way of increasing your 'likes'. Once in a while you can tweet about something that is happening on your Facebook page which will hopefully entice your followers to go over and have a look.

Promote your offers and competitions on other networks

Posting content on your other networks is a great way to pull those users over to your Facebook page. For instance, if you are running a competition or offer on Facebook, make sure you pin your image on Pinterest and tweet about it on Twitter.

Send a direct message to your Twitter followers

Some people are totally against sending direct messages on Twitter, but this can work in directing your Twitter followers to your opt-in page with a compelling offer. You can set up automated direct messages too.

Join a LinkedIn Group

There are groups that exist on LinkedIn that are primarily set up to increase your 'likes' on Facebook. This may be good or not, depending on who your target audience is, but it can definitely help increase the number of your 'likers' and if you are selling B2B, this could be particularly good for you.

Status tagging (shout-outs)

Tagging is when you mention someone in a status update or comment by using the @ sign before their name or page name. When you start writing the person's name, a pop up will appear and you can choose the correct person or page you wish to tag. This will create an instant link. The post to which you added their name or page name to may then be added to their timeline, and any user who clicks that link will be taken to their timeline. When you tag someone they will receive a notification, which is a great way of drawing attention to your page or profile. Also, if you or a friend tags someone in a post or photo which is set to **friends or more,** the post will be visible to their friends as well. You can use this to share other people's content and then tag them in the status update. If you or your page does get tagged, it is a really good practice to go back and thank the person who tagged you.

Another way of using this feature is that if you have photos of events, you can make a folder and then ask your fans to tag themselves in the photos. This is a great way of increasing your reach through their friends' News Feeds.

Invite your fans to leave their Facebook Page URL

This is particularly good if you are selling B2B. People love to network and love any opportunity to promote their business. Inviting people to network on your page is an excellent way of increasing likes and a great way of showing how much you value your fans. You can do this on a specific day of the week or every month. By creating a special branded image to promote this you can also widen your reach when fans share your image.

Use Facebook promoted posts

Promoting your posts with **promoted posts** is an excellent way to increase your reach. You can promote to people who already 'like' your page and to their friends or to a selected audience that you can choose. You will find more details about promoted posts later on.

Add Facebook badges to your website or blog

Facebook has a great little feature called **Badges**. Badges make it easy for you to show off your Facebook profile, as well as your latest status updates, on your website or blog. Simply visit this page. http://www.facebook.com/badges/

Connect your Facebook page with Twitter

To connect your Facebook page with Twitter simply visit here www.facebook.com/twitter . Once you have connected them, all your Facebook posts will go to Twitter with a link back to your Facebook page.

Add your Facebook URL to your videos

Adding a link to your Facebook fan page from any videos you may have on YouTube or Vimeo is a great way of increasing you page 'likes'. If you have a YouTube channel and your main goal on Youtube is to increase your Facebook 'likes' then leave a comment with an incentive to go over and become a fan of your Facebook page.

Add a QR code

You can generate a QR code for your Facebook page, and many sites offer this for free. Once you have your QR code you can place this on any printed material so it can be quickly scanned and your Facebook page 'liked'. This is also great if you are a local business. You can encourage people to 'like' your business page by simply scanning the QR code into their mobile. You can easily set up your QR code by using an app called 'Visual QR code generator'.

Encourage people to check in at your business

With the introduction of the nearby tab and check-in, Facebook offers their users even more opportunities to find businesses near to them and also offers business owners more opportunities to be found. If a user checks-in at your business it will show up in their friends' News Feeds. By using Facebook offers you can create offers and give your fans an incentive to check-in at your business.

HOW TO PROMOTE YOUR PAGE WITH SOCIAL PLUGINS

Social plug-ins increase the visibility of your page outside Facebook and increase the opportunity for people to 'like' your page. Plug-ins basically pull the Facebook experience into your website or blog and create social proof, by letting users see which of their friends have already 'liked', commented on, or shared on your Facebook page. For example, if you visit a website and see your friend's photo on the Facebook plug-in, or if they have commented on the page, you're probably more likely to take interest in that website, 'like' the page too, or buy the product.

Facebook offers eleven social plug-ins, which are detailed below. All the plugins can be found at this link http://developers.facebook.com/docs/plugins/ with instructions on how you or your developer can install them into your website or blog.

The Like Button lets users share pages from your site back to their Facebook profile with one click. The action will appear on their timeline and in their friends' News Feeds.

The Send Button allows users to easily send content to their friends. It allows users to send a personal message to a friend, group, or email. It's a good idea to put the "send" button next to the "like" button.

The Follow Button lets a user subscribe to your public updates on Facebook.

Embedded Posts allows you to embed any public post into your website or blog.

The Share Button allows people to share to Facebook and share with particular friends, groups, or in a private message.

The Comments Plug-in allows your users to comment on any piece of content on your site. The post will appear on your website as well as in the user's News Feed on Facebook. You can put this plug-in in as many places as you wish, including particular product pages on your website or blog site.

If you are commenting on a website or blog post you can post as yourself or as your page, which is a great opportunity to gain visibility for your page.

The Activity Feed plugin shows the most interesting recent activity on your site, using actions ('likes' and recommends) by your friends and other people.

The Recommendations Feed displays the most recommended content using actions by your friends or other users.

Recommendations Bar allows your website users to 'like' content, get recommendations, and share what they're reading with their friends. When a user 'likes' some content or an article on your blog or website, it shows up in their News Feed and their friends' News Feeds.

The Like Box allows you to see how many people 'liked' the page, how many of your friends 'liked' it, and you can view the recent posts. It allows you to 'like' the page without visiting it.

The Login Button shows the profile pictures of the user's friends who have already signed up for your site in addition to a login button. The login button is useful as it gives you information about the audience you are attracting to your blog or website.

The Registration plug-in allows users to easily sign up for your website with their Facebook account.

The Facepile plug-in displays the Facebook profile pictures of users who have 'liked' your page or logged in at your site. This is great for social proof.

There are also third party developers that create plug ins which can be integrated into your page and ones that include plug-ins for multiple social platforms.

HOW TO USE FACEBOOK GRAPH SEARCH TO BUILD YOUR AUDIENCE

Facebook has been slowly rolling in its powerful graph search, and it is currently available to people using Facebook desktop in English.

Graph search lets you carry out more detailed searches and find out more information on Facebook than ever before by letting you find connections between people, places, and things. For instance, you could search for friends with common interests or friends of friends in a certain city.

With graph search you can also look for particular posts and filter posts by author, keywords, location, and comments. Some filers have drop downs that let you refine your search even further. You can also continue to search for keywords and you will see suggested people, photos, pages, and apps that match your keywords. You can put keywords together for things that interest you, for example, restaurants that your friends like. In your search results you will see unique results based on your connections to people, places, and things.

Graph search has opened up even more targeting opportunities for marketeers offering searches with social relevance and has really let them drill down further with searches to find their ideal target audience. Here are some examples of the sort of searches you can perform with Facebook graph search. However, the combinations you can search on are endless.

Find groups than your fans are in: You can search for groups that people who have 'liked' your page have joined and that relate to your page in some way. This can help you network among people with similar interests. For example, "groups of people who like _ _ _ _ _ _" (Page name)

Find pages your fans 'like': Identify other pages your fans 'like', for example, "Pages liked by people who like _ _ _ _ _" (page name).

Find friends who have not 'liked' your page yet: You can put a search query in for the friends who 'like' your page and then you'll be able to work out more easily which of your friends have not 'liked' your page and then send them an invitation.

Find people who 'like' a particular page: Graph search will show you who 'likes' a particular page, even if they are not your friends.

Find pages 'liked' by particular people or pages: This can help you interact even more with particular people or influencers. You can even sort by gender, age, and location.

Find employees of certain companies: For example, you could find out which pages the employees of a particular company 'like'.

Find common interests: You can find out more about your fans' interests and then determine which similar interests your fans have. This can help you produce the right content for your fans. Also, when it comes to advertising you can use this information to target people with particular interests.

CHAPTER FOUR

CONTENT IS KING ON FACEBOOK

ONCE YOU HAVE prepared your page, started to gain 'likes,' and build your audience, this is only the beginning. Once users have 'liked your page, it is unlikely that they will return to your page. In fact, nearly 90% of fans will never return again. In order to build a thriving community of brand advocates and customers who want to share your content, sign up to your newsletter, and buy your products, you are going to need to build trust, loyalty, and likeability. The only way to do this is by communicating with them on a regular basis in the right way and by consistently delivering the highest possible quality content which will grab their attention, appeal to their interests, and add real value to their lives. Once your fans start engaging with your content, you will start building trust and start to convert them into customers.

Even when you start posting on Facebook it is unlikely that your posts are going to be seen by every one of your fans in their News Feed every time, unless you are paying for promoted posts. This is simply because Facebook uses an algorithm called Edgerank, which determines what does and does not show up in a user's timeline. They know that because of the sheer volume of content posted that if their users were to see every post it would ruin their viewing experience. Facebook devised the algorithm to create the best possible experience for their users, and Edgerank helps to ensure that users see what is most important to them and what has the greatest value. There are three variables that are measured to make up this algorithm and these are: affinity, weight, and time decay.

Affinity: Affinity measures the relationship between the viewer and the creator of the content. The closer the relationship, the higher the score. So the more one of your fans interacts with your content, the more likely your posts are going to show in their News Feed.

Weight: Weight measures the value carried by different types of content and the way users engage with that post will also affect the score.

Time Decay: Time Decay is about the age of the post. The older the post, the lower the score. This is what helps your News Feed to stay full of fresh, new content. Approximately 75% of engagement takes place within the first five hours and 60% within the first three hours. The value of the post will decrease as time goes on.

One of your main goals for creating content for Facebook is going to be producing the highest quality content for your audience so that they will engage with that content, thereby creating the highest possible Edgerank score. The higher your score, the more fans will see and engage with your posts. You can check your Edgerank score at this link www.edgerankchecker.com

In order to create the right content you are going to need to have a real understanding of your target audience and deep insight into what interests and motivates them. Once you have this information and put this together with the strategies in this book, there is no reason why you cannot build a thriving community of advocates for your brand on Facebook. In this chapter you are going to learn about the different types of posts, content, and tips on how to help you create the best experience for the fans so you can receive the highest engagement and highest Edgerank.

35 Content Ideas

With the competition out there on the Internet for attention, the only way you are going to win is with high quality content. Content really is king on Facebook. This is even more important now since Facebook is decreasing the number of posts from pages which are visible in the News Feed. You may be wondering how you are going to consistently produce and deliver compelling content to your audience on a regular basis for the foreseeable future. However, once you have picked your topic of interest, you will be surprised how one idea will lead to another and you will be able to find numerous pieces of content to create and post. Here are some ideas for content that can be adapted to any type of business or topic:

1. Relatable content

Relatable content is one of the best and most shared types of content. Relatable content is anything that your target audience can relate to and identify with. It's when your audience sees a piece of content and immediately thinks, "Yes, I can relate to that and this is exactly the way I feel when this happens." It's incredibly powerful because this content is immediately communicating to your audience that you understand them and you feel their pain or joy and can empathize with them. With relatable content you are communicating with them on quite a deep level, which all helps to build relationships and trust. This is why Someecards is so successful. Most of their content is relatable.

2. Emotive content

Evoking an emotional response is an essential ingredient to successful viral content marketing. If you create content that evokes a strong positive emotional response it will help your audience associate that emotion with your brand. Content like this is very memorable, and if you can make people feel something by posting an image, text, or video, this can really help in building your brand and creating powerful associations. Evoking any of the primary emotions, be it surprise, joy, fear, sadness, anger, or disgust, is a certain way to get people sharing your content.

3. Educational content

Posting informative content about your subject is invaluable. This will help you to stand out as a thought leader and expert in your field. If your content is valuable and useful, your followers are likely to keep coming back for more and are likely to share your content too. Remember, your audience is looking to find and share valuable content with their friends and customers, too, and will want to be associated with any compelling content you create.

4. Informative

This could be about letting your followers know about something that is happening, like a webinar, a trade show or event in the area, a special offer, or any information that will be of use or value to them.

5. Entertaining/amusing content

Social media is all about being social and having fun. People love sharing funny stuff. Even if you did not create it yourself but you think it is going to appeal to your target audience then share it. The aim here is to amuse and entertain your audience. Humor is a winner all around. Not only does humor break down barriers, it is also more likely to be 'liked' and shared.

6. Seasonal Content

Posting content related to important holidays and annual celebrations is a really good way to stay connected with your audience. If you have an international audience, being aware of their holidays and religious celebrations will go a long way in building relationships.

7. Inspiring and motivational content

The truth is everyone has a bad day sometimes and needs a little bit of motivation or cheering up. A motivational quote will help to lift your audience and can really help to connect with them. If you know what your audience wants, what they aspire to, and what their frustrations are, then it is likely that you will be able to motivate them by posting content which inspires them. These types of posts are also very shareable, especially if put together with a colorful and inspiring image like a cartoon or photo.

8. Employee and behind-the-scenes content

If you have news about your employees and the great things they are doing, then post it. Maybe they have been involved in a fundraiser or won an employee of the month award. Giving your audience a behind-the-scenes view of your business helps to keep your business and brand looking real and authentic, and it adds human interest.

9. Customer Content

Having a member of the month or including news or content about a customer's business is a great way to spark interest in your posts. Sharing a customer's content not only shows you value your audience but that you can also encourage them to do the same. If you are B2B, you could also invite your audience to network and let them share their page on your page once a month or once a week. This is a great way to offer them value. It also creates loyalty, keeps your page in their mind, and keeps them coming back again and again to visit your page.

10. Shared Content

While it's great to post most of your own content, don't be afraid to share other people's content as long as it is relevant. The more valuable content you share, the more valuable you will become to your audience and the more likely they will be to keep coming back for more. Sharing content is also incredibly important in building relationships with your fans. They are going to be far more open to your brand if you are supporting theirs.

11. Statistics

People love statistics which relate to their niche. If your business is B2B then posting statistics can gain a great deal of interest, especially if they are displayed in a visually appealing way, perhaps with an infographic or graph. They are often shared if they are translated into a useful tip for your followers.

12. Questions

Asking questions about subjects your audience may be interested in is a great way to encourage comments, interaction, and community. People love to share their opinions and thoughts and love the opportunity to communicate, contribute, and be heard. Even if you are posting an image or video, it's a really good practice to ask a question.

13. Top Ten lists

People love lists about who or what is top or best. Lists spark interest and this probably because people like to compare their choices and judgements with others. Some may like to see that their opinions match others and feel they are right in that choice, and others may feel comforted by the fact their choices are not the same and they are unique.

14. Controversial

Posting a controversial statement can spark great conversation and interaction. Remember, people love to voice their opinions, have input, and be heard. It may be a good idea to stay out of the discussion here, as you do not want to lose followers and you need to be sensitive to your audience in order not to upset them, so be careful what topics you pick.

15. Special offers

Social media is a great way to get the message out about the special offers you have running, but you will need to be careful not to post them too often or they just appear like advertising and bad noise in your audience's News Feed. You need to make sure that what you are offering is of real value, that it is exclusive to your fans, and you are offering them a deadline to redeem the offer.

16. Contests and sweepstakes

Contests and sweepstakes are always a great way to gain popularity, grow your audience, build your brand, and build your opt-in email list. With contests, your audience can have great fun with your brand and they can also create high levels of engagement. There are so many different types of contests: photo and video competitions, sweepstakes, comment to win, polls, 'caption this' contests, photo contests, quizzes, and the list goes on. Creating and running contests will be covered in more details later on.

17. Voting polls & customer feedback

Creating a poll is a great way to encourage engagement on social media. Incorporating polls into your Facebook strategy can help give you a deeper understanding of your audience and also offer you valuable feedback about products or services. You can either ask your audience a question and ask them to 'like' or comment or use an app like 'Poll' or 'Polls for Facebook' or 'Polldaddy.'

18. Tips and tricks

Offering a weekly or daily 'Top Tip' can keep your audience hooked and returning again and again for the latest information and are a great way to increase loyalty and build relationships. Tips can be anything from instructions on how to do something to information about a useful app.

19. News and current events

Offering information about the latest news in your area or industry is a certain way to keep people interested and sharing your content. Being current and up-to-date with local news is really useful to your audience and it keeps your business looking fresh. To keep up-to-date with news, subscribe to News Feeds and blogs that offer news on your industry or your local area.

20. Negative content

People always like to hear about what not to do, for example: ten things not to do on a first date or ten things not to say in a job interview. The lists of possibilities for this type of post are endless and can create a great deal of amusement and interest.

21. Music, if you are a musician

If you are a band and want to promote your music, there is no better way to promote your material than by posting links to your music and videos on Facebook.

22. Q & A live session

You can host a live question and answer session on your page. This is a really good way to create conversation and engagement. It also creates a professional, informative, and caring image. You can do this by allotting and promoting a specific time for fans to post their questions in the comment section of your Facebook post. Or you could choose to ask them to post their questions and give them a day when you will be answering them. This way, you get more time to research. In both cases it's a good idea to post an image promoting the session.

23. Broadcast live

By using an application called Livestream, you can broadcast any live event to almost any social destination. You can also watch, 'like,' and share any event that may be of interest to your audience.

24. Fill in the blank posts

Getting your audience involved with your content is a very powerful way of creating engagement. Fill in the blank posts can be a way of creating engagement and conversation, for example:

I love going to _____ on my holidays because...

My Monday morning must have this_____

I always take _____ on vacation.

25. Caption this

Posting a photo and then asking your audience to caption it is a really effective and lighthearted way to drive engagement and you could also turn this into a contest. You can use images from stock photo sites or sites like Flickr Creative Commons. Make sure to choose images that will provoke interest and are humorous or inspiring.

26. Case studies

Case studies are a really effective way to demonstrate how something works with real examples. You can use case studies to show how your customers have used your products or services to benefit them in some way. You can also use them to demonstrate a principle or method of doing something by using other businesses as examples.

27. Internet Memes

Meme comes from the Greek word 'Mimema,' which means something imitated. An Internet meme is a style, action, or idea which spreads virally across the Internet. They can take the form of images, videos, or hashtags. There are plenty of tools and apps out there to help you create memes, such as www.memegen.com and imgur.com, which are popular ones.

28. 'Like' versus share votes

This involves combining two competing images in one post and then asking your audience to vote for which image they choose by 'liking' or sharing. This is a really quick way to expand your reach and get your brand out there. To be successful at this you really need to have a good subject and one that most people identify with.

29. Your blog

Creating regular blog posts is a very effective way of getting the fans onto your blog. Make sure you always include an image to provoke interest.

Asking a question can create intrigue and curiosity.

30. Greetings
Simply posting an attractive image or wishing your fans good morning, good night, or to enjoy their weekend will go a long way in breaking the ice and building relationships. These types of posts help to make positive associations with your brand.

31. Testimonials and reviews
You may have received a review on Google Places or Foursquare or simply a message from someone. Posting about good things that people write or say about you contributes to your social proof and builds trust. Remember, people will believe more about what others say about your business than what you, as the owner, say about it.

32. Share something personal
People really like to connect with the person behind the brand. If you have your own personal brand, then this is really important. Sharing interesting positive snippets about your personal life can really help to build relationships and give an authentic feel to your brand. Sharing your plans for the day or posting the occasional photo of yourself can really help get your audience to know you.

33. Thank your fans
Thanking your fans for their engagement and support shows that you really value and appreciate them. This is not only courteous, but it will help make you stand out from the crowd and encourage your fans to participate and engage with your content in the future.

34. Ask your followers how you can help them
Keeping the lines of communication open by asking your fans what sort of content they want more of is another way of showing your fans that you are there to help them.

35. Your personal recommendations

Sharing anything of value with your fans, like a good book or a useful app, is a great way of offering value, and it helps keep your fans feeling positive about your brand.

THE DIFFERENT TYPES OF MEDIA AVAILABLE

In order to create the best experience for your fans you are going to need to create a good balance of content using the different variety of posts available to you. Facebook gives you the opportunity to post text, images, videos, offers, events, and milestones.

Images

"A picture paints a thousand words."

If you are already a Facebook user then you probably know that an image grabs your attention more than any other post in your News Feed. This is because most of us are visually wired and can identify with an image much more quickly than text. Statistics prove that pictures get more comments, shares, and 'likes' than any other post and that followers are far more likely to click on a link to a website, blog, or watch a video if the post contains a picture. According to Facebook, posts which contain a photo generate up to 180% more engagement. If you are posting a link to your blog or an article on your website, make sure you include a compelling image. You are far more likely to gain interest this way. Images not only get shared more, they also have huge viral potential, get remembered, and also create an emotional connection with your audience.

You don't have to be an expert photographer. You can find images from stock photos and also free sites like Flickr. (Be careful to check the license and what you are allowed to do with the images in terms of changing or adding text, etc.) Adding text can be achieved by using Photoshop or other online graphic design apps which are available and easy to use, like www.picmonkey.com . Some stock photo sites also offer you the functionality to add effects and text to your images.

The ideal size for uploading an image to your News Feed it 403 X 403 pixels. If you are linking to images outside Facebook, for example, on your website or blog, then you should aim to have images that are 1200 X 630, or greater, for optimal display on desktop and mobile devices. Larger images send more traffic to websites than smaller thumbnails.

Videos

As with images, videos are highly shareable, have huge viral potential, and increase engagement. People love videos and a good video can offer a huge amount of entertainment, make learning more interesting, more fun, and easier to understand. Videos are also great at helping build relationships, trust, and rapport with your audience. There really is no better way of introducing yourself and building a personal connection with your audience than with video.

The type of videos you should be posting on Facebook are educational, informative, and entertaining and while there is room for the occasional product video, these really belong on your website or blog.

Facebook allows you to upload your video file and stream it directly on your timeline. You can post links to your YouTube videos or share other people's videos. If you want to upload a video to Facebook from your smartphone, you can do so by attaching it in an email and sending it to your unique Facebook email address. To add a caption, simply write it in the subject line of the email.

Text

Whether you are posting a text only post, an image, or video, it is likely that you will be including some text to either introduce or describe your post. As a general rule of thumb, the shorter you keep it, the more engagement you will receive. While that is not to say that longer posts are unsuccessful, generally speaking, it is best to keep the majority of your posts shorter. According to Facebook, posts between 60–250 characters receive 60% more likes, comments, and shares.

While images are definitely more effective and receive higher engagement, there is still room for text only posts to deliver the occasional tip, a greeting, or to ask a question. There are some pages that are very successful at creating engagement with a large number of text posts, but in the end it always comes down to the quality of the content.

Highlighted Posts

If you have a particularly important post or a really compelling image or infographic that needs space, using a highlighted post is a great way to draw attention. The highlighted post spans the whole width of the News Feed and is an excellent opportunity for you to showcase your story. You can really create the "wow factor" with a highlighted post.

To highlight your post, simply upload your image and hover your mouse on the top right of the post over the down arrow and a drop down menu will appear. Simply click the star on the top right of the post and the picture will span both columns of the News Feed. The perfect image size for a highlighted post is 843 X 403 pixels.

Milestones

Milestones on Facebook are used to mark key moments or major events that you want to promote and showcase with your audience. When you create a milestone, it is displayed with a flag icon and automatically expanded to the width of your News Feed. You can use milestones to mark the opening of a business, the launch of a new product, or the launch of an event. The ideal size for a milestone image is 843 X 403 pixels and Facebook will automatically upload it as a highlighted post to span the width of the News Feed. However, you can choose to display it as a normal size post by clicking the highlight button. You can add a location, date, and story for a milestone post. A good tip for milestone posts is to tag as many people who were involved in the milestone as possible.

Blog Posts

According to research, 70% of consumers click through to a website from a retail blog. Blogs are nearly essential now for any business who wants to get found on the Internet, and social media is another very effective tool to drive traffic to your blog. If you do not have a blog then you need to seriously consider creating one. There are numerous free and paid blogging platforms available and there is a whole chapter covering this very subject later on in this book.

Infographics and diagrams

Infographics provide a fascinating way to present statistical information. They are engaging, very shareable, have huge viral potential, and make figures look far more interesting and easier to understand than a list of numbers. People love statistical information relating to their interest because it helps to confirm or affirm what they already may believe, and it helps to give them more confidence in what they are doing or selling. You do not have to be an expert graphic designer to create infographics. There are numerous applications available on the web which can help you do this. Facebook offers you the ability to post large and wide images with highlighted posts, which are excellent for infographics.

Podcasts

Podcasting is a type of digital media usually comprising a series of audio, radio, or video files. You can subscribe to podcasts as you can to blogs and newsletters. For example, if you download a podcast on iTunes, every time the author produces a new one, iTunes will automatically download it. As with video, they are effective at helping to build trust with the listener and can also help you stand out as an authority or influencer in your niche. They encourage customer loyalty if they are produced on a weekly or very regular basis and are incredibly handy for people who are on the go and want to listen while traveling to work or on the way to a meeting. Facebook is the ideal place to promote your podcast.

Cartoons

Cartoons work very well with humor and relatable content. Posting cartoons that your audience can relate to will help demonstrate that you understand and identify with them. They are a great ice breaker and highly shareable as well. Once shared, they are very likely to appeal to more of your target audience and are a great way to widen your reach. If you have an idea for a cartoon, there are sites like Fiverr.com where you can find creatives who offer this type of service at very reasonable prices.

SlideShare

SlideShare is primarily a slide sharing site, but you can upload PowerPoint, keynote, pdf, and open office presentations. SlideShare is a great way to communicate your message, and it is very straightforward and easy to use. It is also another way to get your content rated, commented on, and shared. Your presentations can be embedded into Facebook and your website or blog.

Ebooks & PDF documents

Turning your content into an ebook is a great way to present your content, and offering a free ebook is a really good way to build your opt-in lists and give your reader something of great value.

Webinars

A webinar is like an interactive online conference or workshop. Webinars are a great way of interacting with your audience and building relationships. They can be used for presenting and training, selling a program or course, or answering questions from your audience. They can be saved and listened to at a later date for anyone who could not make the original date and time. Using Facebook to announce your webinar is a very effective way to promote your online event and get people to sign up.

TOP TIPS FOR POSTING CONTENT ON FACEBOOK

Here are some invaluable tips for posting content on Facebook:

Is this relevant to my audience?

Every time you post anything ask yourself this question, and if the answer is no, then don't post it.

Post frequently

To create the greatest opportunity for your fans to see your posts you will need to post between 2-4 times a day. The average lifespan of a post is about three hours and the majority of engagement happens in the first hour. Some people may only view their Facebook page once a day. Therefore, balancing your content at different times of the day is going to boost your chances of having your post seen by more people. Having said this, quality will always win over quantity, so if you do not have anything really good then don't post it.

Create compelling headlines and introductions

Make sure you always communicate why you are sharing and why you think your post will be particularly interesting to your audience. Not only will this grab your audience's attention, but it also helps to personalize your posts and start a conversation.

Include a call-to-action

Facebook posts that include a call-to-action receive far more engagement than posts that do not. Your fans need a little nudge to remind them to 'like', comment, or share, and offering them a choice is very effective. For example, 'like' to agree or comment if you don't. You need to ask your fans to do what you want them to do.

Questions

People are on social media to be social and interact, and people will interact with people other than their friends if they are given the opportunity to do so. One of the best ways to encourage this interaction is through asking questions. According to statistics, asking questions can double your engagement. These could be questions relating to business or non-business topics/subjects. Questions are great ice breakers, spark conversation, and increase engagement. Whether posting an image, video, or text, asking a question provokes discussion.

Facebook hashtags

A hashtag makes a word, group of words, or phrase into a clickable and searchable link in the Facebook News Feed. Every hashtag has its own unique URL on Facebook, and when you click on one, you will see a feed of posts that include that particular hashtag. To create a hashtag simply put the hashtag sign before the word, or group of words, without leaving any spaces between the words. To make your hashtag easier to read you can capitalize the first letter of each word. Even though hashtags do not work on cellphones you can still post them and they will work on desktops. You need to be careful not to post too many hashtags in one post as it just begins to look uninteresting and your fans will lose interest in what is really being said.

The proper use of hashtags on Facebook will greatly benefit your campaign by increasing your reach on Facebook and giving you further opportunities for your content and page to be found. If you find popular hashtags relating to your topic or subject, using these will increase the possibility of your posts being found.

Pin to Top

There may be some posts that you deem particularly important and want new users to see when they arrive at your page. When you 'Pin to Top' your post will appear at the top of your News Feed on the left and stay there for 7 days. At the end of the period you can pin it to the top again if you wish. To pin a post to the top of the page simply hover over the top right of the post, click on the pencil icon, and then click **Pin to Top**.

'Pin to Top' is a very handy little feature and you could also use it to tempt users to become fans by posting an image with a call-to-action. For example, 'Become a fan to receive the latest updates on.....xyz'. You could also use this function to drive new people to an offer, opt-in sign-up form, or an online or offline event like an exhibition or trade show. You could also use it to post a welcome video or a recording of your most recent webinar. Whatever your top promotional goal for the week is, make sure you use the 'Pin to Top' function to promote that goal.

Promoted Posts

Using promoted posts is the only way to guarantee that your posts will appear in the News Feed of all your fans. By clicking **Boost Post** on the bottom right of your post you can choose to either promote your post to the people who already 'like' your page and their friends or to people you choose through targeting. The cost of your promoted post will depend on the number of people who see your post. You can watch the progress of your promoted post campaign as it runs, and you can stop your promotion at any time. Simply click on the heading **Promoted for $** at the bottom of the post and then click on the 'gear' icon on the bottom right in the next window which is displayed and then click **Stop Promotion**.

How frequently you use promoted posts will depend on your budget. In order to make the best use of your budget you will need to try and make sure you promote only those posts that are likely to create the most engagement. The best way to do this is to watch and see how your fans are engaging with a post before promoting it, and if it looks to be successful, promote it. Entertaining posts are usually the ones that receive the most engagement rather than the more sales-driven posts. However, if you have a really good offer, or have a particular action that you want your audience to take, then using this feature is a really good way of guaranteeing that as many people see it as possible.

When you promote a post, Facebook will automatically create a sponsored story. Friends of people who have taken any action on your post by either 'liking', commenting, or sharing will see that on the right side of their News Feed.

Embedded Posts

Embedding your most popular post in your website or blog can really help to increase your reach and engagement and therefore help to increase your Edgerank score. Simply copy the URL of your post, visit this page, https://developers.facebook.com/docs/plug-ins/embedded-posts, and then paste it into where it says **URL of post,** click on **Get code,** and paste it into your website or blog.

Scheduling Posts

Facebook offers you the functionality to schedule posts in the future, and you can schedule posts for photos, texts, images, and videos. This can assist you in timing your posts and freeing you up so you can really keep on top of your Facebook posts. One day you may want to create images for inspirational quotes and you could then post all of these in advance for as far in the future as you wish. To schedule a post, simply complete your post and then click the clock symbol at the bottom left of the post and enter the year, day, and time. You can also schedule your posts using third party sites like Tweetdec, Hootsuite, and Buffer.

Add emoticons

According to statistics, adding emoticons can increase engagement by up to 33%. It's probably not a good idea to add them to every post, but including these funny little images in the occasional post can really add a personal touch, which can result in more comments and shares.

Add images to an album

Adding images to an album rather than directly to your News Feed can really help to increase engagement. When people see a large number of 'likes' on a post they are more likely to click the 'like' button. Because Facebook groups all the 'likes' for all the images into one total sum in albums, this is great for social proof.

CHAPTER FIVE

CREATING EVENTS, CONTESTS ON FACEBOOK

FACEBOOK EVENTS ARE a great way to share your events and even virtual events like the launch of a new blog, website or webinar.

CREATING AND PROMOTING FACEBOOK EVENTS

Creating an event from your business page is like creating an event from your personal account, except you do not have the ability to send direct invitations to your fans and you cannot send Facebook emails to people who are attending. A way around this is to post your event on your own timeline, join your event from your timeline, and then invite your friends. When you post your event, the fans of your page will be able to invite their friends too.

To create an event on your page click on **Offer, Event +** on your timeline. Add the name and details of the event, the location, the date and time, and also a video or image. Images need to be at least 714 X 264 pixels. You also need to add the link where tickets can be obtained from, and this is where you can put the link to your external website. For business events, it is definitely advisable to have an event page outside Facebook, either on your website or a specific event website.

Facebook does not actually support ticket sales. The most popular ticket sales integration seems to be Eventbrite and Eventpal. Eventbrite offers you the opportunity to connect your events to Facebook and will include a link to your ticketing page, which will also be included as a link in your News Feed.

When you have created your event you can share it with your fans by clicking the **share** button on the top right of your page. Make sure you pin your event to the top of your page.

Promoting your event

To ensure maximum exposure of your event, there are strategies you can put in place to further promote your event, which are as follows:

- **Create buzz prior to creating your event:** Before you do actually create your event on your Facebook page it may be a good idea to create some buzz by announcing the event and advising your fans that more details will be posted soon.

- **Use you cover photo:** Your cover photo is a very powerful way to promote your event and draw the attention of new visitors to your page. You can either encourage your new visitors to click the cover image to be taken to an external link or create an arrow pointing to the events tab underneath the cover photo. When you add your new cover photo it will also show up in your News Feed for your fans to see.

- **Promote your event with Facebook Advertising:** When you create your event you will automatically be offered the opportunity to promote it. Simply click **Promote** and you will be sent to the **Event Responses** page where you can choose the audience you wish to target and your budget.

- **Promoted Posts:** A promoted post is a really effective way of promoting your event to all your fans and their friends, and you can target people who are not connected to your page as well. Simply use your event photo and click on **Boost post** and then make sure you pin this to the top of your page. Make sure you add a call-to-action and ask your fans to share the event.

- **Repost your event:** Reposting during the few weeks before your event at different times of the day will help make sure as many of your fans get to know about your event as possible. You could also post different images and information about the event to keep your fans interested.

- **Create a Facebook offer:** You can offer a discount or some kind of benefit to your fans by posting an offer.
- **Invite your friends:** You can't invite your friends from your page, but if you join your event from your personal timeline, you can then invite your friends. Once your friends have RSVP'd, they will then be able to invite their friends, too, by using the **Invite Friends** tab on the top right hand side of the event page. Make sure, when posting about your event, you allow friends to invite their friends and make it clear to them they can do this.
- **Promote on all your marketing and other social platforms:** Make sure you put details about your event on all your blogs and websites and promote it on your other social media sites too.
- **Email your contacts:** You may have customers who are not fans of your Facebook page so be sure to let them know about your event too. Emailing your contacts also makes sure that as many people as possible see your announcement in case they did not see your post on Facebook.

THE BENEFITS OF RUNNING A CONTEST

Many businesses have found running competitions on Facebook to be hugely successful. Facebook contests and competitions are a great way of both generating engagement and new leads for your business. Since Facebook relaxed their rules and are now letting businesses run competitions directly on their page, running a competition is a whole lot easier, less expensive, and much more available for smaller businesses. Previously you were only allowed to run a competition through a third party app. It's a good idea to check Facebook terms and conditions regarding promotions. For example, Facebook still does not permit 'liking' your page or sharing a post as conditions for entering. You also need to check the rules governing contests in your country or state.

Before creating your contest you need to be clear about what your goals are and what you want to achieve through running one. The main benefits for running a competition on your page are as follows:

- **You can build your audience:** A competition is the quickest and easiest way of increasing the number of 'likes' for your page. However, Facebook terms stipulate that you are not allowed to make it a condition to enter your contest. Simple sweepstakes competitions are very popular for increasing the number of 'likes' to your page.

- **Engagement:** Getting people to share your competition is a sure way to increase engagement and a way to improve your Edgerank. Running photo competitions can create huge engagement and a real buzz for a business with fans sharing and commenting on photos. Some third party apps offer the functionality to prompt entrants to share your contest every time they enter.

- **You can capture email addresses for your opt-in:** This is a huge advantage to creating a contest, and once your fans have joined your opt-in, this is a big step in converting them to customers.

- **Brand awareness and social proof:** Having a large number of 'likers' helps to build your social proof, and any promotion like this will help to increase awareness of your brand.

- **Reward your audience:** When you give your audience the opportunity to win something they really value, this helps to keep them interested, particularly if you offer everyone a money-off coupon as a reward for entering.

- **Drive traffic to your website:** You can create a competition with the aim of driving traffic to your website by asking your audience to find certain information about the products on your website and then complete an entry form.

HOW TO CREATE YOUR COMPETITION OR CONTEST

There are two ways you can create your contest: either directly on your page or by using a third party app.

Creating a competition directly on your page

Running your competition directly on your timeline is not only straightforward it is also less expensive. Contests can create a great deal of interest on your page, especially if you are asking for some sort of engagement or action to be taken on your page. Here are some ideas for creating contests on your timeline:

> **A comments contest:** You can post a photo and then ask your fans to comment on it. This is a really effective way of launching and creating buzz around a new product you may be about to launch.
>
> **Create a 'likes' contest:** The advantage of this type of contest is that it is very simple for people to enter. Simply ask your fans to 'like' a post for the chance to enter.
>
> **Caption this contest:** These types of contests are great fun and give your fans a chance to be creative. Simply upload a compelling image and ask your fans to write a caption. The most original captions wins.
>
> **Fill in the blank contest:** Another fun idea for your fans is to simply pick a subject relating to your brand and then write a sentence and leave a space blank for your fans to complete it.
>
> **Photo contest:** Photo contests are really popular. You can either ask fans to submit their photos by attaching them to a private message or ask them to post them on your wall.
>
> **Questions and answers contest:** This is a really good way of getting your audience to find out about one of your products. Simply ask your audience to answer a question relating to one of your products or services.
>
> **Ideas contest:** Get your fans to participate by asking them for their ideas to solve a problem. You may need ideas for the name of a new product. This type of competition not only increases engagement, it also shows you value your fans' opinions and can really make them feel part of your brand.

For best results, here are a few tips for running a contest directly on your timeline:

Post a good image: Using a good image with a description will help tempt your fans to enter and share your contest. However, you are not allowed to make this a condition of entering.

Customize the tab for your contest page

Create a competition image for your cover photo: Make sure you direct people to where they can enter to win with an arrow to the custom tab.

Create a clear headline and call-to-action: Make it clear in the first sentence of your post what you want your fans to do.

Add a clear description: Make it really easy for your fans to understand how to enter and include a description of the prize. Remember to also include hashtags so your get found, for example: #contest, # competition #win #photocontest #sweepstakes.

Create a page to collect entries: If your goal is to collect email addresses then you will need to create either a page on your website or a separate landing page.

Pick the ideal prize: The type of prize you are going to offer is really important, and you should choose a prize which is related to your line of business. This way your contest is far more likely to appeal to your target audience and you will then attract fans who are going to be more likely to be interested in the type of product you offer. You could even create some buzz and engagement prior to launching the competition by asking your fans what sort of prize they would like to win.

Decide on the duration of the competition: You will need to decide on the duration of the competition. With photo and video competitions, you will need to offer a longer time for entrants to carry out the task. With sweepstakes, the duration of the competition can be much shorter.

Keep competition rules clear and simple: You can either include rules in the post or create an external website page for the rules of your competition and make sure you include the following:

> The number of times a participant is allowed to join
> The amount of time the winner has to claim their prize
> The closing date
> Who is eligible
> How the winners will be selected

- **Include the term 'Void where prohibited':** This ensures you are in compliance with any country or state regulations banning your promotion.
- **Include details of how the winner will be chosen.**
- **Announce winners on your timeline:** For competition results you can now announce the winner on your timeline and require that entrants come back to the page to find out who the winner is.

Creating your competition with a third party app

If you want to launch a competition without the worry of administering it yourself then using a third party is ideal. Apps have many advantages, especially if you want to attract a large number of entrants and want to collect emails and add sharing functionality. For larger audiences and sweepstakes, using a third party not only looks professional, it is easier to administer and you can also collect emails and add functionality for sharing your contest. Here are some of the features and benefits of using third party apps:

Look professional and sophisticated: Third party apps can help to make your whole contest look both professional and **organized,** which helps to create trust with your entrants.

Email capture: By using a third party app you can collect email addresses when your users enter the competition.

Include sharing functionality: Third party apps often include a feature where your entrants are offered the opportunity to share the contest.

They select the winner: Using a third party takes away all the administration involved in selecting and notifying the winner.

'Thank you' coupons: You can easily create a thank you coupon for all your entrants so everyone is rewarded for entering. This also helps to drive sales conversions.

In conclusion, third party apps help you to get more 'likes', more engagement, more conversions, more shares, and more emails.

You can visit some of the following to check out prices and information: www.wishpond.com, www.binkd.com, http://www.easypromosapp.com, http://www.wildfireapp.com, www.votido.com, www.offerpop.com. Wildfire offers a great video demo which is really educational, and many of these providers offer case studies so you can see lots of examples of competitions.

PROMOTING YOUR COMPETITION OR CONTEST

Whether you are creating your own contest directly on your timeline or using a third party app you will still need to gain the maximum exposure possible, here are some ways you can promote your contest:

Create Buzz prior to competition announcement: To create some excitement and buzz before the competition is announced you could offer a teaser asking your fans to watch out for the new competition. You could also post a question and ask your fans what prize they would most value.

Create a promoted post: Upload your image with text about your contest with a link to your competition landing page. You can promote your post to the people who 'like' your page and their friends and to a wider, targeted audience.

Create an ad on Facebook: Creating a Facebook ad can widen your audience enormously. Simply click on the **Adverts Manager** from your page and then **Create Ad** on the top right.

Repost your competition: Reposting at different times during the few weeks before your competition date expires will help to let as many people as possible see the competition in their News Feed.

Announce your contest on all your other social platforms: You can use hashtags on Facebook and Twitter so people who are looking for competitions will find you. You can use keywords like sweepstakes, competitions, contest, win, photocontest, etc.

Pin to top: Make sure you pin your competition image to the top of your page so new visitors to your page will see it.

Change your cover photo: Adding your competition image to your cover photo will ensure that any new visitors see your competition, and it will also appear in the News Feed of your fans.

Encourage your fans to share your event: Adding a call-to-action in your post is a great way to prompt people to spread the word.

Promote on your website or blog: Make sure you put a banner about your competition on your blog and website.

Email your contacts: You may have customers who are not fans of your Facebook page, so be sure to let them know about your competition too. Emailing your contacts also ensures that as many of your fans as possible see your announcement, in case they did not see it in their News Feed.

Advertise with Google Adwords: You can use adwords to drive traffic to either Facebook or a separate competition landing page.

List your contest on contest sites: There are lots of websites where you can enter your contest details.

Promote offline: Make sure you include details about your competition on any of your marketing material, at your point of sale, and on receipts or bills.

Analyzing your results

Most third party applications let you analyze the results by giving information, and they can compare the effectiveness of your competition with Twitter. You will be able to see how the contest has affected your interaction on Facebook by viewing the insights and compare figures before and after the competition. Make sure you measure the number of new fans, contestants, 'likes' and shares per contest, sales of product, and visits to your website.

Tracking these figures will help you in creating new contests and bettering your results in the future. Measuring results will give you a good idea whether or not the contest worked. You may decide that you need to promote more on the weekend or at a certain time of the day.

CHAPTER SIX

DAY TO DAY ACTIVITY

THERE ARE CERTAIN things that you will need to do on a day-to-day basis to run your campaign on Facebook. It is a good idea to allot a specific amount of time and a particular time of day to do this. Here are some of the things you will need to do:

'Liking' your customer's pages

This is important if your customers are business owners themselves. 'Liking' their pages or following your customers will go a long way in building relationships. By 'liking' their pages, you are showing them that you are interested in what they have to say and also helping them to achieve their goals by helping to build their audience.

Showing your audience you value and respect them

If you value and respect your audience they will probably love, respect, and value your business. Be kind, generous, offer as much help and value as possible, reply to their comments, and make it obvious that you value them and are listening to them. Don't be afraid to be yourself rather than a stiff brand with no personality.

Everyone is aiming for shares, 'likes,' and comments, so if you are helping others out by commenting and 'liking' their content, it is going to draw attention to your brand. Once they see you have taken an interest they are more likely to take an interest in your content. This is one area where the reciprocation rule works very well on Facebook. Engaging with content will also draw attention to you and your brand, and you will find that people will click on your name to find out who you are and they may very well subscribe to your channel. Be friendly to your audience, be chatty, authentic, genuine, and embrace the conversation. All this will all go a long well in building a positive image for your brand and will set you apart from others who are continually ambushing their audience with self-promotion.

Follow influencers in your niche or 'like' their pages

Building relationships with key influencers in your niche is invaluable. Not only can you learn from their content but also these people can have literally 1000's of fans so when you start to interact with their content, you are exposed to their fans.

Dealing with negative comments

Every business at some time will have to deal with negativity from followers. Hopefully if you have a good product then this is not going to happen too often. There are 'trolls' out there who have nothing better to do than post negative comments. The best thing to do with them is just ignore them, delete their comments, and block them. However, there will be real customers who have real concerns and complaints and may post negative comments publicly. There may also be people who really want to lash out to gain your attention as quickly as possible and spread the news to their friends too! You need to deal with complaints quickly and be as transparent and authentic as possible. The best thing to do is to apologize and say how sorry you are to hear of the inconvenience they have been caused and offer to continue the conversation and deal with their concern by either private message or telephone. You can then deal with this privately, give your customer the full attention they deserve, and decide on your next course of action or compensation.

CHAPTER SEVEN

ADVERTISING ON FACEBOOK

FACEBOOK HAVE CREATED a highly effective and user friendly advertising platform for their users which has been designed to help businesses advertise to their target audience. As reaching your audience organically (free) on Facebook is becoming more and more difficult paying for the attention on Facebook is becoming more and more necessary especially of you have a particular offer or promotion.

Because Facebook holds such a massive amount of information about their users, including: age, gender, location and interests, you can easily leverage the power of Facebook to reach your target audience. You can even target users based on the groups that users have joined and the pages they have liked, yes you can target the fans of your competition! And targeting adverts to fans of your own Page can really help to drive down the cost of your advertising considerably. You can use Facebook advertising to either advertise your Facebook page or to drive traffic to an external website or blog.

Depending on your advertising objective you can choose any of the following Facebook advertising options:

1.) Page post engagement (Promoted Page Posts.)

Promoted posts ensure that your posts show up in the timeline of the people who have liked your page and their friends and also to a wider targeted audience if you wish.

Page post photo

Text 90 characters

Image Size 1200 x 1200 px

Page post link ad
Text 90 characters
Link title 25 characters
Image size 1200 x 627 px

2.) Page Likes (Get more likes)
You can create adverts to grow your audience on Facebook. This is incredibly important for succeeding on Facebook. Once you have people 'like' your page you have more opportunity to build trust and then convert then into customers.
Text 90 characters
Image size 1200 x 450 px

3.) Clicks to Website (Get more clicks to your website)
Enable you to advertise an external website or blog.
Text 90 characters
Advert image size 1200 x 864 px

4.) Website Conversions
You can create adverts for particular actions for people to take on your website. You will need to use a conversion tracking pixel to measure your results.
Text 90 characters
Advert image size 1200 x 864 px

5.) App Installations (Get more app users)
Offers you the opportunity to create an advert which encourages users to install your app.
Text 90 characters
Advert image size 1200 x 864 px

6.) App Engagement (Increase app engagement)

Offers you the opportunity to create an advert to get more activity on your app.

7.) Event Responses (Increase event attendance)

Offers you the opportunity to create adverts to promote an event.
Text 90 characters
Event Title 25 characters
Image Size 1200 x 450 px

8.) Offer Claims (Create offers that can be redeemed in store)

Offers you the opportunity to either create an offer, or advertising an offer you have already created on your timeline.
Text 90 characters
Offer Title 25 characters
Image Size 1200 x 627 pixels

Creating Your Facebook Ad

Creating your advert is really straight forward, Facebook takes you through a very simple step by step process. You will need to select or upload an image, create a headline and description, select your audience, decide if you want your advert to appear in News feed or alongside it and set your campaign budget. Here are some tips for creating your adverts:

- **Study other adverts** Have a good look at what adverts are appearing on your News feed and which ones attract your attention.
- **Image** Your image is the most important part of your advert, this is what will grab your audience's attention. If you are looking to increase your page likes then Facebook will automatically populate your advert with your Page's cover photo. If then you are going for an advert which is going to appear to the right of your News feed then picking a close up image is going to show up much better. You can also use clear readable type, or funny

pictures. You can find images on Facebook in their library, or other stock photography sites, or search creative commons licensed images. You can use an online image editor like http://www.picmonkey.com to enhance, edit and add effects to your images, if your photoshop skills are not up to much.

- **Headline** You will need to use an attention grabbing headline and the maximum number of characters you can use is 25.
- **Text** (90 Characters) To create an effective advert you will need describe the most important benefit to your audience, create desire by offering a discount or free trial and then end with a call to action for example, 'click here to get this free offer' or 'click here to get this free ebook' or 'RSVP Now'.
- **Create more than one advert** It's definitely advisable to create more than one advert. This way once your campaign is running you can see which one is the most successful and use those that are performing better.

Ad Placement

Make sure your have chosen where you want to display your advert and you have three options:
- **Desktop News Feed**
- **Mobile News Feed (Adverts placed on Mobile tend to do better)**
- **Right Column**
-

To get the most engagement then it is advisable to place on Desktop News feed and in Mobile News Feed.

Selecting your audience

You can define the relevant audience for your adverts by selecting from the following:
- **Location**
- **Gender**
- **Age**

- **More demographics** Demographic options include: Relationship Status, Education Level, Subject, School/University, Undergrad years and Workplaces.
- **Interests** When it comes to interests Facebook will provide a drop down menu of different interests and it is here where you can target people who have liked other pages too. Simply start typing in the name of the Page or Group and Facebook will offer you matches.
- **Connections** You can select people who are already connected to your Page or Group, app or event and their friends or you can exclude people who are connected to a certain Page, Group, app or event.

As you select Facebook will display the number of people you will be targeting. Your audience size should be proportional to your budget otherwise you will not reach everyone in your targeted audience. If you find you are targeting too few people with the interests you have selected then try and include related interests to widen your reach.

Setting up your campaign and budget

Once you have created your adverts and selected your target audience you can set your campaign budget, this can be per day or over the lifetime of your campaign. You can either schedule your advert to run continually or set a start and end date. Next you need to bid and you can either bid for Page likes clicks or impressions. When you bid for impressions you pay for when people see your advert. Once you have completed this section you are ready to start advertising.

CREATE, CAPTURE, CONVERT WITH FACEBOOK ADVERTISING

Throughout this book you will read numerous times about the importance of capturing the email addresses of your prospects and how important it is to obtain their email address by offering them a compelling offer on either a special Facebook landing page, your website or a separate landing page with a compelling offer. With the functionality available on Facebook and easy access to your target audience you can easily set up a lead capture system that works on autopilot and here is how you do it:

Create your special free offer

Firstly you need to think of something that your target audience really want and it needs to be something they would consider really valuable, this could be a free ebook, a short video course or a Webinar about a really hot topic or a special money offer coupon. Webinars and videos can be incredibly effective as they help to create an immediate personal connection with your audience from the start. This can be extremely powerful as most of us like to buy from people they like and trust. When choosing your offer you need to ask yourself this one question: is this valuable enough that my ideal customer would pay for it? If your answer to this question is yes, then this is probably the right offer and you are very likely to convince them to volunteer their email. If your answer is no then you will need to think again. This really is one of the most important parts of this lead generation system and in order to create a really positive first experience with your prospect you need to really wow them with your offer.

Create your landing page

Next you need to create a special landing page with your offer and your email opt-in capture form. You can either ask a web developer to create this for you or use a landing page generator service like, www.leadpages.com , www.launcheffect.com or www.instapage.com or www.unbounce.com . For a monthly fee these websites offer an incredibly user friendly service with numerous templates, design examples and tutorials to help you put your landing page together. Your landing page needs to be specific to the one goal you want to achieve which is to visually promote your offer and then capture the email addresses of your prospects.

Create your thank you page
Most of the websites mentioned and your email service provider will offer you the opportunity to create a thank you page. Your thank you page is a great place to offer your subscribers the opportunity to share your promotion with their friends.

Prepare your email campaign
You email list is one of the most valuable assets of your business and the main aim of your opt-in is to be able to communicate with your subscribers on an ongoing basis so that you can build trust, deliver valuable content and sell your products. If you craft your messages correctly you will be able to do all this without coming over as being pushy or over 'salesy'and continue to deliver content for years to come. If you haven't already done so then you will need to set up an account with an email service provider, for example, www.aweber.com or www.mailchimp.com or www.madmimi.com

Create a compelling Facebook Post with your offer
To create your offer you simply need to create a post in your News feed by uploading a compelling image with an attention grabbing message.

- Upload a compelling image with an attention grabbing message on the image. (Text must not take up anymore than 20% of the image)
- Add a compelling description of your offer. Starting your post with a question can be a very effective way of grabbing attention.
- Add your link to your special landing page.

Select your audience
This is where Facebook really excels and you can really drill down and steer your campaign towards your exact target audience. Simply click on 'Boost Post' and you can target by demographics, interests and in advanced options you can target the fans of other pages as well.

Go

Once your system is set up you are ready to push the button and go. It's really important to monitor your results at this stage to see what works and what does not. You may need to adjust your message, or offer, or graphic until you discover what really works. Once you have it right you have your very own system to create, capture and convert leads into customers and your very own brand advocates.

HOW TO PROFIT FROM REMARKETING ON FACEBOOK

In today's digital world not do you have the opportunity to connect with your target audience through content and advertising you now have the opportunity to show off your products and services again to those people who have shown an interest by visiting our webpage but not actually taken the next step by signing up to an opt-in or buying our product or service. This is what is called remarketing and has to be one of the most powerful methods of marketing available to you today.

Even with opt-in and squeeze pages the fact is that the majority of people who land on your web page will disappear never to be seen again. There could be a number of factors or reasons why these browsers do not take any action:

- They are shopping around for the best deals.
- They are not in a right financial position to make the purchase at that time.
- They are distracted by a telephone call or something else.
- They have not heard of your brand before and are therefore unsure about your product.
- They are just not ready to make the buying decision.

Remarketing gives brands the opportunity to have another go at selling their products by showing adverts to the people who have previously visited their website.

Facebook allows their advertisers to create Custom Audiences from Facebook users who have taken a particular action on their website or mobile app. Advertisers can do this by adding a pixel code to their website and then delivering adverts relevant to the actions the users have already taken on the site. For example, a hotel booking website with the remarketing pixel added could be used to reach a group of people who have been searching for a hotel but never actually made the reservation. The advertiser could come back with an advert offering them a certain discount to tempt them back to make their reservation. A website offering a fashion range could come create an advert offering a discount to those people who had browsed their site but not purchased anything.

This remarketing is also a great way to have another go at getting users who have visited your website to sign up to your opt-in. For instance you could advertise your latest Webinar to those Facebook users who have already visited your website and since they have already visited your brands website they are more likely to sign up.

Facebook also allows you to create Custom Audiences from your current email list or your Mailchimp subscribers. To create Custom Audiences and use these features you will need to select 'Audiences' from the Adverts Manager menu and then select 'Create a Custom Audience'. You then need to select which audience you want to create and then agree to the terms and conditions. You can choose from:

- Data File Custom Audience
- Mailchimp Custom Audience
- Custom Audience from your Mobile App
- Custom Audience from your Website

When you choose the Website option you will need to add your Audience Name and Description and then select whether you want to include all website visitors or those who have visited specific pages only. You then need to set the time the people will be saved in your audience and lastly ask your developer to add the pixel code, supplied by Facebook, to your website.

CHAPTER EIGHT

HOW TO WIN WITH FACEBOOK'S ALGORITHM

FACEBOOK'S RECENT ALGORITHM has made it more difficult for businesses to reach their fans organically (without paying), and it does not look like it will change any time soon. However, there are very positive ways to look at this change, and there are many brands and pages that are doing very well and still receiving huge engagement without having to pay for it. Of course if you want to guarantee that all your fans see your posts then you will need to pay for it through Facebook's advertising reach, but there are ways that you can still reach your fans without paying.

One of the good things about this change is that it has cut out a great deal of unwanted noise. Therefore, users are seeing only what they really want to see in their News Feed and are not constantly being bombarded with posts that that they may not want to see. Facebook takes into consideration the posts that users are engaging with and will show more of these posts in their News Feed. Therefore, if you are creating valuable content that your audience is engaging with, you can actually gain more attention. Here are some tips on how to capitalize on Facebook's Algorithm:

- **Make every post count:** With every update, you need to make sure you stand out from the crowd by creating the best possible content. You also need to make sure that you put maximum thought into the way you craft and write your posts in order to receive the highest engagement. By focusing on engagement and encouraging your audience to comment, you are more likely to show up on their News Feed more often.

- **Create text only posts:** Even though image posts tend to get higher engagement, it is becoming evident that text posts are reaching more people in the News Feed. Asking questions is a great way to spark engagement.

- **Don't give up:** Many businesses are giving up and no longer posting updates, which is a huge opportunity for those who are sticking with it. So do continue posting. By staying the course and continuing to deliver high quality content to your audience, you are showing that you are in it for the long haul. If new people visit your page and see that you are no longer posting content, it's not going to do your brand any good.

- **Ask your audience to sign up:** Let your fans know that because of the new algorithm they are unlikely to see all your posts and, therefore, if they want to continue receiving valuable content, it's a good idea to sign up to your list.

- **Be realistic and set a budget:** If you have specific offers or things you want to say and you want to reach the majority of your fans and other targeted users, you are going to need to pay for it using Facebook's advertising platform. Therefore, be realistic, and if you believe Facebook advertising is a priority, work out how much you can afford to spend and set a budget for the year.

- **Promote your most valuable posts:** Make sure that the posts you promote are those that are going to be the most popular, so check how your post performs organically before you pay to promote it. You can usually tell within the first one to three hours how it is performing.

- **Let your fans know:** You can advise your fans that if they like your content and want to get your updates all the time then it would be a good idea to switch on **'Get Notifications'**. This is found by clicking the down arrow next to the 'like' button.

- **Value your fans:** Never has it been more important to show your fans how much you value them in a truly authentic way. Make sure that if your fans have taken the time to engage with your content that you engage with them and reward them by 'liking' their comments and commenting or answering their questions. If you do this, they are likely to come back again. If you a selling to businesses then make sure you reciprocate and share their content if it is relevant to your audience.

- **Create a group**: Creating a group around a topic which is of interest to your target audience can be an incredibly powerful way of promoting your brand and getting them to read your content and visit your blog.

- **Join Instagram:** You may find your fans are on Instagram as well, so if you haven't already gotten an Instagram account then this is the time to set one up. Instagram is a great way of reaching your fans organically, and you can post to both platforms at the same time.

CHAPTER NINE

MEASURING AND MONITORING YOUR RESULTS ON FACEBOOK

MEASURING AND MONITORING your results and performance against your original goals and objectives on a continual basis is essential. This is where many businesses go wrong. They carry on aimlessly, posting content without checking to see what is working and what is not. Then after 6 months or a year, they wonder why their campaign is making no positive difference at all.

When you measure your results you will discover so much information about your campaign which will allow you to steer it in the right direction to achieve those SMART goals and objectives and stop anything that is not working.

When you originally work out your strategies and tactics for your campaign you will be estimating what you need to do to achieve your goals and objectives. However, as your campaign runs, you will see exactly what you need to do to achieve what you originally set out to do. For example, you may need to increase the amount you spend on advertising to attract new fans or you may need to change the types of posts you make to increase engagement and reach. Perhaps you need to increase the number of competitions you run to increase the number of opt-in subscribers. This is what it is all about. Make your campaign work for you by constantly measuring your success against the goals set and then adjusting your strategies accordingly in order to achieve the results.

You will easily be able to see the number of people who 'like' your page, the number of 'likes' you get for a post, or the number of opt-in subscribers. However, if you want to look at more detailed information, for example, the number of people Facebook is sending to your website or blog or how many of your Facebook fans are converting into customers, you will need to use Facebook Ads Manager, Facebook Insights, and Google Analytics. You can also use sites like Hootsuite and Buffer who provide analytics for Facebook.

FACEBOOK INSIGHTS

Facebook **Insights** are found at the top of your page. Insights are a gold mine of information about how your campaign is performing, and it helps you monitor and understand what is and what is not working on your page and who is engaging with your posts. It also helps you make decisions about the best way to connect with your fans.

The insight layout has six tabs: overview, likes, reach, visits, posts, and people.

The Overview Tab shows what has been happening on your page in the last seven days and focuses on three metrics:

> **Page likes** - Total and new.
> **Page reach**- The total number of people who were shown your page and post.
> **Engagement** - The total number of unique people who engaged with your page as well as the type of engagement, 'likes' or comments. You will also see the last three posts that you created and how they performed.

The Page Likes Tab displays three metrics and shows you how your audience is growing:

> **Total Page** – 'Likes'.
> **Net Likes** – 'Likes' minus 'unlikes'.
> **Where your page 'likes' came from**

If you click on this graph it will show you why and how your 'likes' grew on your page on any day. This may be from ads or suggested pages, pages 'liked', posts by other pages, or by cellphone. You can also drag on the chart to display more than one day.

The Reach Tab

- **Post Reach:** This shows you the number of people who saw your posts and how they saw them, either organic or paid. You can click on the chart to see more information about that day or drag on the chart to select more than one day and you can see what posts were being seen over that time. You can see positive engagement, 'likes', comments, and shares, and also negative information which shows if your post was hidden or whether a fan 'unliked' your page.
- **Total reach:** The total number of people who are shown any activity from your page, including posts from other people and check-ins.

The Visits Tab

- **Page and Tab Visits:** The visits tab shows you a breakdown of where your visits are coming from.
- **Other Page Activity:** Shows you the number of actions people took that involved your page. This could be mentions, posts by other people on your page, offers purchased, and check-ins.
- **External Referrers:** Shows you the number of people who came to your page from outside sources, such as Google or Bing or other social sites etc.

The Posts Tab
This tab is divided into two sections.

- **When your fans are online:** This shows you when the people who 'like' your page are on Facebook. You can put your mouse over a certain day and see when your fans are most likely to see your posts.
- **All posts published:** All posts published shows you all your posts in chronological order, how many people the post reached, and how they engaged and the actions that were taken ('likes', comments, or shares).
- **Post types:** Shows you average post performance based on reach and performance.

The People Tab

- **Your fans:** This gives you demographic information about their age, gender, geography, and language. The age and gender chart shows how popular your page is with a certain age or gender compared to the total Facebook population.
- **People reached & people engaged:** These two tabs break down who has seen and engaged with your post by the same criteria.
- **People engaged**

Check-ins

Soon to be introduced check-ins will show you information about who has checked in.

FACEBOOK ADVERTS MANAGER

Your ads manager is where you can see at a glance how your campaigns are performing and analyze what is and what is not working. It's here that you can view your account and billing information, the number of post engagements, page 'likes', and your ad click through rates. You can also create ad reports. You can access your ads manager by clicking the 'gear' icon at the top of the page and then clicking **Manage Adverts**.

Your ads manager will show you comparisons between your different ads and how they are performing in terms of the number of clicks and the cost. When advertising, it's a really good idea to create quite a number of ads and change various aspects of the ad and then test each over a couple of days to see which are working best.

Facebook Ads Reports

You can generate a number of reports with Facebook ads reports, and you can schedule these reports. You can set the frequency at which you want them created and then have them sent to your email address.

Reports

Facebook lets you create and schedule reports in the ads manager. When you click on **Reports** you can then choose from General Metrics, Website Conversion, and Placement Reports:

> **General Metrics:** With this report you can select the time period you want to view and also customize the metrics so only you can see the information that is important to you.
>
> **Website Conversion:** This report lets you see how many conversions you received as a result of your Facebook ad. You do this with an offsite pixel, and you have to set up conversion tracking pixels on specific website pages to track specific conversions that happen on that page. To do this, go to your Ads manager, **Power Editor,** and then **Conversion Tracking** on the left side column. Give your conversion pixel a name and select a category from the drop down menu and then click **Create.** A pop-up box will appear where you can **View Pixel Code,** and this is the code you need to integrate into the page where you wish to track your conversions.
>
> **Placement Based Metrics:** This report shows the performance of your ad based on the placement of your ad and the devices your ad was shown on. For example, you can see the level of engagement for an ad in the News Feed from a cellphone or on

the right side of Facebook on a desktop. With this report, you will be able to identify which type of device resulted in the highest engagement for your ad.

To view the information that is most important to you simply click on **Edit Columns** and use the column sets to view specific metrics you want to see in the report.

- **General**: Includes reach, frequency, impressions, amount spent, cost per impression (CPM), cost per click (CPC), clicks, click-through rate (CTR), and actions
- **Page**: Includes page 'likes', page engagement, offer claims, and cost per page 'likes'
- **Offsite**: Includes clicks, unique clicks, click through rate (CTR), link clicks, reach, impressions, amount spent, cost per click (CPC), and cost per impression (CPM)
- **App**: Includes app installs, app engagement, mobile app installs, and cost per mobile app installs
- **Conversion**: Includes conversions, checkouts, registrations, cost per website conversions, cost per checkout, and cost per registration
- **Demographic**: Includes your ad performance by age and gender
- **Geographic**: Includes your ad performance by country
- **Placement**: Includes performance broken down by placement, where your ad was shown on Facebook

Old Reports
You can also create the following Old Reports:

- **Advertising performance:** This report includes statistics like impressions, clicks, click-through rate (CTR), and amount spent.
- **Responder demographics:** This report provides valuable demographic information about users who are clicking on your ads.

- **Actions by impression time:** This report shows the number of actions organized by the impression time of the Facebook Ad or Sponsored Story.
- **Inline Interactions:** This report helps you understand the engagement on page posts. It includes metrics like impressions, clicks, and detailed actions such as 'likes', photo views, and video plays that happened directly from your ads.
- **News Feed:** This report includes statistics about impressions, clicks, click-through rate (CTR), and average position of your ads and sponsored stories in News Feed. Use it to analyze the performance of your ads and sponsored stories.

GOOGLE ANALYTICS

In order to track the success of your campaign, it really is essential that you set up a Google Analytics account. With Google Analytics, you will easily be able to track how your campaign is performing in comparison to your other social campaigns, and Google Analytics will be able to give you detailed information about the impact Facebook is having on your business.

Social Reports

Google Analytics provides advanced reports that let you track the effectiveness of your campaign with the following social reports:

- **The Overview Report:** This report lets you see at a glance how much conversion value is generated from social channels. It compares all conversions with those resulting from social media.
- **The Conversions Report:** The Conversions Report helps you to quantify the value of social media and shows conversion rates and the monetary value of conversions that occurred due to referrals from Facebook and any of the other social networks. Google Analytics can link visits from Facebook with the goals you have chosen and your E - commerce transactions. To do this you will need to configure your goals in Google Analytics, which

is found under **Admin** and then **Goals**. Goals in Google Analytics lets you measure how often visitors take or complete a specific action, and you can either create goals from the templates offered or create your own custom goals. The Conversions report can be found in the **Standard Reporting** tab under Traffic Sources > Social > Conversions.

- **The Networks Referral Report:** The Networks Referral report tells you how many visitors the social networks have referred to your website and shows you how many page views and visits, the duration of the visits, and the average number of pages viewed per visit. From this information you can determine which network referred the highest quality of traffic.

- **Data Hub Activity:** The Data Hub Activity Report shows how people are engaging with your site on the social networks. You can see the most recent URL's that were shared, how they were shared, and what was said.

- **Social Plug-in Report:** The Social Plug-in Report will show you which articles are being shared and from which network. The Google + 1 button is tracked automatically within Google Analytics, but additional technical set-up is required for Facebook. Information about how to do this can be found on the Facebook Developers site.

- **The Social Visitors Flow Report:** This shows you the initial paths that your visitors took from social sites, through your site, and where they exited.

- **The Landing Pages Report:** This report shows you engagement metrics for each URL. These include page views, average visit duration, and pages viewed per visit.

- **The Trackbacks Report:** The Trackback report shows you which sites are linking to your content and how many visits those sites are sending to you. This can help you to work out which sort of content is the most successful so you can create similar content and also helps you to build relationships with those who are constantly linking to your content.

Tracking Custom Campaigns with Google Analytics

Google Analytics lets you create URL's for custom campaigns for website tracking. This helps you to identify which content is the most effective in driving visitors to your website and landing pages. For instance, you may want to see which particular posts on Facebook are sending you the most traffic or you may want to see which links in an email or particular banners on your website are sending you the most traffic. Custom campaigns let you measure this and see what is and what is not working by letting you add parameters to the end of your URL. You can either add you own or use the URL Builder.

To do this, simply type "URL builder" into Google and click on the first result. The URL builder form will only appear if you are signed into Google. You then need to add the URL that you want to track to the form provided, complete the fields, and click 'Submit.' You will then need to shorten the URL with bit.ly or goo.gl/ . Once you have set these up you can track the results within Google Analytics.

MANAGING YOUR FACEBOOK CAMPAIGN

There are now numerous tools available on the Internet to help manage your campaign, particularly if you are using other networks to build your business. These will let you organize your multiple social platforms, see all your interaction in the same place, and also let you share your information across several social networks. Here are a few of the most popular, with information on the benefits you can offer.

Hootsuite

Hootsuite is a social media management dashboard that helps you to manage and measure multiple social networks. You can manage up to five accounts for free, and it is designed so you can listen, engage, and manage all from one place. Hootsuite is Internet based, so there's no need to download any software. Other benefits include: scheduled tweets, bulk schedule with a csv file, and built-in analytics so you can measure your progress on multiple networks' social campaigns.

Buffer

Buffer is a free online tool that lets you post to multiple accounts, including Facebook, LinkedIn, Twitter, and Google+, and schedule your updates. It offers automatic URL shortening and basic analytics. Buffer lets you post on your personal profiles as well as your business pages, and it also allows you to use bit.ly links so your followers will not know you are scheduling your tweets. Upgrading allows you to add more accounts and schedule more tweets than the basic free account.

Socialoomph

Socialoomph has an impressive list of features to boost your social media productivity. Not only does it help you manage your Facebook, Twitter, and LinkedIn accounts, it also helps you schedule posts to your blog as well. There are free and premium options available.

Make Twitter Work For Your Business

Alex Stearn

Table of Contents

CHAPTER ONE

GETTING STARTED ON TWITTER

TWITTER WAS CREATED in 2006 as a social networking service and microblogging platform to enable users to create and send messages of up to140 characters known as 'Tweets'. The original founders came across the word Twitter and decided it was perfect. The definition, a short burst of inconsequential information or chirps from birds, but of course it has become a whole lot more!

The service gained popularity incredibly quickly and Twitter has grown into a powerful worldwide news service, it is one of the top ten most visited websites and is used by most journalists and the majority of major brands. Today there are around 215 million active monthly users and 100 million active daily users who are tweeting approximately 500 million Tweets per day and rising. When you consider that news often breaks faster on Twitter than through the media, Twitter becomes hard to ignore when looking to use it to promote any business.

According to a study the way in which people are using Twitter is changing and only half of its active users in the sample had posted a tweet in the last month. This suggests that the other half of its active users are simply using it as a resource for discovery. Twitter users are hungry for information and new ideas that are either going to make their business or life better. The great news for businesses is that the usage is becoming more commercial and there is a now a growing interaction with brands among the Twitter population. Statistics show that people are using Twitter to interact with brands, post positive comments about brands and also to ask friends for advice about products and services.

Smart businesses who have identified that their target audience are on Twitter are using its enormous power to find new customers, generate and convert leads, communicate with their existing customers and build their brand.

Twitter provides huge opportunities for any business to get their brand in front of people they would never have had the opportunity of getting in front of before. You can literally grow your followers from just a few to many valuable contacts, influencers and prospects in only a short space of time. However like any social media platform it has to be used correctly and launching in without a plan and information about your target audience is just going to be a waste of time and resources.

THE BENEFITS OF USING TWITTER FOR YOUR BUSINESS

At first it may seem hard to understand how a service that offers you only 140 characters to say something, could be such a powerful force for marketing. So that you can make the best use of Twitter and to help you identify ways that you can use it to benefit your business, you need to know exactly what its capabilities are. Here are some of the ways you can use Twitter:

- **Lead Generation** The main goal of any business is going to be to generate leads for conversion. On Twitter you have access to literally million of users and the opportunity to find new prospects is enormous. Twitter offers a very informal way of making contact with people and makes it very easy for you to gain attention by simply following users. As long as you have a lead generation and capture system in place your business can benefit hugely from Twitter.

- **To connect with customers** If your customers are on Twitter it is very likely that they will want to follow you, and Twitter offers you an excellent way to engage with your customers. By staying in contact with them you can continue to build loyalty, communicate new offers and when they start interacting with your brand their followers will hear about your brand too.

- **Branding** You no longer need to be a big name to build a brand on twitter. Twitter has evened out the playing field and has made everything possible for businesses both small and large and you can literally get your brand in front of thousands of people. Once you are connecting with customers, providing them with valuable information, answering their questions and taking notice of their comments and complaints you can start building relationships and brand loyalty.

- Drives Traffic to your website or blog By sharing and posting links to useful content videos, blog articles and other useful information you can drive traffic to your website or blog which can drive sales and generate leads.

- **Event promotion** Twitter is a great way to get the news out about your new event or Webinar. With Twitter's functionality you can connect attendees of your event which then helps to promote it to a wider audience.

- **Promotions, offers and contests** Promotions are a very effective way of building brand awareness and also building your opt-in list. Word can spread very quickly on Twitter so it's an obvious choice to use this platform to publicize your latest special offer.

- **Introductions to new contacts and networking** The potential for growing new contacts and connecting with thought leaders in your industry is huge. Twitter's search facility makes it incredibly easy to find people who may be interested in your product or service.

- **Helps to break down communication barriers** If you have found particular people hard to contact by traditional methods, then tweeting a message can work wonders and people are often far more likely to respond or reply to a tweet than a cold call.

- **Monitor real time conversations** With Twitter search and other online tools you can listen to what is being said about your business. Twitter is great for catching potential problems early and gives you the opportunity to fix them and turn them around to a positive result before they get out of hand. By listening into conversations on Twitter you can also discover what your customers like or dislike about your product or service.

- **Customer service** Twitter is a great way for your customers to stay in contact with you and because so many people have smart phones and can access the internet it is often so much more convenient to contact a business via social media. Whether you use Twitter for customer service or not will depend on whether you have the resources available to offer to respond to customers quickly. Many businesses use a separate Twitter handle for their customer service.

- **Boosts your visibility on Google** Twitter profiles are highly ranked on Google for both businesses and individuals, this is probably because the content is current and Google loves fresh content.

- **Publicize Testimonials** If anyone says anything good about your business or brand then retweeting this is great way of spreading the word about your positive testimonials and you can also save them as your favorites.

- **Post your press releases** You can use Twitter as another way of getting your press release in front of the right press contacts.

There are very useful directories available where you can find journalists on Twitter who may be interested in your stories.

- **Helps you keep up to date with news and trends in your industry** Twitter is used massively by the media in all types of industries for finding and publishing breaking news, so it is the perfect place to find out about the latest news and trends in your industry.

- **Helps to drive traffic to your other social networks** Using Twitter to find new followers can be very effective way of driving traffic to your other social networks. It may be that you concentrate your marketing efforts on Facebook but you can use Twitter very effectively to grow your fans on Facebook.

- **Helps you find suppliers and vendors** Twitter is a great way to find new suppliers and find out about them through their interactions and current customer feedback.

- **Find out about your competition** What better way to spy on your competition! Following your competition is probably the fastest way to find out what is going on in your market and keeping up with trends in your industry.

Once you are aware of these benefits you need to think hard about what you want to achieve and what your main goals are for your Twitter campaign. This is incredibly important when it comes to setting up your profile and when you start posting content. This will be covered in more detail in the planning section.

SETTING UP YOUR TWITTER PROFILE FOR SUCCESS

Before launching into strategies and tactics and how to use Twitter it is a good idea to first set up your account and familiarise yourself with how Twitter works. This chapter is going to firstly take you through setting up

143

your account and then give you a tour of the site and an explanation of all the common terms which are used on Twitter. So lets get started!

The great thing about Twitter is that it is incredibly easy to set up and simple to use. Once you have set up your profile you are literally ready to go. To join simply visit www.Twitter.com/signup and you will be asked to enter your full name, email address, password and username. When creating your password make sure you make it as secure as possible by making it at least 10 characters long and including both upper and lower case characters and numbers.

Choosing your username

Your username or Twitter handle is incredibly important and is what makes up your twitter profile URL. You will use it to log into your account and to publicize your twitter presence on all your marketing material. Your username can contain up to 15 characters however it is sensible to keep it as short as possible. Not only is a shorter username easier to remember but it's also easier for other users when they are mentioning you in tweets and it will take up less space. Many brands use either their business name or a shorter version of that name, however, if you yourself are 'the brand' then using your own name is a much better option.

If you find your name has already been taken then you can add numbers or a popular keyword that is used in your niche. You can use capitals to separate words within your username which is great for making your username easier to read and stand out, it also helps to make it more memorable and therefore better for your brand. You can change your username as many times as you like so don't worry if you suddenly think of a better username after creating your profile. However once you have started tweeting and building up your following it's not good idea to change it.

Follow accounts

In the initial set up process you will be offered some accounts to follow simply pick 4 at this stage and you can go back later and follow more.

Add connections

You will then be offered the opportunity to add and follow your current contacts by allowing twitter to search your contacts. It is best to skip this until your account is set up properly.

Add your profile image

Your profile image will display on the left of your profile on desktops and laptops and in the centre of your cover photo on the mobile app. Making the decision whether to go with your logo or a head shot of yourself can be a tough one as there are advantages to both. Studies have shown that using a personal photo is more effective as people tend to prefer to connecting with people rather than logos. If you are your own personal brand then it is a no brainer but if not then you will need to weigh up the pro and cons. Using a logo can bring professionalism, brand loyalty and reputation whereas it is more difficult to build a more personal connection with your followers. Using a personal profile picture will offer a more personal connection but makes it less recognisable as a business account.

A good solution if you cannot make up your mind is to include your logo and a picture of yourself this is a great way of pushing your brand and keeping it personal at the same time. This can be done very effectively by laying your logo either under, over or beside your photo depending on where you are positioned in the photo. First impressions count so you need to upload a really high quality image and if it is a head shot make sure your picture is taken in a well lit area and you are smiling. So many profiles have bad quality photos and they are either blurry or dark and this really is a missed opportunity to create a good first impression. You can upload a JPG, GIF or PNG of either your logo or a headshot of yourself. The recommended image size for your profile picture on twitter is 400 X 400 pixels.

Your Bio

Your Bio is a 160 character description of yourself, it is probably the most important part of your profile and what you say will underpin your whole campaign.

The time when your Bio is most likely to be read is either when you follow another user, they see your profile in the list of another user's followers or if someone clicks on your username in an @mention. The first time they see your bio is probably going to be the one and only time that you are going to be able to grab their undivided attention. This is the time when they are going to make the decision whether or not to follow you and this is where you need to hook them with your concise and compelling description. Your main goal when thinking about creating your Bio is how you are going to get them to follow you and definitely NOT to try and sell to them at this point.

Creating a well constructed, concise and interesting bio is a craft in itself and writing a good one can be the difference between being followed and not being followed. Firstly you need to think about what your target audience are looking for, what motivates them and what are the problems they have and how you can help solve them. When creating your Bio you need to do the following, all in 160 characters:

- **Communicate exactly who you are and what you do** This is so important because this is your chance to pick the right audience. You need to communicate what you do in the most inspiring way and if this matches your prospective follower's main interests they will be more likely to follow you. Try and include keywords that will help you to get found for your subject. This may all seem obvious but you would be surprised how many people are not specific and you are left wondering why you would want to follow them.

- **Add something personal or amusing** This is not only a great ice breaker but also helps you to stay in the minds of your followers and adds a unique quality to your bio. This can sometimes be the difference between a follow or not.

- **Offer them value and benefits** You need to make it clear how your audience is going to benefit by following you.

- **Get them to take action** This is could be the only opportunity you have to get your followers to take any specific action before you have to compete with their busy stream of Tweets from other users. This is where you need to tempt them with something valuable and send them to a landing page where they can redeem your valuable insight or content and then capture their email. A good method of doing this is to get them to ask you a specific question and then send them to a page where they can retrieve the answer. For example, 'Ask me what my best tip for success is?' This is great because it gets your audience to start engaging with you and mentioning you. Simple but so effective.

You may be wondering how you can fit everything you want to say in the 160 given characters so it's a good thing to create short concise phrases or use the pipe | symbol to separate phrases and abbreviations. If you need inspiration then checking out other peoples bios can spark ideas. The best thing to do is write a couple and then ask yourself this question, 'Would I want to follow myself after reading my Bio?'

Website URL

Working out which URL you are going to send your followers to is crucial to the success of your campaign and will depend very much on your goals. Sending them to your homepage may lead to fewer conversions since the page will probably not be specific enough. Many businesses make the mistake of creating a great bio but then send users to a cold homepage with little information relating to their profile, suddenly the experience is over and neither you or your follower receives any benefit at all.

There are great opportunities to continue the your brand experience and communicate your message. Remember people are on twitter to communicate and engage and if they have clicked on that link they want to find out more. You need to ask yourself this, when a follower clicks on my landing page what are they feel and say to themselves when they arrive? Are they going to be disappointed or feel welcomed and valued. You may want to think about a few of the following ideas:

Your Email Opt-in landing page If your primary goal is to capture email addresses then you will need to tempt them with a compelling offer, a free ebook or report to capture their email address. Customizing your page so it is exclusively for your Twitter followers will help to continue the experience and make them feel welcomed and valued. Try and keep this page as uncluttered as possible as capturing the email is the main goal and make it as eye catching and interesting visually as possible.

A Specific Twitter landing page Sending your followers to a warm and inviting page with a welcome message about who you are and what you can do for your followers is a great starting point. Again you can customize it so it looks like it is exclusively for your Twitter followers. Here is a list of things you may like to include on that page:
- Welcome message
- Profile photo
- Invitation to join you on other social networks
- Email sign up
- Your latest tweets
- Call to action

Another Social network Using Twitter to increase your following on your other networks can be very effective. For example, if your main goal is to increase your followers on Facebook then you will need to send them to your a page on Facebook where you are offering some kind of free offer and encourage them to sign up to your email opt-in. This way you can continue your relationship on Facebook and by email. There are numerous third parties that create custom apps like www.heyo.com and www.woobox.com and you can also send a direct message to a new follower to help tempt them to your Facebook page.

A competition landing page Another good way to capture emails is to send them to a competition page. Twitter allows you to run contests without having to use a third party app. However you do need to adhere to the rules of your country or region with regard to running a contest. More on running Twitter contests later.

Twitter landing page templates There are numerous websites which create templates for landing pages which can be linked with your email service provider. Sites like http://unbounce.com/landing-page-templates/ www.leadpages.com or you simply type 'twitter landing page templates' into a search engine.

Your profile name
As well as your username you will also need to add a profile name. You profile name is what is going to be displayed on the following:
- The top left of your profile page
- The first name you will see in Twitter search results in bold
- In email notifications that other users receive when you follow them

You can use up to 20 characters in your name and you are allowed to add spaces and capitals so you can make this name make more sense to other users. You can either match it with your username or if you are using a business name for your username you can use your own name which will make it more personal.

Connecting to Facebook

Twitter gives you the opportunity to connect your Facebook account so that your tweets will automatically be posted to your Facebook page. You need to think carefully about whether you want to do this or not. Twitter has a much higher tolerance when it comes to frequent posting and you can get away with posting far more regularly on Twitter than you can on Facebook. If you are planning to be a power user then it's probably a good idea to keep them separate.

Your Twitter Header

Your twitter header image is a horizontal banner which sits on top of the view that displays your tweets and spans the entire width of your profile. The image size required is 1500 X 500 pixels but you need to take into account that approximately 100 Pixels of the height of your header is taken away by the menus at the top and the bottom of your header so you need to make sure that anything you want visible is kept within the central 400 pixels. You also need to take into consideration that the areas on the far right and left (250 pixels on each end) will not appear on mobile devices and also your profile image will sit in the centre of your header. Since you have so much space you can get really creative here by using an image which will communicate your brand and exactly what you do. However, make sure you keep it consistent with your branding on your other social sites so you are easily recognisable.

To upload an image to your twitter header simply click the gear icon on the top right and then click on **Settings** and then **Profile**.

Getting your account ready for your audience

Before you start actively promoting your page you will need to breathe some life into your profile by adding some interesting tweets.

THE BASICS

Once you have set up your profile it's a good idea to have a look around and find your way around Twitter and your account. If you are not familiar with Twitter then here is a brief run down of the features and functionality available on Twitter and definitions of Twitter terms.

The Twitter Menu.

- **Home** Your homepage is where you will land when you login into your Twitter account. On the right you will find a stream of Tweets from the people that you follow. You will also see the number of your tweets, followers and number of people following you.

- **Notifications** The 'Notifications' tab is where you see your 'Interactions' and 'Mentions'. It's nearly impossible to keep on top of everything that is happening on Twitter all the time as the noise of twitter is constant however the Notifications tab lets you see at a glance who is interacting with you, who has retweeted and favorited any of your tweets and who has mentioned you, it also shows any new followers. This information helps you to keep on top by replying and thanking those people and makes interacting very much easier.

- **The #discover tab** The # discover tab is found at the top of your profile and is a really effective way of finding people and new sources of information that are related to your interests. You will find, Tweets, Activity, Who to follow, Find friends and Popular Accounts. The information here is based on the people you follow and allows you to discover news and stories without having to follow additional accounts.

- **The Me tab** The Me tab is where you manage your profile and settings, view the tweets you have sent, view your 'Favorites' and your 'Lists' and 'follower'and 'following numbers.'

- **The Envelope icon** This is situated at the top right next to the

151

gear icon and this is where you can send a 'Direct Message' and where you can view the messages you have either received or sent.

- **The Gear icon** The Gear icon is where you find you Settings, Keyboard Shortcuts, Help and where you sign in and out of your account. Your settings tab lets you manage your account, design, profile, privacy settings, email notifications, apps, widgets and lets you add your mobile phone to your account.

Twitter Lists

A twitter list is a list compiled by Twitter users to group certain users together. Twitter lists are an incredible time saver and let you cut out the noise from your main feed and view tweets from certain users who you are particularly interested in. You can create your own private or public lists and subscribe to other peoples lists.

- **To create a list** simply go to your **gear icon** and then select **Lists** from the drop down menu and then click **Create list.** You can then enter your list name which is up to 25 characters and choose whether you want it private or public and then click **Save.** To add users to your list or remove them simply click on the **gear icon** next to their name and then select the list you wish to add them or remove them from. You can create a maximum of 20 lists. You can share your list with anyone, https://twitter.com/ username/lists/list_name

- **To subscribe to other peoples lists** simply go to their profile and click on **Lists** and then select the list you wish to view and then click **subscribe** if you want to follow that list.

- **To view tweets from a list** simply go your profile page and click on **Lists** tab and then select the list you wish to view.

- **To add users to a list** Simply visit their profile and click on the gear icon next to the 'Follow' button and then click on ' Add or remove from lists' and then tick the box next to the list you want to add them to. You can even add people that you d not follow, your competition!

Twitter Language

- **Tweet** A 140 character post or status update which can contain a url and an image. Twitter automatically shortens URL'S to 20 characters.

- **Follow** When you follow someone on Twitter you are subscribing to their tweets. To follow someone simply click on the icon 'Follow'.

- **Favorites** Favorites are represented by a small star icon next to a tweet. When you favorite a Tweet the original person who tweeted it will know that you liked it. Favorites are a very useful because they let you bookmark content on Twitter so you can go back later to tweets and take a proper look. You can also use favorites to draw attention to your profile and to highlight great things that other users have said about you in their tweets. Favorites are public so anyone can see what you have favorited. You can favorite anything on Twitter and you can view your favorites any time.

- **@Reply** An @reply is an update posted by clicking the reply button on a tweet.

- **@ Mention** The @ sign is used when you want to mention someone . To mention or refer to another user simply add the @ sign before the user name. Using the @ sign alerts the user to the mention. The @ mention is a very important part of

153

communicating on Twitter and is used to publicly direct a message to a particular user onTwitter. @Mentions are used to start discussions and reply publicly to other peoples tweets. You can use the @mention to thank people for following, to draw attention to a particular user and they are also a great way for you to get noticed by others. NB If you use the @mention at the beginning of the tweet it limits who can see that Tweet. If you are followed by the user and you mention them at the beginning of the tweet the tweet will only be seen by them on their homepage. If you mention someone who does not follow you, it will show up on their mentions tab but not in their tweets timeline . If you put the @mention in the middle of the tweet everybody who is following that user will see that tweet and this is not generally a good idea.

- **Direct Message** A direct message or DM is a private message. You can only receive messages from the people you follow and you can only send messages to the people you follow.

- **# Hashtag** The # hashtag symbol is often used to draw attention to topics and keywords and phrases in tweet. By adding # before a keyword or phrase you have the opportunity to show up in Twitter search for that keyword. Also by clicking a word with the hashtag it will bring up all the tweets with that keyword. Some words marked with hashtags may become very popular and become trending topics.

- **#FF** #FF Stands for follow friday and is a great way to build your following. You will see hundreds and hundreds of people using this phrase on a friday on Twitter and is used as a way of recommending your followers on Twitter to other users.

- **Handle** A Twitter handle is the username url. http:// twitter.com/username.

- **Retweet or RT** A retweet is a tweet that has been reposted again and is used to spread news and share other people tweets. You can retweet by simply clicking retweet below the tweet or the icon with the two arrows. However, adding your own comment and personalising the tweet is always a good idea, this way you can point out the how the tweet is relevant and of value to your followers. To add your own comment you need to copy and paste the tweet into your own tweet box, add 'RT' and then add the @ sign before the Twitter handle and click 'Tweet'. When someone retweets your content it's a great idea to thank them.

- **Trends** Trends are topics which are identified by Twitter as popular and are based on who you follow and where you are located. To find trends click on 'Discover' and trends will appear on the left in a list. When you click on a trend you will see all the tweets including that phrase, keyword or hashtag. You can use trending topics as a way to get found, but your tweet has to be relevant to the trending subject or the hashtag. You can change your trends so that they are not specifically tailored to you by clicking 'Change' next to the word 'Trends'. You can see what is trending all over the world and in specific locations by entering locations in the search box.

- **Handle** A Twitter handle is the username url. http:// twitter.com/username.

- **Promoted Tweets** Promoted tweets are tweets that a business has chosen to advertise.

- **Timeline** A real time list of Tweets.

- **Unfollow** To stop following someone on Twitter.

- **Twitter Mobile App** Twitter's mobile website lets you connect wherever you are and extends the twitter experience to both mobiles and tablets. It's a great way of keeping up with your following and communicating on the go. You can navigate very much like you would do on your desktop or laptop. The app has the following menu items: **Home, Connect, Discover** and **Me** and you can do everything you would do on your desktop. It also lets you set up notifications if you want to be alerted to a particular user's account.

CHAPTER TWO

HOW TO BUILD YOUR AUDIENCE ON TWITTER

TO RUN A successful campaign on Twitter you are going to need to build a sizeable following and this chapter is dedicated to the strategies and tactics you need to implement to do so. The opportunities on Twitter to build your audience are probably greater than on any other network. Because Twitter is an informal social network you can grow your audience very easily and when you follow someone on Twitter it is more than likely that they will to follow you back.

However because the audience on Twitter is so enormous it's even more important that you are very specific about defining who your audience are so you can build a highly targeted following. You need to be discerning and qualify users in some way before you start following them. When you know exactly who your target audience is, what they are looking for, and what motivates them, you will be more likely to find them on Twitter and create the right content for them.

Many businesses start by indiscriminately following as many people as possible in the hope that they are going to catch some potential customers but they end up running into a twitter follower limit with a following of people who are not in the slightest bit interested in what they have to say or sell. Twitter lets everyone follow up to 2000 people but after reaching that number the number of people you are allowed to follow is largely dependent on your follower / following ration. Another reason it is so important to follow the right audience is because if you decide to promote your account with Twitter, advertising suggestions are based on the types of account that you follow.

PROMOTING YOUR TWITTER PROFILE

- **Post your Twitter handle URL on all your sites** Make sure your Twitter handle link is on all your marketing material: your website, blog, Facebook and LinkedIn page. Twitter provides code for buttons at this URL https://twitter.com/about/resources/buttons. There are also third party developers that create plugins which can be integrated into your page, they also offer plugins for multiple social platforms.

- **Embed a timeline into your website** You can easily display your recent tweets with images on your website or blog by visiting this page https://twitter.com/settings/widgets . It's really tempting for your website visitors to press the follow button if they can see how interesting your tweets are. You can also embed public tweets from any user on twitter, favorites from any user, lists that you own or subscribe to and customized search results.

- **Add your Twitter handle to all your promotional information** Make sure you add your Twitter URL to any marketing literature, business cards, brochures, your transport, product packaging, storefront, receipts or anywhere you promote your business.

- **Invite your contacts** Send an email to your current contacts inviting them to join you on Twitter. This is a great way to engage with them and also increase your reach through their contacts. You can search contacts from the 'Discover' tab, simply click on 'Find Friends' and you can search your email address book and then follow them.

- **Invite your followers** Invite your fans and followers from other social networks like LinkedIn and Facebook by posting an image, invitation and link.

- **Add your Twitter link to your email signature** Adding a link to your Twitter page on your email signature is a really effective way of gaining followers, especially if you give your readers an incentive or reason to follow you by offering them something of value or inviting them to join for a competition or sweepstake.

- Add your profile to Twitter directories Directories like <u>wefollow.com</u> and <u>Twellow.com</u> allow you to add your profile so you can gain more followers. There are other directories too, simply type 'Twitter Directories' into a search engine.

- **Leave comments on blogs and articles** Leaving comments and a link to any of your related content and your twitter handle can be a good way of gaining followers who are interested in the same things as you.

- **Write articles for other blogs** Many bloggers are looking for other bloggers to write guest posts, this is a good way of getting in front of a new audiences who may have a similar interests.

FINDING AND FOLLOWING YOUR TARGET AUDIENCE

One of the most effective ways to build your audience on Twitter is to go out and actively find your target audience and then follow them. You not only draw attention to your profile when you follow a user but they are very likely to follow you back if they find your bio interesting. Once they follow you back you will be able to start building trust and building a relationship with your followers. When they start engaging with your content, retweeting, mentioning you and favoriting you, this will naturally increase your reach.

Finding users through Twitter advanced search.

Twitter has an advanced search facility that lets you search users by keyword, hashtag and location, you can find it at this URL <u>https://twitter.com/search-advanced</u> . It's a powerful way of finding users in your town or city and allows you to be very specific with the numerous ways in which you can refine your results. By adding :) or : (you can search positive or negative results. You can add more than one keyword by separating the words with OR and you can search for users within a specific distance of a particular location, for example,by typing in 'near: NYC within:15 mi.' you can find tweets created within 15 miles of New York City. You can even search for tweets which have links by adding the words 'filter:links'.

Twitter allows you to save up to 25 searches which is very handy if you want to follow a certain number of people in one day from that list and then continue again on another day.

Finding new information and followers with #discover

The #discover tab is found at the top of your profile and helps you to find people and new sources of information that have been customized to you, based on the people you follow. It allows you to discover news and stories without having to follow additional accounts.

- **Tweets** Tweets reveal headlines that are breaking on Twitter and those that are being talked about by people like you. It also shows how many times the stories have been retweeted or favorited by your followers or the followers of your followers so it's a great way to find other users with similar interests.

- **Activity** The activity guide shows you how the people who are following you are engaging on Twitter, and shows who they have favorited, retweeted and followed. This is a great way to shut out the noise, find out what's important to people and find new followers.

- **Who to Follow** Twitter suggests accounts that you may like to follow and they are based on your interests and the type of users who you already follow. You may find some real gems here so keep an eye out.

- **Find Friends** Twitter lets you search your email address book to find friends and this works with yahoo mail, gmail, hotmail and aol.

Your competitions' followers

Following your competitors' followers is an obvious way to find your audience, however be careful as your competitors are not necessarily always targeting the right users.

NB Filtered Tweets

You can now choose which timeline to view when viewing other profiles: Tweets, Tweets with photos/video or Tweets and replies. This makes it so much easier for you to find what you are looking for and stops you getting lost in endless text.

USE # HASHTAGS TO FIND AND GET FOUND

The # hashtag symbol is often used to draw attention to topics and keywords and phrases in a tweet. By adding the # sign before a keyword or phrase you have the opportunity to show up in Twitter search for that keyword. By clicking a word with the hashtag symbol it will bring up all the tweets which contain that keyword. Some words marked with hashtags may become very popular and then become trending topics. Hashtags are often used for reporting especially during a disaster or crisis.

The probability of being retweeted and getting found is much higher if you use hashtags. By adding the # symbol to the name of a topic or subject you are more likely to get found by the right audience who are looking for that particular topic. When you have found the hashtag phrase you wish to use you can use this in your tweets and also use it to join in existing conversations on twitter. It's easier to join a hashtag campaign which is already running, but if you wish to create your own here are some tips:

- Find out if the hashtag already exists, the meaning it has (sometimes it can have more than one meaning) and the audience it is appealing to (sometimes it can appeal to a different audience to the one you wish to attract). www.hashtags.org is a site which will tells you if and when during the week a hashtag is popular and if the hashtag is reaching the right audience.

- Try and be as specific as possible so you do not get mixed up with too much other unrelated content.

- Use capitals to separate words as it makes it much easier to read. For example, hashtagsaregreat is much easier to read as HashTagsAreGreat.

- Add your hashtag definition to www.hashtags.org

- Do not use more than 2 hashtags in a tweet.

- Set up an email alert so that you know when somebody uses your Hashtag. You can do this at www.twilert.com

- Write the comment before the hashtag to keep your audience interested.

- Do not over use hashtags as they can become very boring.

Hashtags to find like minded people

Hashtags are a great way to find active users who have similar interests so you can start following them, introduce your brand and start building a relationship with them.

Hashtags to chat

Hashtags are often used so people can get together and chat to people about a particular subject. Tweetchat.com is a great tool to use to chat on Twitter. Simply sign in with twitter and then search for your preferred hashtag and join in the conversation. Tweetchat automatically adds the hashtag to your tweet and you can view all the tweets relating to that hashtag in realtime.

MORE WAYS TO GET FOLLOWERS

Participate in Trending Topics

On the left hand side of 'Discover,' 'Notifications' and 'Search' you will see 'Trends'. Trends are topics that are popular at this moment in time. They are determined by an algorithm set by twitter that is based on who you follow and your location. When you click on a trend you will see all the tweets relating to that trend or hashtag.

You can change the location of your trends by changing your custom settings. Simply click on **Change** next to the word Trends and then click on the word **Change** you can select from any location, locally or worldwide.

Participating in trending topics can be a very effective way of gaining more followers who may be interested in your particular niche or industry . To do this you need to pick a trend that is relevant to your business in some way and then simply post your tweet and related content with the phrase or hashtag. It is against Twitter rules to use trends by posting unrelated content and they run quality checks so that any unrelated content will not appear in search.

Join #Follow Friday

Participating in #follow friday is a great way to increase your followers. You can recommend any of your followers. However do not spam your timeline by mentioning all your followers in a series of separate tweets. The best way to do this is to either Tweet about a single person or a small group to follow and give a reason, for example, #FF *#FollowFriday* @*Yourfollowersusername Tweets great info and a great guy too.* Another effective way to save mentioning too many people is create your own list called #Followfriday and suggest people to follow on that list.

Tweeting frequently and posting really good content

If you are tweeting frequently and posting really good content and people are retweeting, mentioning and favoriting you then this is going to increase your reach and will in turn increase the number of followers. This is a biggie and is covered in detail later.

RUNNING A TWITTER PROMOTION OR CONTEST

There are all sorts of benefits to running a contest on Twitter, including helping to build your audience, increasing your opt-in subscribers, building brand awareness and creating buzz. Before you decide on your contest you need to be clear about your goals, are you trying to increase number of followers, increase your opt-in list, drive engagement or promote a particular product or service.

Twitter does not give many restrictions with regard to running a contest but you will need to look into the Twitter rules and guidelines, the rules of your area or state concerning competitions and contests.

To run a contest you will need to think about the following;

The Prize

In order to attract the right audience your prize or prizes need to relate to your product, or service that you sell so you attract the right specific audience. If you offer something like an ipad then you may get a large number of followers but not necessarily the right ones who are going to add any value to your campaign.

The Type of competition or contest

There are a number of different types of competitions including sweepstakes which you can set up manually or by using and third party application like binkd.com . With these third party sites they will create a landing page for you with your company logo, information about the contest and prizes and they will also select a winner automatically after the competition has ended. Competitions on Twitter can include offering prizes for tweeting a particular update, for following a particular user or for posting updates with a specific hashtag. Other idea for contest include:

- **Follow to win contests** Follow to win contest are exactly what they say they are, participants are asked to follow or follow and retweet to enter. It's a good idea to use the hashtag #FollowToWin.

- **Photo Contests** With photo contests you can ask users to upload and vote on photos. Using a third party app like www.wishpond.com can help with the administration of these types of competition.

- **Creative answer contests and Q & A contests** These types of contests work well and are very straight forward however you should remember to ask participants to mention your username (by adding @ sign to your username)to collect entrants as hashtags are not guaranteed to show up all the results.

The duration of the competition or contest

You will need to decide on the duration of the competition. With photo and video competitions you will need to offer your participants longer to enter than if you were are running a more simple sweepstake.

Landing Page

For all competitions you should have a dedicated landing page which offers information on the prizes and rules. By using sites such as Binkd they will actually create your landing page and administer your contest.

Rules

You need to make sure you include the following:

- The number of times a participant is allowed to join or retweet .
- The creation of multiple accounts that users may create to enter numerous times.
- The amount of time the winner has to claim their prize.
- The closing date.
- Who is eligible.
- How winners will be selected.
- Include the term 'Void if prohibited' to ensure you are in compliance with any country or state regulations banning your promotion.

Promoting your competition

To promote your contest you need to announce it on all your social networks, email your contacts and make sure it is publicized on your website and blog as well. Make sure you include the relevant hashtags #contest or #competition or #win or #PhotoContest or #FollowToWin.

Announce the winner

When you have a winner make sure you announce them via twitter, on your website or by email.

Measure your results

Like any campaign you will need to measure results against your original goals. You can use tools like Hootsuite to measure new followers or Google Analytics to measure traffic to your website.

HOW TO LOSE FOLLOWERS ON TWITTER

You are always going to get a certain amount of fall out from your Twitter account, many will follow and then unfollow just to keep a healthy followers to following ratio. However there may be times that you notice that maybe more of your followers are leaving than you would have hoped. This could be due to any of the following reasons;

Tweeting too often Tweeting too often can be annoying especially if you are not adding any value at all. Tweeting 1 – 5 times a day is optimal but it if you really have great content you can afford to tweet more.

Pushing your product too often This is a certain way to lose followers. People just do not want to hear it.

Repetition Repeating the same content over and over again is just going to bore your followers.

Moaning and being negative This is an absolute no no and is certain to lose you followers.

Not communicating If you are not replying to messages or engaging on Twitter then you are not going to thrive.

Not following back This will certainly put many people off and they may quickly unfollow you.

Inactive If you are nor regularly logging on and posting then many will unfollow you especially with the availability of twitter tools which highlight inactive accounts.

Constantly retweeting If you are constantly retweeting others and do not have your own content then this will probably lose you followers. On the other hand if you never retweet anybody then this is not going to do you any favours either.

Chapter Three

Grow Your Followers with Twitter Ads

TWITTER HAS THREE choices for advertising, Promoted Accounts, Promoted Tweets and Promoted Trends. Promoted tweets and promoted accounts are self service advertising and advertising in both cases can be targeted by location and interests. Promoted Trends are reserved for brands with large advertising budgets and are managed by Twitter's advertising department. To access Twitter advertising simply go to the gear icon on the top right and click on '**Twitter Ads**'.

Promoted Accounts

Promoted accounts will expose your profile to a larger number of people and are a great way to increase your follower numbers. Once you have new followers you have the opportunity to generate leads, build trust, drive website traffic and increase brand awareness. Twitter determines who your profile is exposed to by selecting the type of accounts that would be interested, based on your current followers. You can also target your adverts by location, interest, usernames and gender.

Promoted accounts are displayed in the 'Who to follow' widget on the left hand side of your homepage and on 'Notifications' and on the 'Who to follow' page. They also appear on search pages and on profile pages as part of the 'similar to you' widget. As with most social media advertising you set your budget and you only pay for results so you only pay when targeted users actually follow you. Promoted accounts are a great way of standing out from the crowd and really do get your account noticed.

PROMOTED TWEETS

Another way to advertise on Twitter is by promoting your tweets. Promoted tweets are normal tweets that will be seen by a wider audience and are displayed at the top of relevant search results and will appear in a user's timeline just once. Twitter will only allow promoted tweets to appear in the users timeline if the Tweet is going to be of interest or relevance to the user.

To get the best out of promoted tweets you need to decide what your goal is and then drive results by including a call to action. You could use promoted tweets to do any of the following:

- Drive traffic to your website or blog with a link to your best content and you opt-in sign up form
- Offer coupons and deals
- Generate leads using lead generation cards
- Promote sales and special offers
- Promote a competition
- Promote your event or a new product
- Put yourself in front of key influencers

Creating your Promoted Tweet campaign

Creating your campaign is very straight forward. Simply name your campaign and then select how you want to target either by keyword, interest or specific accounts and by location.

You can either manually select the tweets you want to promote or Twitter will automatically select 5 of your most engaging tweets. You can customize where you want your tweet to be promoted, in user's timelines or in search results or both and you can select which devices to appear on and the audience gender you wish to target. You then need to set your total budget for your campaign and a daily budget and set the maximum amount you are willing to spend per engagement. You only pay for results including: if the user clicks on your tweet, follows you, favorites, retweets or replies to your tweet.

PROMOTED TRENDS

Promoted trends appear at the top of trending topics. When a user clicks on a promoted trend they will see all the tweets relating to that trending topic with the advertisers tweets at the top. Promoted trends offer massive exposure but are really only relevant to businesses with huge advertising budgets.

TWITTER LEAD GENERATION CARDS

Twitter lead generation cards are now available to all businesses. They help you to get more from your promoted tweets by helping you to capture leads with a form which is situated within a user's timeline. They are like an embedded landing page within Twitter. When the user expands the tweet they will see a description of the offer and a call to action, their username and email will already be pre-filled on the cards. The great thing about cards is users can do all this without having to leave twitter and they can securely leave their email address. Some businesses have found them very effective at capturing email addresses of contest entrants.

Before you get started make sure you are clear about your goals and why you want to collect the leads. You may want to generate new leads for an ebook, or more subscribers for your opt-in, or you may wish to collect entries for a contest, or promote a special offer.

Set up is very straight forward. Simply click on the 'Creatives' tab and then click on 'Cards' and then 'Create Lead Generation Card'. Here you can add a compelling image (150 X 600 px), a short description, a call to action and a URL and your privacy policy URL. You need to make it very clear in your description how users will benefit and your image should demonstrate the value you are offering. Once you have saved your card and started your campaign your leads will be collected within your

Twitter ads account. You can download your leads at any time. If you have a CRM system (customer relationship management system) or an email service provider like www.mailchimp.com you will need to integrate and sync with them. To sync properly you will need to make sure your custom fields names match. Once set up, your leads will be uploaded directly to your database. Once you have the user's email you can follow up with them by email about the products they are interested in, or add them to your opt-in list.

Twitter provides you with useful card analytics such as a cost per lead card which can help you optimize your card designs.

CHAPTER FOUR

CONTENT IS KING ON TWITTER

IN ORDER TO build a thriving community of brand advocates and customers who want to share your content, sign up to your newsletter and buy your products you are going to need to build trust, loyalty and likeability. The only way to do this is by communicating with them on a regular basis in the right way and by consistently delivering the highest possible quality content which will grab their attention, appeal to their interests and add real value to their lives. Once your followers start engaging with your content, you will start building trust and start converting them into customers.

Content really is king on Twitter and in order to create the right content you are going to need to have a real understanding of your target audience and deep insight into what interests and motivates them. Once you have this information and put this together with the strategies in this book and there is no reason why you cannot build a thriving community of advocates for your brand on Twitter. In this chapter you are going to learn about the different types of content, the different types of media you can use and tips on how to create the best experience for the followers so you can receive the highest engagement.

29 IDEAS FOR CREATING CONTENT ON TWITTER

You may be wondering how you are going to consistently produce and deliver compelling content to your audience on a regular basis for the foreseeable future. However, once you have picked your topic of interest, you will surprised how one idea lead will lead to another and you will be able to find numerous pieces of content to create and post. Here are some ideas for content that can be adapted to any type of business or topic:

1. Relatable content

Relatable content is one of the best types of content and one of the most shared types of content. Relatable content is anything that your target audience can relate to and identify with, it's when your audience sees a piece of content and immediately thinks, "Yes, I know exactly what they mean by that and that is exactly how I feel when that happens." It's incredibly powerful because this content is immediately communicating to your audience that you understand them and you feel their pain or joy and you can empathise with them. With relatable content you are communicating with them on quite a deep level which all helps to build relationships and trust. This is why Someecards is so successful, most of their content is relatable.

2. Emotive content

Evoking an emotional response is an essential ingredient to successful viral content marketing. If you create content that evokes a strong positive emotional response it will help your audience associate that emotion with your brand. Content like this is very memorable and if you can make people feel something by posting an image, text or a video this can really help in building your brand and creating powerful associations. Evoking any of the primary emotions be it surprise, joy, fear, sadness, anger or disgust is a certain way to get people sharing your content.

3. Educational content

Posting informative content about your subject is invaluable, this will help you to stand out as a thought leader and expert in your field. If your content is valuable and useful then your followers are likely to keep coming back for more and are likely to share your content too. Remember your audience are looking to find and share valuable content with their friends and customers too and will want to be associated with any compelling content you create.

2. Informative
This could be about letting your followers know about something that is happening like a Webinar, a trade show or n event in the area, or a special offer, or any information that will be of use or value to them.

3. Entertaining/amusing content
Social media is all about being social and having fun, people love sharing funny stuff. Even if you did not create it yourself but you think it is going to appeal to your target audience then share it. The aim here is to amuse and entertain your audience, humor is a winner all round and not only does humor break down barriers it is also more likely to be liked and shared.

4. Seasonal Content
Posting content relating to important holidays and annual celebrations is a really good way to stay connected with your audience. If you have an international audience then being aware of their holidays and religious celebrations will go a long way in building relationships.

5. Inspiring and motivational content
The truth is everyone has a bad day sometimes and needs a little bit of motivation or cheering up. A motivational quote will help to lift your audience and can really help to connect with them. If you know what your audience wants, what they aspire to and what their frustrations are then it is likely that you will be able to motivate them by posting content which inspires them. These types of post are also very shareable especially if put together with a colorful and inspiring image like a cartoon or photo.

6. Employee and behind the scenes content
If you have news about your employees and the great things they are doing then post it. Maybe they have been involved in a fundraiser or they

have won an employee of the month award. Giving your audience a behind the scenes view of your business helps to keep your business and brand looking real and authentic and it adds human interest.

7. Customer Content

Having a follower of the month or including news or content about a customer's business is a great way to spark interest in your posts. Sharing a customer's content not only shows you value your audience but can also encourage them to do the same. You can also offer to mention your followers on #Follow Friday or add to a 'Follow Friday list'. This is a great way of offering them value, it also creates loyalty and keeps your Twitter account in their mind.

8. Shared Content

Whilst it's great to post your own content, don't be afraid to share other peoples content as long as it is relevant. The more valuable content you share the more valuable you will become to your audience and the more likely they will keep coming back for more. Sharing content is also incredibly important in building relationships with your followers, they are going to be far more open to your brand if you are supporting theirs. As long as you are giving your audience good content then it does not matter where it is coming from. You do not necessarily need to retweet all the time either, you can add your own comment and post a link to any piece of content you want.

9. Statistics

People love statistics which relate to their niche. If your business is B2B then posting statistics can gain a great deal of interest especially if they are displayed in a visually appealing way like with an infographic or graph. They are often shared if they are translated into a useful tip for your followers.

10. Questions

Asking questions about subjects that your audience may be interested in is a great way to encourage comments, interaction and community. People love to share their opinions and thoughts and love the opportunity to communicate, contribute and be heard. Even if you are posting an image or video it's a really good practice to ask a question.

11. Top Ten lists
People love lists about who or what is top or best. Lists spark interest and this is most probably because people like to compare their choices and judgement with others. Some may like to see that their opinions match others and feel they are right in that choice or others may feel comforted by the fact their choices are not the same and they are unique. You can create your own lists on list.ly and also get your users to join in by adding to the list which is a great way to increase engagement.

12. Controversial
Posting a controversial statement can spark great conversation and interaction, remember people love to voice their opinions, have an input and be heard. It may be a good idea to stay out of the discussion here as you do not want to lose followers and you need to be sensitive to your audience in order not to upset them so be careful with what topics you pick.

13. Special offers
Twitter is a great way to get the message out about the special offers you have running, but you will need to be careful not to post them too often or they just appear like advertising and bad noise in your audience's news feed. You need to make sure that what you are offering is of real value, that it is exclusive to your followers and you are offering them a deadline to redeem the offer.

14. Contests and sweepstakes
Contests and sweepstakes are always a great way to gain popularity, grow your audience, build your brand and build your opt-in email list. With contests your audience can have great fun with your brand and they can

also create high levels of engagement. There are so many different types of contests: photo and video competitions, sweepstakes, comment to win, polls, caption this contest, photo contest and quizzes and the list goes on.

15. Voting polls & customer feedback

Creating a poll is a great way to encourage engagement on social media . Incorporating polls into your Twitter strategy can help to give you a deeper understanding of your audience and also offers you valuable feedback about products or services. There are apps you can use to help administer your poll like www.Polldaddy.com or www.polleverywhere.com .

16. Tips and tricks

Offering a weekly or daily 'Top Tip' can keep your audience hooked and returning again and again for the latest information and are a great way to increase loyalty and build relationships. Tips can be anything from instructions on how to do something, to information about a useful app.

17. News and current events

Offering information about the latest news in your area or industry is a certain way to keep people interested and sharing your content. Being current and up to date with local news is really useful to your audience and it keeps your business looking fresh and up to date. To keep up to date with news subscribe to news feeds and blogs that offer news on your industry or your local area.

18. Negative content

People always like to hear about what not to do, for example: 10 Things not to do on a first date or 10 things not to say in a job interview, the list of possibilities for this type of post are endless and can create a great deal of amusement and interest.

19. Music if you are a musician

If you are a band and want to promote your music then there is no better way to promote your material than by posting links to your music and videos on Twitter.

.

20. Q & A live session

Hosting a live question and answers session on Twitter is a really good way to create conversation and engagement. It also creates a professional, informative and caring image. You can do this by choosing a hashtag and then allotting and promoting a specific time hashtag for your followers to post their questions. When it is time to go, Tweet that you are ready to go and post an image, then do a search for your hashtag and check your tab and then start answering questions.

21. Broadcast live

By using an application called live stream you can broadcast any live event to almost any social destination. You can also watch, like and share any event that may be of interest to your audience.

22. Welcome Followers

Welcoming your followers in a Tweet is a great way of showing them they are valued. It exposes them to your followers which can help them to get followed and hopefully they will reciprocate and you in turn will be exposed to their followers.

23. Caption this

Posting a photo and then asking your followers to caption it is a really effective and light hearted way to drive engagement and you could also turn this into a contest. You can use images from stock photo sites or sites like Flickr creative commons, make sure to choose images that will provoke interest and are humorous or inspiring.

24. Case studies

Case studies are a really effective way to demonstrate how something works with real examples. You can use case studies to show how your customers have used your products or services to benefit them in some way. You can also use them to demonstrate a principle or method of doing something by using other businesses as examples.

25. Internet Memes

Meme comes from the greek word 'mimema' which means something imitated. An internet meme is a style, action or idea which spreads virally across the internet. They can take the form of images, videos or hashtags. There are plenty of tools and apps out there to help you create memes such as www.memegen.com and imgur.com which are popular ones.

26. Tweet a Pin

If you have a good pin or image on Instagram then tweet it.

27. Your blog

Creating regular blog posts is a very effective way of getting your followers onto your blog or website. Make sure you always include an image to provoke interest and asking a question can create intrigue and curiosity. Also pointing your users to other blogs is a great way of adding value and also building relationships with the blogger.

28. Greetings

Simply posting an attractive image or a wishing your followers good morning, good night or to enjoy their weekend will go a long way in breaking the ice and building relationships. These types of posts help to make positive associations with your brand.

29. Testimonials

You may have received a review on Google Places or Foursquare or simply a message from someone. Posting about good things that people write or say about you contributes to your social proof and builds trust. Remember people will believe more about what others say about your business than what you as the owner says about it.

THE DIFFERENT TYPES OF MEDIA

In order to create the best experience for you followers you are going to need to create a good balance of content using the different variety of posts available to you. Twitter offers you the opportunity to post text and images, and you can also post links to videos, podcasts, websites, blogs and videos.

Images

'A picture paints a thousand words'
If you are already a Twitter user then you probably know that an image grabs your attention more than any other post on your timeline. This is because most of us are visually wired and most of us can identify with an image much more quickly than text. According to statistics Tweets with photos receive 35% more engagement than Tweets without. Followers are far more likely to click on a link to a website or blog or watch a video if your post contains a picture. If you are posting a link to your blog or an article on your website then make sure you include a compelling image, you are far more likely to gain interest this way. Images not only get shared more, they also have huge viral potential, get remembered and also create an emotional connection with your audience.

With Twitter you can now really show off your brand visually and you can now include up to four photos in one Tweet which will be displayed in a collage in your followers' timeline. If they want to take a closer look they can click on each image to expand and images are even included if you get retweeted. You can tag up to 10 people in one image and names will be displayed alongside the photo.

You don't have to be an expert photographer you can find images from stock photos and also free sites like flickr (be careful to check the licence and what you are allowed to do with the images in terms of changing or adding text, etc.) Adding text can be achieved by using photoshop or other online graphic design apps which are available online and which are easy to use like www.picmonkey.com . Some stock photo sites also offer you the functionality to add effects and text to your images.

Your image file size can be up to 3MB and Twitter accept GIF, JPEG and PNG files.

Text

To ensure that whatever you are posting on Twitter is effective, then you will need to add an introduction or text of some sort. Posting a question can be a really good way of driving engagement. There are lots of tips in the next section about how to create effective tweets.

Videos

As with images video is highly shareable, has huge viral potential and increases engagement. People love videos and a good video can offer a huge amount of entertainment, make learning more interesting, more fun and easier to understand. Videos are also great at helping to build relationships, trust and rapport with your audience and there really is no better way of introducing yourself and building a personal connection with your audience than with video.

The type of videos you should be posting on Twitter are educational, informative and entertaining and while there is room for the occasional product video these really belong on your website and/or blog.

Blog posts

According to research 70% of consumers click through to a website from a retail blog. Blogs are nearly essential now for any business who wants to get found on the internet and social media is another very effective tool to drive traffic to your blog. If you do not have a blog then you need to seriously consider creating one. There are numerous free and paid blogging platforms available and there is a whole chapter covering this very subject later on in this book.

Infographics and diagrams

Infographics provide a fascinating way to present statistical information. They are engaging, very shareable, have huge viral potential and make figures look far more interesting and easier to understand than a list of numbers. People love statistical information relating to their interest because it helps to confirm or affirm what they already may believe and helps to give them more confidence in what they are doing or selling. You do not have to be an expert graphic designer to create infographics, there are numerous applications available on the web which can help you create infographics.

Podcasts

Podcasting is a type of digital media usually comprising a series of audio, radio or video files. You can subscribe to podcasts as you can to blogs and newsletters. For example if you download a podcast on itunes every time the author produces a new one, itunes will automatically download it. As with video they are effective at helping to build trust with the listener and can also help to make you stand out as an authority or influencer in your niche. They also encourage customer loyalty if they are produced on a weekly or very regular basis and are incredibly handy for people who are on the go and want to listen while travelling to work or on the way to a meeting. Twitter is to the ideal place to promote your podcast.

Cartoons

Cartoons work very well with humor and relatable content. Posting cartoons that your audience can relate to, can help demonstrate that you understand and identify with them. Cartoons are a great ice breaker and highly shareable as well. Once shared they are very likely to appeal to more of your target audience and are a great way to widen your reach. If you have an idea for a cartoon and you are not an artist them there are sites like Fiverr.com that offer creative services at very reasonable prices.

SlideShare

SlideShare is primarily a slide sharing site but you can upload powerpoint, keynote, pdf and open office presentations. SlideShare is a great way to communicate your message and very straight forward and easy to use. It is also another way to get your content rated, commented on and shared and your presentations can be shared on Twitter and embedded on your website or blog.

Ebooks & PDF Documents

Turning your content into an ebook is a great way to present your content and offering a free ebook is a really good way to build your opt-in lists and giving your reader something of great value.

Webinars

A webinar is like an interactive online conference or workshop. Webinars are a great way of interacting with your audience and building relationships as they let you connect personally with your audience. They can be used for presenting and training, selling a programmer or course or answering questions from your audience. They can be saved and listened to at a later date for anyone who could not make the date and time. Using Twitter to announce your Webinar is a very effective way to promote your online event and get people to sign up.

How to Create Effective Tweets

Getting your Tweet right is the key to maximising the full potential of twitter. When you are trying to direct people to a blog or article you need to make your tweet so compelling that they click on the link. Make your tweets unique, interesting and try and make them appeal emotionally to your audience. When creating your tweet you need to think 'excellence' and when you read your tweet back you need to ask yourself the following:

Is this going to grab my audience's attention?
Is it going to make my followers curious enough to click on the link?

Is it compelling enough to be retweeted?

Is it going to help me reach one of my goals?

To create tweets that really do work here are a few tips:

Use questions or interesting headlines to draw attention to your tweet Questions are a great way of gaining attention because it can make the user feel that you are addressing them directly. Here are some example questions:

> Need help with your .... ?
>
> Can't find that......?
>
> Want to find out more about.....?
>
> Wondering why your business is not ....?
>
> Are you tired of ..... not working ?

Write for your audience Write with your audience in mind by using words like 'you' and 'your'. When you do this it looks like you are directly addressing each follower.

Keep it short and sweet Shorter tweets are more likely to be read than lengthy ones. Research shows that tweets with less than 100 characters receive more engagement. The aim is not always to tell them everything in a tweet but to get them to click the link. If your goal is be retweeted then keeping your tweet less than 100 characters leaves space for them to add a username and a comment.

Be specific Be specific and keep to one subject, you have plenty more tweets to create.

Provide a link Try as often as possible to include a link to your valuable content.

Include a call to action Wherever possible include a call to action, for example, 'click this link' or 'share this,' 'Click here to download!' Asking

185

your followers to retweet can generate up to four times more retweets but don't overuse it and when you do ask for retweets make sure it is for your most valuable content.

Use humor Humor is a great ice breaker and highly sharable. Twitter is definitely a place for humor and it is a fact that brands which use humor are followed more than those that do not.

Include an image where possible Simply click on the blue compose tweet button, tap on the camera icon and select your image.

Use hashtags Add one or two Hashtags relating to your subject and add them at the end of your tweet.

Use Lists and numbers Using lists and numbers can be a really effective way of adding interest to your tweets, for example, 10 effective ways to…….. Or 5 reasons to …..

Include Keywords Try and include keywords in your tweets as often as possible so that when people are searching they will be more likely to find and follow you .

Is this relevant to my audience? Every time you post anything ask yourself this question and if the answer is no then don't post it.

Scheduling your Tweets If you are going to be a power user on Twitter and post regularly then scheduling your tweets may be a very good idea. Scheduling tweets is a great way to free you up especially if you are going away for a while or you simply want to stay on top of your tweeting. Scheduling allows you to be stay consistent and spread your tweets out evenly throughout the day and also free's you up to engage with other people.

Twitter has now introduced scheduled tweets exclusively for its Ad users, which allows users to schedule tweets for up to a year in advance. You can access this on the top left at the twitter ads icon and then click on the 'Creatives tab'. Here you can create a tweet and add an image, location or card and then you can either set as an organic tweet (without paying for promotion) or as a promoted tweet.

There are other online tools that can schedule your tweets Hootsuite, Tweetdec and Buffer, more about this later.

CHAPTER FIVE

COMMUNICATING FOR SUCCESS ON TWITTER

CONTRARY TO POPULAR belief Twitter is not just a broadcasting channel but a social networking site. If you want to get broadcasted on Twitter then you need to get Social and interact too.

A great deal of this book has been dedicated to building your audience and creating high quality content. However in order to build a community of people who are potentially going to buy your products or start talking about you then you are going to need to get social, interact with your followers and nurture your following. When you are targeting the right audience you can be confident that all time you are spending interacting and communicating with them is going to create new customers and ambassadors of your brand.

To nurture your audience you need to value them by welcoming them, offering them amazing content, helping them by either offering them solutions or sharing their content. You can only do all this by communicating with them and this is where you can really stand out by building a real community with your followers. If you are really good to your followers then this will most definitely be reciprocated and as a result you will widen your reach even more.

The first thing you need to do is listen to your audience by reading tweets on your homepage and you can then start communicating with them. You can communicate with users and reply to their tweets by clicking on the reply icon and you can mention people by using @mention. You can send direct messages and also you can support your followers or any user

189

by retweeting them or favoriting one of their tweets.

@Mention The @mention is a very important part of communicating on Twitter and is used to publicly direct a message to a particular user on Twitter. @Mentions are used to start discussions and reply publicly to other peoples tweets. You can use the @mention to thank people for following, or to draw attention to a particular user and they are also a great way of getting you noticed by others.

The Power of The Retweet

Retweeting is what has made Twitter into such a powerful social media platform. A retweet is when somebody shares your content or you share somebody else's content. Retweets look like any other tweet except that they have the retweet icon with the username next to it under the tweet.

One of your main aims on Twitter should be to get as many retweets as possible which will increase your reach . Creating valuable content and building good relationships with your followers by retweeting and engaging will help to get you retweeted.

When you retweet another user's content it's a great way to show support, get noticed and engage on twitter. It's very much like the share button on Facebook. People feel honoured when you retweet their content because it means their tweet has some value and their content will have more chance of being seen by others. If you want a particular follower to notice you then it's a good way to draw attention to yourself.

You can retweet anyone whether or not they follow you or you follow them. To retweet just click the 'retweet' button under the tweet. If you wish to add your own comment you simply click 'reply' and add the letters RT with the username and then copy and paste the tweet with your comment.

To see who has retweeted any of your tweets simply type

rt@yourtwitterhandle into the search box and you will see who has retweeted and then you can thank them. If you retweet anyone you follow you can see this in your profile timeline. If you retweet someone you do not follow this will show up on your profile and home timeline. You can remove a retweet that you have made by simply clicking on 'retweeted' below the tweet.

Use 'Favorites'.

When you favorite a tweet you are not only showing your support to a follower but you can also draw attention to the original person who posted the tweet. When a user favorites your tweet it you can see it in your 'Notifications' tab.

Sending Direct Messages

A Direct Message is a private message that you can send through Twitter. You can send a DM to anyone that follows you and you can receive DM's from people who you follow too. There are two schools of thought when it comes to sending direct messages to new followers. Some people find them invaluable for welcoming new followers and building relationships and others are totally against sending them at all. It is a fact that many direct messages are sent out full of self promotion and as a result many people avoid reading them. However, for the numbers that do, I am of the belief that it is definitely worth sending a direct message as long a you are genuinely trying to spark up a personal connection with new followers and offering something of genuine value. Direct messages can be a great first step to building your opt-in by sending them to a custom Twitter landing page, or another social media platform like Facebook and offering them an ebook or report. Whatever you do, do not try and sell to them at this stage.

Auto Direct Messages.

If you are looking to gain a high volume of followers and feel you do not have the time or resources to send a DM to all your new followers then using an automated service like www.socialoomph.com is definitely

191

worthwhile.

Here are some tips for sending direct messages:

- **Make sure you are following them** If you send a DM to anyone make sure you are following them or they will be unable to send you a message back. Also it really looks impolite if you have sent them a message but have not even bothered to follow them, they will be quite likely to unfollow you immediately.

- **Be Personal** Wherever possible try and make your messages as personal as possible. You can do this by using their name or using the words 'you' or 'your', or asking them a question. You could also comment on something that you may have in common with them.

- **Be Original** Sending something a bit different from the norm is far more likely to get you noticed.

- **No Sales pitch** Do not push your products and services or they will be considered as spam and you are likely to lose your follower.

- **Provide value** If you do include a link then make sure it is worth their while and adds value.

- **Offer to connect on another network** You may find that you prefer one particular platform like Facebook for instance. Twitter can be a great way to find new Facebook fans especially if you have it set up with an offer so you can encourage users to sign up to your email opt-in.

- **Make it short and simple** Shorter messages work better and are more likely to be read.

- **Ask a question** This is a great way to start a conversation. Make sure you respond when they reply though. Encouraging interaction like this may lead to increased clicks to your website or blog.

- **Use a unique link** If you use a unique link you can track how many followers have followed that link and test how effective your message is.

- **Monitor and change your message** The best way to work out whether sending Direct Messages is working is to continually monitor your results. If you do not thinking you are gaining then keep testing by changing the content of your message until you are achieving results you want.

- **Keep track of your unfollow rate** If you start to lose followers maybe you need to change the content of your DM.

- **Reply to direct messages** This really depends on how many you are getting but there could a great opportunity here to connect by replying to a user and thanking them for your message.

MORE TIPS ON GETTING THE MOST OUT OF TWITTER

Now you know how to create great tweets and you know how to communicate on Twitter there also are many other ways you can make your campaign successful on Twitter. To make the most effective use of your time the best thing to do is set aside a particular amount of time each day to interact and carry out certain tasks. Here are some tips on how to get the most out of Twitter:

Listen first before you tweet

It's common knowledge that effective sales people listen to their customers or prospects, they then try to understand their requirements or needs and then direct them towards a solution. This is the same for Twitter, you need to listen to what your target audience are saying which will help you to understand and communicate with them in the best possible way. When you start interacting with other people and their tweets you will find they will start listening to you. If you give, give, give on Twitter, you will really stand out from the crowd.

Acknowledge, communicate and join conversations

Make sure you build acknowledging others into your Twitter strategy. Make it a daily ritual to view your twitter stream and comment and interact with users. It's really easy to just add an @ to a username and acknowledge a user. Retweeting is a great way of recognising people and when you 'favorite' someone they get notified which is a great way of drawing attention to your profile.

Appoint and select your Tweeters carefully

Make sure that whoever you appoint to tweet, truly understands your business and your brand so they are able to communicate your brand's personality and voice correctly.

Tweet about your high quality content

If you are going to be successful on Twitter then you need to try and create as much of your own high quality content as possible. This could be anything related to your topic in the form of blog posts, videos, infographics, slides, podcasts, images or webinars.

Tweet quality and not quantity

The more you tweet with valuable information and content the better. How often you tweet will depend very much on the time and the resources you have to create valuable content but as a general rule between 1 – 5 times a day is deemed optimal. Certainly do not tweet for the sake of tweeting as this will not win you followers.

Use the Pinned Tweet feature

Once you start using Twitter you will realize how fast the feed can go and your best tweets can get lost. Twitter now lets you pin your most important tweet to the top of your feed so your new followers can see what you are about and you can display your most useful or informative tweet at the top of the feed. This is particularly good if you have found it difficult to communicate your message in the 160 characters provided in your bio as you can use the pinned tweet as an extension of your bio. The pinned Tweet also offers you the opportunity to highlight your most important offer.

Thank new followers

If you want to thank followers for following you then it is probably best to do this by direct message, this way you do not create unnecessary tweets and jam your feed with boring content. Many do use the @mention to do this but ask yourself this question, when reading somebodies else's Tweets when you are deciding whether or not to follow someone, do you really want to read a load of thank you messages.

Follow back

It's best practice and good etiquette to follow people back on Twitter. It makes for good relationships and promotes engagement. You can always unfollow at a later date if you feel you are not gaining any value.

Unfollow people who are not following you back

In order to help you keep a positive follower to following ratio you need to keep an eye on those who are not following you. Unless you are gaining any value then unfollow because they will see your tweets. You may also want to keep following a user if you really want to attract their attention and get them to follow you back and you can do this by retweeting them you mentioning them. However, do not overdo this as this will just be considered as annoying behaviour.

Participate in trending topics

Trending topics are highly visible to many people. If you participate with the right content then you are more likely to get found.

Be consistent

You cannot expect success on Twitter in a few weeks. You need to be in for the long haul, you need to be consistent and invest time. Many fall by the wayside but those who are consistent and continually monitor their results reap the benefits.

Be a resource for your niche

Provide as much useful information as possible so users keep coming back for more. This also helps to build your brand.

Help others

Helping others and offering solutions to their problems can go a long way to building relationships. You can find out by searching for your industry keywords and the word 'help'.

Reply to Direct Messages and mentions

Replying to direct messages and mentions is an essential if you want to engage, connect and start building relationships. It's worthwhile allocating a fixed time each day to do this. If you do not have the time to reply to direct messages then prioritise by replying to the most important ones, but replying is courteous and a great way to show your followers that you value them.

Follow influencers

If you follow the right people on Twitter you will attract the right people. Following influencers in your niche not only helps you to gain knowledge but also exposes you to their followers and more like minded people.

Constantly be on the look out

As you use Twitter you will notice who are the good tweeters and what type of tweet or information grabs your attention. Make sure you take a note of these really good tweets and attention grabbing headlines and see if you can incorporate them into your tweets.

Be positive all the time

Most people are not interested in negative information and moans and groans. It stands out like a sore thumb and is guaranteed to lose you followers.

Repost

Not everyone is going to see your posts all of the time. If you are crafting well written tweets and posting good content then you want to get as many people to see it as possible. You can change your tweet content to give it a fresh look or add a different image. Repeating your tweets at different times of the day is essential on Twitter and if you have an international audience repeating each post four times a day at regular intervals is a good idea. Some people may disagree but by doing this your posts are far more likely to be seen by more people.

Give referrals

The rule of reciprocation works here. Whatever you give you usually get back.

Use Twitter Lists

Lists help you to organize your Twitter stream. When you get more and more followers your stream can become very busy, Twitter lists allow you to keep on top of top tweets and content and filter out the noise. If your Twitter lists are organized properly you can really help to increase your exposure. If for instance you create a list of your industry influencers you may find that other people follow this list.

Make your last tweet really good

If you are do not have the time or resources to be very active on Twitter then make the last tweet that you post particularly good and make sure it has a link to a page which has both valuable content and a email capture form.

Schedule your posts

If you are planning to be a power user on Twitter then you will probably need to schedule your posts and there are many effective tools you can use to do this including: Tweetdec, Hootsuite and Buffer.

Automated blog posts

There are tools available which will automatically update your Twitter feed with your and other people's blog posts. www.twitterfeed.com is good for automated posts. With www.twitterfeed.com you can set up a free account and simply add the URL or the RSS feed URL of your favorite blogs. You can specify what you want to show in the tweet, how often it updates, whether you want to include the title description and whether you want to prefix or suffix the tweet with the username.

If you are choosing the right blogs that appeal to your niche then they are likely to appreciate the quality content. If you do not have the time to create blog posts on a regular basis but still want a regular presence on twitter then this is a great way to constantly feed your followers with quality content while keeping the feed active all the time. You need to be careful with this if you using this to post your own blog links as you may find that just after you post your's another post is submitted and your post is no longer at the top of your feed.

Don't feed Twitter to Facebook

Twitter has the capacity to tolerate more posts per day than Facebook. Feeding your twitter posts into Facebook will just upset your audience and are likely to lose you your Facebook fans.

Notifications

A great way of keeping up to date with the most important people or organizations you follow is to turn on notifications. Simply go to the users profile on your mobile and then click on the gear icon and turn on notifications.

CHAPTER SIX

DAY TO DAY ACTIVITY

THERE ARE CERTAIN things that you will need to do on a day to day basis to run your campaign on Twitter. It is a good idea to allot a specific amount of time and a particular time of the day to do this. Here are some of the things you will need to do:

Following your customer's Twitter

This is important if your customers are business owners themselves. Following your customers will go a long way in building relationships. By following you are showing them that you are interested in what they have to say and also helping them to achieve their goals by helping to build their audience. By setting up a special list for your customers you can easily check their tweets and support them by retweeting whenever you wish.

Showing your audience you value and respect them

If you value and respect your audience they will most probably love, respect and value your business. Be kind, generous, offer as much help and value as possible, reply to their comments and make it obvious that you value them and are listening to them. Don't be afraid to be yourself rather than a stiff brand with no personality.

Everyone is aiming for likes, shares and comments so if you are helping others out by commenting and liking their content it is going to draw attention to your brand and they are more likely to take interest in your content. This is one area where the reciprocation rule works very well on Twitter. Engaging with content will also draw attention to you and your brand and you will find that people will click on your username to find out who you are and are very likely to follow you. Be friendly to your audience, be chatty, authentic, genuine and embrace the conversation. All this will all go a long well in building a positive image for your brand and will set you apart from your others who are continually ambushing their audience with self promotion.

Following influencers in your niche
Building relationships with key influencers in your niche is invaluable. Not only can you learn from their content but also these people can have literally thousands of followers, imagine if they follow you back and then share your content!

Dealing with negative comments
Every business at some time will have to deal with negativity from followers. Hopefully if you have a good product then this is not going to happen too often. There are 'trolls' out there who have nothing better to do than post negative tweets, the best thing to do with them is just ignore them and block them.

However there will be real customers who have real concerns and complaints and may post negative tweets publicly, there may also be people who really want to lash out to gain your attention as quickly as possible and spread the news to their friends too!

You need to deal with complaints as quickly as possible and be as transparent and authentic as possible. The best thing to do is to apologise and say how sorry you are to hear of the inconvenience they have been caused and offer to continue the conversation and deal with their concern by either private message or telephone. You can then deal with this privately, give your customer the full attention they deserve and decide on your next course of action or compensation.

Check your lists

Make sure you remember to check your lists on a regular basis. This way to can keep on top of the conversation without having to read every tweet. You may not be following some of the people on your lists so this way you get to see what they are saying occasionally.

CHAPTER SEVEN

MEASURING AND MONITORING YOUR RESULTS ON TWITTER

Measuring and monitoring your results and performance against your original goals and objectives on a continual basis is essential. This is where many businesses go wrong, they carry on aimlessly posting content without checking to see what is working and what is not. Then after 6 months or a year they wonder why their campaign is making no positive difference at all.

When you measure your results you will discover so much information about your campaign which will allow you to steer your campaign in the right direction to achieve those SMART goals and objectives and stop anything that is not working.

When you originally work out the strategies and tactics for your campaign you will be estimating what you need to do to achieve your goals and objectives. However as you campaign runs you will see exactly what you need to do to achieve what you originally set out to do. For example, you may need to increase the amount you spend on advertising to attract new followers or you may need to follow more people per day. You may very well need to change the types of Tweets to increase your number of retweets. Perhaps you need to increase the number of competitions you run to increase the number of opt-in subscribers. This is what it is all about, making your campaign work for you by constantly measuring your success against the goals set and then adjusting your strategies accordingly in order to achieve the results.

There are numerous tools you can use to measure your Social campaign including Twitter analytics, Google Analytics and other third party sites like Hootsuite and Buffer.

TWITTER ANALYTICS

To view Twitter analytics you will need to set up an advertising account. Once you are set up you can view the following:

Timeline activity dashboard. At a glance you can view your activity on Twitter, how many followers, mentions and unfollowers you have over time and also lets you view the number of interactions (Favorites, retweets, replies) you are getting for any tweet.

Followers. Followers shows you how your followers have grown or declined over the last four months and also offers you insights about their interests, location, gender and engagement.

Website. This allows you to embed code into your website so that you can view the traffic that Twitter sends to your website from your tweets.

GOOGLE ANALYTICS

It really is essential that you set up a Google Analytics account. With Google Analytics you will easily be able to track how your campaign is performing in comparison to your other social campaigns and Google Analytics will be able to give you detailed information about the impact Twitter is having on your business.

Google Analytics Social Reports.

Google Analytics provides advanced reports that let you track the effectiveness of your campaign with the following social reports:

- **The Overview Report.** This report lets you see at a glance how much conversion value is generated from social channels. It compares all conversions with those resulting from social.

- **The Conversions Report** The Conversions Report helps you to quantify the value of social and shows conversion rates and the monetary value of conversions that occurred due to referrals from Twitter and any of the other social networks. Google Analytics can link visits from Twitter with the goals you have chosen and your E - commerce transactions. To do this you will need to configure your goals in Google Analytics which is found under **Admin** and then **Goals**. Goals in Google Analytics let you measure how often visitors take or complete a specific action and you can either create goals from the templates offered or create your own custom goals. The Conversions Report can be found in the Standard Reporting tab under Traffic Sources > Social > Conversions.

- **The Networks Referral Report** The Networks Referral report tells you how many visitors the social networks have referred to your website and shows you how many page views, visits, the duration of the visits and the average number of pages viewed per visit. From this information you can determine which network referred the highest quality of traffic.

- **Data Hub Activity** The Data Hub activity report shows how people are engaging with your site on the social networks . You can see the most recent URL's that were shared how they were shared and what was said.

- **Social Plug-in Report** The social plug-ins report will show you which articles are being shared and from which network. The Google '+1' button is automatically tracked but if you want to discover what is happening with Twitter sharing buttons on your site then you will need to ask a developer to set up your Analytics and add specific code to your site. Information on how to do this is available in the Google Developers site. With the Social Plug-in report you will be able to see which is the most popular content and then you can create more of this type of content. If you have added either the 'AddThis' or 'ShareThis' Plugins to your site they will also automatically report your on site activities as well.

- **The Social Visitors Flow Report** This displays the initial paths that your visitors took from social sites through your site and where they exited.

- **The Landing Pages Report** This report displays engagement metrics for each URL. These include page views, average visit duration and page views and pages viewed per visit.

- **The Trackbacks Report** The Trackback report shows you which sites are linking to your content and how many visits those sites are sending to you. This can help you to work out which sort of content is the most successful so you can create similar and also helps you to build relationships with those who are constantly linking to your content.

Tracking Custom Campaigns with Google Analytics

Google Analytics lets you create URL's for custom campaigns for website tracking. This helps you to identify which content is the most effective in driving visitors to your website and landing pages. For instance, you may want to see which particular posts on Twitter are sending you the most traffic or you may want to see which links in an email or particular banners on your website are sending you the most traffic. Custom Campaigns let you measure this and see what is and what is not, working by letting you add parameters to the end of your URL. You can either add you own or use the URL Builder.

To do this simply type 'URL builder' into Google and click on the first result. The 'URL builder' form will only appear if you are signed into Google. You then need to add the URL, that you want to track, to the form provided and then complete the fields and click 'Submit'. You will then need to shorten the URL with bit.ly or goo.gl/ . Once you have set these up you can track the results within Google Analytics.

OTHER THIRD PARTY APPS

There are many sites available to assist you with measuring and monitoring on Twitter like www.socialbro.com www.tweetreach.com and www.bufferapp.com www.twentyfeet.com .

CHAPTER EIGHT

TWITTER AUTOMATION TOOLS

THERE ARE A wealth of extremely useful tools that can really help to put power behind your Twitter campaign. The amount of time you have available for twitter will depend on your budget and resources, but making use of some of the online tools available will not only save you time but also help you to find your target audience, keep on top of trends in your local area and also help you to maintain a healthy follow/follower ratio.

Tweetdec

Tweetdec is a social media dashboard for the management of Twitter accounts. It helps to show you at glance what is happening on your Twitter accounts by dividing information into easily viewable columns. You can create columns for mentions, direct messages, lists, trends and favorites plus you can follow and unfollow all from one place. To help keep organized you can schedule your tweets on tweetdec and it also supports URL shortening. With tweetdec you can even mute users to eliminate unwanted noise

Hootsuite

Hootsuite is a social media management dashboard that helps you to manage and measure multiple social networks. You can manage up to five social accounts with a free account. Hootsuite is designed so you can listen, engage, analyze and manage all from one place. Hootsuite is internet based so there is no need to download any software. Hootsuite allows you to schedule your tweets and bulk schedule with a csv file and it also has built in analytics so you can measure your progress.

Buffer

Buffer is a free online tool that lets you schedule your tweets and post to multiple accounts, Twitter, Facebook, LinkedIn, and Google+. Buffer offers automatic URL shortening and basic analytics. Upgrading allows you to add more accounts and schedule more tweets than the basic free account. If you are using Facebook as well, it is useful to know that you can also post to your personal profile as well as your business page.

Twitterfeed

With www.twitterfeed.com you can set up a free account and add RSS feeds and Twitterfeed will automatically update your timeline with yours and other people's blog posts. If you do not have the time to create blog posts on a regular basis but still want a regular presence on twitter then this is a great way to constantly feed your followers with quality content while keeping the feed active all the time. If you are choosing the right blogs that appeal to your niche then your followers are likely to appreciate the quality content.

To use simply add the URL or the RSS feed URL of your favorite blogs. It's a great way of offering your audience regular content as long as you are choosing quality blogs. You can specify what you want to show in the tweet, how often it updates, whether you want to include the title and description and whether you want to prefix or suffix the tweet with the username. You can also specify to display posts with certain keywords.

You need to be careful with this if you are posting your own blog links as you may find that just after you post yours another post is submitted and your post is no longer at the top of your feed. Make sure you only choose quality blogs and also that you do not choose blogs that post to often as this can be annoying for your followers.

Socialoomph

SocialOomph has many useful features you can utilize to offer a really good experience for your followers and effectively manage your campaign at the same time. It offers many features which can help you do the following:

- Schedule tweets
- Track and notify you about keywords
- Review and Follow back
- Automate Direct Messages
- Search with advanced search facilities

Tweetadder

To use Tweetadder.com you need to download, purchase and register your copy of Tweetadder, you then add your Twitter username and then authorise Tweetadder to use your account. Once set up you can use the following features:

- **Search** Tweetadder helps you to find and follow people who share your same interests. You can search by tweet or profile or location. You can search the followers of a user and you can also search Twitter lists.

- **List Cleaning** Tweetadder lets you see the users who are following you and then you can follow them back. The unfollow users section allows you to clean up your list by allowing you to search your list to see who is following you, who has stopped following you, who is inactive or over noisy. You can these choose to unfollow them if you wish.

- **Send out Tweets** Tweetadder has the ability to send out tweets from your account from a pre added list of tweets and can also automatically send out tweets from an RSS feed. You can also automatically retweet predetermined users.

- **Send out messages** Tweetadder can automatically send out thank you messages to new followers and send out direct messages.

Socialbro.com

Socialbro is a tool to manage and analyze your Twitter community in terms of where they are from, what they like, when they tweet and how influential they are. It helps you to find followers so you can target prospective customers and it also analyzes when your followers are online and when is the best time to tweet.

Manageflitter

Manageflitter helps you to work smarter and faster on Twitter by helping you find out who unfollowed you on twitter and finds accounts that are active and inactive plus it helps you to find new followers.

Friendorfollow.com

Friendorfollow.com is another site that lets you see at a glance who is not following you back with thumbnail pictures of users.

Tweetreach

Tweetreach shows you how far your tweets are reaching and provides an easy real time way of finding, analysing and reporting the reach and exposure of your campaign.

Twitter Directories

Twitter directories are a great way to find users and get found too. Twiends.com, twellow.com and wefollow.com are all directories where you can register your username and select the categories you wish to be found under.

Topsy.com

Topsy.com searches and analyzes any topic published on Twitter. It lets you pull data for any hashtag, term or username for you or your competition.

Twitaholic.com
Twitaholic.com shows you the top 1000 accounts on Twitter. You will find many celebrities and influencers in certain industries. It can be quite time consuming to use though as it does not give you any profile information so you need to look at each individual profile.

Whatthetrend.com
Whatthetrend.com tells you whats trending all over the world on Twitter.

Useqwitter.com
Useqwitter.com is a really great service that lets you keep on top of who is unfollowing you by sending you a notification email every week.

Trendsmap
Trendsmap.com is a great way to see what is trending in your area. Simply register and sign in with twitter, add your location and the trending topics for your area will show up on a map.

Followerwonk
Followerwonk.com helps you find new followers by keyword, location, URL and name. It also helps to analyze your account and give you more information about who your followers are, their location and when they tweet. It's really straightforward to use and you simply sign up with your twitter account.

Twitter Fan Wiki
Gives you a list of similar apps available to use with Twitter.

Make Google+ Work For Your Business

Alex Stearn

Table of Contents

CHAPTER ONE

GETTING STARTED ON GOOGLE +

GOOGLE'S VERY OWN social network Google + was created in 2011 to help individuals communicate and share information. It is currently the second largest social network with over 540 million active users. Google + is a similar idea to the other social networks, however, as the king of search it has made finding, sharing and engaging with content even more effective and innovative.

Google + offers a myriad of features including the +1 button, personal profiles, business pages, communities, events and Hangouts (live video chat for up to 10 people). Google + differs from Facebook in that you can follow anyone without that person having to accept a friend request. Google + also offers a unique way to share information with the different people in your life with 'Circles'. Circles allow you to organize people into different groups so that you can easily select who you want to share your posts with.

In terms of functionality Google + with its unlimited resources and expertise will get better and better for its users, its already seamlessly integrated with other Google products like YouTube, GMail, Google Docs and Google Analytics. Even though it does not look like it will overtake Facebook in terms of connecting with friends and family, there are definitely valuable opportunities to be had here with regard to search engine rankings and connecting with new audiences, especially in niche markets. More and more businesses are signing up to Google + every day and businesses can no longer afford to ignore Google + especially with the number of benefits it offers for marketing and promotion.

BENEFITS OF USING GOOGLE + FOR YOUR BUSINESS

Before you get started you really need to understand the features and benefits that Google + can offer for marketing your business. You will then be able to work out whether Google+ is for you, whether your audience are active on Google + and how you can use Google + to achieve your overall marketing goals. Here are some of the benefits that Google+ offers to businesses:

Exposure and recommendations with the +1 Button

Whether or not you decide to create a business page on Google + you need to add the +1 button to your website. The +1 button allows your business to be recommended by anyone with a Google + profile and helps build your brand by creating social proof. When someone +1's your website this action will be added to your count which will be seen by others. When someone has you in their circles and views content that you have +1'd, your +1 may be highlighted next to the +1 count. Also if anyone +1's your website they can share it with their circles on Google +. To add the +1 button to your website simply add the +1 tag to your site which can be found at this page

https://developers.google.com/+/web/+1button/

Major exposure for local businesses on Google

If you have a bricks and mortar business you can merge your Google + business page with Google + local, which means you can benefit from being listed on Google maps and take advantage of all the social features that a business page offers as well. When anyone searches for your business it gets displayed prominently on the right side of Google search with address, photos, reviews, opening times and an option to follow your page. This gives you more opportunities to get found, engage with your followers and build a wider audience.

Your ranking in Google search

Google + is strongly integrated with Google search and having a business page will help improve your search rankings. When your Google + page is verified with your website, your site is more likely to be ranked in Google search and every time your page is +1'd or if your content is shared this will also have a positive effect on your search ranking.

To connect with your customers

Google + is growing at a phenomenal rate and currently has 345 active 'in stream users' and growing fast. It is safe to say that some of your customers and prospects are likely to be using Google + and therefore it will be a good place to connect, communicate and promote your brand.

Opportunities for targeting specific groups

Because you can organize your contacts into circles, Google + makes it possible for you to target your posts to particular individuals or groups which is incredibly powerful for marketing.

A real opportunity to grow your contacts

Google+ offers real opportunities to connect with new people. Google + is full of professional people who genuinely want to connect to like minded people and it's a great place to get yourself known, build a reputation and expose your work. You can follow people and add them to your circles without asking permission and although they will not see your posts in their stream you can still comment on and share their posts. This is a great way to draw attention to your profile and start building relationships.

Helps to publicize and distribute your content

When you post new content on Google + it will almost immediately get discovered, crawled and indexed by Google and therefore is more likely to get found. With your own profile or a Google + business page you can publicize your blog content and widen your reach through sharing and engagement.

Immense editing power

Unlike any of the other platforms, Google + offers you complete control over what you post and you can edit and make changes and updates whenever you like. If you press the button to share a post and suddenly realize you made an error you can simply change it. You can also disable comments for your posts and delete any of your posts. Google has a reputation for offering the most relevant and up to date content, so by giving their publishers this functionality it makes information even more accurate and up to date.

More engagement with Hangouts

Google Hangouts offer live video chat for up to 9 people. This has opened a whole new world for businesses and personal brands. You can now connect with your audience in a unique way and host virtual meetings, video conferences, coaching sessions, live broadcasts and live demos. This service is completely free and Hangouts can be recorded and viewed at a later date.

Helps connect you to influencers

With Google + you can add anyone to your circles and although they will not be able to see your content you can still see, comment on, and share their content. This in turn can draw the attention of those influencers to your profile.

Communities help you to engage with like minded people and find your audience

Google + Communities offer huge value to businesses and brands and provide a great place for them to listen and engage with their target audience. By creating a Google + Community around a subject relating to your brand you can bring people together to connect and interact, while at the same time building your brand.

Helps you to promote your personal brand

If you are a personal brand then Google + is a powerful platform to grow your brand. Your profile is automatically set to public and you can control who sees your content more easily than on any other social network. The about section on you profile is a great place to write about your business, so when anyone looks at your profile you can promote your business as well.

Promoting events

Google + offers many features for promoting both online and offline events and offers full integration with Google Calendar and Google Hangouts. Google+ also offers a sophisticated way of sharing event photos by allowing real time and mobile sharing of photos for anyone attending the event.

Offers a new and high quality audience

The opportunities for businesses to find and engage with their target market are made much easier through pages, Hangouts and communities. Google + is attracting numerous businesses who are seeing the advantages for search engine optimization with posting their content on a business page. This has created more opportunities for businesses to connect with a high quality audience who are all keen to widen their reach by connecting and interacting with each other. Google + certainly has its own personality and has a wealth of friendly and interesting people to connect with who are also posting great content.

The Google + image

Google + has developed a very professional image linked to high quality discussions and content and it is developing a reputation as a place where businesses can be heard.

Currently no monetization

Up until now Google has not monetized this platform so there are still big opportunities to get your posts in front of your audience without having to incur advertising costs. Of course you can promote your page with Google Adwords if you wish.

Social Reporting

Because Google + is seamlessly integrated with Google Analytics you can measure and analyze your social campaign in detail. Social reporting lets you measure the value of conversions with 'The conversions report' and lets you measure your actual results against the social media goals.

Integration with other Google services

Google is tying all its products together and Google + integrates seamlessly with the other Google services, for example, Gmail, Google Docs, Google Drive, Google Calendars, YouTube and search. You only need one password for all these services which makes using Google services so much easier.

Your Google ads show your Google + endorsements

If your Google + Page is linked with your website and you advertise with Adwords, your listing will display endorsements for your page by showing the number of followers you have on your page which helps to create social proof.

A great place to learn

There is an extremely high number of knowledgable and creative people on Google + which makes it a great platform for not only finding information and learning but also for connecting with those people who may be able to help you and get the answers you need about certain subjects.

SETTING UP YOUR PERSONAL PROFILE

Google + offers you valuable yet free real estate, for your business and there are huge opportunities for your business to get found with both your personal profile and your business page, especially if they are optimized properly.

To get started on Google + you will need to set up a Google account .

You will need to upload a really good profile picture and preferably one that you use on all your social networks to tie in with your personal branding. The ideal size is 250X 250 pixels and will be displayed as a circular image on your profile. At this stage you will be prompted to invite all your contacts on Yahoo, Gmail and Hotmail, you will be offered suggestions of people to circle and will also be able to search for people you know. However, it is best to skip this and come back to it once you have set everything up properly. You will be then asked to fill in some basic information about your school, employer and where you live. Once you have completed the set up process you can go back to any part of your profile to complete or edit it at any time.

Tagline
Creating a good brief description about who you are is essential, as this is what will appear directly under your profile name in Google search results.

Introduction
When creating your introduction it is important that you write for the reader and not just fill your introduction with keywords in the hope that this will help with your search rankings. This will not only put your potential followers off but Google will also recognise this. You can also add links, your website or blog link and links to your other social platforms and you can smarten up your introduction text with underline, bold and bullet points. You can also add some really good keywords for your business and link them back to related content on your website. Above all write for your customer, make it very readable and interesting.

Your Cover Photo
Google + provides a sizeable canvas to promote yourself, this area gives you a great opportunity to both visually tell your story and promote your brand. This is where you can make a good first impression with a great image. It is advisable to use an image which will somehow connect with your audience emotionally and that will help to build a powerful and

memorable connection with your audience.

A very important thing to consider when designing your cover photo is that the majority of times your profile will be viewed on Google+ is when someone hovers over your name. When anyone hovers over your name, a hover card will appear with a miniature representation of your profile, it's like a virtual business card. This is why your cover photo becomes such an important area to promote your brand and offers you the opportunity to really express who you are and what your offer. The more active you become on Google + the more people will your hover over your name and view your profile, therefore whatever image or text your decide to put on your cover photo, it needs to stand out enough to be easily seen or read on the small hover card.

The recommended size for your cover photo is 1080 X 608 and maximum is 2120 X 1192. To get the best effect it's a good idea to keep it as clean, simple and uncrowded as possible. Make sure you view your profile on your mobile too, by downloading the app for either android or iphone.

To optimize your cover photo for search, you need to rename your image file with some good keywords relating to your business and separate them with hyphens. Also when you upload your image add a caption description, call to action and URL to your website.

Profile Photos
When you add your profile picture it is best to add a close up picture of your face. When you click on your profile photo and then click on the profile photo under the picture, you will arrive at another page where you can add more photos of yourself. This is a great branding opportunity for you to add more pictures of yourself or perhaps images of people using your product.

NB When someone hovers over your profile image on a post then some information about you will appear, you can control what you want your visitors to see here and this can be edited in the 'work' section of your 'about' section under the heading 'employment'. You can also add your website link.

Advertising your Google + URL (Shortening it !)

Your Google + URL includes a long stream of numbers which is not good for advertising or promoting you Google + account on your website or blog. However, Google now provides you with a custom URL which you can find by clicking 'Get URL' at the top of your profile.

FINDING YOUR WAY AROUND GOOGLE +

Once you have set up your profile and before you start posting and promoting, it's a really good idea to have a look around and familiarise yourself with Google+. Once you get to know Google + you will find how much it has to offer and how straight forward it is to use. This section will give you a quick introduction to finding your way around Google + and an explanation of the terms which will be mentioned throughout this book.

Your Stream

When you arrive at your homepage you will see your stream. Your stream is where you view all your posts from the people in your circles and where you create your posts for your own stream.

The horizontal menu

The horizontal menu along the top shows your circles: All, Friends, Family, Acquaintances and more (a drop down list of all the circles you have created). With this menu you can control which posts you see. So by clicking **All** you see posts from everyone including the pages that you have +1'd. By clicking **Friends** you will see posts from just your friends.

Google includes posts that they think you may be interested in, 'What's hot and recommended' and you can comment and +1 any of this content.

The Services Menu

When you hover your mouse over the **Home** button a vertical menu along the left hand side will appear which displays all the services offered on Google + and allows you to manage your profile, etc. Here is an overview of this menu:

- **Home** Takes you back to your stream.

- **Profile** Takes you to the page where you can view, manage and edit your own profile.

- **People** This page displays the people you have added to your network and the people who have added you. It allows you to find people for your network and allows you to manage and organize your contacts into circles.

- **Photos** Here you can upload and manage your photos by putting them into albums, keeping your photos safely backed up on Google+ and choosing who you allow to actually see those photos. Google will automatically enhance your photos and lets you highlight particular photos in an album.

- **What's Hot and recommended** Google includes posts that they think you may be interested in and you can comment and +1 on any of this content. You can also control how much you see of this. Simply click on 'What's hot and recommended' and then click on the gear icon alongside it and you can choose to see either more, standard or fewer posts. If you do not want to see any simply untick the box 'Show posts in home stream'.

- **Communities** Communities on Google + are where people can join together to discuss and share ideas about the things that they love and are passionate about. You can create your own communities or join communities.

- **Events** Google + Events lets you create events, invite your circles and then comment and share photos of that event.

- **Hangouts** A Hangout is a free live video chat service for up to 9 people at a time. Google can effectively switch the view to the person who is chatting. As well as creating your own Hangout you can view live Hangouts and stream and record them for viewing later so even if you are having a Hangout with just a few people, potentially you can have thousands viewing the Hangout after it has taken place, which offers amazing opportunities for businesses. More detail about Hangouts later.

- **Pages** Google + offers you the opportunity to create pages for your business. Creating a page means your customers and prospects can follow and interact with your posts and offers you yet another opportunity to get found in search and widen your reach.

- **Local** Google + Local helps you to discover and share places. You can get recommendations based on your circles and your location, you can view pages, read Zagat reviews and find reviews from people you trust. If you are a bricks and mortar business then it is important that you show up in Google + local.

- **Games** Fun Fun Fun! When you have a spare moment there are a host of different free games to play.

- **Settings** Here is where you can control your privacy settings and control who sends you notifications. Literally you can control everything you want, or do not want, to see on Google+ in this setting section.

Google Circles for specific targeting

Circles are a very unique and important feature of Google + and can be used to both organize what you see in your stream and to target your posts to different groups of people. Google + recognises that we all have different contacts from different circles or walks of life. These could be, close friends, school friends, college or university friends, family, business contacts, customers and prospects etc. Google + also recognises that these people are not necessarily interested in the same things and that when you post content you may only want particular people to see that content.

From the very beginning when you add anyone to your network you have to add them to a circle and you can add anyone to a circle, it is similar to clicking the 'follow' button on Twitter. You can either add them to one of the default circles, friends, family and acquaintances or create a new circle that you have specially created (your circle names can only be seen by you). When you add them to a circle they may be notified (if they have their notifications switched on) and then they can choose whether or not they want to add you to one of their circles.

Circles are such a great feature because it means every time you post a comment or content you can choose exactly who can see it by simply ticking the boxes of the circles you want to include. This is one advantage that Google +has over Facebook in that you can easily and selectively message people. For instance your customer probably does not want to see the latest picture of your granny, so you would simply select your family circle. On the flip side your friends and family may not want to see every one of your business posts. You can even lock your posts if you do not want a photo or link to be shared.

Viewing other peoples posts

When it comes to viewing other peoples updates then circles are a very effective way of filtering information so you can concentrate on what you are interested in. You can choose to view content from different 'Streams' or you can view all content from all your circles if you wish. In terms of organization this is a great feature and helps you to cut out the noise and helps you to view posts from the people you deem to be the most important to you.

Managing and sharing your Circles

You can manage your circles by clicking the **People** tab and then **Circles**. Once you have them in your circles you can move them around by dragging and dropping them into other circles. For instance you may have a prospect that has recently become a customer and therefore want to move them to your 'customer' circle. You can also remove people if you wish by simply going to the **People** tab and then clicking on **Circles** and then click the **X** in the upper right hand corner.

Circles are versatile, they are great for targeting information to particular groups and also for organising and finding new people. You can also share your circles with others by simply clicking on the circle you wish to share and then under the tab **Actions** click **Share Circle**. You could for instance create a circle of people around a specific interest and then share it to help other people find people......don't forget to add yourself!

The + 1 button

The way that people are searching for information about products and services is changing. More and more, people are looking for recommendations and social proof. Google have recognised this and in order to give us even better results when searching they have embraced this fact and created something that will easily display recommendations, the Google +1 Button.

Google introduced the + 1 button to help people find the things they love and care about and share them with their friends, family and contacts and to help them create even more relevant results in Google search. The Google +1 Button is now appearing in more and more places on the web, on web pages, blogs, news articles and Google + pages. It is literally hit millions of times a day all around the world!

The +1 button is very similar to the Facebook 'like' button and is used to show your appreciation for any thing you find on the web that has the +1 button featured on it. To use the +1 button you need to have a profile page on Google+. When you click the + 1 button you are quickly giving something your signature of approval, so that when any of your family or friends in one of your circles stumbles upon something on a website, or blog, or Google search, or Google adverts they may see that you +1'd it. This is where social proof comes into play and based on your +1 or 'your recommendation' this may help another person to decide whether or not they are going to buy something.

When you +1 something on the web you will be given the option to share this with any of your circles on Google + and then it will be collected in your +1 tab on your profile. You can display that tab on your profile if you wish by simply selecting it on your profile settings, then click on 'Settings' and then under the 'Profile' heading you can check the +1 box.

CHAPTER TWO

CREATING YOUR BUSINESS PAGE ON GOOGLE +

A GOOGLE + page provides your business with a public identity on Google, here you can post content and engage with an audience of people who have chosen to click the 'follow' button. By interacting with your audience on your page you can build trust, build relationships, develop your brand and widen your reach. Google + pages work similarly to Google + personal profiles, you can add people to circles, edit your profile, share content on Google +, +1 comments and photos within Google + and create and join Hangouts. You can post content and direct them back to your website or blog for updates about your business and you can send messages to particular groups of people. However Google + Pages cannot currently +1 other pages and you cannot share to extended circles.

Before your set up your page you need to be clear and specific about what you want to achieve by creating a business page on Google +. You can use your Google + page as a marketing tool to do many things including: finding new customers, building your brand, promoting events and special offers, building your opt-in and driving traffic to your website or blog.

To create your page simply go to your homepage and click on **Pages** tab and click on **Create a page**. You will need to select your business type from the 5 given options and then select the category that your business falls into from the drop down menu.

Note for local businesses

If you select **Local Business** or **Place** Google will allow you to search for your business on Google maps. If it is not already listed on Google maps you can enter all the details. Google will prepare a verification postcard with a pin number to send you by post to verify your business. If you do find your listing on Google maps you will need to verify by phone or post, this is so Google can make sure you are authorised to manage this business page.

You will then need to add your business name and web address details and agree to the terms and conditions. To complete your page you will need to add your profile picture, cover photo, your contact information, an introduction, a tagline and then link your website to your page by adding a line of code to your website. Linking your website will make your site eligible for 'Google + Direct Connect' which means by putting the + sign before your page name you can navigate straight there to your page from Google Search.

Your Cover Photo

Your cover photo is the most valuable area of marketing real estate on your page. This is where you can really shout out and promote your brand and use this space to communicate visually exactly what your business is about and how you can help your ideal customer. Many businesses miss out on this opportunity by just uploading a fairly generic image without any message and the visitor is left feeling they have no real reason to press the follow button. This is not what you want. When it comes to your cover photo you have two main goals; to get your visitors to follow you and to get your followers to sign up to your email opt in.

1. To get your visitor to follow you

When someone follows you one Google + you get the opportunity to stay in touch with them by posting updates which they will see in their stream. In many cases the first time your visitor arrives at your page may often be the only time they actually see your page in its entirety, after that they may not have a reason to actually return to the page itself. It is therefore of paramount importance that whatever you put on your cover photo impacts your ideal customer enough to get them to like your page. In order to do this you need to grab their attention by choosing a compelling image and creating a message that connects with them emotionally. Your message needs to let them know immediately that they have arrived at the right place by stating clearly how you are going to help them or offer them a solution to their problem. The right image and the right message is a winning combination and if you are targeting the right audience they are very likely to press the follow button.

2. To get your visitor to sign up to your email opt-in

One of the most important things to realize with any social media profile is that you don't actually own it, changes are taking place all the time and although social media is incredibly powerful there is nothing more important than building your own list of ideal customers. Your next goal is therefore to get your visitors to opt-in to your email list, this way you have permission to communicate with them on a regular basis through their email inbox.

The other effective way of collecting leads is to send your fans to a page on your website where you have a compelling offer and a form to capture their name and email address. You can use your cover photo to promote your offer by adding the details of your offer to your cover photo. When you click on any cover photo you are then taken to a page with the cover photo image and a comment area. This is where you can add the details and benefits of your offer together with the URL of the webpage with your offer and your email capture page. You can then add a call to action to your cover photo with the image of a button on your cover photo. When your follower or visitor clicks on the button image they will be taken to the page with the details of the offer.

However, a word of caution here, you do need to think very carefully about how and what you are offering here as the audience are very different on Google + and they love Google + because there is an abundance of high quality content and it is not full of advertisements. If your cover photo is one great big advert then this may not gain you the followers you want. You therefore need choose an offer which is going to delight your ideal customer as soon as they see it.

Designing your cover photo

The recommended size for your cover photo is 1080 X 608 and maximum is 2120 X 1192. To get the best effect it's a good idea to keep it as clean, simple and uncrowded as possible. Make sure you view your profile on your mobile too, by downloading the app for either android or iphone.

To optimize your cover photo for search, you need to rename your image file with some good keywords relating to your business and separate them with hyphens. Also when you upload your image add a caption description, call to action and URL to your website.

You profile photo

You need to upload a square image of your logo (minimum 250 X 250 pixels) which will be displayed within a circular frame. Some logos just don't seem to work in a circle so you may want to bring in just a recognisable part of your logo to fit in with the circle.

The About section

- **Tagline** Unless you are a local business your tagline will appear below your business name in search and on your hovercard which displays about 35 characters of your tagline. This is where your can give people a quick idea of what your business is about and is an ideal place to put your slogan, a motto or a short message you may want to convey to your audience.

- **Introduction** This is where your need to write about the benefits you can offer your customers. Although you need to write the introduction for your audience you still need to try and include keywords from your industry to help you to get found in search.

* **Links** Make sure you add all your links where your business is present on the internet; other social networks, your website, blog and YouTube channel. You can add custom links by adding explanatory text which link to your URL's.

Your Google + custom URL

Your Google + URL includes a long stream of numbers which is not very good when it comes to advertising or promoting your page on any of your marketing material. However, Google + now provides you with a much simpler custom URL which you will find by clicking **Get URL** at the top of your profile.

A tip for those working from home or on the move

Here is a tip if you work from home. Even though every business must have a physical address you can still create a local page and hide your physical address. You do this by going to **Pages** and then click **Edit business information** on the page you want to edit and then click on the pencil icon next to address. At the bottom of the form tick the box **I deliver goods and services to my customers at their location** and then remove the tick from the box which says **I also serve customers at my business address**. Your address will then be hidden.

Getting your page ready

Before finding your audience and circling them you need to add some interest to your page by adding photos, videos and articles and then creating some interesting posts for your target audience. The whole subject of creating content will be covered in a separate chapter.

Page Manager

You can add multiple page managers to your page, simply click **Pages** from your personal profile and then click **Manage this page** and then **Add managers to your page** and you can then invite the people you want to manage your page. You can remove managers simply by clicking on the **X** associated with their name.

CHAPTER THREE

BUILDING YOUR AUDIENCE ON GOOGLE +

WHEN YOU HAVE your personal profile and your business page set up and you have posted some status updates you will be ready to start building your audience. You will first need to start building your audience on your personal profile before your business page, this way you can start building your reputation on your personal profile and share updates from your business profile to your personal profile. This chapter is split into two sections:

1. Building your audience on your personal profile.

2. Building your audience on your business page.

Of course building your audience will go hand in hand with creating content. As more and more people +1, comment and share your content you will grow your audience. However the strategies in this section will help you to start laying the foundations which will give you a firm base for you to build on.

NB. Please note as there are two parts to 'Building your Audience' you may find certain parts repeated. As this book may be used as a reference book it was felt necessary to include certain information in both sections.

BUILDING YOUR AUDIENCE ON YOUR PERSONAL PROFILE

Building your audience on your personal profile is incredibly important on Google + particularly if you are a personal brand. Here are some tactics to build our audience:

Create some circles

It is very likely that you are going to build a sizeable audience on Google + so it's important to organize your followers into circles from the very beginning. If you leave this until later, it is likely to get very confusing and you will probably forget why you circled people in the first place. Organising your contacts into circles will not only help you to target specific groups but will also keep you focused when it comes to choosing who you want to follow.

Here are some examples of circles you can create:

• One for women and one for men (this may be particularly important if you have products that are more suited to either gender)
• Prospects
• Customers
• Suppliers
• Influencers
• Countries or regions. This is of paramount importance if you are going to be posting to different time zones and don't worry if you are using Hootsuite to schedule your post because they allow you to post to different circles too.

The People Tab

Google + offers a number of ways for you to find and connect with people. To start searching you need to click on the **People** tab on your homepage menu. When you are adding your connections a drop down menu will appear which lets you select which circles you wish to add them to. Once you have added them they will receive a notification to say you have added them to your circles. (Unless they have their notifications switched off.) When you add someone they can decide whether they want to add you or not. They will obviously not see any of your posts until they have added you to one of their circles.

From the **People** tab Google makes suggestions for you based on the people you know. You can add contacts from your Gmail, Yahoo or Hotmail, simply click on **Connect services** and you can get started. You can search people you know based on where you work, or used to work, or the school, college or university you attended. To do this simply click on **Find co-workers** and **Find classmates** and you can search based on the years you attended those establishments.

Find people with Google+ Search

The main search at the top of the page lets you search for people, pages, posts, and communities. Simply add your specific term in the search box and it will bring up everything relating to that. This is a really a good way of finding people you know and finding people with the same interests. When you add people make sure you create a circle and name it 'leads'. Once you have done this you can select to read the posts from this particular stream and start interacting with their posts.

Join Communities

This is a great way to find people with similar interests. For example, if you are selling a gardening product then you could join a gardening community or even create your own (more about this later). You can interact and engage with other members by commenting on their posts and by providing valuable content for the community. People who are in these communities are generally happy to hear from you as long as you are posting content which is of interest or value to them. This is a great way of showing yourself off as an expert in a particular area of interest as well, however, this is definitely not a way to push your products and will be considered as spam if you do.

Follow your customer pages or profiles

If you know of anyone (customer, associate, friend,etc) who has a page then if you follow them you may find they add you to their circles and follow you.

Add great content and value

Once you start posing really good content and people start interacting with that content by commenting and sharing you will increase your reach and build trust and respect from your current following.

Connect with influencers

Google + makes it incredibly easy to connect with influencers. Here are some ways you can try and connect with them and draw attention to your profile.

- Add them to a circle.
- Mention them in a post.
- Comment on a photo they have commented on.
- Comment on a photo they have posted.
- Comment on a photo they are tagged in.
- Send an invitation to an event or a 'Hangout On Air'.

Attend public Google + Hangouts hosted by industry experts

Attending these types of events can get you noticed by the person who has created the Hangout and by other viewers and helps to start building relationships.

Circle back

When people add you to their circles then it is courteous to circle them back and you can even send them a private message welcoming them. This type of practice is always going to create good will and help to expand your reach. You can always remove them from your circles at a late date if you wish.

Host a Hangout on air

Hosting a live video event, if done properly, can attract attention during and after the event on YouTube and Google + . Hangouts on air are ranked very well on Google + and offer you yet another way to get found and start building your influence.

Your Email Signature
Add your profile, page and community URL to your email signature and any other marketing material like business cards, etc.

Add Google+ Buttons to your website or Blog
You can find all the badges and widgets for your profile and your page here: https://developers.google.com/+/web/badge/. Simply add the code to your website or blog. Some businesses have reported an increase in followers of up to 40% by adding a badge to their business website, articles and blogs.

Cross promote on your other social networks
You can invite your connections from your other networks like Facebook and Twitter. It's another way to connect and share your content as these connections will have different connections on Google + so it's a great way of increasing your reach amongst those people too.

Directories
You can use directories to find people on Google + like www.circlecount.com www.womenofgplus.com www.gglpls.com www.gpeep.com/

Find shared Circles
There are people who have actually compiled circles of people to share on Google + and you can either add them to your existing circles or create new ones. Not everyone will circle you back but many will and even if they do not, you can start commenting on their posts. You could also ask the person who compiled the circle to add you to the circle. There are a number of ways to find shared circles as follows:

- Simply type in 'Shared Circles' into Google search.
- Visit the page 'Shared Circles on G+' found here goo.gl/sdDFQi
- You can find people with similar interests on a shared document

here goo.gl/vzs33L

Create your own circle to share

Simply creating a circle around of topic which your niche will be interested in and then add yourself. To do this simply go to the **People** tab, create your circle and search for yourself in the search box and then drag yourself into the circle.

Suggested list of circles you could be added to

In your introduction in the about section of your profile you can add a list of suggested circles that people can add you to with a heading: Suggested circles you can put me in.

Take any action and interact

If you take any action on other posts you will get noticed by the post creator and their audience. This can be a comment , share , +1 or a + mention.

Use Hashtags

A Hashtag is the symbol # with a word. As with Twitter and now Facebook, Hashtags can be used to find content and get other people to find your content. They are particularly useful to get you noticed by people outside your circles. To place a Hashtag within a post, simply complete your post and then add the # symbol with a word (no spaces allowed), when the text turns to blue you have created a Hashtag. If you click on a Hashtag in a post, Google + will load more posts with that Hashtag.

BUILDING YOUR AUDIENCE ON YOUR GOOGLE + PAGE

Your Google + Page works in a similar way to your profile so the tactics you use to promote your page will be similar to those used to promote your personal profile, so there will be some overlaps here. As with your personal profile you need to make sure you create some circles before you start building your audience so that you will be able target your posts to specific groups.

Share your business page on your personal profile

Once you have created your business page and added some interest with videos, images and a few posts you can then share your page on your profile. Simply add a message on your post like, 'Follow our Google+ Page to get the latest........'

Link your page to your website

This is a great way to drive traffic to your page. Google + offers clear instructions to link your page to your website on the help pages 'Link to your website'. Doing this will help Google determine the relevance of your site to a query on google search and therefore will help with your Search engine optimization.

Add people and businesses to your circles

If you click on the **People** tab from your page you will not find the options for adding people as you do on your profile. However you can still search people and organizations and then add them to your circles. When the search results appear you can either press the 'follow' button for businesses or the 'add' button for people. These people or businesses will be notified when you add them (unless they have their notifications switched off). This is again a good way of drawing attention to your brand. Google + offers you four circles to get you started, Following, Customers, VIP's and Team members but you can add as many of your own as you like. Once you start interacting with their posts by either +1ing, commenting or sharing you may find they will add you to their circles.

Join Communities

As a business page you can also create, join and participate in Google+ communities.

Host a Hangout On Air (HOA)

More about this later, but hosting a live video event, if done properly, will attract attention during and after the event on Google + and YouTube. To host a HOA on a Google + page you need to connect it with your YouTube account.

Add great content and value

Once you start posting valuable and interesting content for your target audience and they start interacting with it by +1ing, sharing and commenting you will increase your reach through their circles. This subject is covered in detail later on.

Your Email Signature

Find your custom profile, page and community URL and add it to your email signature and other offline promotional material.

Add Google + Buttons to your website or blog

You can find all the badges and widgets for your profile and your page here https://developers.google.com/+/web/badge/. Simply add the code to your website or blog.

Cross promote on your other social networks

You can invite your connections from your other networks like Facebook and Twitter. It's yet another way to connect and share your content and also these connections will have different connections on Google + so it's a great way of widening your reach.

Linking your Google + page with your AdWords campaign

By linking your Google + page with your Adwords campaigns all your +1's from your website, your page and your adverts get added together and appear as a single total. By enabling 'social extensions', consumers will be able to see all the recommendations your business has received.

Directories

You can use directories to find people on Google + like www.circlecount.com http://www.womenofgplus.com/ www.gglpls.com www.gpeep.com/

Find shared Circles

There are people who have actually compiled circles of people to share on Google + and you can either add them to your existing circles or create new ones. Not everyone will circle you back but many will and even if they do not you can comment on their posts. You could also ask the person who compiled the circle to add you to the circle. There are a number of ways to find shared circles as follows:

- Simply type in 'Shared Circles' into Google search.
- Visit the page 'Shared Circles on G+' found here goo.gl/sdDFQi
- You can find people with similar interests on a shared document here goo.gl/vzs33L

Create your own circles to share

Create a circle of interesting people around a subject popular in your niche and then add your page. To add your page simply go to your **'People'** tab, create a circle, search for your page in the search box and then drag your page into the circle.

Take any action and interact

If you take any action on other posts you will get noticed by the post creator and their audience. This can be a comment , share , +1 or a + mention. The +1 function cannot be turned off and will get sent as a notification.

Use hashtags

A Hashtag is the symbol # with a word. As with Twitter and now Facebook, Hashtags can be used to find content and get other people to find your content. They are particularly useful to get you noticed by people outside your circles. To place a hashtag within a post simply complete your post and then add the # symbol with a word (no spaces allowed) when the text turns to blue you have created a hashtag. If you click on a hashtag in a post, Google + will load more posts with that hashtag. The first three hashtags are displayed on the top right of your posts and once you click on one it will flip around and show you other content with that hashtag.

Connect with influencers

Google + makes it easy to connect with influencers. Here are some ways you can try and connect with them.

Add them to a circle.

- Mention them in a post.
- Comment on a photo they have commented on.
- Comment on a photo they have posted.
- Comment on a photo they are tagged in.
- Send an invitation to an event or a 'Hangout on Air'

Circle back

When people add you to their circles then its courteous to circle them back and you can even send them a private message welcoming them. This type of practice is always going to create good and will help to expand your reach. You can always remove them from your circles at a late date if you wish.

Post articles within Google +

Google + offers you the ability to write longer, more detailed and formatted posts which can be found within Google + and in Google search. Sometimes keeping people within Google + rather than sending them to an external blog can help to build your audience by encouraging engagement within the platform.

Find shared Circles

There are people who have actually compiled circles of people to share on Google+ and you can either add them to your existing circles or create new ones. If you don't find them interesting then simply delete them or the circle in its entirety. There are a number of ways to find shared circles as follows:

- Simply type in 'Shared Circles' into Google search.
- Visit the page 'Shared Circles on G+' found here goo.gl/sdDFQi
- You can find people with similar interests on a shared document here goo.gl/vzs33L
-

Not everyone will circle you back but many will and even if they do not you can comment on their posts. You could also ask the person who compiled the circle to add you to the circle.

Use Google Ripples

Google Ripples creates an interactive graph of each of your public posts on Google + and show you how your posts have rippled throughout the network. To view your ripples simply click the drop down arrow at the top of your post and click **View Ripples**.

You will be able to view who has publicly shared a post or URL and the comments they have made and the statistics about how your post was shared. Viewing your Ripples will help you to discover new people who are already interested in your content. You can also view ripples on other peoples posts! This is a great way to find people who are interested in the type of content and you offer.

You may find that there are particular people who are always sharing your content and it may be a good idea to create a circle for these people. Once you know who these 'Superfans' are you can pay particular attention to them by sharing, commenting or + 1'ing their content.

CHAPTER FOUR

CONTENT IS KING ON GOOGLE +

IN ORDER TO build a thriving community of brand advocates and customers who want to share your content, sign up to your newsletter and buy your products you are going to need to build trust, loyalty and likeability. The only way to do this is by communicating with them on regular basis in the right way and by consistently delivering the highest possible quality content which will grab their attention, appeal to their interests and add real value to their lives. Once your followers start engaging with your content, you will start building trust and start converting them into customers.

Posting excellent content on Google + is not only going to help increase your followers on Google + but is also likely to put you in a winning position in Google's organic search. Content really is king on Google + and in order to create the right content you are going to need to have a real understanding of your target audience and deep insight into what interests and motivates them. Once you have this information and put this together with the strategies in this book, there is no reason why you cannot build a thriving community of advocates for your brand on Google +. In this chapter you are going to learn about the different types of content, the different types of media you can use and tips on how help you create the best experience for your followers so you can receive the highest engagement.

Whether you are looking to focus on your personal profile or your business page you will need to consistently produce and share high quality content with your audience on a regular basis. To do this you will need to create a posting calendar and Google gives you the perfect tool to do this. With **Google Calendar** you can color code your entries, set reminders, add documents and images and share with your colleagues if you wish. This will be covered in more detail in the planning section of the book.

On Google+ you can share photos, a link, video or events and Google + gives you much more editing power than any other network. You can for instance delete or change text after it has been posted and you can format your text and use bold, add italics and strikethroughs to make it stand out.

30 IDEAS FOR POSTING CONTENT ON GOOGLE +

You may be wondering how you are going to consistently produce and deliver compelling content to your audience on a regular basis for the foreseeable future. However, once you have picked your topic of interest you will surprised how one idea lead will lead to another and you will be able to find numerous pieces of content to create and post. Here are some ideas for content that can be adapted to any type of business or topic:

1. Relatable content

Relatable content is one of the best types of content and one of the most shared types of content. Relatable content is anything that your target audience can relate to and identify with, it's when your audience sees a piece of content and immediately think, "Yes, I can relate to that and this is exactly the way I feel when this happens". It's incredibly powerful because this content is immediately communicating to your audience that you understand them and you feel their pain or joy and you can empathise with them. With relatable content you are communicating with them on quite a deep level which all helps to build relationships and trust. This is why Someecards is so successful, most of their content is relatable.

2. Emotive content

Evoking an emotional response is an essential ingredient to successful viral content marketing. If you create content that evokes a strong positive emotional response it will help your audience associate that emotion with your brand. Content like this is very memorable and if you can make people feel something by posting an image, text or a video this can really help in building your brand and creating powerful associations. Evoking any of the primary emotions be it surprise, joy, fear, sadness, anger or disgust is a certain way to get people sharing your content.

3. Educational content

Posting informative content about your subject is invaluable, this will help you to stand out as a thought leader and expert in your field. If your content is valuable and useful then your followers are likely to keep coming back for more and are likely to share your content too. Remember your audience is also looking to find and share valuable content with their friends and customers and will want to be associated with any compelling content you create.

4. Informative

This could be about letting your followers know about something that is happening like a Webinar, a trade show or event in the area or a special offer or any information that will be of use or value to them.

5. Entertaining/amusing content

Social media is all about being social, having fun and people love sharing funny stuff. Even if you did not create it yourself but you think it is going to appeal to your target audience then share it. The aim here is to amuse and entertain your audience, humor is a winner all round and not only does humor break down barriers it is also more likely to be liked and shared.

6. Seasonal Content

Posting content relating to important holidays and annual celebrations is a really good way to stay connected with your audience. If you have an international audience then being aware of their holidays and religious celebrations will go a long way in building relationships.

7. Inspiring and motivational content

The truth is everyone has a bad day sometimes and needs a little bit of motivation or cheering up. A motivational quote will help to lift your audience and can really help to connect with them. If you know what your audience wants, what they aspire to and what their frustrations are then it is likely that you will be able to motivate them by posting content which inspires them. These types of post are also very shareable especially if put together with a colorful and inspiring image like a cartoon or photo.

8. Employee and behind the scenes content

If you have news about your employees and the great things they are doing then post it. Maybe they have been involved in a fundraiser or they have won an employee of the month award. Giving your audience a behind the scenes view of your business helps to keeps your business and brand looking real, authentic and adds human interest.

9. Customer Content

Having a member of the month or including news or content about a customer's business is a great way to spark interest in your posts. Sharing a customer's content not only shows you value your audience but can also encourage them to do the same.

10. Shared Content

Whilst it is great to post most of your own content, don't be afraid to share other peoples content as long as it is relevant. The more valuable content you share the more valuable you will become to your audience and the more likely they will keep coming back for more. Sharing content is also incredibly important in building relationships with your followers, they are going to be far more open to your brand if you are supporting theirs.

11. Statistics

People love statistics which relate to their niche. If your business is B2B then posting statistics can gain a great deal of interest, especially if they are displayed in a visually appealing way like with an infographic or graph. They are often shared if they are translated into a useful tip for your followers.

12. Questions

Asking questions about subjects that your audience may be interested is a great way to encourage comments, interaction and community. People love to share their opinions and thoughts and love the opportunity to communicate, contribute and be heard. Even if you are posting an image or video it's a really good practice to ask a question.

13. Top Ten lists

People love lists about who or what is top or best. Lists spark interest and this is most probably because people like to compare their choices and judgement with others. Some may like to see that their opinions match others and feel they are right in that choice or others may feel comforted by the fact their choices are not the same and they are unique. You can create your own lists on list.ly and also get your users to join in by adding to the list which is a great way to increase engagement.

14. Controversial

Posting a controversial statement can spark great conversation and interaction, remember people love to voice their opinions, have an input and be heard. It may be a good idea to stay out of the discussion here as you do not want to lose followers and you need to be sensitive to your audience in order not to upset them so be careful with what topics you pick.

15. Special offers

Google + is a great way to get the message out about the special offers you have running but, you will need to be careful not to post them too often or they just appear like advertising and bad noise in your audience's stream. You need to make sure that what you are offering is of real value, that it is exclusive to your followers and you are offering them a deadline to redeem the offer.

16. Contests and sweepstakes

Contests and sweepstakes are always a great way to gain popularity, grow your audience, build your brand and build your opt-in email list. With contests your audience can have great fun with your brand and they can also create high levels of engagement. There are so many different types of contests: photo and video competitions; sweepstakes; comment to win; polls; caption this contest; photo contest and quizzes; and the list goes on.

You can display a link in Google + to promote a contest or promotion off Google +. If you are solely responsible for the promotion and compliance with local and federal laws however you cannot run contests, sweepstakes directly on Google +. If you do want to promote a contest off Google+ make sure you read Google + terms and conditions. www.**google**.com/+/**policy**/pagesterm.html

17. Voting polls & customer feedback

Creating a poll on Google + is really easy and takes only a couple of minutes, it's also great for creating a bit of fun and engagement.

i.) Simply type your question in the posting area, where it says 'share what's new', and ask your audience to + 1 their choice in the comments below.

ii.) Then share the post.

iii.) Write the possible answers to your post in the comments below the post.

iv.) Disable the comments.

v.) Wait for the answers to come in.

18. Tips and tricks

Offering a weekly or daily 'Top Tip' can keep your audience hooked and returning again and again for the latest information and are a great way to increase loyalty and build relationships. Tips can be anything from instructions on how to do something to information about a useful app.

19. News and current events

Offering information about the latest news in your area or industry is a certain way to keep people interested and sharing your content. Being current and up to date with local news is really useful to your audience and it keeps your business looking fresh and up to date. To keep up to date with news subscribe to news feeds and blogs that offer news on your industry or your local area.

20. Negative content

People always like to hear about what not to do, for example: 10 Things not to do on a first date or 10 things not to say in a job interview, the list of possibilities for this type of post are endless and can create a great deal of amusement and interest.

21. Music if you are a musician

If you are a band and want to promote your music then there is no better way to promote your material than by posting links to your music and videos on Google +.

22. Q & A live session

You can host a live question and answers session on your page. This is a really good way to create conversation and engagement. It also creates a professional, informative and caring image. You can do this by allotting and promoting a specific time for followers to post their questions in the comment section of your post. Or you could choose to ask them to post their questions and give them a day when you will be answering them, this way you get more time to research if you need to. In both cases it's a good idea to post an image promoting the session.

23. Broadcast live
By using an application called livestream you can broadcast any live event to almost any social destination. You can also watch, like and share any event that may be of interest to your audience.

24. Welcome Followers
Welcoming your followers in an update is a great way of showing them they are valued. It exposes them other followers which can help them to get followed and hopefully they will reciprocate and you in turn will be exposed to their followers.

25. Caption this
Posting a photo and then asking your followers to caption it is a really effective and light hearted way to drive engagement and you could also turn this into a contest. You can use images from stock photo sites or sites like Flickr Creative Commons. Make sure to choose images that will provoke interest and are humorous or inspiring.

26. Case studies
Case studies are a really effective way to demonstrate how something works with real examples. You can use case studies to show how your customers have used your products or services to benefit them in some way. You can also use them to demonstrate a principle or method of doing something by using other businesses as examples.

27. Internet Memes
Meme comes from the greek word 'mimema' which means something imitated. An internet meme is a style, action or idea which spreads virally across the internet. They can take the form of images or videos. There are plenty of tools and apps out there to help you create memes, the most popular of which are www.memegen.com and imgur.com which are

popular ones.

28. Your blog

Creating regular blog posts is a very effective way of getting your followers on Google + to visit your website or blog. Make sure you always include an image to provoke interest and asking a question can create intrigue and curiosity. You can either direct your audience to your external blog or write a blog post within your post which can help to build your audience. Google+ offers immense editing power within the platform so you can format your posts and use bold, italic and strikethrough. You can also share Google documents on Google +. Also pointing your users to other blogs is a great way of adding value and also building relationships with the blogger.

29. Greetings

Simply posting an attractive image or a wishing your followers good morning, good night or to have a good weekend will go a long way in breaking the ice and building relationships. These types of posts help to make positive associations with your brand.

30. Testimonials

You may have received a review on Google Places or Foursquare or simply a message from someone. Posting about good things that people write or say about you contributes to your social proof and builds trust. Remember people will believe more about what others say about your business than what you as the owner says about it.

On Google+ you can share photos, a link, video or events and Google + gives you much more editing power than any other network. You can, for example, delete or change text after it has been posted and you can format your text and use bold, add italics and strikethroughs to make your text stand out.

THE DIFFERENT TYPES OF MEDIA

In order to create the best experience for your followers you are going to need to create a good balance of content using the different variety of posts available to you. Google + offers you the opportunity to post text, images, videos, Events and links to podcasts, websites, blogs and videos.

Images

'A picture paints a thousand words'

If you are already a Google + user then you probably know that an image grabs your attention more than any other post on your timeline. This is because most of us are visually wired and most of us can identify with an image much more quickly than text. Statistics prove that pictures get more interaction than any other post and that your followers are far more likely to click on a link to a website or blog, or watch a video if your post contains a picture. If you are posting a link to your blog, or an article on your website then make sure you include a compelling image, you are far more likely to gain interest this way. Images not only get shared more, they also have huge viral potential, get remembered and also create an emotional connection with your audience.

Images on Google + are a big part of the Google + experience and there are a multitude of talented photographers and creatives uploading amazing images. However, you don't have to be an expert photographer you can find images from stock photos and also free sites like Flickr (be careful to check the licence and what you are allowed to do with the images in terms of changing or adding text, etc.) Adding text can be achieved by using photoshop or other online graphic design apps which are available online and are easy to use like www.picmonkey.com . Some stock photo sites also offer you the functionality to add effects and text to your images.

Google + also offers all its users 'Auto Awesome photos and movies' which creates fun versions of your photos and videos. Auto Awesomes are generated automatically when you upload images and videos, if they

260

match certain criteria and you turn Auto Awesome on or off in settings. Here is a list of Auto Awesome effects:

- **Eraser** If you take a sequence of 3 or more photos in front of a landmark with movement in the background, Eraser will give you an image with all the moving objects removed. This is great when you are taking photos in a crowded place and cannot get a shot without background movement

- **Action** If you take a series of shots of someone moving (dancing, running,or jumping) Auto Awesome will merge them together into one action shot so you can see all the movements in one shot.

- **Pano** If you are taking a series of photos with overlapping landscape views, Auto Awesome will put them together into a panoramic image.

- **HDR** High Dynamic Range is a process of taking multiple exposures of the same image. When you merge these together, the result is a greater range of shadows and light in the photo. Uploading three similar images at different exposures will create an HDR image for you.

- **Motion** If you have taken a series of photos in succession (at least five) Auto Awesome will put these photos together into one short animation.

- **Smile** If you have taken a few group photos, Auto Awesome will choose the best shots of each person in your image and merge them into one great shot.

- **Mix** If you have taken a series of portraits with similar background elements, Auto Awesome will compile these photos

261

together into a photo booth style grid. This works best with close-ups of faces.

- **Movies** You can create Auto Awesome movies from the Google photos app for Android. These are short films created automatically by editing together the videos and photos you create around an experience. You can choose the photos and video you want to use and Google will do the rest. You can change the theme, style and background music and you can shorten, reorder or remove scenes.

Animated Gifs

An animated GIF (Graphics interchange format) is a graphic image on a webpage that moves and is made up of a series of images that are displayed in succession, looping back to the beginning when the last frame has been displayed. Google + is where the GIF action is taking place. Because they are more immediate than a video and they do not require you to press a play button a GIF offers instant gratification. GIF's can be more compelling than just a plain image and can really catch the eye and convey ideas and emotion and they have huge viral potential.

GIF's can be used for all manner of things including humor, art and also they are very good to quickly show how to do something. If you have a great video then it's a good idea to create an animated gif with a URL to the video, this is yet another way of getting your video found. It's a very good idea to get familiar with making GIFs and it is actually very straight forward. There are numerous tutorials on how create GIFs online and there are easy to use free GIF generators on the web such as: www.imgflip.com/gifgenerator and www.picasion.com

Text

Whatever you are posting on Google + to make it effective then you will need to add an introduction or text of some sort. Posting a question can be a really good way of driving engagement.

Videos

As with images, video is highly shareable, has huge viral potential and increases engagement. People love videos and a good video can offer a huge amount of entertainment, make learning more interesting, fun and easier to understand. Videos are also great at helping to build relationships, trust and rapport with your audience and there really is no better way of introducing yourself and building a personal connection with your audience than with video. The type of videos you should be posting on Google + are educational, informative and entertaining and while there is room for the occasional product video these really belong on your website, blog.

Blog posts

According to research 70% of consumers click through to a website from a retail blog. Blogs are nearly essential now for any business who wants to get found on the internet and social media is another very effective tool to drive traffic to your blog. If you do not have a blog then you need to seriously consider creating one. There are numerous free and paid blogging platforms available and there is a whole chapter covering this very subject later on in this book.

Infographics and diagrams

Infographics provide a fascinating way to present statistical information. They are engaging, very shareable, have huge viral potential and make figures look far more interesting and easier to understand than a list of numbers. People love statistical information relating to their interest because it helps to confirm or affirm what they already may believe and helps to give them more confidence in what they are doing or selling. You do not have to be an expert graphic designer to create infographics there numerous applications available on the web which can help you create infographics.

Podcasts

Podcasting is a type of digital media usually comprising a series of audio, radio or video files. You can subscribe to podcasts as you can to blogs and newsletters. For example if you download a podcast on itunes, every time the author produces a new one, itunes will automatically download it. As with video they are effective at helping to build trust with the listener and can also help to make you stand out as an authority or influencer in your niche. They also encourage customer loyalty if they are produced on a weekly or very regular basis and are incredibly handy for people who are on the go and want to listen while travelling to work or on the way to a meeting. Google + is an ideal place to promote your podcast.

Cartoons

Cartoons work very well with humor and relatable content. Posting cartoons that your audience can relate to can help demonstrate that you understand and identify with them, they are a great ice breaker and highly shareable as well. Once shared they are very likely to appeal to more of your target audience and a great way to widen your reach. If you have an idea for a cartoon and you are not an artist them there are sites like Fiverr.com that offer creative services at very reasonable prices.

SlideShare

SlideShare is primarily a slide sharing site but you can upload powerpoint, keynote, pdf and open office presentations. SlideShare is a great way to communicate your message and very straight forward and easy to use. It is also another way to get your content rated, commented on and shared. Presentations can be shared on Google + and embedded on your website or blog.

Ebooks & PDF Documents

Turning your content into an ebook is a great way to present your content and offering a free ebook is a really good way to build your opt-in lists and gives your reader something of great value.

Webinars

A Webinar is like an interactive online conference or workshop. Webinars are a great way of interacting with your audience and building relationships. They can be used for presenting and training, selling a programme, or course, or answering questions from your audience. They can be saved and listened to at a later date for anyone who could not make the date and time. Using Google + to announce your Webinar is a very effective way to promote your online event and get people to sign up.

TIPS FOR POSTING ON GOOGLE +

Creating compelling content will get the more engagement, more shares and more followers on Google+ however there are other things you can do to help make your posts more successful too and here are a few tips:

Post frequently

The emphasis on Google + is definitely quality over quantity however you do need to post at least once a day. Only you can gauge how often you will be able to create and post your own quality content, however Google+ is a powerful community and therefore sharing other peoples content will not only help you to deliver regular content, but will also help to build relationships with the creators of that content.

Post at the right times

Studies have shown that the best time to post on Google + is during work hours between 9am and 11am, this seems to emphasize that this is really a platform being used by business people. There is a gentle build up of traffic in from 6am until 11am and then it starts to drop off in the afternoon. Once you start building your audience you can use an app called Timing + which will actually analyzes the last 100 posts on your account and identifies when is the best time to post for your particular account. Obviously you need to take into consideration where your target audiences are located and post according to their local time.

Is it Good?

Before you post anything ask your self this question, is this going to be useful or interesting to my audience, or help them or make their life or business better in some way? If the answer is no then don't post it.

Always post a comment

Links that are posted without comments receive lower engagement. Always create a small introduction before posting a link describing why this is useful to your audience. Asking a question can also be a very effective way of introducing an update and creates engagement.

Add a title

Adding a title will immediately give your audience an idea of what your post is about and will help to grab their attention. You can make it bold by adding an asterisk before and after the heading.

Optimize on your post headings and your descriptions

The first sentence of your post becomes your title post so try and include a few relevant keywords in the first sentence to optimize for Google + search and the main search engines.

Use a URL shortener

When you add your link use a URL shortener to shorten your link, not only does this save you space but also allows you to track how may people have clicked on your link. You can use the Google URL shortener at goo.gl or bitly.com

Absolutely add an image

Adding an eye catching and interesting image will encourage sharing and more engagement. Using full size (800 X 600 px) images rather than small images or thumbnail links will stand out far more.

Passion, passion, passion

If you are passionate about your subject then this is going to be communicated in your posts which will make your content irresistible to the your audience.

Add Hashtags to your Posts

Adding a few popular hashtags to your posts will make them far more easily found by other people who may be searching for particular subjects. Make sure your content is relevant to the subject of your post or blog article. The first three of your hashtags will be displayed on the top right of your post so make sure you choose your most important three hashtags first.

Mix it up

Try to mix your posts up by using the different types of media to create interest, for example: informative infographics; inspiring videos; images; podcasts and Hangouts. All these types are highly shareable too.

Format your text

Formatting can help order your post. You don't need to over do this, but highlighting your heading and a few keywords will help to draw your audience's attention.

- To make your text bold simply add * at the beginning and end of the word, for example *BOLD*
- To add italics simply add underscore before and after the world, for example _italics_
- To create a strikethrough Put a dash before and after the word -STRIKETHROUGH-

Mention people in your posts

When you mention someone in your posts it will draw their attention to your post and depending on how they have set their notifications they may even get a message saying you have mentioned them. This is a very useful way to grow your followers. To mention someone simply put the

+ or @ sign before their name. You may want to do this if you share someone else's blog with your audience, or thank a co-author of your own blog. Another useful way to grow your followers. But do not overuse it as it can be regarded as spam! Before you mention someone, ask yourself this question, is mentioning this person either courteous or useful to them ? If the answer is no then don't mention them.

Interact with your commenters

When you post your aim is to create interaction an engagement so when your audience do interact then it's really important to interact back and continue those conversations.

Use Circles to your advantage

If you have segmented your audience properly into different circles you can really use this to your advantage. You can post relevant content to the audience which is going to be most interested in that content. This way you can hit the right people with the right content most of the time. One really simple tip for creating circles is to create one for women and one for men, this is so simple yet so powerful. This allows you to tailor and craft your messages so you can target specific audiences with different products and services. You can create circles for as few or as many people you wish.

CHAPTER FIVE

GOOGLE + OFFERS, GOOGLE EVENTS, HANGOUTS AND HANGOUTS ON AIR

GOOGLE + OFFERS local businesses in the USA a new way to reach potential customers, Google Offers and it lets mobile users find your offer and visit your business to claim the offer straight away. If you are the owner of a verified local Google+ page you can set up your offer in just minutes through your dashboard. Simply locate the Google offers tab on your dashboard and click 'Create an Offer'.

You can choose from a variety of offers, such as buy one get one free, product discounts and dollar off. You can tailor make your offer with images and terms and conditions and then publish your offer to be made available for free on the Google Offers app and website, wallet app and Google+, for no charge as long as it complies with Google policies. To reach even more customers you can set a monthly budget and distribute your offer on Google Maps and Google Offers subscriber's emails.

GOOGLE + OFFERS

Google + offers local businesses in the USA a new way to reach potential customers, Google Offers and it lets mobile users find your offer and visit your business to claim the offer straight away. If you are the owner of a verified local Google+ page you can set up your offer in just minutes through your dashboard. Simply locate the Google offers tab on your dashboard and click 'Create an Offer'.

You can choose from a variety of offers, such as buy one get one free, product discounts and dollar off. You can tailor make your offer with images and terms and conditions and then publish your offer to be made available for free on the Google Offers app and website, wallet app and Google+, for no charge as long as it complies with Google policies. To reach even more customers you can set a monthly budget and distribute your offer on Google Maps and Google Offers subscriber's emails.

GOOGLE + EVENTS

Whether you are organising a company meeting, Webinar or a public event, Google + events offers unique features to help you organize and promote your event. Here are some of the benefits and features of using Google+ Events:

- **Online and offline events** You use Google + events to create events either offline or online, For example a Hangout or a Hangout on air (Public event).

- **Invite everyone** You can invite people who are not on Google + as well as those that are.

- **Integrated with Google Calendar** Google + events are fully integrated with Google Calendar . You can see the events you have created, events that you have been invited to and events that you have already replied to. The event will also appear in the Google Calendar of all the people in your circles that you have invited.

- **Photo Sharing** Photos can be uploaded and shared from all devices including mobiles and you can choose whether or not your attendees are allowed to upload photos to one shared collection or not.

- **Invitations** You can choose whether or not your guests are allowed to invite other guests.

- **Event and Hangout reminders** Your invitees will automatically get sent a reminder about the event the day before or when a Hangout begins unless they have disabled this type of notification in their settings.

Creating an Event on Google+

Simply click on Events and you will be offered the option to 'Create an event' or 'Plan a Hangout'. To get started click 'Create Event' and the event form will appear. You can either choose from a theme or add your own image. By adding your own image you can brand your event and add your event name and message so you can grab your audience's attention. The image size required is at least 940px x 280 px.

You will then need to complete the event form and add the name of your event, times, start and end dates, location and details about your event in the title. Then choose who you wish to invite from your Circles and your email list.

CREATING GOOGLE HANGOUTS AND HANGOUTS ON AIR

Google + Hangouts have really made anything possible in terms of connecting and broadcasting live to individuals and groups of people on video, and anyone with a verified account who has installed the plug-in and has a webcam can stream Hangouts on Air live to YouTube, their Google+ profile and their website. This amazing technology has opened up numerous opportunities for businesses to connect with their customers and prospects. Hangouts on Air automatically get ranked and creating a Hangout on Air is yet another way to get found more easily.

Hangouts

Hangouts can be used for private video chats or video conferencing with up to 9 other people or just text chat with another person or a group of people. Hangouts are only visible to the people who are invited and are useful for groups of friends who want to communicate or for companies who want to run private company meetings. They are not recorded or streamed to YouTube or your profile. Hangouts are found on the top right of your Google + profile and and are found in green text in quotes.

Hangouts on Air (HOA)

'Hangouts on Air' are found in the drop down menu on the left of your Google + profile and you can also create a Hangout on Air from the 'Events' tab. With Hangouts on Air you can have up to 10 people participating, but the difference is they are publicly viewable to an unlimited audience and they are automatically streamed to your YouTube account and your Google + profile. Having a 'Hangout on Air' is like having your very own TV programme with the added advantage that you can actually interact with your audience and it's free!

With Hangouts on Air you can run your own Webinar without incurring the high costs which are usually involved in running one and without the restrictions on audience numbers. Also there is no need to download any special software for those who just want to watch and listen.

One of the best things about Hangouts on Air are they are incredibly straightforward and you do not need any technical knowledge to run a very professional looking meeting or presentation. You can share your screen and upload your slides from SlideShare by simply selecting the SlideShare option and you can also install a Q & A app which allows viewers to ask questions during the HOA. When you turn the Q & A app on, you will see an area to the right of the HOA where your viewers can post their questions and you can answer them.

When you start your hangout and before you start broadcasting, you can take the URL and embed on your website, blog or Facebook for live streaming. After your Hangout is over it will be visible for anyone to watch, unless you have chosen for it not to be.

The opportunities for marketing are limitless. You don't even have to be live on camera to do a 'HOA'. You can do a slide presentation and then stream it to YouTube. Here are a few ideas for using Hangouts on Air:

- **Run a Webinar** A huge money saving when compared to the well known online meeting services, and your audience do not have to download any software and they can ask questions if the Q & A app is installed.
- **Run a press conference**
- **Customer service session**
- Customer meeting, especially useful for overseas customers.
- Q & A sessions. (These sessions build rapport and trust as well as customer satisfaction.)
- A Product launch and demonstration.
- **Product demonstrations**
- **Consulting sessions**
- **'How to.........' videos**
- **Teaching videos/ language teaching**
- **Private coaching sessions**
- **Presentations / Slide shows**

Creating Google + HOA's

To create an HOA you need to make sure your computer has the supported browser and minimum processing and bandwidth requirements. Most PC's and Macs will have this, but it is a good idea to check in Google + Help for more information about 'Hangout system requirements'. These are the steps involved in starting and broadcasting a hangout.

- **Install Link with YouTube and verify** When you originally click the 'Create Hangout on Air' button you will need to install the latest version of the Google + voice and video plugin. Simply follow the simple on screen instructions. In order to stream your hangouts to YouTube and so your HOA can be recorded, you will need to link your Google + page or profile to your YouTube

channel. Both your Google + and YouTube accounts must be
linked to the same Gmail account. You will then need to verify
your YouTube channel, this will allow you to have unlimited
length videos. If you do not verify it, you are limited to 15
minutes of video. To verify your channel go to your YouTube
settings and click verify and they will simply send you a text
message with a verification code. You can start a HOA from
either your Google+ page or your profile. Also when you use
your page, your HOA will be connected with your own personal
YouTube account unless you have linked your page to a separate
YouTube account.

- **Click 'Start a Hangout on Air'**

- **Name your HOA** Try to use a name that will grab your
audience's attention and inspire them.

- **Now invite people from the drop down options** (these may
include your Circles, friends and family). You cannot invite public
(non Google+ users) to participate but they will be able to view
the Hangout when broadcasting on YouTube.

- **Click 'Start the Hangout'** Your Hangout will begin but you will
not be broadcasting and your Hangout will not be recording. You
can check to see if your camera angle and lighting is all ok before
you start broadcasting. This is when you can stream your
Hangout live on another website by embedding your Hangout
link, this is found on the bottom right of the screen along with
your YouTube event page where people can watch your HOA. If
you want to send your participants a link so they can directly link
to the hangout then you can get this from the top of the screen
and then you send this out by email or text.

- **Press 'Start Broadcasting'** A live player of your broadcast will be posted on your Google + homepage and your HOA will also run on your YouTube channel.

- **Control your Hangout on Air** When you create a hangout then you are in control of what people hear and see. You can mute people if they are noisy or you can click on a persons video to make that person appear on the main screen.

- **Open Chat** You can open up a chat window where your participants can communicate. If you want people who are just viewing to be able to communicate or chat then you can let them do that either on YouTube, the comments on your blog, or on Google +

- **Edit your recording.** You can edit your recording on YouTube when it is finished and your post will be updated on Google+ automatically.

Tips for Creating Hangouts on Air.

- Watch some HOA's to get an idea of what can be achieved and what seems to work.

- Be clear about what goals you want to achieve by hosting a HOA, and be clear about how your audience are going to benefit.

- **PLAN PLAN PLAN** Make sure you plan and know exactly what you are going to say and how you are going to present your HOA. If you are going to use slides then practice sharing your screen and using the slides. Also plan how you are going to involve and draw your participants into the HOA.

- **TEST TEST TEST** Before you start broadcasting you will need to practice and test the various features available to make yourself familiar with both audio and video settings. Make sure all the screens you want to show are open and ready to share. To practice simply choose a group with no one in it or select yourself when you select your invites and don't press 'Start Broadcast'.

- Make sure you are hardwired with your internet connection and that you use an ethernet cable. WiFi is not good enough and you may experience screen freezing or other quality issues.

- You can share your screen with your audience, simply click the screen share option on the left menu and then click the screen you wish to share. You can also upload slides to SlideShare and share with your audience. When you select that SlideShare option your face will appear in a small screen at the bottom of the screen while your slides show at the top. You can also share documents on screen with Google Drive.

- To avoid audio feedback (a terrible ringing or screeching noise) use a headset microphone, this will also block out noise from the tapping of a keyboard which can be very distracting for the end user. To control audio settings click on the gear icon on the top right.

- Make sure you light up your area. Natural light is good but if you do have a light source make sure it is behind the webcam and facing you.

- For optimal performance it maybe a good idea to install Chrome browser since it is a Google product .

- If you do not want your HOA to be watched you can simply delete it from your google + profile and then make it private on your YouTube account.

- Brand your HOA. You can brand your HOA and add your name and business name to the lower third of your screen so it is visible to your audience. You can do this with the 'Lower third app' which is part of the 'Hangout Toolbox ', a third party app which can be found on the left toolbar. If you do not see this you just go to 'View more apps' and search for 'Hangout toolbox'. You can then add your lower third text or upload a custom branded image. You can also ask your participants to do this so your audience are clear about who everyone is.

- Make sure you are ready and looking professional. Remember this is a live representation of your brand. So make sure your background area is as tidy and bright as possible and practice your presentation skills.

- Make sure you are centred on the screen and that while broadcasting you look at the camera above your screen so it looks like you are looking at your audience and not at your screen.

- As a creator of the Hangout you can control who is being seen on the main screen. You do this by clicking on the thumbnail image of anyone in the Hangout and that then shows their screen.

- Use Hangout chat (this is found on the left menu) and is used for you to chat with your participants. This is not seen by the public and is not recorded. If you would like to offer the opportunity for your audience to interact and ask questions during the Hangout on Air then simply turn on the Q &A app which is found in the left column.

- Use the cameraman app to control who is on air. This is the video icon which is found when you hover over someones thumbnail in the film strip. Participants will see anyone who has been hidden, but the public will not.

- If someone behaves inappropriately at your Hangout you can simply hover over their thumbnail and eject them.

- Mute yourself when you are not talking. Ask people to mute their microphones as well when they are not speaking. As the creator of the Hangout you can mute a participant if they are noisy.

- You can edit your video after broadcasting, with the YouTube video editor. You can combine videos, trim your videos to custom lengths, add approved music and customize with special tools and effects. http://www.youtube.com/editor.

- Arrange for your participants to join 20 minutes before broadcast so you can prepare them and answer any questions before hand.

- Make sure you leave enough time at the end of the event for Q&A's

PROMOTING YOUR EVENT OR HANGOUT ON AIR

Build your audience

Before you start creating events make sure you have built up your audience so you can invite as many people as possible from your Circles.

Schedule and publicize your HOA with an Event

To schedule your HOA and let your audience know about it well in advance, simply click on the 'Events' tab, then 'Event Options' and then 'Advanced' and then click on 'Make this an Event on Air' (this is usually used for offline public events), then click on 'Show more options' where you will be able to add more detailed information. Make sure you make it clear here that the event is an online event. Google + does not give you the URL of your HOA until it has started however, there is a simple way around this. You can either add the URL for your Google + homepage or add your YouTube URL for the HOA. http://www.youtube.com/user/*username*/live (Replace username with the name of your YouTube account). This way people will be directed to your YouTube account where the HOA will be streaming. Make sure you are specific about the time of your HOA so that when your attendees arrive at the address, the HOA is taking place. If it is not taking place they will be directed to the homepage.

Add a good image promoting the HOA and complete the event form with all the information. You can then select who you want to invite and the HOA will appear on the Calendar of anyone who uses Google Calendar.

Create some Buzz
Start talking about your event or Hangout four to five days before the date and post an image.

Promote with your embed Code
When you start your HOA you will find an embed code at the top of the Hangout which you can shorten. You can embed this link into your website or blog and onto Facebook. Make sure you embed it before you hit the broadcast button!

Promote on all your social networks
Advertise your HOA on your other social media networks. You could use a promoted post on Facebook.

Create a publicity Video
Create a short teaser video advertising the subject matter of the HOA to create some buzz about the event. You can create a short 'Hype' Video at http://www.hypemyhangout.com/

Optimize your HOA on YouTube for after event views
Make sure you optimize your video on YouTube. Simply visit your video manager and make sure you fill in your description, and use all your keywords, so this broadcast gets found long after it is broadcasted.

Send out emails
Send out invitations to your email contacts and your opt-in list.

Advertise it on your website or blog
Add an image or text to your blog advertising your online event .

Advertise on Adwords
By advertising your event on Adwords and using keywords that will catch your target audience, you can grow your following on Google +.

Ask your participants to promote it
Ask your participants to invite their circles and ask them to share your promotional images and also add them to their website or Blog.

Communities
Sharing information about your Hangout on any relevant communities that you are a member of is a great way to get people to watch your HOA.

Share on SlideShare
After your event has taken place you can upload it to SlideShare which can help to drive additional traffic.

CHAPTER SIX

BUILDING BRAND AWARENESS WITH GOOGLE +

COMMUNITIES

GOOGLE COMMUNITIES OFFER endless opportunities for you as an individual or a business to connect with new people and engage about the subjects in which you are interested. They are an amazing way to expand your reach, build awareness and make new contacts. As a business you can either join existing communities and share your content and interact, or create your own.

JOINING A GOOGLE + COMMUNITY

Joining communities that are related to your industry can be a very effective way to make new contacts and build your brand. By sharing valuable content and getting involved in discussions you can build relationships, build trust and establish yourself as a thought leader.

As well as engaging and making new contacts, communities can be a good source to discover information about your target audience and also to solve problems. As a member of a Google + Community you can read and listen to conversations, ask questions and find out exactly what your target audience want, what motivates them and what is important to them. Communities can also be a very good source of inspiration for content creation as well and you will find the more you listen the more ideas you will come up with.

For a small business joining well run and established communities can often be a much better option than creating your own, you can start engaging straight away without having to administer the group and build the membership. You can either join a community as yourself or your page however posting as yourself will open up more doors to networking as people generally prefer to communicate with a face rather than a logo. When you join communities you will find that most of the good ones will not tolerate blatant self promotion and carrying out this practice is a sure way to get yourself removed. When you start searching for communities to join you will see quite quickly that many are of little use and just full of businesses plugging their own products with little engagement or discussion. This type of community is unlikely to be of any use to you or your business. Here are some tips for participating in communities:

Choose the right communities
There are many really good Google + Communities which are full of activity and discussion, however there are also ones that are full of spam and self promotion which are not being moderated properly. You need to be selective when deciding which communities to join, a quick scan of the stream will probably be enough to tell you if it is worth joining.

Choose to display your public community posts in your profile
If you choose to display your community posts on your profile they will show up in the stream of anyone who is a member of that community and has circled you . Your community posts will not show up in other people's streams unless they are a member of the community and they have circled you but they will appear on your Google + profile.

Circle people.
Adding community members to your circles will help you to promote your profile or your page.

Comment and Tag +1
The more involved you are by interacting with posts the more valuable you will become to the other members of the community who are

posting. You can do this by commenting within the community and also by tagging them and posting their content in your profile if it is relevant to your audience. When you tag them it is likely they will be notified unless they have their notifications switched off. This will draw their attention to you and your profile and they may also reciprocate when you post a link to one of your articles.

Post valuable content.
Once you are established in the group and have contributed by joining discussions you can start posting your own relevant content if you are allowed. By posting top quality content which will offer value to members, you will not only draw attention to your blog or website but also start to build authority and trust. Make sure you have a compelling offer available on your blog or site to encourage opt-in subscribers.

BENEFITS OF CREATING YOUR OWN COMMUNITY

By creating communities around subjects that relate to your products you can create a very powerful platform to communicate and interact with your target audience and help to build awareness of your products. Communities will help you to create interest and buzz for your products or services as long as you are not continually plugging your products.

Before creating your community you need to be clear about the goals you want to achieve and whether you can afford to invest the time it takes to build and maintain a successful community. Even though setting up a community on Google + is extremely easy it also requires a full commitment of your time and not only do you need to keep on top with content creation but it also takes time to manage and moderate the community. It's definitely a good idea to join a few first to see what is involved and how they work. Here are some of the main benefits you may want to think about before setting those goals:

Creates awareness of your brand or product
The members of your community will be aware who is running the

community which will create awareness without having to push your product or service on your members.

Helps you or your brand to build authority on industry related subjects

Many Google + users join communities to gain knowledge about a particular subject and to have their questions answered. Providing answers to these questions through blog articles or other media gives you the opportunity to stand out as an authority or expert in your particular field. This in turn will help to build your brand and build trust and recognition for providing help.

Market Research

Communities are a great platform for market research. Here you can find out so much information about what your customers want by listening to what they are saying and the questions they are asking. You can also conduct market research by posting polls.

Great news for Search engine optimization

Posting relevant content it is yet another way of getting found in search, and content that is posted on a Google+ community which is public is almost always immediately indexed and ranked on Google search. If you are searching on Google for answers to certain questions you will find that the answers often come up in within Google + communities.

Drive Traffic to your website or blog

As the subjects and interests grow you will find more opportunity to share relevant articles on your website or blog. Make sure you have a compelling offer on your blog or website to either build your opt-in list or promote a special offer.

Expands your reach

Engaging with active member will increase your reach particularly if you are publishing their content on your blog as a guest blog or sharing their content on your profile.

Ties in with Google Hangouts

Google Hangouts can be used in conjunction with Google communities for face to face public discussion. Communities are a great way of publicizing a Hangout as long as the subject is relevant.

Communities integrate with your newsfeed

Communities behave similarly to circles so you can post updates to your community from your profile page without having to visit your community page.

Customer Service

Your community can also be used as a customer service platform and becomes an obvious place for your customers to come and make their complaints. This can work both for and against you, but in most cases situations can be turned around to a positive result if handled professionally and being transparent can go a long way in building trust with your members.

SETTING UP YOUR OWN COMMUNITY

If you decide to go ahead and create a community then you need to carefully think about which subjects and topics are most dear to your target audience and whether there is the demand to create one. If there are similar communities available then you need to work out whether, by creating another, you will be able to offer any unique content and any added value to your audience. If the answer to this is no then you need to move on to a different subject. In choosing your subject you also need to be sure that you are going to have enough material to sustain your community over a long period and keep the conversation going. When you have chosen your subject you are ready to set up your community.

Step 1

Before setting up your community you need to decide whether to create it from your personal profile or from your business page. A big consideration to take into account here is that if you do create it from your page not only will your page name with logo show up as the owner of the community, but also people will be able to follow your page directly from your community page. This will immediately increase awareness of your brand. If you create it from your personal profile you will not show up as the owner of the page.

To set up your community, simply hover over the home button on your profile and then click on **'Communities'** and then click **'Create community'** on the top right.

Step 2: Select the type of community
You next need to select the type of community you want to create. Once you have selected you cannot change it, so you need to think carefully which type of community is going to work for you out of the four available types which are as follows:

- **Public** (anyone can join). These are used for general interest groups and fan clubs.

- **Public** - Moderator approval needed to join but everyone can see the posts. These are good for a group who wants to share their content but only approved members can create it. However if the group becomes very popular then just monitoring the new memberships can be time consuming in itself.

- **Private** - Can be found through search and people can request to join. Only members can view posts. This is for groups who only want their members to create and see the posts. Could be used for associations, drama groups or orchestras or any similar types with an active group of members.

- **Private and hidden from search**. You can only join if invited and only members can view posts. This could be for a family or private work group or private coaching group.

Step 3: Choose an obvious but unique name

The name of the community needs to be immediately obvious to potential members who are looking for a particular subject. If you already have a Google + page then make sure you have a different name and try and make it as unique as possible so it cannot be confused with other community pages with the same subject. You can change your community name up until you have 500 members.

Step 4: Choose a tag line

Add a brief clear description of your community making it clear to users how it can benefit them. Make sure to include some good keywords for the search engines.

Step 5: Public or private

This is where you decide whether you want your community to be searchable. If you are using this to increase brand awareness then make it public.

Step 6

Click on '**Create community**'

Step 7: Add a Photo.

To add your image simply click the gear icon where the image should be and then from the drop down menu click on '**Edit community**' and then '**Pick a photo**'. Make sure you choose a photo which is a true representation of the community. The image should be 250 X 250 pixels.

Step 8: Add information into the About section.

The 'About' section will appear at the top of your community page. To add information about the community click on the gear icon and then '**Edit community**'. There is space on the left to add information, add links and the location. You can add more detailed information about the community here, its mission and guidelines about posting content and how you want the community to be run. You can list the organization behind the community and add links, contact numbers and email addresses if you wish. Make sure you include industry keywords so you can catch the people who are looking for communities around your subject. You can also add Hashtags to make your community even more searchable.

If you have useful information that you know your audience is going to want to know, you can create articles on your website and then provide the links to these articles on your 'About' section. This will ensure maximum exposure of this information and help to drive traffic to your website and increase exposure of your brand.

Step 9: The Rules

Adding rules is important and contributes to the smooth running and value of the community. You can add a line about blatant self promotion and how this is considered as spam and that it will be removed by moderators.

To make your rules visible on the community page you can create a post with your community rules and then get the link from the post and add it to the '**About this community**' section. You can add a title to the link, for example: Community Rules - Must Read. You need to be clear from the start what actions will be taken if rules are not followed, for example, either removal of posts or total ban from the community. Here are some rules that you may to consider adding to your community:

- Be more than excellent to one another! This community is about learning, shared interests, openness and helping each other. Above all show respect, keep it positive and have fun.
- No commercial postings allowed. Any such postings will be removed.

- Please use categories in your postings where possible to keep content organized.
- Please feel free to post or share relevant content. However, the community does not welcome off topic or non relevant postings which will devalue the community.
- No Link only posts please. If you are posting a link to a relevant article please write a short sentence of introduction in the post.
- If you think there is a category we have missed, please contact us.

Step 10: Adding Content

Before you start inviting people to join your community you need to add content. You can do this by adding interest categories. Simply go to the gear icon and then click '**Edit**' and you can add as many categories as you like about subjects or topics relevant to your community. In order to get the ball rolling you will then need to create some posts for each category. Make sure that wherever you send members to read your articles you have a compelling offer and an email capture form so that you can build your opt-in list.

Once your categories are set up then members can post their updates according to the categories which helps to keep discussions well ordered and on topic. Here are some ideas for categories you can create which will help to spark interest and engagement. Depending on your subject there may be many categories which are relevant to your community, however here are a few generic ideas to get you started:

- Community Rules - Must Read
- Questions / Help Needed
- Member introductions
- Discussions
- Introduce yourself to the community. (If the community gets very busy then you may want to delete this as you may well get members turning off their notifications.)
- Latest news

- Photos
- Videos
- How to's and Tips & Tricks
- Topic headings
- Jobs
- Help needed

Once you have created your categories you can rename and move them around depending on their popularity or delete them if you wish.

FINDING YOUR WAY AROUND AND MANAGING YOUR COMMUNITY

The Gear icon

From the gear icon you can do all the following: Invite people, share community, edit community, manage members, leave the community and report abuse. As an owner you have more options than members.

The community search bar

The search bar allows you to find information within the community, really useful for when the community is growing and getting really busy.

Managing Member permissions

If you click on **'Manage members'** from the gear icon you can access the control settings for member permissions and view whether they are an owner, moderator or member .

What owners can do

- Add Moderators
- Add and edit categories
- Remove posts
- Remove members from the community
- Ban members from the community
- Delete the community

What moderators can do

Once your community is set up you will need to think about managing your community and selecting moderators. Moderators are very important and are there to moderate the content and quickly remove spam or inappropriate content that will quickly devalue the community if not removed.

You can promote a member to a moderator at any time and they can do any of the following:

- Add and edit categories
- Remove posts
- Remove members from the community
- Ban members from the community

Managing Notifications

You can simply turn notifications by email on or off. If you are the owner or moderator you may need to keep this 'on'. For communities where you are just a member you may want to turn this off, as emails can be constant. If set to 'on' you will be also be notified on your mobile device and on your toolbar.

Create an email filter in Google Mail

If you are receiving a great deal of mail from communities then it is a good idea to set up a filter in Gmail so your mail from communities is sent to a separate folder and not to your inbox where it may take over your mail and become unmanageable.

PROMOTING YOUR COMMUNITY FOR SUCCESS

You have your community set up, you have posted some interesting content and you know the basics about managing your page, you are now ready to start inviting people and promoting your community for growth. Here are some tips for building your community:

Invite people on Google +

Google + makes it very easy for you to invite your contacts. On the top left of the community simply click on the gear icon and then on '**Invite people**' and you can invite all sorts of people from your circles but make sure you only invite those who you think will be interested in the subject.

Announce your community on other social networks

This is a great way to bring in new contacts from outside Google + especially if you want to build your audience and engage on your own profile.

Share your community with Google + followers

Simply share your community publicly from your profile or Google + page.

Get a vanity URL for your community page

Your Google + URL includes a long stream of numbers which is not good for advertising or promoting on your website or blog. Google will provide you with a shorter URL for your community.

Promote your community on all your marketing channels

Make sure you add your link to your community to your email signature, business cards, YouTube account and any other material.

Add your community URL to blogs and articles

This is a great way of finding people who have similar interests. If you post your community URL in the comments section of someone else's blog you are very likely to get some new members. Be careful here that your comment is relevant to the blog subject or it will be considered as spam.

Join similar groups on Facebook and LinkedIn

Once you are a member of other groups you can invite or announce your community page there as long as group rules do not stipulate that you are not allowed to do this. If you do this be careful not to be too pushy and do it as a 'by the way' sort of comment.

Invite thought leaders
Inviting thought leaders and interesting people within your industry will not only add interest and value to your community but will also attract other members.

Send out emails
Send an invite to people on your opt-in list and your other customer mailing lists.

RUNNING YOUR COMMUNITY
Now you have your community set up this is where the hard work starts. Here are some tips for running an interesting and engaging community:

Posting interesting content
It is important for you and your moderators to regularly post relevant content and other media content for example, images and videos. This will immediately create structure and direction for the community. You can post either directly on your community page or from your profile where you can select your community from the drop down menu where you can choose to post to your community.

Welcome people
You can welcome your new members by tagging them in a post and asking them to write a brief introduction saying why they have joined the community and what they are particularly interested in. This is a great ice breaker and can help to get conversations going and can also give you new ideas for content creation.

Engage with your members
Make sure you make comments and interact with members. People like to

feel they are being heard and that their input is appreciated and if you can make your members feel confident to keep posting and commenting you will build a thriving community.

Monitor your community
Make sure you check in at least once a day to see that the right sort of content is being posted and people are not spamming or self promoting.

Create discussions & ask questions
Asking questions is a great way to create engagement with your members. Make sure you post specific questions in relevant subjects to promote discussion.

Create a poll
Polls are always great fun and can be created easily. You can ask for a + 1 or comment.

i. Simply type your question in the posting area, where it says 'share what's new' and ask your audience to + 1 their choice in the comments below.

ii. Then share the post.

iii. Write the possible answers to your post in the comments below the post.

iv. Disable the comments.

v. Wait for the answers to come in.

Host a weekly Hangout on Air
What better way to build relationships than meet people face to face. If you host a regular weekly Hangout this will keep people coming back every week and keep the community active and engaged.

Post a weekly video
Posting a weekly or monthly video is great for building your brand and again keeps people coming back again and again. The content will depend very much on your subject but make sure it offers value to your

members. This is a big commitment of time so make sure you have the resources and a plan of your content before you announce this regular slot. Not keeping to a regular commitment will devalue your community.

Keep looking and listening
Keeping your eye on other communities and what they are doing will help to inspire you.

Offer exclusive promotions
Offering your community a once in a while exclusive promotion will make your members feel valued while also helping to promote your brand. Make sure you do not do this too often though, or it will certainly turn your members off and work against you. You have to remember at all times that this is a community and not a business page.

CHAPTER SEVEN

DAY TO DAY ACTIVITY

THERE ARE CERTAIN things that you will need to do on a day to day basis to run your campaign on Google +. It is a good idea to allot a specific amount of time and a particular time of the day to do this. Here are some of the things you will need to do:

Following your customer's Pages

This is important if your customers are business owners themselves. Following their pages or following your customers will go a long way in building relationships. By +1'ing their Pages, you are showing them that you are interested in what they have to say and also helping them to achieve their goals by helping to build their audience.

Showing your audience you value and respect them

If you value and respect your audience they will most probably love, respect and value your business. Be kind, generous, offer as much help and value as possible, reply to their comments and make it obvious that you value them and are listening to them. Don't be afraid to be yourself rather than a stiff brand with no personality.

Everyone is aiming for shares, +1's and comments so if you are helping others out by commenting and liking their content it is going to draw attention to your brand and they are more likely to take interest in your content. This is one area where the reciprocation rule works very well on Google +. Engaging with content will also draw attention to you and your brand and you will find that people will click on your name to find out who you are and they may very well circle you. Be friendly to your

audience, be chatty, authentic, genuine and embrace the conversation. All this will all go a long well in building a positive image for your brand and will set you apart from your others who are continually ambushing their audience with self promotion.

Following influencers in your niche
Building relationships with key influencers in your niche is invaluable. Not only can you learn from their content but also these people can have literally 1000's of followers, imagine if they follow you back and then share your content!

Dealing with negative comments
Every business at some time will have to deal with negativity from followers. Hopefully if you have a good product then this is not going to happen too often. There are the 'trolls' out there who have nothing better to do than post negative comments, the best thing to do with them is just ignore them, delete their comments and block them.

However there will be real customers who have real concerns and complaints and may post negative comments publicly, there may also be people who really want to lash out to gain your attention as quickly as possible and spread the news to their friends too!

You need to deal with complaints as quickly as possible and be as transparent and authentic as possible. The best thing to do is to apologise and say how sorry you are to hear of the inconvenience they have been caused and offer to continue the conversation and deal with their concern by either private message or telephone. You can then deal with this privately, give your customer the full attention they deserve and decide on your next course of action or compensation.

CHAPTER EIGHT

MEASURING AND MONITORING YOUR RESULTS ON GOOGLE +

MEASURING AND MONITORING your results and performance against your original goals and objectives on a continual basis is essential. This is where many businesses go wrong, they carry on aimlessly posting content without checking to see what is working and what is not. Then after six months or a year they wonder why their campaign is making no positive difference at all.

When you measure your results you will discover so much information about your campaign which will allow you to steer your campaign in the right direction to achieve those SMART goals and objectives and stop anything that is not working.

When you originally work out your strategies and tactics for your campaign you will be estimating what you need to do to achieve your goals and objectives. However as your campaign runs you will see exactly what you need to do to achieve what you originally set out to do. For example, you may need to increase the amount you spend on advertising to attract new followers, or you may need to follow more people per day. This is what it is all about, making your campaign work for you by constantly measuring your success against the goals set and then adjusting your strategies accordingly in order to achieve the results.

You can measure your activity within Google + and see the activity on your posts (found on the drop down menu on the top right of your post). You can also view your Ripples in the same drop down menu which will show you how your posts are being shared and shows your reach on Google +. There are many tools available to measure your campaign on Google + including Google Analytics which gives excellent reports on how Google + is working with your website and also you can use third party sites like Hootsuite, Buffer and GPlusData Pro.

SOCIAL REPORTS WITH GOOGLE ANALYTICS

One of the terrific things about Google + is that it is seamlessly integrated with Google Analytics and provides social reporting which is designed to help measure the effectiveness of your social campaigns by showing how your visitors are engaging with your content within Google + with+1's and shares. And even better if your Google + page links back to your website and also uses Google Analytics a card will appear in your dashboard that displays the number of visits, the number of unique visitors and the number of pageviews

The Overview Report This report lets you see at a glance how much conversion value is generated from social channels. It compares all your conversions with those resulting just from social.

The Conversions Report The conversions report helps you to quantify the value of social and shows conversion rates and the monetary value of conversions that occurred due to referrals from Google + and any of the other social networks. Google Analytics can link visits from Google + with the goals you have chosen and your E - commerce transactions. To do this you will need to configure your goals in Google Analytics which is found under 'Admin' and then 'Goals'. Goals in Google analytics let you measure how often visitors take or complete a specific action and you can either create goals from the templates offered or create your own custom goals. The Conversions report can be found in the Standard Reporting tab under Traffic Sources > Social > Conversions.

The Networks Referral Report The Networks Referral report tells you how many visitors the social networks have referred to your website and shows you how many page views, visits, the duration of the visits and the average number of pages viewed per visit. From this information you can determine which network referred the highest quality of traffic.

Data Hub Activity Report The Data Hub activity report shows how people are engaging with your site on the social networks. You can see the most recent urls that were shared how they were shared, and what was said.

The Social Plug-in Report The social plug-ins report will show you which articles are being shared and from which network. If you have Google "+1' buttons and the Facebook 'like' buttons on your site you will be able to see which buttons are being clicked for which content. This way you will be able to see which is the most popular content and then you can create more of this type of content. Google Analytics automatically reports '+1' activity that takes place on your site. If you have added 'AddThis' or 'ShareThis' Plugin to your site they will also automatically report your on site activities.

The Social Visitors Flow Report This report displays the initial paths that your visitors took from social sites through to your site and where they exited.

The Landing Pages Report This report displays engagement metrics for each URL. These include page views, average visit duration and pages viewed per visit.

The Trackbacks Report The Trackback report shows you which sites are linking to your content and how many visits those sites are sending to you. This can help you to work out which sort of content is the most successful so you can create similar and it also helps you to build relationships with those who are constantly linking to your content.

TOOLS TO HELP YOU MANAGE YOUR CAMPAIGN
Although you can be included in an unlimited number of circles, Google

+ sets a limit of 5000 for the number of people that can be included in your circles. There is also a daily limit for adding people to circles and if you reach this Google + will temporarily stop you from adding more people to your circles.

There are now some clever tools available to help you find circles and manage your circles. Here is a brief run down on some of the tools available and what they do.

Circlecount.com

In addition to finding a wealth of information about the most popular accounts and the most followed and shared circles you can also see activity on your account that you would not see by just looking at your Google + account. www.circlecount.com provides you with a detailed follower graph where you can view your ranking based on your number of followers. You can view which circles you have been included in and who added you. With this information you can then search for them on your Google + account and send a message thanking them for adding you.

Circloscope.com

Once you get going on Google + you will realize it is easy to get to the 5000 member mark quite quickly. Circloscope.com is a chrome extension which will help you to manage your circles, by identifying and removing people who are either inactive or not following you back, it can also find duplicates and provide lists of people who are engaging with your posts. With the paid version you can add people to your circles, and remove people from your Circles, in bulk.

Replies and more

Replies and more is a chrome extension. Its function is to primarily save you time by allowing you to simply 'reply to author' with a click. It also allows you to reply to people who have commented on a post, you simply hover over your mouse next to the name of the person who commented and the 'reply' link is made visible. It also installs a drop down menu under the share icon which lets you share your post to Facebook and Twitter and email.

Doshare

If you use Hootsuite then you will know that it cannot be used for updating your personal profile or community pages. Doshare is another chrome extension which lets you do this and allows you to write and schedule your posts and also post links to Google + from any tab in Google chrome. You can also use Doshare to automatically number and reference your posts, this informs your followers whether they have missed any posts in any given day.

Make Pinterest Work For Your Business

Alex Stearn

Table of Contents

CHAPTER ONE

GETTING STARTED ON PINTEREST

PINTEREST HAS TO be the most, exciting, delicious, beautiful and captivating of all the social media platforms. When you initially set up your account, if you haven't already done so, it won't surprise you that this was the fastest site in history to cross the 10 million member mark.

The marketing possibilities and opportunities are endless and a dream come true for businesses of all kinds because the typical person who is using Pinterest not only shops but they also tend to be high spenders too.

Once you discover how this platform is being used by millions for their personal use and truly appreciate why Pinterest has grown and continues to grow at this incredible rate you will see why this platform may be one of the most powerful forces for marketing your business.

WHAT IS PINTEREST?

Pinterest is a social bookmarking tool and content sharing site used to 'pin' images, videos and other objects found on the internet to a virtual pin board. People join to create, organize and share the collections of the things they love and then share them with their friends if they wish.

When you join Pinterest you can literally take images from the internet with the click of the 'pin it' button and pin them to a board. Pins always link back to the website source. A board is where you organize your collection of pins by topic/subject of your choice.

The site seems to make everything possible for its users by helping them to create the lifestyle they are striving for on a pin board. Their pin board is like a personal statement saying here are some of the beautiful things that I love and make me who I am or and this is how I want my life to be.

Pinterest is great for personal use because you can create boards about anything you like and can collect as much information as you like and then find it all in one place. It's like having your own personal magazine, the main difference being it consists only of the things you love.

The concept seems so simple yet Ben Silberman and his co founders have surpassed excellence and made the Pinterest experience completely unique, beautiful and fascinating for their users. It is no wonder it took four months and 50 working variations of the site before they came up with the final grid design. Another of the main features of the site is the 'Infinite Scroll'. The never ending page lets users browse more and more images without having to click buttons and waist time waiting for pages to load.

The founders were also very discerning about how they built their initial audience realising the beauty of the site would result mainly from the images pinned. What emerged was a growing community of mid western young american women pinning ideas for weddings, home design and recipes. However, the audience has grown into much more.

As a child, Ben Silberman was fascinated with nature and was a great collector of everything from insects to stamps. "What you collect says so much about who you are" he said in an interview.

When you log into your account you are welcomed by your home feed which is made up of images from all those you are following, it's this beauty and simplicity which makes Pinterest so unique and so appealing to its users. It was designed to be visually appealing with a minimum of text. It is the ultimate window shopping experience which makes it a dream come true for businesses. "When you open up Pinterest," Ben Silberman says, "you should feel like you've walked into a building full of stuff that only you are interested in. Everything should feel handpicked for you."

Pinterest is also a social platform and like all the others you can follow, share your content by repinning , make comments and tag users. However the similarities stop there and Pinterest succeeds with the uniqueness of its product and a very different audience. The majority of Pinterest users are actively looking for inspiration and whether they are looking for wedding ideas, home and interior ideas, fashion ideas or recipes they are ready to buy. Pinterest boasts very high sales conversion rates.

Once 'Pinners' have found what they like there is a good chance they will visit the website source, share by repinning on one of their boards and then someone else will see it on their board. This is what makes Pinterest so viral.

WHY IS PINTEREST SO GOOD FOR BUSINESS?

Pinterest has become a social media platform which is hard to ignore for businesses selling directly to consumers and for those selling to other businesses. While starting as a hang out for middle class American women looking for lifestyle inspiration it is now become much more. Every day millions of people are using Pinterest to look for inspiration, buy products and connect with others who have similar interests. The majority of users are still women residing in the US but Pinterest is now growing a much stronger presence in Canada, Australia and the UK. To help your decide whether you think it could be a part of your marketing plan here are some of the main reasons why using Pinterest to market your business maybe very good idea:

Excellent traffic referral

Pinterest is a top generator and referrer of website traffic and statistics report that buyers referred to sites by Pinterest are 10% more likely to buy. Businesses who have installed the 'Pin it' button have seen big increases in traffic.

Easy to find and target your audience

Since the whole Pinterest concept is interest based and you can search by interest, finding your target audience and building up a community of people who are very likely to be interested in your products has been made possible.

A new and interested audience

Pinterest's fast growing audience is very different from other social media networks because users are using the site for inspiration. Unlike Facebook or Twitter their first priority for being on Pinterest is probably not to be social but to actively search out new products. This makes this audience one that is much more ready to purchase. Pinterest offers a delicious visual experience for users and the average time spent on Pinterest is one hour. Moreover statistics are proving that Pinterest is a major player when it comes to people purchasing. According to www.comscore.com Pinterest buyers spend more money, more often, and on more items than any of the other top 5 social media sites.

Higher Spending audience

It has been reported that Pinterest shoppers spend more per session, in comparison with Facebook shoppers.

Levels the playing field

With Pinterest your frustration of getting your products out there can be over. Everything is possible for everyone and you don't have to be a big brand to compete and if you have a new product, a new gadget or invention there seems to be no better place to showcase it. Because of the amazing visual experience that the site layout offers, every business has the opportunity to make their products look appealing. Pinterest is all about discovery and a great place for your potential customers to discover what you have to offer. Once you find your target audience the chances are that their friends will have a similar taste and suddenly you have a growing community.

Simplicity
The beauty of Pinterest is its simplicity and it has mastered visual sharing. Pinterest has managed to leverage the strength of social proof and word of mouth advertising with the simplicity and visual power of images.

Branding
Because of its visual nature Pinterest offers businesses the perfect platform to build their brand with images that reflect their brand.

Information about customers
No other social media site gives you as much insight into what your customers' interests and desires are, as Pinterest. Pinterest is where their members go to showcase what they are passionate about and then share it with their friends. Simply by visiting your audience's profiles and looking at their pins and boards will give you so much information about their lifestyle and desires. Getting to know them like this will not only help you tailor your marketing efforts but also help you to build on the products that you can offer .

The path from seeing a product to buying it is shorter
Visitors from Pinterest convert into customers much faster than from any other social network. It seems that the step from seeing to buying is more natural and displaying your products doesn't come over as being pushy because the visual display of images is what Pinterest is all about. The saying, 'A picture paints a thousand words' truly comes into play on Pinterest.

Huge Viral Potential

Pins flourish virally and currently 80% of pins are repins which means a huge amount of sharing is going on and shared images are being circulated more than new images are being uploaded. User engagement on Pinterest is very high and this is because of the visual nature of the platform. It seems it is totally addictive and users can't stop sharing.

Your content has a long shelf life

Because Pinterest is interest based rather than timeline based your content will be still relevant and shared long after it has been posted.

Easy to manage & less costly

The great thing about Pinterest is it is simple and because your content stays current for longer, managing this platform is very much easier than the other social networking platforms as you are not under the constant pressure of time.

Website integration

Pinterest is so easy to integrate into your website. By simply placing a button on your site your visual content can be instantly shared with others. Literally one image from your site could be shared and repinned hundreds of times.

Facebook and Twitter integration

Users can now automatically post pins to their Facebook news feed and Twitter accounts.

Search engine optimization

Pinterest is indexed by Google and is another way to get found and a good way of obtaining valuable back links to your site. After all if people are pinning your pins, then this means people like your content and this is what Google are looking for and Google likes websites with authentic back links.

Is Pinterest Relevant for your Business?

Only you will be able to tell whether it will be worth investing your time and resources on this platform and it mostly comes down to whether your customers are on Pinterest or not, and what you are selling. The majority of users are still women residing in the US but Pinterest is now growing a much stronger presence in Canada, Australia and the UK. Here is a list of the top ten categories on Pinterest:

- Home
- Arts and Crafts
- Style/ Fashion
- Food
- Inspiration/ Education
- Holidays / Seasonal
- Humor
- Products
- Travel
- Kids

However, whether you are going to invest a great deal of time in Pinterest or not then adding the 'Pin it' button to your site or images is essential and the first thing you should do. This way anyone who visits your site can 'pin' your images. Many sites have seen an influx of traffic from Pinterest without even having the 'Pin it' button but installing that button will open up yet another source of traffic. To find out whether any of you images from your website have been pinned you can type this URL into your browser http://Pinterest.com/source/YOURSITE.com

Seeing Pinterest from the customers perspective

Before setting up your account it's a really good idea to familiarise yourself with Pinterest and start seeing how and why people are using this platform for their own personal use. Using it for your own personal discovery just for a couple of hours or so will really help to make everything in this book easier to understand and all the strategies and tactics mentioned will be much clearer. The idea is to pick some topics that you are interested in, create some boards, (secret boards if you wish) start following some profiles and start pinning images from websites.

Once you start using it and start enjoying the experience you will see this platform from the perspective of the customer. You will see the ease at which relaxed browsing of visuals converts so easily into sales and see how online communities are built. By doing this hopefully you will see and fully appreciate why this platform is having such a positive impact on businesses. It's a great confidence booster too and the strategies explained in this book will be much clearer and easier to understand. So before you go any further go on have a go.

SETTING UP YOUR ACCOUNT

Pinterest is highly addictive, it is jam packed with amazing images and before you know it you have been dragged into its beauty and a short session has suddenly turned into a 2 hour pinning session! It can be a big time waster which is fine if you are in your own leisure time but if you are using it for your business you need to have clear goals and strategies in place in order to make the most of this platform for your business. Ultimately your goals will be to drive traffic to your website, build your opt-in list, convert followers to buyers and build your brand. These goals are easily achievable with Pinterest but before jumping in and randomly pinning images there is a method to using this social media to reach its full marketing potential and create an outstanding Pinterest experience for your followers. When you start putting the strategies and tactics that you learn into practice you'll be surprised at how quickly it jumps into first place in driving traffic to your website or blog, generating leads and increasing sales. So lets get started!

Setting up your Pinterest business account

If you already have a personal Pinterest account that you are using for business and you already have a good number of followers then it would be a good idea to convert your account to a business account rather than start from scratch. The Terms and Conditions state that if you wish to use the site for commercial use then you need to set up the account as a business account and agree to their business Terms and Conditions.

To convert your account simply login to your account and then visit the Pinterest for business section found here http://business.pinterest.com/ and click on the text 'convert here'. You will then be taken through the setting up process where you will be asked to select your business type and complete the about section, website name, business name and then you will need to agree to the T&C's.

If you are new to Pinterest or have decided to set up a new account for business you simply visit this URL http://business.pinterest.com/ Setting up your account is very straight forward. You will be asked to select your business type and add your business name and add a username. Your username will become your Pinterest URL , http://pinterest.com/username and you are allowed up to 15 characters. It's a good idea to use your business name as your username, however, if it doesn't fit then you can either use an abbreviation or something that is simple and easy to remember.

You will then be asked to upload your logo or photo. A head shot may be preferable if you are a blogger or a personal brand as often people prefer to connect and follow individuals rather than brands. However for some businesses a logo will be better and will help to promote a more corporate identity. Whatever you choose its advisable to keep it consistent with your brand on other social profiles so your brand is easy to recognise and connect with. Your Pinterest profile picture dimensions are 160×165 pixels.

The 'About' section
The about section is one of the first things users will see when they land on your page and is also a hot spot for search engine optimization.

Google ranks Pinterest accounts highly and since the appearance of Pinterest accounts in search is largely based on the content of profiles, the about section is very important. You have up to 160 characters for this section so make the most of these by using as many keywords from your niche as possible. If you are going to use your brand name then you can personalize your account by adding your name or the names of those who will be managing your account.

Verify your website

Next you will need to verify your website. This establishes a link between your website and Pinterest and confirms that you are the owner of your website and will give you access to your analytics too. To do this simply click on the pencil icon in the top right hand corner of the name box and then enter your web address in the website field and click verify. You can verify with an HTML file or a META tag. Pinterest gives clear instructions on how to do this but if you are still having problems your web designer will be able to do this is five minutes.

Link to your other social media profiles

Make sure you add links to your Facebook and Twitter profiles. Once you have added those and allowed Pinterest to obtain information from these accounts you can post to these sites. You will also be notified when one on your followers joins Pinterest. You can only link to your personal profile on Facebook if you want to link to your Facebook Page then you can do this using an app.

Add the 'Pin it' button to your website

Next you will need to add the 'Pin it' button to your website and next to any images that you want to share. Pinterest gives you the code to embed at www.pinterest.com/about/goodies you can choose from various 'Pin it' or 'Follow' buttons. Now anyone who visits your website will be able to press the 'Pin it' button on your site and then share your content on any of their boards. By viewing your Pinterst analytics you will be able to view how many of your pins have been pinned from your website, how many people saw those pins and how many people clicked through to your site as a result of seeing those pins. You will be notified every time someone repins one of your pins.

Installing a 'Pin it' button on your browser

To pin directly from your browser simply install Google Chrome and install the 'Pin it' button to your toolbar, once installed you can pin any image from any site and Google Chrome makes it even easier now, you only have to mouse over an image now and you will see the Pin It button.

Installing the 'Pin It' Button to your mobile browser

This is incredibly handy especially if you are using Pinterest to organize your own interests. To add simply follow these steps:

- Open up Safari in iPhone or iPad and go to http://www.pinterest.com
- Add a bookmark by tapping on the icon that looks like a box with an arrow coming out of it.
- **Select 'Bookmark' from the selection of icons and then change the title from Pinterest to 'Pin It' and tap 'Save' on the top right.**
- **Tap on the icon that looks like an open book and select 'Edit' and then 'Pin It'**
- **Below the title, you will see a box to add the bookmark's address. Delete the Pinterest URL and paste the following code:**
-

```
javascript:void((function(d){var
%20e=d.createElement('script');e.setAttribute('type','text/
javascript');e.setAttribute('charset','UTF-8');e.setAttribute('src','//
assets.pinterest.com/js/pinmarklet.js?r='+Math.random()
*99999999);d.body.appendChild(e)})(document));
```

(If you are reading the printed version of this book then simply

search

for this code on Google)

Creating a really good looking account

Whether you have decided to convert your existing account or set up a new business account you need to create a really good looking account. When users arrive on your profile it needs to be interesting, eye catching and inviting.

To help get you started here are some Pinterest basics.

PIN BASICS

Before you get going and start creating your boards here are some pin basics:

What is a pin?

A pin is a visual bookmark of an image or video. The pin has a description and a link back to the original webpage or blog.

How to pin an image

You can pin an image in three ways:

- **Clicking the 'Pin it' button.** Many sites have a 'Pin it' button. You simply click this and then Pinterest offers you a selection of images from that webpage to pin in a pop up box. Once you have selected the image you can select the board you wish to add it to and then add a description. Pinterest takes the original URL to link the image to. You can install the 'Pin It' button onto the toolbar of your browser by simply going to www.pinterest.com/about/goodies. Once you have installed this you can pin any image from any site.

- **Uploading an image.** You can upload an image from any file on your computer. Simply click on + sign situated on the top right and then '**Upload a Pin**' on the drop down menu. This is very handy if the image does not exist on your website but you still want to pin interesting images.

- **Manually adding a pin.** Instead of using the 'Pin it' button you can manually add the pin by clicking 'Add Pin' on the top right drop down menu and then adding the URL of the page where the image is. You will be offered all the images on that page and then you select the image you want and click 'pin it'.

Repinning an image

If you see an image that you like on Pinterest you can repin that to any of your boards simply by clicking the 'Pin it' button and you can add your own description. That pin that you have repinned will show up in the newsfeed of your followers and this is how your pins can spread virally. This is a similar action to a retweet on Twitter.

A Board

A board is a virtual pin board where you organize your pins by topic. Boards can be secret or public and you can have as many as you like, they are incredibly useful for anyone who wants to organize, keep and find things in one place. Popular collections/boards include: recipes, wedding ideas, films to watch, books to read, gift ideas, home decorating ideas, fashion ideas, inspirational quotes, gardening ideas, interesting articles, and the list goes on and on.

As a business you can use brands to show off your products and anything related to your brand that your audience may be interested in and anything you want associated with your brand. Pinterest is incredibly powerful when it comes to promoting your brand because this is where you can really go to town in visually representing it.

To create a board simply click the **+** symbol and '**Create board**' and then add a name and a description.

Follow

Like Twitter and Facebook you can follow other users on Pinterest and you can either follow profiles or particular boards. You can sign up with Facebook or Twitter which makes it easy to find and follow friends who are already using Pinterest.

Like

You can like any pin without having to follow the profile or board. When you like something on Pinterest it will not appear in your Newsfeed, however the owner of the pin will get notified.

Comment

If you want to leave a comment on Pinterest then you need to click on the pin to enlarge it and then you can leave a comment in the box provided.

Pinterest on Mobile

Pinterest is big on mobile, in fact statistics show that 75% of its usage is coming from mobile. With the mobile app you can pin on the go from anywhere and the app offers a similar Pinterest experience to that which you will find on the web.

The Pinterest Business Blog

Pinterest has produced a blog for businesses and this is a great way to keep up to date with what is going on with Pinterest and the great things that brands are doing on Pinterest and also they will be broadcasting Webinars on the blog. This blog will continually give you new ideas for you to apply and drive your business and you can follow this blog at http://businessblog.pinterest.com/

CHAPTER TWO

CONTENT IS KING ON PINTEREST

NOW YOU HAVE set up your profile and added your 'pin it' button(s) to your website you are ready to set up your boards. Whether or not you have an image rich business you will need to create some initial boards in order to give a good visual impression when your potential customers arrive on your profile. Your profile needs to be interesting, eye catching and inviting.

Pinterest is not just about showcasing your products. While your ultimate goal is to sell your products it's also about understanding your customer and finding out what makes them tick. Randomly creating boards that you think may be interesting is not going to work. To be successful in creating the visual experience your audience is looking for you will need to plan the experience you want to create and then how you are going to put your boards together to best promote your products. Later on in this section you will discover some ideas for creating your boards but first you will need to consider and research your target audience and your competition.

RESEARCHING YOUR TARGET AUDIENCE

Hopefully by the time you have created your profile you will already have a clear idea of who your ideal customer is. However Pinterest is going to give even more information about your customers which will not only assist you with your marketing on Pinterest but with all your social media platforms.

Never has it been so easy to research what your customers are interested in than with Pinterest. You can literally gain huge insight into what makes they like and what their interests and desires are by simply looking at their boards and seeing what they are pinning and repinning. To find out what your potential customers are interested in, simply type a generic term for your product into the search box and it will bring up all the images relating to that search. If you look under the image you can see how many times it has been repinned and by whom. Simply click on the name of somebody who has repinned that image and it will bring you to the profile of that pinner. You will then see all their boards and what they are interested in.

Here is an example. I typed the term 'wedding flowers' into search and I came up with lots of images of flowers. I picked an image which had been repinned 19 times and then clicked on the name of one of the users who had pinned this image. When I arrived at this particular lady's profile she had 5 boards and these were the titles: 'Love this,' 'Planning our new kitchen,' 'Going to the chapel and we're going…' 'New home inspiration' and 'This year I would like to wear'. That's a huge amount of information about a user and what they are interested in.

This information is like gold and it's worth spending a great deal of time looking around and seeing what your audience are pinning and repinning. Viewing more than a few profiles is going to give you invaluable information and insight into what your audience are looking for before creating your own boards.

Here is a list of questions you should asking yourself about your audience when planning your boards:

Who are the audiences you need to connect with?
Are these audiences using Pinterest?
Are they following your competition on Pinterest?
What are they interested in? What are they pinning?

What are they looking for ?

What sort of topics would appeal to them?

What are the problems they have that they need solving?

Your competition on Pinterest

You can find out a great deal of information about your target audience from your competition as well. See what they are pinning and see what their followers are liking and pinning and repinning. It maybe they are not doing a great job and maybe you will see ways you can do it better. It's definitely worthwhile spending time researching as many of your competitors or other businesses offering similar products.

PREPARING YOUR WEBSITE OR BLOG

The first thing you need to do before producing any fresh content is go back to your blog or website and image check your content and check whether it has a pinnable images. If you do not have images on your website then nothing can be pinned, nothing can be repinned and none of your content has the potential to go viral.

If you are a product based business then you are probably going to have enough material . However, if you do not have an image rich site and you really want to leverage the full power of this platform to drive sales then you are going to need to create your own original content and images to go with that content.

If you already have valuable articles or any valuable content on your site which do not have an image then you need upload a relevant image to the your website or blog so it can be shared on Pinterest. You will also need to decide how you can incorporate these images in your overall board strategy. There are three ways you can create content on Pinterest:

i.) You can repin content

ii.) Pin directly from websites and blogs

iii.) Create your own pins

Each method has its advantages and uses, however research has shown that 80% of content on pinterest is repinned. While this shows how viral and how successful sharing is on Pinterest it also demonstrates the huge opportunity there is for creating fresh content on Pinterest. Like with any social media Pinterest is not the total marketing solution it's another tool to use to drive traffic to your website for sales or to build your opt-in list. Whatever web page you are pinning from, you need to make sure that it is clear where the product can be bought and that your opt-in sign form is prominent with a clear incentive to join.

CREATING OUTSTANDING PINS AND BOARDS

As time goes by you will be adding more and more pins and boards to your profile but to get started it's advisable to set up at least 5-10 boards with at least 10 pins on each board. Your aim here is to delight your target audience and create an enjoyable experience for them by giving them what they love. Once you have done your research you will have a good idea what is going to appeal to them.

You may not have too many of your own images to begin with but this is fine as you can pin or repin from other profiles or websites. You can set up some really impressive initial boards with a view to adding your own content at a later date which will add to the experience.

When creating your boards, organization is paramount and you need to think about how you are going to make it as easy as possible for users to find what they are looking for. To create a board simply click the **+Add** at the top next to the Pinterest logo and then click **Create Board.** Here are some tips for creating your boards

Create secret boards

It's good practice to create secret boards and then change them to public when you are ready to go public. This way you can be confident that your boards are ready to publicize. Remember though you cannot go back to secret once you have gone public.

Themed boards

Organising your boards and making them interest specific is going to be much more effective than just bunching a load of unrelated pins together. Theming your board around a top category is beneficial if you have the relevant products or services.

Naming your boards

Board names are really important and a good unique board name will enhance your Pinterest experience and encourage people to follow you. Users are not usually searching for brands they are searching for topics so you need to be specific when naming your boards. Being inspirational, unique funny and a little bit different is paramount on Pinterest. Board names which are original, unique, quirky or funny have the potential to go viral so this is where you can get really inventive and imaginative. Even businesses that are considered to be quite uninspiring can really get creative and use Pinterest to make their business more interesting and stand out with really interesting board titles and relevant content.

As well as creating names which are interesting and attention grabbing you need to make sure you optimize your board descriptions for search purposes by including the relevant keywords from your niche.

Make the most of your cover images

Make sure you select the best images for your board covers and make sure they are your images if possible. You can change the cover image anytime.

Board organization

It is important to position your most important boards to the top so that when a user lands on your profile they see your best and most relevant content at the top. Boards can be moved and reorganized by simply dragging them into the new position.

CREATIVE IDEAS FOR YOUR BOARDS

With the competition out there on the internet for attention the only way you are going to win is by inspiring your audience with high quality images and content on Pinterest. You may be wondering how you are going to consistently produce and display compelling images to your audience on a regular basis for the foreseeable future. However once you have picked your topics of interest you will surprised how one idea lead will lead to another and you will be able to find ideas for numerous boards and images to create and pin.

Product boards

If you are an image rich business or have tangible products for sale then the first board you will want to create is one with your products. Depending how many products you have, you may wish to create more than one board. You could create one board with all your images included and then also include certain product images on other boards that may be related to other board topics. If you have images of your products actually being used by customers then these can be very effective for promoting a type of lifestyle.

Business resources that your clients will love

If you are selling to other businesses, then your audience will find anything to do with helping them in their business of value. Posting informative content about your subject is invaluable, this will help you to stand out as a thought leader and expert in your field. If your content is valuable and useful then your followers are likely to keep coming back for more and are likely to share your content too. Remember your audience are looking to find and share valuable content with their friends and customers too and will want to be associated with any compelling content you create. Creating a board of useful tips is incredibly effective especially if the original source of the pin is from your site or one of your landing pages with a picture of your product or an incentive and form to join your opt-in list.

328

A Board to Help

Whatever you are selling then there will be a subject or subjects that will help your audience. Maybe you are in real estate and then a board about how to get your house ready for a sale would be very useful. If you are in fashion then you can create a board about how to accessorise or maybe fashion tips or even tips about color matching. Instructions on how to do things is very big on Pinterest. If you can create boards to help others and include pins with instructions on how to do certain things which appeal to your target audience you are probably onto a winner with regard to the viral sharing of your content. This can be incredibly powerful for your branding.

Relatable Content Board

Relatable content is one of the best types of content and one of the most shared types of content. Relatable content is anything that your target audience can relate to and identify with, it's when your audience sees a piece of content and immediately thinks, "Yes, I can relate to that and this is exactly the way I feel when this happens". It's incredibly powerful because it means that your content is communicating to your audience and showing that you understand and empathise with them and you feel their pain or joy. With relatable content you are communicating with them on quite a deep level which all helps to build relationships and trust. This is why 'Someecards' is so successful, most of their content is relatable.

Product user boards

Ask your customers to pin pictures of themselves using your product or what they have produced using your products. This could be anything from nail polish to paint.

Seasonal boards

Creating boards for your brand based on the seasons are a great way to market your products, for example: Christmas Day, Mothers Day, Fathers

Day, Easter, etc. Make sure you position your seasonal boards so they are at the top at the right time of year, and when they are out of season then position them at the bottom.

Collaborative boards

Collaborative boards are boards that you invite other users to pin to. The benefits of a collaborative board are endless. It's a great way to increase exposure as it introduces you to the followers of those you are collaborating with and helps to build relationships and follower numbers. Bloggers can invite other bloggers, businesses can invite their employees. You may wish to invite users to pin about a common interest to encourage networking. If you are promoting a joint event or fund raiser, creating a collaborative board can increase your reach no end.

To create a collaborative board you simply create the board and then click 'Edit' and you will be able to add the email address or the username of those people you wish to invite. To invite users to join a collaborative board you need to follow them and then send them an invite, however be careful not to spam other users by sending more than one invite. To encourage collaboration leave a comment in the description field to say that you welcome other pinners and to ask interested users to leave a comment with their user name so you can send them an invite. You can also let your followers know that you are doing this on your other social networks. If you do create collaborative boards then you will need to monitor the content on the board carefully, since any pin that is added will appear on your feed.

'How to' boards

Because of the visual nature of Pinterest a series of 'how to' images can make a very effective board. You can also pin tutorials and Webinars. For example, if you are selling toys for children then maybe you could make visuals about how a child can make a model or toy. If you are selling produce or an ingredient then a 'how to' image about how to make something with that ingredient is an obvious winner.

Testimonial boards

If people are saying good things about your products and services then pinning those comments will create credibility and social proof for your business.

Infographics and graphs

People love statistics especially if they are portrayed in an easy to understand way with eye catching images. Infographics and graphs are really popular on Pinterest particularly with B2B businesses, they are very shareable and have great viral potential too.

Inspiring and motivational boards

The truth is everyone has a bad day sometimes and needs a little bit of motivation or cheering up. A motivational quote will help to lift your audience and can really help you to connect with them. If you know what your audience wants, what they aspire to and what their frustrations are then it is likely that you will be able to motivate them by posting content which inspires them. These types of post are also very shareable especially if put together with a colorful and inspiring image like a cartoon or photo.

Event boards

You can create boards about exhibitions and events in your industry and also publicize your own events by displaying images from an event that has already taken place. Collaborative boards work very well with events and you can get different people pinning their perspective of an event.

History boards

A history board of your business and how it has developed through the years can add huge interest, credibility and authenticity to your profile. You could also create a board with the history of your industry.

Entertaining/amusing content

Social media is all about being social and having fun, and people love sharing funny stuff. Even if you did not create it yourself but you think it is going to appeal to your target audience then share it. The aim here is to amuse and entertain your audience, humor is a winner all round and not only does humor break down barriers it is also more likely to be liked and shared. Funny stuff is one of the top ten categories on Pinterest.

Color boards

Organising your boards into colors can be very effective especially if you are involved in design, fashion or home style. Creating color themed boards with products that compliment your products, are a great way to grab your audience's attention.

Your current content

If you do not have your own tangible products as such but do have articles or other types of written content then you will need to pin all these. Make sure you create interesting and unique images for any of your content which will encourage your blog visitors to pin your image.

Complimentary product boards

Create boards with products that compliment your product. For example, you may be selling laptops, so pinning anything related to laptops like lap top cases will increase your reach on Pinterest. If you own hotel then you can pin information about places of interest that are local to your hotel, you may even get those places reciprocating and pinning your hotel or establishment. If you are a wedding cake maker you could pin local wedding suppliers and hopefully they will reciprocate too.

Video Boards

If you have a YouTube channel then these videos are ideal for pinning. Make sure you use the word video in the title of your board. Simply copy the short code for your video from YouTube (click share and YouTube will give you a short URL to copy) and then paste it into the '**Add Pin**'

URL Box. There are so many ideas for videos, 'how to' videos, product demonstrations, talking head videos and funny videos. Creating a collaborative board for videos is an excellent way to share content and gain new followers. People are always looking for ways to publicize their videos. You could also create a board where people have submitted videos for a competition where they are using your product.

Behind the scenes
Giving your audience a behind the scenes view of your business helps to keep you business and brand looking real and authentic and adds human interest. People love to see the production process and watch how the product was made before they buy.

Employee boards
An introduction to your team will help to humanise your brand and adds a personal touch. Followers will have a sense that they have already met your staff, particularly if you include videos. It also shows your followers that you value them and want them to get to know your business in a more personal way. If you have news about your employees and the great things they are doing, then post it. Maybe they have been involved in a fundraiser or they have won an employee of the month award.

Non Industry Boards
Creating boards about other popular topics can help to widen your reach, but be careful here as you may just be wasting time on an audience that is not actually interested in your products.

Customer success boards
Highlighting your customers' successes or including case studies on a board is a great way of displaying social proof. You also keep your customers happy by giving them free promotion and they are very likely to share your pin on one of their boards so you reach their followers too.

Local boards

If you are a local business then pinning other businesses or attractions in the area is a very good idea. If for instance you are a florist, then pinning images of local wedding venues and other wedding suppliers in the area is a great way to create interest around your whole subject. It also attracts the attention of these other suppliers to your business.

To help you give you ideas for boards and see what other brands are doing Pinterest has put a page together made up of brands who have been successful on Pinterest. You can view these at this URL http:// business.pinterest.com/success-stories/

CREATIVE IDEAS FOR PINS

The opportunities and ideas for creating pins are endless but here are a few ideas to get you started:

Product images

Make sure your products photos are really beautiful. It may be worthwhile to get these done by a professional if you haven't done already, to really help emphasize and highlight the beauty and uniqueness of your product.

Step by step images

A tall image made up of three or four images showing step by step instructions or the development of a product are really effective and very popular.

Inspirational or motivational images

An inspirational quote or motivational tip set in a beautiful picture is always a winner on Pinterest. If you are using images then making the best use of the space available is crucial. www.pinstamatic.com is a great tool for creating this type of image.

Pictures that make you go Awww!

Images of cute animals and children are a real winner on Pinterest.

Before and after images
These are particularly effective for creatives who do makeovers, like interior designers, hairdressers, beauticians and stylists.

Trending topics
Creating pins relating to trending topics is an obvious choice especially if they relate to your niche. You can find out what is trending on Pinterest with www.repinly.com where you will find a huge amount of information about the most popular pinners and pins.

Offers and competitions
Creating attention grabbing images for any of your latest offers or competitions that you are running on Pinterest or any other social networks will really help to increase your reach. Pinterest is a great way to get the message out about the special offers you have running, but you will need to be careful not to post them too often or they just appear like advertising and bad noise in your audience's news feed. You need to make sure that what you are offering is of real value, that it is exclusive to your followers and you are offering them a deadline to redeem the offer.

Above all be unique
Pinterest users love new fresh interesting and original content, so if you can be unique in your pin creation and put your own stamp on your pins, this will go along way in creating content that is more likely to get shared and go viral.

CREATING YOUR PINS
Once you have a good idea of the boards you wish to create you can start your own. There are a wealth of tools, apps and websites than can assist you with creating amazing pins. This is where you have the potential to create pins that may go viral and suddenly you may have thousands of eyeballs looking at your product or brand. Here are some

tips for creating pins:

Image Size
You can pin JPG, PNG or GIF image files. Pinterest does not limit the vertical size of images but the maximum horizontal width size is 554 pixels and anything over that will be resized. The minimum size for an image is 84 Pixels. When pinning from other websites the minimum image size is 100 X 200 pixels. According to research tall images are more likely to get repinned, however it's a good idea to keep height of images under 5000 pixels so the user does not have to scroll down as it is then unlikely that they will scroll back up to comment, like or repin.

Image Quality
Since Pinterest is all about the visual experience then image quality is really important. Because there are so many creatives on Pinterest the standard of images is extremely high, so any images that you pin need be of a very high quality in order to compete. Most smart phones will have good cameras but you need to make sure the light is right and the image is clear and not blurry.

Watermark your image
Watermarking your image not only promotes your brand but also helps to protect you from image theft. It doesn't have to be a large watermark and can be placed in the bottom left or right corner so not to spoil the main picture. Sites like www.watermark.com let you generate watermarks for your images for free. Image theft is always going to be a problem and although you cannot completely stop it you can take steps which will deter the majority from trying.

Stock Photography
Sites like www.shutterstock.com istockphoto.com and www.bigstockphoto.com provide a huge selection of photos on any subject. Make sure you read the terms and conditions with regard to whether or not the images can be used on Pinterest. Some of these sites

also offer photo editing tools so you can add effects and text to images.

Use images from photo sharing sites

Photo sharing sites like www.flickr.com and compfight.com offer a great selection of images that are free. Make sure you select images with the Attribution licence and also credit the photographer.

Text on Graphics & Photo Editing

Adding text to graphics is one of the most effective ways to get your images repinned. A good image itself is eye catching but sometimes by adding text you can clarify exactly what the pin is all about and pinners appear to love this. Photoshop is the obvious choice for doing all sorts of wonderful things to images but if you are not an expert then there are other image editing sites like www.picmonkey.com and www.canva.com which are incredibly easy to use and create an extremely professional result.

Infographics

Infographics are the latest sharing craze on Pinterest and other social networks. They have great viral potential and can really shout out your brand particularly if you use your corporate colors. Simply type 'Infographic tool' into Google search and a whole host of different sites will come up to help create infographics.

Pin your videos

You can pin all your videos. YouTube videos are easily pinned by simply using the 'pin it' button. Pinterest supports YouTube and Vimeo.

Online graphic design & marketing services

Sites like Fivver.com which is an online services marketplace, offer inexpensive graphic design and marketing services. This incredibly useful site offers services all starting from $5 including logo design, caricatures, cartoons and other many other design services.

Online pin creation tools

Sites like www.pinstamatic.com and www.pinwords.com offer free tools for creating instant pins. These tools make Pinterest possible for those of us who are more creatively challenged! You can create quotes in different styles, add text to your images and create sticky note images. Studio Design is an iPhone app which has different filters, fonts and shapes to enhance your images and you can upload them while on the go. You can also create a pin of your location which is linked to Google maps and create a pin of your website or your Twitter profile. Another handy pin creator is Someecards which lets you create your own card.

Be camera ready

Once you adopt the photo mindset on an everyday basis you will start to notice all sorts of photo opportunities within your business and outside. Taking your own photos not only saves you money it also gives you the unique fresh content that pinners will love. As you get used to Pinterest you will find it is all about discovery. Be on the lookout for interesting things that will inspire your audience.

Faces

Images without human faces seem to get shared more times than those with faces.

Be colorful

Color images are more likely to be repinned than black and white images.

Pin Orientation

Images with vertical orientation perform better than horizontal.

Be authentic

Users on Pinterest tend to prefer backgrounds that are real rather than objects which have been superimposed on artificial backgrounds.

ADDING DESCRIPTIONS TO YOUR PINS

It's very important to add good descriptions to all your pins. With every pin you have the opportunity to add a description of up to 500 characters even if you are repinning an image. Every description area is prime real estate for your business. The optimum length for a pin description is probably between 100 and 200 characters. If it is under 140 it can be tweeted too! You can add your own descriptions or you can quickly autofill the description with the description from the website you pinned the image from. To do this simply highlight the text you wish to copy and then click the pin it button and you will find the text in the description box which saves time.

Optimising your pin descriptions

To get the most out of you pins you will need to take the following into consideration when writing your descriptions:

- **Write for your audience** What is really important is that the image description is interesting and you can write why you feel your pin is interesting. The main priority is to get your visitors so interested that they want to find out more and visit your website. You can be quite inventive with descriptions and a good description that outlines benefits of a product or tells a story can really capture the attention of the audience.

- **Keywords in descriptions** You will need to optimize all your descriptions for Pinterest search by including keywords from your niche. If you are a local business it will be important to add your town or city. This will also work well for Google and Bing Search.

- **Include Price information** According to research, pins with price tags get more likes, so adding prices is definitely a good idea. People naturally want to know if they can buy it and how much it is. You can add prices to all your images by just adding the currency sign. Once you add a price, your products automatically get added to the gift section and the price will be added to the top right hand corner of the image.

- **Add a Call to action.** Including a call to action is essential. You can include this in the image or in the description. Statistics show that images with a call to action result in 80% more interaction. Examples are 'click here' for more information' or 'Feel free to repin this image' or 'repin this'

- **Add your descriptions to repins** It's good practice to create your own descriptions for images that you repin as it can give your perspective relating to your business.
- **Keywords on your web page** It is really important that if you are pinning from your own website then the page you are pinning from contains the relevant and similar keywords to that of your description. Pinterest seems to take this into consideration in their search results and they obviously do this so that users receive the best search experience and are taken to relevant web pages.
- **File names** It's always a good idea to be as descriptive as possible in the actual file name of the image for search purposes.

BEST PINNING PRACTICES

Pin at least once a day Try and pin or repin at least once a day so you can give your followers fresh content in their feed.

Space out your pins. When you post try not to flood the stream otherwise this can overwhelm your followers especially if it's just more of the same thing. Flooding the stream not only looks like blatant self promotion, it's boring and takes away from the unique Pinterest experience of variety and discovery and doing this will lose you followers. Hootsuite's app, ViralTag, is an excellent tool for scheduling pins you find online but you cannot schedule repins or upload original pins.

Be authentic
Use your pins to show your brands values and your brands vision, personality and what is important to your brand. Pinterest is incredibly powerful when it comes to creating, developing and promoting your

brand. You also need to be careful not to pin or repin anything that does not fit in with your branding.

Avoid blatant self promotion
Simply pushing your products and services all the time will not work. When creating pins keep in mind the lifestyle you are trying to promote with your products or services. You can create much more interest by pinning images from other sources.

Do not link pins to affiliate links
Under Pinterest terms and conditions you cannot link directly to affiliate links, however you can embed links to your own website or blog and then link your pins to those pages.

Download the Pinterest iPhone and Android app
If you're an iPhone user, the free Pinterest app lets you pin pictures with your location, directly from your phone.

Time Management
Like any of the social networks Pinterest takes time and it is easy to get dragged into the site and spend literally hours and hours browsing the interesting material available. Once you have set up your initial boards you will need to allocate a certain amount of time each day and then try and keep to that, so you do not waste too much time. Setting a timer is a good idea.

HOW TO USE RICH PINS
Rich pins are pins that allow retailers to add extra information to the images that people pin. There are five different types of rich pin, Product Pin, Place Pins, Article Pins, Recipe Pins and Movie Pins.

- **Place Pins** include a map, address and phone number
- **Article Pins** include headline, author and story description
- **Product Pins** include pricing, availability and where to buy.

Pinners also get notified when an item drops in price

- **Recipe Pins** include ingredients, cooking times and serving information and recipe search filters help Pinners to find the recipes they are looking for
- **Movie Pins** include information about ratings, cast members and reviews

To get started with rich pins you will need to prepare your website with metatags and then get your Rich Pins validated and then apply to get them approved on Pinterest. You probably want to get a developer to help you if you are not technical. For more information you can visit this page https://developers.pinterest.com/rich_pins/

CHAPTER THREE

BUILDING YOUR AUDIENCE ON PINTEREST

LIKE ANY OTHER social media network Pinterest is a traffic source and a tool to find new customers. Once you have created your initial boards you will be ready to find and build your audience so that you will be able to do the following:

- Drive traffic to your website
- Promote and sell your products
- Build your opt-in list
- Increase exposure to your products
- Build your brand

Here are some strategies to building your followers on Pinterest:

Install the Pinterest follow button on your website

Make sure you have installed a Pinterest follow button on your website and also install 'Pin it' buttons next to the products on your site as well, if possible. There is still a concern amongst pinners about copyright and about whether or not you are allowed to pin images, so making your website visitors aware that they are welcome to pin your images will go a long way to get people to share your images. You can make it obvious to your visitors by including a call to action, for example, ' Feel free to pin'. You can find buttons at this link www.pinterest.com/about/goodies where you can choose from a selection of widgets to embed on your site including: the pin it button, follow button, pin widget, profile widget and board widget which lets you display up to thirty of your favorites board's latest pins.

343

Connect your Facebook and Twitter accounts

When you joined Pinterest you may have linked your Twitter and your personal Facebook profile. If you have done this then you will be notified whenever one of your friends joins Pinterest. You can choose to share your Pins on Twitter and Facebook every time you add a pin you can click on the pin to share it. This will increase your reach through your friends, but not a good idea if you are pinning regularly, as it may put your Facebook friends off.

Announce your presence on your other social networks

Create a post for Facebook, Twitter, Google + and any other social networks announcing you are on Pinterest and invite people to follow you.

Select a Pinner of the month

Selecting a 'Pinner of the month' is an incredibly powerful way to encourage pinners to pin and repin your content on Pinterest. This not only helps to grow your reach on Pinterest but also helps to grow your followers. The reason this is so powerful is pinners will be desperate to win that spot as they will gain huge publicity among your followers if they get picked as your 'Pinner of the Month' and in turn you will gain huge exposure amongst their followers. It's a win win for both parties.

Win 'Pinner of the Month'

If you are a personal brand then winning a' Pinner of the Month' competition could offer you huge exposure. Make sure you pick a brand that has the right audience for your brand and is not directly in competition with you.

Email your contacts

Invite your current customers or the people who have joined your opt-in list. Remember every follower you gain on Pinterest has the potential increase your reach by drawing in their contacts and more like minded users with similar interests and therefore helps grow your following.

Cross promote with friends.

If you have friends on Pinterest then ask if they can repin some of your pins on their boards and offer to do the same for them.

Use search to find your target audience

By using the search facility you will be able to find your target audience on Pinterest. Simply type your term into search and it will bring up the images relating to that term, under that image you will see details about how many times an image has been pinned and by who. By following either their profile or one of their boards the user will be notified. Going out of your way to repin their images especially if they are the actual source of the image rather than repinning what they have repinned will really bring your profile to their attention. If you do not want to be too overwhelmed in your feed by too many pins from the same user then following just one of their boards may be better.

Repinning and sharing

Everyone is aiming for repins so if you are helping others out by repinning their content it is going to draw attention to your brand and they are more likely to take interest in your content. This is one area where the reciprocation rule works very well on Pinterest. Engaging with content will also draw attention to you and your brand and you will find that people will click on your profile to find out who you are and you may very well end up with another follower. The more you share the more others will see your actions. Repinning is one of the most social activities on Pinterest, it's how users build their network of followers and works especially well if your business is B2B. Other businesses will appreciate that you are promoting their product by repinning and this is how you can start to build a really good community.

Liking other pins

Liking is also a really good way to connect and draw attention to your brand. Maybe you don't want to repin because a pin doesn't fit in with your brand or any of your boards but you can still like it.

Commenting on pins

Commenting on pins is a really excellent way of engaging with the community. Once you start interacting you will create interest in your own content too, other people will see your comments and may be drawn to come and have a look at one of your boards. The more you participate and get involved the more you will grow your following which makes for more eyeballs on your content. Be careful not to comment too much at one time, Pinterest may consider this as spammy behaviour and suspend your commenting privileges.

Comment on popular pins

This section can be found here http://www.pinterest.com/popular/ You need to make sure you are writing thoughtful comments and not too many for the reason mentioned above.

Contribute to other boards

This is a great way to get noticed . Contributing to popular boards with interesting pins will put you in front of even more users and help contribute to your follow count.

Mention / Tag other users

You can draw attention to people and your profile by tagging them and they will be sent an email notifying them. Simply add the @ sign before their profile name. This really helps to build rapport in your community. You can recommend a pin to someone, start a conversation or ask questions.

Advertising on Pinterest

Pinterest are now introducing Promoted Pins. Promoted Pins work in a similar way to Facebook promoted posts and basically advertisers can pay to get their pins to show up higher under certain categories. The platform is currently experimenting with certain businesses this but will soon be rolled out to other businesses in due course.

CREATING A CONTEST ON PINTEREST

One way of building your following is to run a Pinterest competition. Competitions can also help you to grow your opt-in list, drive traffic to your website, promote a new product and build your brand. If you need inspiration then type the words competition, or, contest, into Pinterest search and have a look at some of the competitions currently running. Pinterest has tightened up their terms and conditions regarding promotions and this is most probably because they want to preserve the Pinterest experience which is all about discovery, creativity and interests. If you want to create a contest or competition it's probably a very good idea to use a third party as they will ensure that the terms and conditions are met. Here are the steps you need to take to create your competition or contest:

Decide on the type of competition

The type of contest you wish to run will depend on your goal and whether you wish to increase your following, build your opt in list, increase exposure or promote a particular product. Creative contests tend to gain more engagement while sweepstakes may gain you more followers. Here are a few ideas about the types of contest you may wish to run:

- **Photo or video contest** Create a board which allows your entrants to upload an image or video. Ask your audience to submit their videos or photos of them using your product. This is great for creating engagement and buzz and entrants will often want to share and shout about their own creations with their friends and followers which will increase your brand reach even further.

- **Pin Now Contest** Simply ask your entrants to create a board with the board name you have chosen and ask them to choose their favorite products from your website. To administer this you will need to create a landing page to administer the contest and ask entrants to complete an entry form and share their board URL on the form. Alternatively you can ask them to pin just one of their favorite images from your site and complete an entry form. **NB** Under Pinterest terms and conditions you cannot ask entrants to pin something from a predefined selection of pins. You should not require a minimum number of pins and you cannot name your competition 'pin it to win it'.

- **Sweepstakes** Sweepstakes are a great way to build your opt-in list. Rafflecopter.com lets you set up contests in minutes and offers an easy entry process.

- **Blog or website contest** If your competition is all about launching a new product you may want to simply send your audience to a landing page where they find out about your product and then have to answer a question and leave a comment on your website or blog. (Not on Pinterest as one of their Terms and Conditions states: 'Don't Encourage spammy behaviour, such as asking participants to comment'.)

Whatever the type of competition you choose to run be sure to keep it simple and easy to enter, the easier it is to enter the more entrants you will get. Also make sure your competition's landing page is optimized for mobile and tablets. You can do this by using a third party app like www.wishpond.com or www.woobox.com or www.shortstack.com These apps also help to keep track of entries, assist in selecting a winner and ensure that you keep within the Pinterest terms and conditions.

Decide on a significant prize

The prize needs to reflect the effort that you expect your audience to put in and obviously the bigger the prize the more people will enter. Also you need to pick a prize that will appeal to your target audience so when they do start following they will actually be interested in your pins and engage with your content. The 'Win an iPad' competitions can draw large numbers of followers but they don't necessarily attract the right audience and promote your product. To keep your audience happy it's also really good to give your entrants a reward for entering like a small gift or maybe money off coupon.

Create a landing page
Create your contest landing page on your website or blog with a description of the contest, entry instructions, competition entry form, terms and conditions and closing date. You will need to be clear how you will be picking the winner.

Create your competition pin & description
You will need to create a compelling image to promote your contest on Pinterest. Adding clear title text to the image and the description field promoting contest will help to increase the numbers of entrants. Your description needs to clearly describe what the competition is all about, what the prize is and when the closing date is. Including a date will also help to get your contest found as people may well enter a search terms like 'contest September 20_ _. Try and include as many keywords as possible including words like competition, sweepstake, win, giveaway , promotion.

Add a value
If your prize has a monetary value then add this in the description with currency sign and it will then show up in the top right of the image.

Promote your contest
You will need to create some buzz to draw attention for your Pinterest contest. Here are some ideas how you can do this:

- Invite your subscribers from your opt in list

- Announce your contest on your other social networks
- Create a board for other peoples competitions as well as your own to help drive traffic to yours, example 'September contest on Pinterest'
- Add your contest pin at different times of the day and create different images of the prizes to promote the same contest
- Promote on your blog or website
- Use Facebook advertising
- Create some information about your competition in print for the customers who visit your business to take away. This could literally be just a note on a receipt

Pick a winner

You can run a sweepstake and choose a winner from all the entries. www.random.org offers a service that selects winners of competitions. Alternatively you can appoint a panel of judges to pick the best board or use another third party contest app.

Pin a picture of the winner or winning pin

This is a great way to make your contest look authentic especially if you are planning to launch another one. You can also include the information in the pin to introduce yet another contest. People are very suspicious about contests so by doing this you will give users the confidence that the contest is real and they are more likely to enter.

Delete the contest when it's over

There is nothing worse than visiting a page with an out of date contest, it's disappointing for your followers and will leave them with a negative feeling about your business. Make sure you delete the pin when it is over or replace the content on the web page with a new contest or a picture of the winner.

Check on competition terms

This is a big one. Make sure you are aware of the rules for contests in your own state, region or country and make sure you read Pinterest guidelines about marketing and the do's and don'ts for running a contest http://business.pinterest.com/en/brand-guidelines Here are a list of Don'ts taken from that page;

- Suggest that Pinterest sponsors or endorses you or the contest.
- Require people to add Pins from a selection—let them add what they like.
- Make people Pin your contest rules. This is a biggie.
- Run sweepstakes where each Pin, board, like or follow represents an entry.
- Encourage spammy behaviour, such as asking participants to comment.
- Ask people to vote with Pins, boards, or likes.
- Overdo it: contests can get old fast.
- Require a minimum number of Pins. One is plenty.
- Call your contest a "Pin it to win it" contest.

If you use Pinterest as part of a contest or sweepstakes, you are responsible for making sure it complies with all legal requirements. This includes writing the official rules, offer terms and eligibility requirements (eg: age and residency restrictions), and complying with marketing regulations (eg: registration requirements and regulatory approvals). These rules can vary from place to place, so please work with a lawyer or other expert to make sure you're in compliance. You should also always comply with Pinterest's Terms of Service.

CHAPTER FOUR

MEASURING AND MONITORING YOUR RESULTS ON PINTEREST

MEASURING AND MONITORING your results and performance against your original goals and objectives on a continual basis is essential. This is where many businesses go wrong, they carry on aimlessly posting content without checking to see what is working and what is not. Then after 6 months or a year they wonder why their campaign is making no positive difference at all.

When you measure your results you will discover so much information that will allow you to steer your campaign in the right direction to achieve those SMART goals and objectives and also to stop anything that is not working.

When you initially work out strategies and tactics for your campaign, you will be estimating what you need to do to achieve your goals and objectives. However as your campaign runs you will see exactly what you need to do to achieve you original goals. For example, you may need to change the types of posts you make to increase engagement and reach. Perhaps you need to increase the number of competitions you run to increase the number of opt-in subscribers. This is what it is all about, making your campaign work for you by constantly measuring your success against the goals set and then adjusting your strategies accordingly in order to achieve the results.

To help you measure your results Pinterest offers very good analytics and also you can use Google Analytics. There are other tools available on the net but these two should be sufficient.

Pinterest Analytics

With the launch of the new Pinterest analytics tool you can now measure the success of your marketing efforts and really see whether it is working for your business. You can see which pins are getting shared, how many pins are getting pinned from your website and you can learn about what pinners like.

Once you have verified your website you can access analytics on your business account for free. Analytics is accessible from the top right in the drop down menu. If you already have an active account then you need to make sure you switch to the new look which is situated at the bottom of the drop down menu .

Pinterest analytics will help you understand how pinners are engaging with your content. Once you are into your analytics dashboard you will be able to access all sorts of useful information.

- **Pins** The average number of things pinned from your website.

- **Pinners** The average number of unique people who have pinned from your website.

- **Repins** The average number of times pins from your website have been repinned.

- **Repinners** The average number of unique people who repinned your pins on Pinterest.

- **Impressions** The average number of times your pins appeared in feed and search for boards on the web.

- **Reach** The daily number of unique people who saw your pins on Pinterest.

- **Clicks** The average number of clicks to your website from Pinterest.

- **Visitors** The average number of unique people who visit your site from Pinterest.

- **+/- %** Percent increase or decrease from your current date range to a previous date range.

You can also see your websites most recent pins and most repinned pins and most clicked pins.

GOOGLE ANALYTICS

Google Analytics will be able to give you detailed information about the impact Pinterest is having on your business.

Google Analytics Social Reports

Google Analytics provides advance reports that let you track the effectiveness of your campaign with the following social reports:

The Overview Report

This report lets you see at a glance how much conversion value is generated from social channels. It compares all conversions with those resulting from social.

The Conversions Report

The Conversions Report helps you to quantify the value of social and shows conversion rates and the monetary value of conversions that occurred due to referrals from Pinterest and any of the other social networks. Google Analytics can link visits from Pinterest with the goals you have chosen and your E - commerce transactions. To do this you will need to configure your goals in Google Analytics which is found under **'Admin'** and then **'Goals'**. Goals in Google Analytics let you measure how often visitors take or complete a specific action and you can either create goals from the templates offered or create your own custom goals. The Conversions report can be found in the Standard Reporting tab under Traffic Sources > Social > Conversions.

The Networks Referral Report The Networks Referral report tells you how many visitors the social networks have referred to your website and shows you how many pageviews,visits, the duration of the visits and the average number of pages viewed per visit. From this information you can determine which network referred the highest quality of traffic.

Data Hub Activity The Data Hub activity report shows how people are engaging with your site on the social networks . You can see the most recent URL's that were shared, how they were shared and what was said.

The social visitors flow report This report displays the initial paths that your visitors took from social sites through your site and where they exited.

The landing pages report This report displays engagement metrics for each URL. These include pageviews, average visit duration and pageviews and pages viewed per visit.

The Trackbacks Report The Trackback report shows you which sites are linking to your content and how many visits those sites are sending to you. This can help you to work out which sort of content is the most successful so you can create similar and also helps you to build relationships with those who are constantly linking to your content.

Tracking Custom Campaigns with Google Analytics
Google Analytics lets you create URL's for custom campaigns for website tracking. This helps you identify which content is the most effective in driving visitors to your website and landing pages. For instance you may want to see which particular links are sending you the most traffic from

Pinterest or you may want to see which links in an email are sending you the most traffic. Custom Campaigns let you measure this and see what is and what is not working by letting you add parameters to the end of your URL. You can either add you own or use the URL Builder.

To do this simply type 'URL builder' into Google and click on the first result. The URL builder form will only appear if you are signed into Google. You then need to add the URL, that you want to track, to the form provided and then complete the fields and click 'Submit.' You will then need to shorten the URL with bit.ly or goo.gl/ . Once you have set these up you can track the results within Google Analytics.

Make LinkedIn™

Work For Your Business

Alex Stearn

Table of Contents

CHAPTER ONE

GETTING STARTED ON LINKEDIN

WITH OVER 200 million members in 200 countries and an average member income of over $100,000 LinkedIn is now the worlds largest and fastest growing professional networks with its main objective being to connect business people.

The immediate thought that usually comes to mind when thinking about LinkedIn is for recruitment and job search however it has proven to be much more. LinkedIn is not only where senior executives are headhunted and serious job seekers hang out, it is also where a great deal of business takes place. Research shows that a whopping 80% of members influence buying decisions in their companies and also members have more trust in business information they receive on LinkedIn than on any other social networks. More and more businesses are joining and seeing the additional benefits LinkedIn has to offer for building their business. Here are some of the main benefits for business:

Business development & networking

No other network offers such a high number and high calibre of business people on the internet. The opportunities to network and make new contacts are endless. LinkedIn's advanced search function allows you to search for people based on a variety of criteria which allows you to reach out to specific industry professionals including customers, suppliers and employees.

A powerful lead generation tool

Because of its huge business membership LinkedIn is a very powerful source and generator of leads for any business and LinkedIn can be used to find and connect with potential customers. There are many areas that you can use LinkedIn to generate leads as follows:

- Building your personal connections
- Participating in LinkedIn Groups
- Creating your own LinkedIn group
- Creating a Company Page on LinkedIn
- Using Linkedin's powerful search for sourcing leads and contacting new prospects

Increases your business' exposure with a company page

LinkedIn offers you the opportunity to create a page for your company where you can upload detailed descriptions of your products and services for free which will help to increase your brand's exposure amongst a network of professional people. Having a company page is like having another website except with a ready made audience that is linked to your business profile and potentially exposed to an audience of business professionals.

Increases credibility

Linked in offers a great opportunity to receive recommendations for your business from clients, business partners and suppliers which can be viewed on your page. This is a powerful way of building credibility and social proof with potential connections.

Website Traffic

LinkedIn is responsible for driving a higher proportion of social traffic to corporate websites compared to any other social networks.

Content Sharing

LinkedIn offers you the opportunity to share your content, your news and developments in your industry.

Group Participation

With LinkedIn you can participate in groups which are centred around specific topics in your niche. By joining and participating in groups you can share your expertise with other members, comment on topics and join in conversations. All of these actions can help to build relationships with potential customers and key influencers and help to build your brand.

Group Creation

Creating, promoting and maintaining your own group on LinkedIn will increase your exposure, influence and credibility within your niche and is great way to connect with customers and potential customers. Creating a group which is active and full of discussions and great content can help you to stand out as a thought leader, help to build your brand and gives you credibility for bringing like minded people together.

Industry news

LinkedInToday helps you stay on top of whats going on in your industry and offers you the most popular articles that are being shared on your network. You can have these updates sent to your email. Being in the know and up to date with the latest trends and news assists you in your own content creation which you can also share on other networks too.

Recruitment & Job Search

LinkedIn in offers both recruiters and job seekers some of the best information for searching for people, together with regular job news and updates.

Google favorites

LinkedIn profiles and company pages are very well ranked in Google search.

Builds personal brands

LinkedIn is excellent for building a personal brand based on your professional and educational background. It allows members to view your experience and qualifications and helps build trust through credibility and history. No other network offers this amount of information about a person's education and work experience.

It's all business

LinkedIn stands out from all the other social platforms because it's all about business. People are on Linkedin are in a business mindset and ready to discuss and do business.

CREATING YOUR PERSONAL PROFILE ON LINKEDIN

You need to think of your LinkedIn profile as your own professional website, there to promote your skills, knowledge, personality and your own personal brand. LinkedIn profiles are generally ranked in first or second page for your name in Google and as with every other social media network your profile needs to be fully optimized for LinkedIn search and for Google search.

To register for your account you will need to input some basic information including your name and address and your most recent position with dates. LinkedIn will then offer you the opportunity to find your current email contacts that are already Linkedin members. It is best to leave this until your profile is fully completed and optimized.

At the next step Linkedin will send you an email to verify your account. You can then choose if you want a basic account (free) or a premium (paid) profile. A free account is sufficient to start with and allows you to take advantage of the many benefits and opportunities that Linkedin offers to their members. You can upgrade your membership at any time if you require any of the additional features a paid account has to offer.

Optimising your profile for success

Once you have completed the initial sign up process you will need to complete all the sections to optimize your profile. It's worth putting a great deal of time and thought into creating an interesting, personable and authentic profile. LinkedIn is all about your professional self and lets you really go to town selling yourself with the profile features it offers. Simply click on '**Profile**' and then '**Edit Profile**' and you can add your photo, summary, work experience details and skills and expertise.

When it comes to uploading your profile picture, make sure the image you have is a high quality one and represents you in the most friendly and professional way possible.

When it comes to optimising your LinkedIn profile it's really important to complete every section in detail. The more complete your profile the higher you will appear in LinkedIn search. Here are some tips on completing the various sections on your personal profile:

Your professional headline

Your professional headline is found below your name on your personal profile, it is shown when you ask another member to connect with you. The headline is automatically populated by LinkedIn with your job title but you have the opportunity here to be really ahead the competition by being specific about what you offer and the value you can bring to your customers. You have 110 characters to entice your audience by writing something creative and compelling. Remember your headline is your first opportunity on LinkedIn to break the ice and start a relationship with anyone who is viewing your profile so you need to use this headline to reach out to them and grab their attention. So many individuals miss out on this marketing opportunity by not making it obvious how they can be of assistance and of benefit to their potential customers. Sometimes adding a little humor can work and not only gains attention but also helps people to remember you.

Be sure to include powerful keywords from your niche as it will affect how you are shown in Google and LinkedIn search results. You may even want to mention your business name or what country, area or region you are in, especially if your business is of a more local nature. If you are stuck for inspiration the best thing to do is check out other profiles and headlines.

Custom profile background/Cover photo

Premium members can now upload a custom profile background. This in itself is a huge motivation to sign up as a premium member on LinkedIn and an excellent way to stand out on LinkedIn and promote your brand. You can either choose from LinkedIn's gallery of images or upload your own, the cover photo area is 1400X425 pixels.

Personal Summary

Your personal summary is an extension of your professional headline and is a great white space to tell your story preferably in the first person. You have 2000 characters to communicate your personality, expertise and the value you can provide. The best summaries that stand out are usually inventive, authentic and interesting. You need to tell your audience who you are, what you do and how you can help them. This is also a great place to provide information about your interests beyond business, as it makes your profile more interesting, unique, memorable and personal to you. You can add videos, SlideShare presentations and other files to your summary which really help to showcase your work. You can also add a video which is particularly good if you are a personal brand, after all there is no better way of breaking the ice and helping people get to know you than by creating and including a short introduction video.

When it comes to writing make sure your paragraphs is short and snappy, in order to keep your audience interested. You can also add bullet points, stars or fun bullets by copying and pasting them into your summary from a word document.

Don't forget to add a friendly call to action and asking people to contact by email will help to encourage connections and make you more approachable.

Before completing your personal summary it's definitely worthwhile having a look around at some other profiles in your niche and seeing which ones grab your attention and which ones send you to sleep!

Experience

This is like your resume, it's important here to add all your positions, education, skills, expertise and responsibilities including any major achievements. Again to make it easier to read you can add bullet points by pasting from a word document.

Skills and expertise

You can add up to 50 skills to your profile. Once you have added these skills they will be added to your personal profile so when your connections view your profile they will be able to view your skills and they will be offered the opportunity to endorse those skills. Skills with the most endorsements will be listed first. Receiving endorsements is a great way to build your credibility and your professional brand. You can choose not to display any endorsements if you wish.

If people are writing recommendations for you or endorsing certain skills then it is good practice to reciprocate if you agree that they have the skills they have listed.

Education

You can add all the educational establishments that you attended and all your qualifications together with documents, files, images and videos.

Visually enhance your profile with videos, images and documents

LinkedIn now gives you the opportunity to showcase your work and experience by adding images, videos and documents to your summary, experience and education section. This is an incredibly powerful way of helping you to tell your story in a visual way. Adding a short and well made video will help to make a more personal connection especially with new connections and help to give them more insight into who you are. A video is also an instant ice breaker and makes it easier for people to remember you. To begin sharing simply click 'Edit' on your profile and follow the prompts.

Choosing your most visible and prominent sections
LinkedIn allows you to change the position of the summary, experience, education and skills sections with the arrow you will find to the right of each section. You can select which is the most important section and place it at the top.

Extras
On the right of your profile in edit mode you can add extra information: Organizations, Honours and Awards, Test Scores, Courses, Patents, Certifications, Volunteering and Causes, Publications, Projects and Languages.

Edit contact information
In this section you can add one or more twitter accounts, telephone, email, an instant messaging address and up to three web/blog addresses. You can add keyword anchor text to your website address if you wish by choosing 'other' in the drop down list and then adding the keywords that will then become your anchor text.

Asking for recommendations
A recommendation helps to illustrate your achievements and shows information about why other people have enjoyed working with you. A recommendation is a comment written by another LinkedIn member in their own words to endorse another member. These recommendations matter and can be used by other members when deciding whether or not to do business with you or employ you. Recommendations not only add

credibility to your profile ,but according to data, users with recommendations are more likely to appear in searches on LinkedIn.

You can request a recommendation by simply sending a request to another member. Simply click 'Edit Profile' at the top of the page and a drop down menu will appear, you can then click 'Ask to be recommended' You will then be offered a form to complete where you choose the job or education that you want to get recommended for and you are also able to select the connections you want to send your request to. LinkedIn offers a standard message to send with your request, however by adding a personal message and asking your connections to recommend you for something specific, they will be far more likely reply. When they do reply you can choose whether you want to display the recommendation or hide it.

Customize your public profile URL

When you register LinkedIn will give your personal profile A URL made up of your name and some letters and random numbers. You will find your LinkedIn URL just under your profile picture. You can enhance your personal brand by creating a custom URL which is easier to remember and easier to display on emails and other places where you wish to promote it.

To customize it simply move your cursor over 'Profile' and then click 'Edit Profile' then click 'Edit' next to your URL under your profile picture. On the top right you will see a box 'Your public profile URL' and you need to click on 'Customize your public profile URL'. Your URL can contain between 5 and 30 letters and numbers, but no symbols, spaces or special characters. You cannot change more than three times in a six month period.

Updating your personal profile

If you want to update your personal profile on LinkedIn but do not want your changes and updates to show up in your connections feed, you can temporarily turn off ' **Activity broadcasts**'. Simply click on '**Privacy and Settings**' which is situated on the drop down menu when you click on your photo on the top right of your profile. Then click on '**Turn on/ off your activity broadcasts**' and then remove the tick from the box.

Viewing your public profile

Your public profile is the profile that can be viewed by people outside LinkedIn. You can view this by clicking '**Edit Profile**' and then click on '**Manage public profile settings**'. LinkedIn allows you to fully control what is displayed on your public profile and you can customize the view if you like and even set it so that none of it is public if you wish. On this page you can also obtain profile badges so that your profile can be viewed on your website, blog or email signature.

ADDING CONNECTIONS & BUILDING YOUR PERSONAL NETWORK

On LinkedIn your personal network is made up of connections. These connections are called 1st ,2nd and 3rd degree. You can easily identify what type of connection they are as an icon is displayed by their name. You can mage your connections from the '**Network**' tab at the top of your profile.

1st degree connections are those who are directly connected to you and have either sent you an invitation that you have accepted or they have accepted your invitation to connect . 2nd degree connections are those who are connected to your 1st degree connections. 3rd degree connections are a wider network of people connected to your 2nd degree connections. To contact people outside your network you will need to send InMail and this comes with the premium membership.

Once you have successfully set up your profile and company page you will be ready to start making connections. The more connections you have the more chance you have of connecting with a wider network.

Here are some tips to building your network:

Invite Connections.

The quickest and easiest way to add connections is to send an invitation to your email contacts through LinkedIn. To start simply visit your profile home page and click '**Network**,' then '**Add Connections**'. LinkedIn will take the email that is associated with your account and you will then need to give LinkedIn permission to access your email address book. LinkedIn will match your contacts with those that are already members and then offer you the opportunity to send invitations to those contacts who are not on LinkedIn. Your invitation will include a standard LinkedIn message, but it's definitely beneficial to tailor your message to each individual contact.

You can invite your existing contacts by uploading your own contacts file or by sending out individual invitations. It is recommended that you only send invitations to those people you know well and trust.

You can also send invitations from the '**People you may know**' area on the right side of your profile page. Simply click connect next to their name, you can also use LinkedIn search to find people you know. Once they have received and accepted your invitation to connect they will become a '1st degree connection.' Remember every connection you make offers you the potential to connect to even more people.

Converting 2nd and 3rd degree connections to 1st degree connections

As you become more active on LinkedIn by updating your status, interacting, joining groups and getting to know people you will be able to send out invitations to your 2nd and 3rd connections. Be careful not to send out invitations to people who you do not know as they can report this as spam and LinkedIn only have to be notified a few times and they will close your account.

Get introduced to 2nd Degree connections

By getting introduced by your 1st degree connections you can reach out to 2nd degree connections. As a free member you can get up to 5 introductions per month and as a premium member you are allowed up to 35 per month, depending on your level of membership. To find people more connections in your niche you can use the advanced search feature. Simply complete the search form and the results will display a list of members and whether you share any connections with those people. Next to where it says 'Connect' there is a down arrow with a drop down menu, simply click on ' **Get introduced**' and you will be shown which of your 1st degree connections have this contact as their 1st degree connection. You can then choose who you wish to introduce you to this new contact and send them a request to be introduced.

Accept Invitations to connect

The more connections you have the more opportunity you have to expand your network and increase exposure to your brand or personal brand. This is of course up to whether you accept or not, beware though of spammers who quite often stand out because they have not got a complete profile.

Send a reply when accepting invitations

A great way to break the ice and start building relationships with new connections is to send them a message. The content will obviously depend on how well you know them but this is a great way of keeping the conversation going.

Find Alumni

You can search who you were at college with by adding the name of the establishment and the years you were there. You can find the 'Alumni tab' under the 'Network' tab.

Send an InMail

If you are a premium member you are allowed to send between 3 and 25 InMails per month depending on the level of membership you have. This means you do not need to be introduced by a connection and you can reach out to other members directly. In order to get the best response from your InMails make sure your first InMail to a new contact is just a brief enthusiastic and professional introduction of yourself, your goal for your first InMail is just to start a conversation. You could also mention a member that you both have in common. Once you have started the conversation you can then continue the conversation and focus on the benefits you can offer them or how you can help them in some way.

Use Advanced Search

LinkedIn offers a very sophisticated search facility that lets you find people in specific positions or industries. Premium members can use up to 8 extra advanced search filters.

Send a message to an Openlink member

Whether or not you are a premium member you can still reach out to any member if they are a member of the Openlink network. If they are part of the Openlink network they will have a badge displayed on their profile or in any search results that they are in. The icon looks like a small ring of dots. You can send a mail by simply clicking '**Send InMail**' on the members profile.

Share and comment on other peoples posts

Actively contributing to other peoples discussions and status updates is invaluable and can only increase your visibility to your 1st, 2nd and 3rd degree connections.

Start or join LinkedIn groups

Participating in LinkedIn groups is a very effective way to make new connections. By interacting, commenting and asking questions you can start up new conversations and increase your visibility on LinkedIn.

Follow other companies

If you follow the company pages of your connections and actively comment and share their content you will increase your visibility to their followers. By supporting their pages they are more likely to participate and share your content.

Create a post on your Facebook fan page

Announcing your presence on Facebook and inviting your fans to connect with you on LinkedIn will open up new opportunities of connecting with their connections on LinkedIn too.

Follow up on people you meet

What better way to stay connected with someone you have recently met than by sending them an invitation to connect on LinkedIn when you get back to your office.

Endorse skills for your connections

Endorsing your 1st degree connection for their skills is are a great way of showing support and recognising them for their expertise. If you give endorsements to your connections they are more likely to reciprocate and also are more likely to think kindly towards you and interact with your content.

Recommend your connections

Recommending your connections for certain things helps them to win clients and get hired and it also strengthens your relationships with your network. Your connections are more likely to recommend you if you have already recommended them. To recommend simply click on the connection you want to recommend and then click on the down arrow (next to send email) and then click 'Recommend' You can recommend your connection as a colleague, service provider, business partner or student. You then need to complete the recommendation form and press send. You can recommend someone who is not on LinkedIn too and they will be invited to create a profile on LinkedIn.

You can request recommendations for yourself by going to 'Privacy and Settings' situated in the drop down under your photo on the right and then click on '**Manage Your Recommendations**'

Post regular updates

Creating conversations and staying engaged with your connections is key to building trust, credibility, building more connections and building your brand. It's a good idea to connect with your audience at least once a day. Being active on LinkedIn will gain you more visibility, when a connection interacts with your updates these actions will be seen by their network which will increase your reach and your potential to gain a new followers.

You can include up to 600 characters in an update and you can include a link or upload a file attachment. Unlike your company page you do not have the opportunity to upload an image file but you can share links and LinkedIn will automatically shorten your links.

Your updates will remain at the top of your profile until it is replaced by another one. When you post an update you can choose who sees your post. You can choose to share your updates with Public and Twitter, just Public or just your 1st degree connections. Only the first 140 characters of your update will show on Twitter.

Updating your status on your personal profile

LinkedIn is very different to Twitter and Facebook and is purely a professional network and so updates also need to be professional. However, be careful not to overdo the self promotion, as it will just turn your followers off.

Here are some ideas for status updates:
- A description and link to one of your blog articles.
- Update on what you are doing, or ask what others are doing.
- A link to a new blog article that you found interesting and think would appeal to your network.
- A useful quote.
- A link to a pin on Pinterest .
- Tips, advice and useful information about your industry.
- A link to a YouTube video.
- A request to connect on your other social networks.
- An update about your business or press release.
- An update on what you are currently working on.
- Ask a question to spark conversation.
- Share useful online tools you may use to help you with your business.
- Comment on business books you are reading.
- Share posts and articles from top influencers on LinkedIn.

BENEFITS OF A PREMIUM ACCOUNT

Benefits of upgrading your account to a premium account.

The LinkedIn basic account offers many benefits to the user however if you want to use LinkedIn as a sales generation tool and send InMails or allow any member to message you then you will need to upgrade your account to a premium account. LinkedIn offers different premium accounts and you can tailor their services and benefits towards whatever you want to use Linkedin for. You can check your account type in your privacy settings and view the different account types available on the 'compare account types' tab.

- Business - For general business use
- Job Seeker
- Sales Navigator - For sales professionals
- Talent Finder
- Recruiter

Having a premium account can assist you in sourcing new sales leads and finding key decision makers, with its advanced search facility. Premium accounts offer the following features and benefits:

Custom profile background and larger profile picture

As a premium member you can now upload a larger profile photo and your own custom header. You can either upload your own branded backround or choose from LinkedIn's gallery of background images.

InMail

InMail allows you to contact users that you are unable to contact with a free account. LinkedIn offers between 3 and 25 InMails per month depending on the subscription type. You don't need any introduction and you can attach your profile with your message when contacting people. If a user does not respond to an InMail within seven days on the eighth day LinkedIn will credit you with an additional InMail. You can purchase additional InMails too. You can check your InMail status in 'Privacy and Settings'.

Stand out on search results

As a premium member you will stand out in search results and your profile will be displayed twice as big as non premium members.

More search results

As a premium member you can get more search results, up to 700 contacts depending on the membership you have. You can also save more searches and more alerts if there are new people who have fallen into the search criteria of your saved searches. To access your saved searches simply visit the advanced search and click on the gear icon on the top right of the page. With premium membership you can make your searches even more specific with up to eight advanced search filters.

Keyword suggestions

LinkedIn will give you top keyword suggestions for your profile summary which are optimized and will help you to get found more easily in search.

Who's viewed my profile

You can see who has viewed your profile on the right side of your homepage. As a paid member you can view the profile of anyone who has viewed your profile in the last 90 days. If you do not have a paid option you can only view up to five profiles and see the number people have viewed your profile in the last 90 days.

Premium badge

As a premium member you can display a badge that shows to other members you are a premium member. You can choose to display this or not. This can be found on your 'Privacy & Settings' tab. Badges are displayed on your profile and in search results.

Openlink

The Openlink network allows any member to contact you by InMail completely free whether they are a premium member or not. Openlink opens you up to more networking opportunities and lets other professionals know that you do not mind them reaching out to you. You can choose whether you want to be included on the Openlink network or not. If you want to be part of this network then you need to display the Openlink badge on your profile, this option can be found on your 'Premium Badge Settings' and the badge looks like a small ring of dots.

Lead Builder

The Lead builder is available with the premium account for sales professionals and allows you to create and save lists of prospective customers using more advanced search criteria. You can find lead builder when you click on **'Advanced'** next to the search bar.

THINGS YOU NEED TO KNOW

LinkedIn 'Contacts' and organising your contacts and connections.

LinkedIn Contacts is a feature that is available to all members and allows you to organize your contacts in one place. When you click on '**Contacts**' from your 'Network' tab you will see a list of your connections and also you may see photos of your connections who have birthdays or a have a new job or photos of the people you have set reminders to contact. In 'Contacts' you can add profiles that you have saved and add more information to these profiles. This information can only be viewed by you. You can view your contacts however you want by pulling them up based on different criteria. For example you could pull up members with the same tags or pull up your connections only.

You can add contact information, notes and details about how you met. You can also add information and tags. Tags are simply keywords that help you organize your contacts. You can also set reminders for yourself to contact and stay in touch with a connection or contact.

Pulse

LinkedIn Pulse is a source of professional news which is tailored to you and it is where you can discover and share compelling content related to the topics you are interested in, or the industry you are in. Updates and articles from the influencers you follow will appear in your updates feed. You can choose which Channels or Influencers you wish to follow. Simply go to the 'Interests' tab and select '**Pulse**' and then '**All Influencers**' or '**All Channels**'

Restrictions to using Linkedin

LinkedIn does enforce their terms of service and if members do not adhere to them they can be restricted. This can happen if you send one too many invitations that are marked as spam, or a number of users have indicated that they do not know you. This can happen quite easily and LinkedIn will often remove the restriction if it's your first time. You need to visit the help centre and type in 'Account Restricted' to have this restriction lifted.

To avoid being restricted do not send invitations to people you have had no contact with and if you want to connect, then send a personalized introduction message first by InMail and then ask them if it is ok to send them an invite to connect. Don't send one unless they reply.

The Help Centre

LinkedIn provides a wealth of information about their network. You can find out anything about LinkedIn simply by accessing the help centre which can be found on the menu under your profile picture on the top right of your profile.

CHAPTER TWO

CREATING YOUR COMPANY PROFILE ON LINKEDIN

LINKEDIN OFFERS AN incredibly effective platform for promoting your business and your products with company pages. Company pages perform very well in searches for company searches on Linkedin and there are huge opportunities for generating leads. Once you have set up your company page you can post updates directly from you company page to your followers and like and comment as your company too. You can showcase your products and services or other content, generate social recommendations, send traffic to your website and generate leads.

As long as you have your own a domain email address then you can create a company page on LinkedIn. Simply move your cursor over 'Interests' on the top of the page and then click on **'Companies'** and then click **'Add a Company'** and simply add your company name and email address and then LinkedIn will send you an email so that they can verify your company.

When creating your description it will need to be optimized for both LinkedIn search and Google Search. Google displays up to 156 characters of your description, so you need to make the beginning of your description includes the facts which are going to be useful to your ideal customer. You can add your website and company specialities and your logo and a company homepage image. Since your 'about' section will be situated at the bottom of your page it's a good idea to add a message to your homepage image.

Here are the image sizes for your images which can be PNG/JPEG/GIF format:

- **Company Homepage Image** - Minimum 646 x 220
- **Company Standard Logo** – 100 x 60 (Image will be resized to fit)
- **Company Square Logo** 50 x 50 (Image will be resized to fit)
- **Product pictures** 100 X 80 pixels

CREATING A SHOWCASE PAGE

If your business is quite complex and has multiple products and you want to deliver different messages to different audiences then showcase pages can be incredibly useful. However before you look at setting one up you need to work out if they are really going to benefit your business, as it will take more resources to build separate audiences and it may be that your company page is sufficient for your needs. Showcase pages are dedicated pages that let you segment and deliver multiple brand messages to specific audiences. You can create up to ten showcase pages and they work in a similar way to company pages, you can advertise your showcase page and analyze your performance with LinkedIn analytics.

Creating a showcase page is very straight forward. Simply go to your company page and then click on the down arrow next to the 'Edit' button on your company page and then click 'Create Showcase Page'. You need to create a showcase name, add a page description (75 to 200 characters), a showcase website URL, your industry and upload images as follows:

Hero Image Minimum: 974 X 330 Pixels
Logo: 100 X 60 pixels. Image will be resized to fit.
Square logo: 50 x 50 pixels. Image will be resized to fit.

Your showcase page will display any other company showcase pages and will show that your showcase is part of your company page.

CREATING A SPONSORED UPDATE

Sponsored updates work similarly to promoted posts on Facebook and let you promote your company updates to targeted users who are not yet following your company page, allowing you to grow your reach and build awareness. They can be used for lead generation or to promote an event, a blog post, a new product or a giveaway that you are using to build your opt-in. Before you decide to promote your post, make sure you have a clear objective in mind. If your objective is to drive engagement then it's a good idea to see how your update is performing without promotion and then if you think it is doing well, sponsor it. Here are some tips for your sponsored update:

- Keep to one specific topic with one URL.
- Use a compelling image.
- Create a compelling headline.
- Make sure you have a good landing page with your offer an opt-in sign up form if you are looking to grow your subscribers.

To create a sponsored post simply create and post your update as normal and then click on '**Sponsor update**' under the post. You will then be taken to another page where you can choose to either '**Create an ad**' or '**Sponsor an update**'

Select '**Sponsor an update**' and then name your campaign and select the company page and the update you wish to sponsor. You will then be taken to another page where you can select the audience you want from the following criteria; location, companies and job title. You then to select your budget and then 'Save'. You can pay for sponsored updates based on the number of members who see your update (CPM) or the number of clicks they receive (CPC).

Once you campaign is up and running you view the performance of your sponsored update in '**Analytics**' which will show you the following:

- **Impressions** The number of times each update was shown to members

- **Clicks** The number of clicks on your company name, logo or your content.

- **Interactions** The number of times people have liked, commented on, and shared.

- **Engagement %** The number of interactions and the number of clicks and followers gained, divided by the number of impressions.

- **Followers Acquired** How many followers you gained by promoting each update.

- **Reach** A graph displaying the number of times your updates were seen organically and through paid campaigns on a daily basis.

- **Engagement** A graph displaying the number of times members clicked, liked or commented and shared your content both organically and through paid campaigns.

BUILDING YOUR AUDIENCE ON YOUR COMPANY PAGE

In order to drive engagement on your company page you will need to build your followers. LinkedIn has stated that you need at least one hundred and fifty followers to drive engagement. Here are some tactics to attract and gain followers for your page.

Adding Social Plugins to your sites

To enable users to share your content and add follow buttons for your website or blog you can find the code at this page https://

developer.linkedin.com/plugins

- **The Follow Button** Adding the company follow button to your website will assist you in growing your LinkedIn company page community so you can engage with your target audience, develop relationships, and acquire leads. By simply clicking the Follow Company button, users will automatically begin following your company page. Status updates you post from your company page will now show up on your follower's homepage feed. By encouraging your audience to like and share and interact with your content you will be spreading the word to their followers as well.

- **The Member Profile Plug in** You can also bring your LinkedIn member profile to your site. This immediately adds a personal touch to your website and you helps to promote your own personal brand.

- **Share Button** 'InShares' are a bit like Facebook 'likes' and twitter 'retweets' Using the share button allows professionals to share your valuable content among their connections and when people share your content it is added to the Linkedin ecosystem, and your content is shown to those who are interested in this type of content. This will offer you more visibility and more traffic from professionals.

- **The Recommend Plugin** This plugin enables users to recommend your products and services to LinkedIn's professional audience, and drive traffic back to your site.

Post regular updates to your company page
Encourage lively interaction on your page by regularly posting valuable and interesting content to your company page. Content creation is covered in more depth later on in the book.

Invite your friends, family and co-workers
Inviting the people you already have a relationship with is a good way to start to build your initial following and to encourage engagement.

Run an email invitation campaign
Inviting your current contacts and opt-in subscribers to your company page is yet another way to stay in contact and build relationships and more trust with those contact.

Announce to your connections
Once you have created your company page you can post an update on your personal profile announcing that your company page is up and invite your connections to follow.

Announce your company page on your other social networks
Inviting your followers from other social platforms to join the conversation will often appeal to your followers as it's an additional way for them to interact and make new connections as well.

Participate in LinkedIn Groups or create one
Participating in groups is a powerful way to drive people to your company page and promote your brand. You can mention your company page as long as it has useful information that is relevant to any group discussion taking place. Creating your own group can be a very powerful way of promoting your company page on LinkedIn.

Promote your page with Linkedin ads
LinkedIn offers targeted advertising opportunities. Your adverts can appear throughout LinkedIn and you can target your adverts to members in specific industries, companies and regions. The ability to target people with certain job titles makes LinkedIn advertising even more effective. Once these targeted members become followers or interact with your content on your company page then their connections will see these

action widening your reach further.

To advertise simply click on '**Business Services**' from your home page and then select '**Advertising**' and you can choose from '**Create an ad**' and '**Sponsoring an update**'. You can use text, images or videos and you can set your budget and stop your ads at any time.

Follow other companies

If you follow other businesses on LinkedIn then those businesses may very well reciprocate and follow you back. Once you start interacting with these pages other members may come and check out your company page. Please note that you can only follow a page as an individual and not a company.

Employees

Ask your employees to create their own personal profile which is linked to the company as their employer, this way you will increase the reach of your business. Once they have linked then they automatically become profiles that can follow your page, comment, like and share your posts.

Add your company page link to all your content

Make it easy for people to interact with your company page by adding it to all your content, white papers, pdf's and email signatures.

Post updates to your personal profile

Encourage your connections to follow your company page by posting occasional details about your business on your personal profile. This is especially effective if you have an image and a link to a useful article on your website or blog.

Follow your connections

When you make a new connection and then follow their business they may well reciprocate and follow your page.

Consider upgrading to a paid account

You may at this stage decide that upgrading to a paid account is going to give you additional contact options for building more connections.

CHAPTER THREE

CONTENT IS KING ON LINKEDIN

IN ORDER TO build a thriving community of brand advocates and customers who want to share your content, sign up to your newsletter and buy your products you are going to need to build trust, loyalty and likeability. The only way to do this is by communicating with them on regular basis in the right way and by consistently delivering the highest possible quality content which will grab their attention, appeal to their interests and add real value to their lives. Once your followers start engaging with your content, you will start building trust and start converting them into customers.

Content really is king on LinkedIn and in order to create the right content, you are going to need to have a real understanding of your target audience and deep insight into what interests and motivates them. Once you have this information and put this together with the strategies in this book there is no reason why you cannot build a thriving community of advocates for your brand on Linkedin. In this chapter you are going to learn about the different types of post, different types of content and tips on how help you create the best experience for your connections and followers so you can receive the highest engagement.

31 IDEAS FOR CREATING CONTENT ON LINKEDIN

You may be wondering how you are going to consistently produce and deliver compelling content to your audience on a regular basis for the foreseeable future. However once you have picked your topic of interest you will surprised how one idea will lead to another and you will be able to find numerous pieces of content to create and post. When you post your status updates on your company page your followers will see these updates on their homepage feed and they can comment, like or share your content. Your aim here is to amplify your message in order to grow your following. The more actions that your followers take with your content the more likely your page will be seen by other Linkedin members. According to Linkedin this type of engagement on company pages is responsible for over a third of impressions. Here are some ideas for content that can be adapted to any type of business or topic:

1. Relatable content

Relatable content is one of the best types of content and one of the most shared types of content. Relatable content is anything that your target audience can relate to and identify with, it's when your audience sees a piece of content and immediately thinks, "Yes, I can relate to that and this is exactly the way I feel when this happens". It's incredibly powerful because this content is immediately communicating to your audience that you understand them and you feel their pain or joy and you can empathise with them. With relatable content you are communicating with them on quite a deep level which all helps to build relationships and trust. This is why Someecards is so successful, most of their content is relatable.

2. Emotive content

Evoking an emotional response is an essential ingredient to successful viral content marketing. If you create content that evokes a strong positive emotional response it will help your audience associate that emotion with your brand. Content like this is very memorable and if you can make people feel something by posting an image, text or a video, this can really help in building your brand and creating powerful associations. Evoking any of the primary emotions be it surprise, joy, fear, sadness, anger or disgust is a certain way to get people sharing your content.

3. Educational content

Posting informative content about your subject is invaluable, this will help you to stand out as a thought leader and expert in your field. If your content is valuable and useful then your followers are likely to keep coming back for more and are likely to share your content too. Remember your audience are also looking to find and share valuable content with their friends and customers and will want to be associated with any compelling content you create.

4. Informative

This could be about letting your followers know about something that is happening, like a Webinar, a trade show or an event in the area, or a special offer, or any information that will be of use or value to them.

5. Entertaining/amusing content

Social media is all about being social and having fun, people love sharing funny stuff. Even if you did not create it yourself but you think it is going to appeal to your target audience then share it. The aim here is to amuse and entertain your audience, humor is a winner all round and not only does humor break down barriers it is also more likely to be liked and shared.

6. Seasonal Content

Posting content relating to important holidays and annual celebrations is a really good way to stay connected with your audience. If you have an international audience then being aware of their holidays and religious celebrations will go a long way to building relationships.

7. Inspiring and motivational content

The truth is everyone has a bad day sometimes and needs a little bit of motivation or cheering up. A motivational quote will help to lift your audience and can really help to connect with them. If you know what your audience wants, what they aspire to and what their frustrations are, then it is likely that you will be able to motivate them by posting content which inspires them. These types of post are also very shareable especially if put together with a colorful and inspiring image like a cartoon or photo.

8. Employee and behind the scenes content

If you have news about your employees and the great things they are doing then post it. Maybe they have been involved in a fundraiser or they have won an employee of the month award. Giving your audience a behind the scenes view of your business helps to keep your business and brand looking real and authentic and adds human interest.

9. Customer Content

Having a member of the month or including news or content about a customer's business is a great way to spark interest in your posts. Sharing a customer's content not only shows you value your audience but can also encourage them to do the same. If you are B2B you could also invite your audience to network and let them share their page on your page once a month or once a week. This is a great way to offer them value, it also creates loyalty, keeps your page in their mind and keeps them coming back again and again to visit your page.

10. Shared Content

Whilst it's great to post most of your own content, don't be afraid to share other peoples content as long as it is relevant. The more valuable content you share, the more valuable you will become to your audience and the more likely they will keep coming back for more. Sharing content is also incredibly important in building relationships with your followers, they are going to be far more open to your brand if you are supporting their's.

11. Statistics

People love statistics which relate to their niche. If your business is B2B then posting statistics can gain a great deal of interest especially if they are displayed in a visually appealing way, for instance with an infographic or graph. These are often shared if they are translated into a useful tip for your followers.

12. Questions

Asking questions about subjects that your audience may be interested in is a great way to encourage comments, interaction and community. People love to share their opinions and thoughts and they love the opportunity to communicate, contribute and be heard. Even if you are posting an image or video it's good practice to ask a question.

13. Top Ten lists

People love lists about who or what is top or best. Lists spark interest and this is most probably because people like to compare their choices and judgement with others. Some may like to see that their opinions match others and feel they are right in that choice or others may feel comforted by the fact their choices are not the same and they are unique.

14. Controversial

Posting a controversial statement can spark great conversation and interaction, remember people love to voice their opinions, have an input and be heard. It may be a good idea to stay out of the discussion here as you do not want to lose followers and you need to be sensitive to your audience in order not to upset them so be careful with what topics you pick.

15. Special offers

Social media is a great way to get the message out about the special offers you have running, but you will need to be careful not to post them too often or they just appear like advertising and bad noise in your audience's news feed. You need to make sure that what you are offering is of real value, that it is exclusive to your followers and you are set a deadline to redeem the offer.

16. Contests

Running a contest is a great way to generate leads and widen your reach on LinkedIn. If you want to use LinkedIn to run a competition you will need to create a Landing page outside LinkedIn to house your rules and entry details. It is very important for you to look into the rules governing contests in your state or country, often using a third party application to run your competition can be a very good idea.

17. Member feedback

Asking your followers their advice, or for feedback on a new product is a great way to create engagement and also makes your audience feel they are valued.

18. Tips and tricks

Offering a weekly or daily 'Top Tip' can keep your audience hooked and returning again and again for the latest information and are a great way to increase loyalty and build relationships. Tips can be anything from instructions on how to do something to information about a useful app.

19. News and current events

Offering information about the latest news in your area or industry is a certain way to keep people interested and sharing your content. Being current and up to date with local news is really useful to your audience and it keeps your business looking fresh and cutting edge. To keep up to date with news, subscribe to news feeds and blogs that offer news on your industry or your local area.

20. Negative content

People always like to hear about what not to do, for example: 'Ten Things not to do on a first date' or 'Ten things not to say in a job interview', the list of possibilities for this type of post are endless and can create a great deal of amusement and interest.

21. Music if you are a musician

If you are a band and want to promote your music then there is no better way to promote your material than by posting links to your music and videos on LinkedIn.

22. Q & A live session

You can host a live question and answers session on your page. This is a really good way to create conversation and engagement. It also creates a professional, informative and caring image. You can do this by allotting and promoting a specific time for followers to post their questions in the comment section of your LinkedIn update. Or you could choose to ask them to post their questions and give them a day when you will be answering them, this way you get more time to research if you need to. In both cases it's a good idea to post an image promoting the session.

23. Broadcast live

By using an application called Livestream you can broadcast any live event to almost any social destination. You can also watch, like and share any event that may be of interest to your audience.

24. Fill in the blanks posts

Getting your audience involved with your content is a very powerful way of creating engagement. 'Fill in the blank' posts can be a way of creating engagement and conversation, for example:

I love going to _____ on my holidays because…

My monday morning must have _____

I always take _____ on holiday.

25. Caption this

Posting a photo and then asking your audience to caption it is a really effective and light hearted way to drive engagement and you could also turn this into a contest. You can use images from stock photo sites or sites like Flickr Creative Commons, make sure to choose images that will provoke interest and are humorous or inspiring.

26. Case studies

Case studies are a really effective way to demonstrate how something works with real examples. You can use case studies to show how your customers have used your products or services to benefit them in some way. You can also use them to demonstrate a principle or method of doing something by using other businesses as examples.

27. Internet Memes

Meme comes from the greek word 'mimema' which means something imitated. An internet meme is a style, action or idea which spreads virally across the internet. They can take the form of images, videos or hashtags. There are plenty of tools and apps out there to help you create memes such as www.memegen.com and imgur.com which are popular ones.

28. Like versus share votes

This involves combining two competing images in one post and then asking your audience to vote for which image they prefer by liking or sharing. This is a really quick way to expand your reach and get your brand out there. To be successful at this you really need to have good subject and one that most people identify with.

29. Your blog

Creating regular blog posts is a very effective way of getting your followers onto your website or blog. Make sure you always include an image to provoke interest and asking a question can create intrigue and curiosity.

30. Greetings

Simply posting an attractive image or a wishing your followers good morning, good night or to enjoy their weekend will go a long way in breaking the ice and building relationships. These types of posts help to make positive associations with your brand.

31. Testimonials

You may have received a review on your website or Google Places or simply a message from someone. Posting about good things that people write or say about you contributes to your social proof and builds trust. Remember people will believe more about what others say about your business than what you as the owner says about it.

THE DIFFERENT TYPES OF MEDIA AVAILABLE

In order to create the best experience for you followers and connections you are going to need to create a good balance of content using the different variety of posts available to you. LinkedIn offers you the opportunity to post text, images and links to SlideShare presentations, videos, blog posts and websites.

Images

'A picture paints a thousand words'

If you are already a LinkedIn user then you probably know that an image grabs your attention more than any other post in your newsfeed. This is because most of us are visually wired and most of us can identify with an image much more quickly than text. Statistics prove that pictures get more comments, shares and likes than any other post and that your followers are far more likely to click on a link to a website or blog or to watch a video if your post contains a picture. Even though you cannot post images on your personal profile, you can post them on your company page and then share them on your profile. If you are posting a link to your blog or an article on your website then make sure you include a compelling image, you are far more likely to gain interest this way. Images not only get shared more they also have huge viral potential, get remembered and also create an emotional connection with your audience.

You don't have to be an expert photographer, you can find images from stock photos and also free sites like flickr (be careful to check the licence and what you are allowed to do with the images in terms of changing or adding text, etc.) Adding text can be achieved by using photoshop or other online graphic design apps which are available online and are easy to use like www.picmonkey.com . Some stock photo sites also offer you the functionality to add effects and text to your images.

Videos

As with images, video is highly shareable, has a huge viral potential and increases engagement. People love videos and a good video can offer a huge amount of entertainment, make learning more interesting, more fun and easier to understand. Videos are also great at helping to build relationships, trust and rapport with your audience and there really is no better way of introducing yourself and building a personal connection with your audience than with video.

The type of videos you should be posting on LinkedIn are educational, informative and entertaining and while there is room for the occasional product video these really belong on your website or blog.

Text

Whether you are posting a text only post, an image or a video, it is likely that you will be including some text to either introduce or describe your post. As a general rule of thumb the shorter you keep it the more engagement you will receive. Whilst that is not to say that longer posts are unsuccessful, generally speaking it is best to keep the majority of your posts shorter.

While images are definitely more effective and receive higher engagement there is still room for text only images to deliver the occasional tip, a greeting or to ask a question.

LinkedIn Long-Form-Posts

Soon to be available to all LinkedIn members long form posts which allow you to create long posts on LinkedIn's publishing platform and share them with your network. You can add photos and videos and edit and delete your posts as and when you require. If your posts are shared by your network they can reach a wider audience and anyone outside your network can follow you from your post and receive your updates too.

Blog posts

According to research 70% of consumers click through to a website from a retail blog. Blogs are nearly essential now for any business who wants to get found on the internet and social media is another very effective tool to drive traffic to your blog. If you do not have a blog then you need to seriously consider creating one. There are numerous free and paid blogging platforms available and there is a whole chapter covering this subject later on in the book.

Infographics and diagrams

Infographics provide a fascinating way to present statistical information. They are engaging, very shareable, have huge viral potential and make figures look far more interesting and are easier to understand than a list of numbers. People love statistical information relating to their interest because it helps to confirm or affirm what they already may believe and helps to give them more confidence in what they are doing or selling. You do not have to be an expert graphic designer to create infographics there are numerous applications available on the web which can help you create infographics.

Podcasts

Podcasting is a type of digital media usually comprising a series of audio, radio or video files. You can subscribe to podcasts as you can to blogs and newsletters. For example if you download a podcast on itunes, every time the author produces a new one, itunes will automatically download it. As with video podcasts are effective at helping to build trust with the listener and can also help to make you stand out as an authority or influencer in your niche. They also encourage customer loyalty if they are produced on a weekly or very regular basis and are incredibly handy for people who are on the go and want to listen while travelling to work or on the way to a meeting. LinkedIn is to the ideal place to promote your podcast.

Cartoons

Cartoons work very well with humor and relatable content. Posting cartoons that your audience can relate to can help demonstrate that you understand and identify with them, they are a great ice breaker and highly shareable as well. Once shared they are very likely to appeal to more of your target audience and are a great way to widen your reach. If you have an idea for a cartoon and you are not an artist them there are sites like Fiverr.com that offer creative services at very reasonable prices.

SlideShare

SlideShare is primarily a slide sharing site but you can upload powerpoint, keynote, pdf and open office presentations. SlideShare is a great way to communicate your message and very straight forward and easy to use. It is also another way to get your content rated, commented on and shared and your presentations can be embedded into LinkedIn and your website or blog.

Ebooks & PDF Documents

Turning your content into an ebook is a great way to present your content and offering a free ebook is a really good way to build your opt-in lists and gives your reader something of great value.

Webinars

A Webinar is like an interactive online conference or workshop. Webinars are a great way of interacting with your audience and building relationships. They can be used for presenting and training, selling a programme or course, or answering questions from your audience. They can be saved and listened to at a later date for anyone who could not make the date and time. Using LinkedIn to announce your Webinar is a very effective way to promote your online event and get people to sign up.

Tips for Posting on LinkedIn

Post frequently

The number of posts you create will depend on the amount of valuable content you have, but anything between 1-5 times per day is optimal. According to LinkedIn, statistical information updates which are posted in the morning receive up to 45% more engagement.

Headlines and Descriptions

Make sure your headlines are attention grabbing and your descriptions are brief and to the point. Try and include a question or a call to action wherever possible.

Questions

People are on LinkedIn to interact and get noticed so they will interact with other members if given the opportunity. One of the best ways to encourage this interaction is through asking questions. These could be questions relating to business or other interests. Questions are great ice breakers, spark conversation and increase engagement. Whether posting an image, video or text, asking a question will provoke discussion and engagement.

Include a Link

Wherever possible include a link to an external blog, website or document.

Include an image

Try and include a compelling image in your post wherever possible. Images attract more attention and interest than plain text and are more likely to get shared and commented on.

Pin to top

LinkedIn allows you to highlight your most important updates at the top of your page. It's a good idea to put your most popular post here or a post regarding your latest offer, promotion or event that you want to promote.

Is this relevant to my audience?
Every time you post anything ask yourself this question and if the answer is no then don't post it.

Sponsored updates
To increase your reach and to promote specific offers or events use sponsored updates.

Schedule posts
Hootsuite and Buffer allows you post directly to your personal profile and your company page from your dashboard.

Follow your company page
Make sure you add yourself as a follower of your company page so you can share updates on your personal profile.

BENEFIT FROM LINKEDIN'S PUBLISHING PLATFORM
As a member you will be shortly able to publish long-form-posts on LinkedIn's publishing platform. LinkedIn are slowly rolling out the new publishing platform to all its members. This does not mean that you become a LinkedIn influencer but your post will become part of your professional profile and can be viewed in the posts section of your profile. You can share your posts with your connections and they can like, comment and share your posts which will help to distribute your post beyond your network. If other members outside your network see your post they can also choose to follow you from your long form post and receive updates when you publish another post. Long-form-posts are public and are searchable both on and off LinkedIn so even non members will be able to see you posts.

To create a long-form-post simply go to your 'Share an update' box and then click the pencil icon and it will take you to the publishing tool. You can add links, visuals and embed videos. Once your post has been created you can edit it or delete it if you wish, and you can view stats for your long form post as well.

To view your posts simply click 'Profile' at the top of your page and then find the 'Posts' section and then click any of your posts and then click 'See your posts and stats'. You can choose to hide or flag any abusive comments.

Long-form-posts are all about sharing your professional expertise. If you want your posts to get distributed beyond your network then you need to stay away from promotional posts and keep your posts centred around creating value for your audience. LinkedIn determines quality of posts by their algorithm and other factors and some high quality posts may get tagged and distributed through LinkedIn Pulse and emails but there is no guarantee of this.

Here are some tips for creating long-form-posts

- Keep your posts relevant to your expertise and around subjects that your target audience are interested in.

- Share your posts on other networks, such as Twitter, Facebook and Google+, You can automatically share with Twitter by checking the Twitter icon on the publishing tool.

- Share your posts with relevant LinkedIn Groups.

- Publish frequently.

- Engage on the platform by liking and commenting on other member posts.

- Include an image wherever possible to add to the visual experience.

- Ask a question at the end of your post to encourage discussion and engagement.

- Grow your following so you can increase your reach.

Chapter Four

LinkedIn Groups

LinkedIn Groups offer a place for their members who are in the same industry or niche to share information, share content, make connections, network and post job vacancies. As a member of LinkedIn you can join up to 50 groups at one time and after that you would have to withdraw from one in order to join another. However, even though you can join up to 50 groups this may spread you very thin and being very active in a just few groups maybe a better use of your resources than trying to participate in many.

LinkedIn Groups offer you the opportunity to:

- Connect and interact with other members.
- Join discussions.
- Share your knowledge and build authority, influence and credibility.
- Become a top influencer.
- Source information and increase your knowledge.
- Expand your reach and find followers for your company page, your website or blog. However LinkedIn Groups should not be used to blatantly promote your product or service.

Joining a Group

One of the advantages of joining a group is that members appear in the search results of that group. So if you go to a group and click the number stating how many members the groups has you can see whether any of your connections are already members.

To find groups simply click 'Interests' on the top menu of your profile and then click 'Groups' on the drop down menu. You will then be able to search groups under keywords that you enter and start filtering and viewing results. You can view 'Open Groups' without joining but you can only view content of 'member only groups' after you have joined.

There are over a million groups on LinkedIn so you can afford to be selective when choosing the groups you want to join. Before joining, you need to work out what your goals are, are they to build connections and relationships or to gain knowledge from key influencers or to establish yourself as a thought leader? If your main goal is to drive traffic to a website or blog then you need to find groups that allow you to post links.

When searching for groups you can view a description of each group together with the group statistics which include the number of members and the number of discussions and comments that have been made. Joining smaller, lively groups with lots of interaction may be more advantageous than joining larger ones with little activity, this is where quality can sometimes outweigh quantity. The demographics are important too, joining a group when the majority of its members are international maybe a complete waste of time for you if you are a local business. Viewing the groups activity feed will help you see whether the group relevant to you or not and whether you think you could be able to contribute in some way.

Once you have made your selection and joined you can then introduce yourself and start commenting and joining in with discussions. If you want to build influence then it is important to stay active and engage with members and contribute to discussions. LinkedIn keeps track of the interaction that takes place in groups and appoints 'The Top Influencers of the week'. You can view 'The Top Influencers' at the top right of the group page, these are the people who have contributed and participated in discussions and liked and commented the most. This is a huge opportunity for exposure for you and your brand if you are appointed.

LinkedIn Discussions

LinkedIn discussions are a great way to communicate with others in your niche and build connections. To start a discussion simply hit the 'Discussion' link at the top and add the title for your discussion and a description. You can add an article or ask a question. You can also post relevant content with a link to your company page, website or blog and you can post this to your group and Twitter if you like. Your group may also have a special section for adding promotions and jobs.

You can participate in discussions by liking and commenting and you can also follow a particular discussion. You can choose to be notified by email whenever anyone comments on that particular discussion.

Starting a poll

LinkedIn allows you to start a poll which is an effective method of driving engagement and shows that you are interested in people's opinions rather than just self promotion. To start a poll simply click 'Discussions' and then click the poll icon for when your poll expires.

Promotions

If the group allows, you can post promotions which are visible to the group for up to 14 days.

Group Settings

When you click on the 'i' button on the top right of the group you can find out all about the group and also you can manage your settings. Here you can also manage whether you want an email to be sent to you for every activity within the group or whether or not you want to allow other members to send you messages.

Member only groups

Member only groups have a padlock displayed next to the group name and are groups that can only be seen by other members. They can only be seen by the group members and they will not appear in search.People often create closed groups for their customers and use them as a forum.

Don't get SWAM'ed

SWAM stands for 'Site Wide Auto Moderation'. If you are SWAM'ed it means that all your posts and comments are not posted automatically and have to be approved by the group owner before it can be made visible. This can happen if a group owner marks your posts as 'requires moderation' or you get blocked from a group. LinkedIn have introduced this to limit the abuse of groups on the platform.

If you are SWAM'ed then your posting privileges will be limited across all LinkedIn groups and not just the group where you were SWAM'ed. Make sure you read the rules for all the groups you join and then adhere to those rules. If you do get SWAM'ed the only thing you can do is write to the group owner or write to LinkedIn customer support asking them to reconsider.

THE BENEFITS FOR STARTING YOUR OWN GROUP

Creating your own group on LinkedIn has a multitude of benefits particularly if you are B2B. Here are some of the benefits you can enjoy by creating your own group on LinkedIn:

Raises your profile

As a group creator your name will be clearly featured as the owner of the group and running a successful group will help you to be considered as a thought leader. The more you contribute to your group by interacting and offering valuable content the more you will build your credibility and be considered as an expert in your niche.

Lets you send weekly emails to your members

As a group creator you can send emails to your members every week. This is a great opportunity to gain attention by sending your members the links to your top quality content relating to the group subject.

Drives traffic to your website or blog

You can drive traffic in a few ways:

- Adding your URL to the group profile is great exposure as most people will click on this link when deciding whether or not to join the group.
- Include your URL in the groups welcome message.
- Include your URL when sending valuable content to your members once a week.
- By creating discussions within the group and including your URL.

Creates community

Many people love to be part of a community and join other like minded people in discussions. If you are the creator of a thriving LinkedIn group and community by bringing people together and helping them make connections you will be looked on very favourably by your members. In turn this will create trust and good will towards you and your brand.

Expands your personal network

Creating a group is a great way to build connections. If your group is active then members are going to want to connect with you because you are the authority and you are likely to receive numerous invitations to connect on LinkedIn.

Generates leads and sales

When you send out your initial welcome email and thank members for joining you can include details and benefits of joining the group and also a brief background and description of yourself and your business. You could also invite them to join your newsletter or invite them to connect on other social networks.

BEFORE YOU CREATE A GROUP ON LINKEDIN

Actually creating a group is very straight forward, however before you going ahead and create one you should realize that growing and managing a successful takes huge commitment and can be quite extremely time consuming. Here are some things you need to do and take into consideration before creating a group on LinkedIn:

Join other groups.

Joining and involving yourself in groups which are managed by others is a great way of getting to know how groups work. By joining popular and active groups you will see what the group administrators are doing to make it so successful and see how you can adapt ideas to your group to bring value to your members.

Consider your resources

Do you have the resources required to manage and administer an active group? As well as posting discussions and creating content you will also need to approve members and regularly monitor the group so you do not get spammers and irrelevant discussions being posted by others. You may need to allocate a number of staff members to administer the group. If the group is not managed properly this will actually work against your brand.

Define and set your goals

You will need to look closely at your overall marketing goals for your business and see whether creating a group is the best way of achieving those goals in comparison to other methods. The topic needs to be specific but also wide enough to allow for unlimited content creation and discussion. There is huge amount of competition out there and in order to attract high quality members then it needs to be really original. When choosing your topic or subject you will need to consider the following:

- What subjects are going to offer your target audience the most value?
- What subjects are going to help you best achieve your goals?
- Are there other groups about this subject? And if so, is there room to create another group and can you bring more value than the current group/groups?
- How you can make your group unique?

Create an excellent plan

When your group is running you will need to aim to post at least one discussion per week with related content and you will need to decide on whether you are going to allow others to post discussions and content or just comment. You will also need to plan the announcements that you are going to send out once a week, the content you are going to include and work out how you are going to generate leads from these announcements without being too self promotional.

Build a landing page or website for your group

Creating a landing page about your group on your website or even creating a website for your group is essential. This way you can offer members something of value in return for their name and email addresses. Even though you are permitted to send out an announcement to your group members every week you will not have access to their email addresses. Having these email contacts will give you control over how you can connect with your members.

Search Groups

Before creating your group, search the groups section to see how other groups are listed and what makes certain groups stand out. Make sure you use the search feature at the top of your homepage as opposed to the group directory, this way you will be able to search by type and see the way the groups are listed. The group directory will only show you groups listed alphabetically.

CREATING A GROUP ON LINKEDIN

To create your group simply click **'Interests'** then select **'Groups'** and then **'Create a group'** Here are some tips for creating your group:

Your Group Logo

You can create your own logo for the group and you can upload a PNG, JPEG or GIF image. The logo will appear as a thumbnail beside the group name, on the group search page and on the top right of the actual group page. When creating your custom logo try and keep it in line with your corporate branding and, as it is quite small try, and make it as striking as possible without too much text.

Your group name

Your group name will be displayed in bold together with your summary and logo in the search results page. Your group name is very important and offers you the opportunity to be unique and also to get found within LinkedIn. You will need to consider what keywords your target audience are going to be searching for when looking to join a group, these key words are what are going to drive your results in the LinkedIn search so you will need to try and include these in your name. Be careful not to use a famous name or a trade mark or your name will be taken away from you and you could open yourself up to a legal headache.

Select your group type

You are given seven group type options to choose from; alumni, corporate group, conference group, networking group, non profit group, professional group and other.

Group Summary

When anyone searches for your group your summary will appear in the Groups directory along with your group name and logo. Only about 140 characters of your summary will be displayed so you will need to be brief and to the point and need to include, the purpose of the group, the name of your target audience and the benefits of joining the group.

Description

Your description is featured on your group profile page which can be accessed by clicking on the 'i' on the top left of your group. You need to make it very clear what the group is for, what the main focus of the group is, and the benefits your group is going to offer your members when they join. Including keywords from your niche will also help you to be found within search, this is also a good place to display your group rules.

Website URL

One of your main goals for creating a group is going be to generate leads. LinkedIn groups offer you, as a group owner, the perfect opportunity to build your opt-in list and capture leads with a view to converting your group members into customers. To do this you will need to create a landing page for your group with an offer to tempt members to join your opt-in. You can also use this landing page as your group website and include your blog and any online or offline events you wish to promote.

Membership

You will then be asked whether you want to offer members '**Auto-Join**' or '**Request to Join**' Asking members to 'Request to Join' can make your group appear more valuable, make it more exclusive and help control spam. However you will need to consider whether you have the resources to administer this. You will also be offered options about whether or not members can invite other members, whether they are allowed to display their logo and whether you want your group to be featured in the group directory.

Language

Select your language.

Location

You can select a particular geographic location for your group.

Twitter announcement

If you tick this box then your group will be announced on the twitter account which is linked to your LinkedIn profile.

Agreement

Read the terms of service and then check the box.

Create group

You will be offered the option to 'Create an Open Group' or a 'Create a Members-Only Group'. Creating an open group will make your group more visible and easier to promote. Members only groups only allow other members to see the content.

When you have created your group you will automatically be offered the opportunity to send out invitations to your connections and contacts and you can also upload a contact file as well. It is best to skip this section and give yourself some time to familiarise yourself with the group admin panel, learn about the features and possibilities available and add some content before sending out invitations.

GETTING YOUR GROUP READY TO LAUNCH

When you arrive at your group page you can set up and manage everything about your group in the admin panel under the **'Manage'** tab.

Creating custom emails

As the group manager or owner you can set up your own custom emails, simply click on 'Templates' and you will be offered the following:
- Request to Join message
- Welcome Message
- Decline Message
- Decline and Block Message

Group Rules

As the owner of your group you can create your own group rules. You can add rules in the '**admin panel**' and they will be displayed under the 'i' tab but it is also a good idea to put them in your description and add them to the welcome email you will send to your new group members. This way as many people get to see the rules as possible. Many groups are a target for spammers and it is easily visible when a group is badly managed.

It is good practice to first write an introduction about what the group is about, the aims of group, the benefits of the group, why you are creating rules, and also what types of actions and content will be welcomed in your group. Here are some examples of rules you may wish to make:

No spam, self promotion or direct sales pitches are allowed. Members will be immediately removed from the group if these practices are carried out.

- **No Off Topic Posts** All posts made must be related to the 'Subject' of the group. Any posts which are not will be deleted.

- **No Spamming** Please do not post solicitations about your product or service. Any post like this will be deleted.

- **Job Posts** Please post job postings under the 'Jobs' tab

- **Politics and Religion** No religious or political discussions are allowed.

- **No Inappropriate Postings and comments** No threatening, abusive, discriminatory or harassing comments.

Group Settings

In Group settings you can manage your permissions about what your members are allowed and not allowed to post. Here you can manage who can post discussions, polls, jobs and promotions and whether or not you are going to screen discussions posted by others before approving their inclusions.

Creating niche sub groups

Setting up niche sub groups is a great way to broaden your base and attract new people, however only do this if you have the resources available as it's time consuming enough to run the main group. Sub groups are a great way to offer your members value by giving them the opportunity to promote their product or service and also keeps them from self promoting on the main discussions page.

MANAGING YOUR GROUP

To build a high quality, active and engaged group you will need to do the following:

Promote your group

A group is no good without members and you will need to commit to spending time building your group membership to get the momentum going. The next section of this chapter is dedicated to the subject of how to build your group membership.

Post a weekly discussion

You will need to regularly post discussions in your group to create interest. Your discussions need to be about something on topic and about something that your audience relates to and that will provoke discussion. Discussions that provoke an emotional feeling can be very effective. Joining other groups is a very useful way of finding ideas for discussions and you may find a pattern in what works and what does not.

You can also allow your members to post their blogs if related to the subject. LinkedIn Group Digest emails go out daily or weekly to members depending on the activity of the group. The names of people who have created discussions are included in this email, so you want to make sure your name is turning up in that email as often as possible.

You can further promote your discussions by featuring your discussions as the managers choice. To do this click on the title of the discussion and then click on '**Add to Manager's choice**' underneath the profile picture. You can select up to ten discussions to add to the manager's choice and they can be discussions created by any member depending on whether your group allows its members to post discussions. The manager's choice will displayed at the top of your group page, on the carousel and in the group digest emails.

Welcome message

Automatically send your members a welcome email and ask them to introduce themselves to encourage engagement.

Send out a weekly announcement

As a group manager or owner you can send out one announcement to your group per week, to your members who have chosen to receive emails. You can include a subject up to 200 characters and a message of up to 4000 characters with URL's. Sending out weekly announcements to your group is proven to be a great way to boost your lead generation if done correctly. You need to make sure you create an attention grabbing headline and share really useful content and encourage members to sign up to your opt-in by offering them a free ebook, or invite them to attend an online event. Announcements are also automatically posted as a featured discussion within the group so you can comment and add to the discussion. Make sure you send a test one to yourself first which will give you an idea of how it will appear to your audience.

Post a weekly question

Asking open questions is a great way to create interest and encourage comments and discussion.

Comment on discussions

Commenting and engaging with group members will show your members you appreciate their input and will make them feel valued and will encourage them to contribute again.

Create LinkedIn polls

Polls create a quick and easy way for people to engage and create conversation and interest. You need to make sure you create a question that your audience will be passionate about. You can specify up to five answer choices for your poll. Simply click on the poll icon to the right of the activity bar and complete the short form.

Encourage active users

Make sure you encourage active users by quoting them and drawing attention to them and sharing their content.

Monitor posts

You will need to monitor posts and discussions for spam and misuse. Your group will lose value if it is left open to spam and self promotion from members.

PROMOTING YOUR GROUP

Invite your connections or contacts

To send invitations from within the admin panel simply click on **'Manage'** then **'Send Invitations'** on the left menu. You can also design your own email with your group branding and send it to your contacts. Make sure you outline the benefits of your group and what you will be offering.

Allow group members to send out invitations

You can allow your members to send out invitations to join your groups by choosing the option **'Allow members to invite others to join this group'** in Group Settings'

Announce on your personal profile and your company page

Announce your group creation on your company page with an image and share on your personal profile too.

Promote your group on your blog or website

There is no plugin for this but writing an article about your group with the group logo and a clear invitation to join your group on LinkedIn can be an effective way to promote your group to new members.

Invite Influential People

Invite the most influential people in your niche to join your group.

Engage in other groups

By joining other groups and contributing with rich and valuable content you will increase the likelihood of people visiting your profile and joining your group. This is a very powerful way of encouraging people to join your group without being too self promotional.

Announce your groups on other social media platforms

Your followers on other networks will probably feel honoured to be invited to join your group on LinkedIn. Make sure you post a compelling image.

Make it part of your connection process

When people send you an invitation to connect, send them a message with an invitation to your LinkedIn group and the benefits of joining your group.

Add to your email signature

Add your group name, logo and description to your email signature.

Be a good host

Be a good host by involving yourself in discussions, helping people and managing the group well.

CHAPTER FIVE

ADVERTISING ON LINKEDIN

WITH ITS HIGH quality audience made up of professionals, senior executives, entrepreneurs, business owners and decision makers LinkedIn is a powerful platform for advertising and reaching your exact target audience. You can develop highly targeted campaigns and reach professional audiences in particular industries, companies and positions and you can tailor make your adverts to those audiences. LinkedIn also allows you to analyze your results so that you can continually make improvements to your campaigns. When people are using LinkedIn they are of a business mindset, and sales conversions can be higher than on any other social network.

Before launching into your first campaign you will need to define your goals. These could be to increase your reach past your current followers on your company page, to drive traffic to your website or blog or generate leads for conversion. You will also need to work out what your expectations are, and the sort of result you hope to achieve.

To drive a successful campaign you will need to create a customized landing page or a page on your website where your audience can take some kind of action. You may want them to join your opt-in, or complete a form in exchange for some valuable content in the form of an ebook, or maybe you have a special offer you would like audience to take up. Whatever it is you need to make sure you have a plan of action to catch these prospects rather than just sending them to a page where they may continue to another website never to be seen again.

Creating your campaign

LinkedIn adverts can be found throughout the LinkedIn platform, and up to three text, image or video adverts can be seen on profile pages, home pages, inbox, search results and groups.

To start simply click **'Business Services'** on the top right of your profile and then click **'Advertise'** and then **'Get Started'** on the next page. You can choose to either **'Create an advert'** or **'Sponsor update'** .

Creating your advert

With a Linkedin advert you can target your audience with either text, an image or a video advert. You can create up to 15 advert variations per campaign so you can test different headlines, descriptions, images and different calls to action and see which ones are the most effective. Before you go ahead and create your adverts, it's a good idea to view adverts on LinkedIn and see which ones catch your eye and grab your attention.

- **Campaign name** The first thing you will need to do is choose your campaign name. Creating a name which relates to the audience you are going to target for this particular campaign will help you when it comes to analysing your results and you will easily be able to pinpoint which campaigns are performing better than others.

- **Select your Media type** You will then be offered the option to choose a basic advert(text and image) or a video advert.

- **Advert Destination** Here you can select whether you want to send your audience to your website or your customized landing page or your company page.

- **Create your headline** You have 25 characters to grab your audiences attention and write a strong, brief and specific headline. This is where you can need to offer something useful to your audience or offer some kind of solution to a common problem your audience may share. It needs to be unique and appeal in some way to the emotions of your audience, sometimes a simple question can work very well.

- **Description** You have 75 characters to compose a message so it needs to be concise, to the point and relevant to the landing page to which you are sending your audience. It's here you need to expand on your headline, add a call to action and give them even more reason to click your advert.

- **Your Image** The maximum size for an image is 50 x 50 pixels and you can either use an image relating to your product or your company logo. The space for the image is very small so your image needs to be a close up shot.

- **Video adverts** Video adverts work exactly the same as text adverts except instead of adding an image you can upload a video. When a user clicks the advert, a 30 second video will play and after the video is complete the user can click through to the URL. Videos allow you to expand on your message and they can inspire, educate and sometimes persuade your audience members more effectively than just an image.

- **Targeting** The next step is to select your target audience and this is where you can utilize the power of LinkedIn and the incredible amount of information they hold about their professional members. You can select your audience by location, company type or company name, job title, school, skills, gender, group and age. As you select your audience the figure on the top right will indicate the number of people you will be targeting. You can get as specific as you like, you can even choose specific company names if you like and LinkedIn will also offer you a pre-selection of categorised companies. Groups are a hugely effective way of targeting your audience because they let you target members through their interests.

- **Campaign Options** Just before you are ready to go live with your adverts you need to choose your campaign options. The great thing about LinkedIn adverts is they are self serve and you are totally in control of your budget. You can turn your campaign on or off whenever you like and increase or decrease your bids depending on your budget. You can choose a daily budget and choose whether you prefer to use CPC (cost per click) or CPM (Cost per 1000 impressions) and LinkedIn will suggest a bid.

- **Lead Collection** Lead collection is a free add on that lets people who have viewed your advert, request contact with you. Members that click on your advert will see a lead collection bar above your website that asks them if they wish you to contact them. You will then get an email that notifies you when you have received the lead and you can subsequently reach out to them with a personal email.

Measuring the effectiveness of your adverts

The dashboard will show you the effectiveness of your adverts. You will be able to see the number of impressions, the number of click through rates and the number of clicks. In order to run an effective campaign your click through rate needs to be at least 0.025% and the more relevant your advert is to your audience the higher your click through rate will be.

CHAPTER SIX

DAY TO DAY ACTIVITY

THERE ARE CERTAIN things that you will need to do on a day to day basis to run your campaign on LinkedIn. It is a good idea to allot a specific amount of time and a particular time of the day to do this. Here are some of the things you will need to do:

Following your customer's LinkedIn

This is important if your customers are business owners themselves. Following their company pages on LinkedIn will go a long way in building relationships. By following you are showing them that you are interested in what they have to say and also helping them to achieve their goals by helping to build their audience.

Showing your audience you value and respect them

If you value and respect your audience they will most probably love, respect and value your business. Be kind, generous, offer as much help and value as possible, reply to their comments and make it obvious that you value them and are listening to them. Don't be afraid to be yourself rather than a stiff brand with no personality.

Everyone is aiming for likes, shares and comments so if you are helping others out by commenting and liking their content it is going to draw attention to your brand and they are more likely to take interest in your content. This is one area where the reciprocation rule works very well on LinkedIn. Engaging with content will also draw attention to you and your brand and you will find that people will click on your name to find out who you are and may want to connect with you. Be friendly to your

audience, be chatty, authentic, genuine and embrace the conversation. All this will all go a long well in building a positive image for your brand and will set you apart from your others who are continually ambushing their audience with self promotion.

Following influencers in your niche

Building relationships with key influencers in your niche is invaluable. Not only can you learn from their content but also these people can have literally thousands of followers, imagine if they follow you back and then share your content!

Dealing with negative comments

Every business at some time will have to deal with negativity from followers. Hopefully if you have a good product then this is not going to happen too often.

You need to deal with complaints as quickly as possible and be as transparent and authentic as possible. The best thing to do is to apologise and say how sorry you are to hear of the inconvenience they have been caused and offer to continue the conversation and deal with their concern by either private message or telephone. You can then deal with this privately, give your customer the full attention they deserve and decide on your next course of action or compensation.

CHAPTER SEVEN

MEASURING AND MONITORING YOUR RESULTS ON LINKEDIN

MEASURING AND MONITORING your results and performance against your original goals and objectives on a continual basis is essential. This is where many businesses go wrong, they carry on aimlessly posting content without checking to see what is working and what is not. Then after 6 months or a year they wonder why their campaign is making no positive difference at all.

When you measure your results you will discover so much information about your campaign which will allow you to steer your campaign in the right direction to achieve those SMART goals and objectives and stop anything that is not working.

When you originally work out your strategies and tactics for your campaign you will be estimating what you need to do to achieve your goals and objectives. However as your campaign runs you will see exactly what you need to do to achieve what you originally set out to do. For example, you may need to increase the amount you spend on advertising to attract new followers, or you may need to change the types of posts you make to increase engagement and reach. Perhaps you need to increase the number of competitions you run to increase the number of opt-in subscribers. This is what it is all about, making your campaign work for you by constantly measuring your success against the goals set and then adjusting your strategies accordingly in order to achieve the results.

LinkedIn Analytics

LinkedIn analytics provides you with metrics and trends for your company page and is split into two sections; Company Updates and Followers.

Company Updates

Company updates has three sections; Updates, Reach and Engagement.

Updates

Shows a table with the most recent updates as follows:

- **Preview.** This shows the first few words of a post.
- **Date.** The date each update was posted.
- **Audience.** Indicates whether the update was sent to followers or targeted.
- **Sponsored.** Shows which campaign or campaigns you have sponsored an update in.
- **Impressions.** The number of times each update has been shown to LinkedIn members.
- **Clicks.** The number of clicks on your company page, logo or your content.
- **Interactions.** The number of times people have liked, commented or shared an update.
- **Engagement %.** The number of interactions, clicks and followers divided by the number of impressions.
- **Followers acquired.** How many followers you gained by promoting an update.

Reach

This displays a graph showing the number of times your updates were seen either organically or through a paid campaign. You can select your preferred date ranges from a drop down menu.

Engagement

This displays a graph showing the number of times members clicked,shared or commented your organic or sponsored content.

- **The Followers Section.** The followers section is divided into five sections and show where your followers are coming from.
- **Type.** A daily record of the total number of LinkedIn members following your page.
- **Organic.** Followers to your page that you gained without advertising
- **Acquired.** Followers you gained on your page through sponsored updates or company follow adverts.
- **Follower Sources.** The top five places where your followers are coming from as a percentage of your total followers. This could be from search, company page, mobile or paid sources.
- **Follower Demographics.** A breakdown of who is following your company page by seniority, industry, job function and company size.
- **Follower Trends.** This shows how your number of followers has changed over time.
- **How you compare.** This shows you the number of followers compared to other companies.

GOOGLE ANALYTICS

If you want to look at more detailed information, for example, the number of people LinkedIn is sending to your website or blog or how many of your connections and followers are converting into customers you will need to use Google Analytics. Google Analytics provides advance reports that let you track the effectiveness of your campaign with the following social reports:

The Overview Report. This report lets you see at a glance how much conversion value is generated from social channels. It compares all conversions with those resulting from social.

The Conversions Report. The conversions report helps you to quantify the value of social and shows conversion rates and the monetary value of conversions that occurred due to referrals from LinkedIn and any of the other social networks. Google Analytics can link visits from LinkedIn with the goals you have chosen and your E-commerce transactions. To do this you will need to configure your goals in Google Analytics which is found under '**Admin**' and then '**Goals**'. Goals in Google Analytics lets you measure how often visitors take or complete a specific action and you can either create goals from the templates offered or create your own custom goals.

The Conversions report can be found in the Standard Reporting tab under Traffic Sources > Social > Conversions.

The Networks Referral Report. The Networks Referral report tells you how many visitors the social networks have referred to your website and shows you how many page views, visits, the duration of the visits and the average number of pages viewed per visit. From this information you can determine which network referred the highest quality of traffic.

Data Hub Activity Report. The Data Hub activity report shows how people are engaging with your site on the social networks. You can see the most recent URL's that were shared, how they were shared and what was said.

Social Plug-in Report. The Social Plug-ins report will show you which articles are being shared and from which network. The Google + 1 button is tracked automatically within Google Analytics but additional technical set up is required for LinkedIn, Twitter and Facebook, you can find out how to do this on the Facebook developers site. Other sites like 'AddThis' or 'ShareThis' offer plug-ins as well which automatically report sharing.

The Social Visitors Flow Report. This report shows you the initial paths that your visitors took from social sites through to your site and where they exited.

OTHER MANAGEMENT TOOLS

Hootsuite

Hootsuite is a social media management dashboard that helps you to manage and measure multiple social networks including LinkedIn. You can manage up to five accounts for free and it is designed so you can listen, engage and manage all from one place. Hootsuite is internet based so there is no need to download any software. Other benefits include scheduled tweets and bulk schedule with a csv file and also has built in analytics so you can measure your progress on multiple social networks.

Buffer

Buffer is an online tool that lets you post to multiple accounts including, LinkedIn, Facebook, Twitter and Google+. Buffer lets you schedule your updates and offers automatic URL shortening and basic analytics. With Buffer you can post on your personal profiles as well as your business pages and also allows you to use bit.ly links so your followers will not know that you are scheduling your tweets. Upgrading allows you to add more accounts and schedule more tweets than the basic free account.

Socialoomph

Socialooph has an impressive list of features to boost your social media productivity. Not only does it help you manage your LinkedIn, Twitter and Facebook accounts, it also can help you schedule posts to your blog as well. There are free and premium options available.

CHAPTER EIGHT

SLIDESHARE

ANY BOOK ABOUT LinkedIn would not be complete without a section on the incredibly powerful platform SlideShare. SlideShare is the worlds largest community for sharing private and public presentations and helps discover people through content and content through people. LinkedIn acquired the professional content sharing platform in 2012 for approximately 119 million in cash and stocks which demonstrates how valuable SlideShare is for business. SlideShare presentations can be viewed on the website, on hand held devices and they can be embedded on websites as well. Files can be uploaded in the following formats, Keynote, Powerpoint, PDF or OpenOffice presentations and it also supports videos and Webinars.

SlideShare boasts over 60 million visitors a month and its community is predominantly professional and educational which makes it an incredibly powerful platform for B2B's. The most tagged words on SlideShare are business, market, social media, trends and research.

BENEFITS OF SLIDESHARE

Features in Google search

SlideShare presentations are very highly ranked in Google's organic search which can offer your business yet another way of being found. All Slideshare presentations are ranked and indexed and information you present on SlideShare is far more likely to be found than on your own site.

Straight business

People are on this site to have their business questions answered and therefore any presentation that solves their business problem or helps them in some way is going to be valued by the audience, and a business product will be well received by this audience.

Website traffic & lead generation

SlideShare can boost traffic to your website or blog and can be highly effective in generating new leads. It can also be a great contributor to your sales funnel to drive traffic and build your opt-in list.

People love images

People do love images and slideshow presentations make learning fun, easy and enjoyable. If you can get your audience to enjoy a learning experience with you, then you are half way there in terms of building a following who may then watch your next presentation.

SlideShare spreads virally

Since anyone can share or embed a SlideShare presentation they often spread virally through social networks such a LinkedIn, Facebook, Google + and Twitter.

Connect with new people

SlideShare enables you to upload your ideas and connect with new people who can often help you with new ideas.

Brand awareness

As with all visual presentations you can publicize and promote your brand by offering relevant and interesting content or answers to questions on topics that your niche are interested in.

Excellent for the camera shy

SlideShare could be describe as the YouTube of slides. If you are not happy about standing in front of the camera, slides are the next best thing in terms of positioning yourself as a thought leader.

Cost effective content creation
Creating slide presentations can be a great deal cheaper than video creation particularly if you are not creating your own videos.

Integration with LinkedIn and Facebook
Both these networks offer integration and LinkedIn will display your most recent presentation on your profile and send out a notification to your network advising them that there is new content.

SlideShare lead capture
For members who sign up for one of the pro versions of SlideShare there is the ability to activate the user friendly lead capture form. This allows you to obtain information about your followers. You can also incorporate a system where you can grow your opt-in list.

Measure your success
Through SlideShare analytics you can measure shares on other social media like LinkedIn, Twitter and Facebook. You can find out which pieces of content are giving you the most views and the location of your viewers. You can also see which sites and blogs are giving you the most views.

Great visibility for your blog
You can upload your blog to SlideShare. If you are new to blogging then this could be a great way to increase the visibility of your blog and get some new followers.

SETTING UP YOUR PROFILE
To set your profile up for SlideShare it is recommended to set up the free version. You can sign up for pro version later if required where there are some excellent extra marketing features.

Make sure your profile name and picture is consistent with your brand. SlideShare offers you the opportunity to select from eight business types and gives you up to 100 characters for your profile name. This is really useful because you can get really descriptive here and you can include your name and business name and use your personal profile picture which would really help to personalize your brand. It is your profile name that is mostly promoted within SlideShare. You can change your business type and profile name anytime but you can not change your username. For best results your image needs to be square 96 X 96 pixels. You can add a really decent keyword rich 'about' section (up to 700 characters) and you can connect your Twitter, LinkedIn and Facebook profiles which will be displayed under your about section. In the sharing section you are also offered the options to automatically share your presentations with Facebook and LinkedIn.

SlideShare also lets you display your Twitter feed on your profile, simply go to the drop down menu on the top right and Click **'View my profile page'** then on the bottom of this page you can add your Twitter handle and you can choose to display your feed. This is another way to increase you reach and gain followers on Twitter too.

The pro version of SlideShare allows you various levels of branding your profile and you can use preset themes or create your own. The level of investment will be dependent on how much you are going to use the platform.

TIPS FOR CREATING GREAT PRESENTATIONS

Sharing your slides on SlideShare is going to increase the reach and put your product or service in front of a new audience of business professionals. If you are creating the right content you will be reaching a highly targeted audience of potential customers. If your presentation is good enough you may even get featured on the home page as one of the top presentations of the day. Before you get started it is essential to spend some time checking out as many SlideShare presentations as possible, and this way you can get a feel for what works and what does not. Here are some top tips for creating great presentations on SlideShare:

Know your goals

Be clear on what your goals are in creating your presentation. If it is generating leads, then it's a good idea to the pro version which will help you capture leads.

The type of presentations

The best presentation will be about subjects that your audience are interested in and that your audience want to know more about. It could be the answer to a question they need answering. Ask yourself if this is going to add value in some way, is it going to be useful, helpful, or make their life easier in some way? As this is a pretty savvy audience you will need to give them specific answers and high quality information.

Grab attention with your headline and first slide

- Write a really good attention grabbing headline . Use headlines like
- Top ten tips to …..
- The tip five things……
- The ultimate guide to……
- The complete guide…..
- Five ways to solve…….
- Seven secrets you should know to………
- Top five ways to make your customers love you.

Your first slide should be highly engaging and visually appealing. By using an extraordinary fact to open your presentation or asking a question like, 'Did you know that……….' is a great way to get your viewers to click the next slide.

Add a description and tags

Write a compelling description which is keyword rich and add highly relevant tags. It's good idea to include your contact information and any other relevant information.

Plan your presentation and your slides

Try and sift out what is really important and keep to one message per slide. Storytelling is one of the best ways to gain engagement and keep your audience's attention throughout the presentation to the end.

Make your slides very visual

People remember images much more easily than text. You can source images from image libraries and also sites like flickr. Make sure you check the image license first before using any images!

Make sure you include keywords in your slides

SlideShare sources text from slides for search purposes and if you include keywords your presentation is more likely to be found on Google.

Do not crowd your slides

Adding too much information will only make them look confusing. Whitespace is a good thing! Generally people can only cope with one piece of information at a time.

Keep a consistent theme

Keep to a few colors and a modern font style. Doing this will make your presentation look far more professional and pleasing to the eye. It is also a good idea to keep your presentation in line with your corporate identity.

Add Audio or video

Adding narration to your presentation can make it much more personal and engaging. You can now add audio via an app on ipad called

9slides.com . You simply import the presentation and then record audio and video on your ipad and then post it back on the web. Video is under utilized on SlideShare and what many people do not realize is that you are very much more likely to get your video viewed on SlideShare than on YouTube, so make sure you always upload your videos to SlideShare. Creating a talking head video for SlideShare is a great way to start a more personal connection with your followers and viewers.

Add a call to action
All links on SlideShare presentations are clickable . You could use paywithatweet.com to help share the word about your presentation or direct your viewers to a free offer and opt-in page or ask them to follow you on SlideShare. If you are uploading a video you could ask them to join your YouTube Channel.

BUILDING YOUR FOLLOWERS ON SLIDESHARE

As with all the social media networks you need to build your targeted audience on SildeShare, here are some tips about how to do this:

Your Website or Blog
Insert the SlideShare button on your website or blog. You can find the badges and the code to embed in your website or blog http://www.slideshare.net/widgets/minibadge
You can also embed your presentations on your website too, which can also help you to grow your followers. Remember the majority of website traffic disappears into the ether so any way you can catch a website visitor and continue a relationship is good.

Connect and comment
The more people you connect, the more likely you will be to find new contacts. The first place to start is with your current contacts, it is likely that some of them will already be on SlideShare and if you follow them they will probably follow you back. As soon as you follow a user they will get an email notification and a link so that they can follow you back.

Commenting on other peoples presentations is a great way to start conversations as well as exposing your account to others who have commented on a presentation.

Advertising

Driving traffic through an Adwords campaign to one of your presentations is a great way to generate and capture leads. You can either include your own call to action at the end of the presentation or embed a SlideShare generation form in the middle or at the end of your presentation.

Share share share

As discussed earlier you can choose to automatically share your presentations with Facebook and Twitter. It is also advisable to share with your other networks like Pinterest. You can also embed your presentation in your linkedIn profile and you can even convert your SlideShow to video and upload it on YouTube for your community there.

Send email to your contacts

You could also advise your contacts by email that you have a profile on SlideShare and direct them to your presentation.

LEAD CAPTURE

As mentioned earlier one huge benefit of SlideShare is that you can actually capture leads and view and download them as a csv. To do this you will need to sign up to the Pro version. You then need to select the pro dashboard and then under the word **Capture** select the words **Turn on.**

When the lead capture is turned on visitors will have the option to submit their information on an easy to complete form which then allows them to receive more information about your products. You will need to give your form a title and a message, so you need to be clear about what your goal is before you do this. The fewer questions you ask the more

442

likely your viewer is to complete the form.

Make Instagram Work For Your Business

Alex Stearn

Table of Contents

CHAPTER ONE

GETTING STARTED ON INSTAGRAM

"INSTAGRAM IS A fast, beautiful and fun way to share your life with friends and family." This is Instagram's official description but is now a whole lot more and with 150 million users and still growing, Instagram has become a powerhouse for marketing any brand and has the ability to connect on an emotional and personal level.

The Instagram mobile app was launched in 2010 solely as a photo sharing site and managed to gain 100 million users in just over 2 years. In June 2013 it incorporated video sharing, allowing its users to create and share video lasting up to 15 seconds. In September 2012 Facebook acquired Instagram with its 13 employees for $1 billion in cash and stocks, it was the largest acquisition deal to date!

Instagram's unique feature is that it confines images to a square shape and allows its users to add digital filters to enhance their photos and then share them with their friends or followers. Users can also share their images on other social networks like Twitter, Facebook, Tumblr and Flickr.

In order to appreciate how Instagram can work for businesses it is essential to understand why Instagram is so successful. The answer is that Instagram has combined the power of the image with the power of social media and the launch of iphone and android devices with their high quality camera and video capability. Users can now easily take pictures of what they love and see, and then share them with their friends and followers and other social networks instantly. Everything about the app is simple, immediate and fun and users can take quite ordinary pictures and quickly make them into something quite remarkable with the filters and effects. The single feed lets users focus on just one single image which they can like and comment on easily.

Instagram has opened up a whole new world of intrigue, discovery and interaction and people get to see things that they would not ordinarily see and connect with people they wouldn't usually connect with. It is no wonder it is now one of the most popular mobile apps in the world.

As one of the fastest growing social networks Instagram is definitely a platform that marketeers and business owners need to pay attention to. Like Pinterest, Instagram has let businesses build their brands through the power of the image and has given businesses the ability to build their brand by connecting with their followers in an emotional and personal way. Some businesses have literally been able to catapult their business from little to well know in no time all. With a constant stream of photos that personalize and represent their business' personality they are now able to connect with their prospective customers in a whole new way by delivering a new visual experience and creating memorable brands. Brands like Top Shop, Gucci ,Virgin, Burberry, Audi, Starbucks, Red Bull and Levi's all realized the power of the Instagram early on and continue to grow their audience and keep them interested with regular uploads.

Images are hugely important to brands for marketing as most people are visually wired and images tend to appeal to the emotions. Beautiful and interesting shots can quickly attract followers, show off a product and help users identify and relate with a brand much more easily than with text. Images are also far more likely to be remembered and by reaching their audience with images in a fun light hearted way, brands can encourage interaction. With behind the scenes images businesses can offer their followers a degree of transparency and authenticity which helps them to build trust. When people feel personally connected with a brand or business they are more likely to purchase from that brand when they are ready to buy.

Instagram's audience is quite young compared with that of Facebook and Twitter and the majority of users are between 18 and 35 so it is the perfect platform for any small business who wants to promote their product or service to this younger audience on a smaller budget. Another really amazing statistic is that over half of its users use Instagram daily. Instagram users just love the platform and it is all very much about soul, emotion and personality. It's not until you start using the platform yourself that you can truly appreciate and experience the thriving and positive communities that are present on Instagram and realize the possibilities for promoting any business.

Like all the social media platforms Instagram takes time, dedication and commitment. Although it is simple to use you still need to find ideas and create a good deal of content to succeed on this platform. Posting photos has to be frequent but not as frequent as other platforms. Once a day is probably optimal but some brands are even successful posting less often.

THE BENEFITS OF INSTAGRAM FOR BUSINESS.

Before you go ahead and set up your account you need decide exactly what you want to gain for your business from Instagram and you need to have a clear idea of what your goals and objectives are. Here is a list of possible benefits and uses of Instagram for business:

To find new customers increase
If you have products which are aimed at the 18 −35 age group then you are most probably going to find them on Instagram. The percentage of male to female users is fairly evenly split. There are exceptions to this in the Far East where the audience is female dominated and in Saudi Arabia where it tends to be male dominated.

To stay in contact with your customers

What better way to stay in contact with your customers and keep them coming back to buy your products than by posting images. It's less intrusive and probably more interesting than email and keeps your product or service fresh in their mind. Also a great way to communicate new products and new offers .

Drive traffic to your website or blog

If you find the right audience for your products and you are posting beautiful images of those products then it is natural that your followers are going to want to check out where they can buy those products. Instagram is the perfect place to showcase your products and get traffic to your website.

To increase overall awareness of your brand

If you know who your audience are and you know their needs and desires you can connect with your audience emotionally by giving them the content they want and then connecting with them emotionally. Once you have been successful doing this you can really succeed in building your brand. Posting photos on a regular basis is a sure way to widen your reach and introduce your brand to new potential customers in a visual way. Once you have new followers you can build their trust by keeping in contact visually and they will be more likely to remember you when they next go to make a purchase.

Market Research

Similar to Pinterest, Instagram can given you huge insight into your target audience and what they like. If you find and follow your audience on Instagram you can discover so much information about them with the images that they post. The more information you find out about our audience the more likely you will be able to give them what they want. When you connect with them emotionally through the type of images that they can identify with then you will be onto a winning formula.

To promote a new product or event

If you have built up a loyal following and you have a new product, book or event to launch what better way to introduce it than with a simple image or sequence of images. Posting images will constantly remind your followers to go take a peep at your website or go along to your event.

Build a stronger social presence on other platforms

Instagram is an excellent place to find more of your audience and can be a great way to build your following on other social networks like Facebook or Twitter.

Build subscribers on your opt-in list

Email is still one of the most powerful tools in converting leads to customers. Instagram can be a very effective way to get followers to join your opt-in as long as you have the right system in place. To do this you need to drive your followers to an external page and offer them an incentive to join your opt-in.

To create viral photos & videos

There is no better way to increase awareness of your brand than by creating viral content. Photos or videos of cute kittens, animals, babies and animals doing funny things are incredibly viral. If you are good at finding and creating images like this, then it could be a very effective way of getting your brand noticed.

To integrate with other social platforms

You may find that Instagram works well with other platforms. You could for instance use Facebook or Twitter to promote a contest on Instagram.

To connect with your audience personally

The Instagram 15 second video functionality is a great way to connect with your followers and make a personal connection without having to worry about high video production costs. You can say and demonstrate a great deal in these bite size videos. Also because your followers know they are only short videos they may be more likely to watch.

SETTING UP YOUR PROFILE

Setting up your Instagram is free, quick and easy. Simply download the app from the app store if you have an iphone, or Google play if you are on Android. You will need to set up your account with a user name and password and then fill out the profile information and upload your profile image with either your logo or a photo of yourself.

Your username is like your signature and needs to clearly represent your brand and be similar to your usernames on other social networks. Try and make your username as short and easy as possible for users to type in and if possible make sure your name is the same as your username.

When it comes to adding your website address you need to remember that your profile is the only place that allows for clickable links and the only place for your website URL. Instagram does not allow for clickable links in posts, comments and captions. You need to take this into consideration when deciding which web page you are going to be sending your followers to.

Having the right bio can really help to increase the number of followers you have and you have 150 characters to tempt them to do this. When creating your bio you need to think about what your audience wants and the sorts of things that they are interested in and then mention these. Try and include keywords from your niche and make it as interesting and punchy as possible. You can also use emoji characters if you want to brighten up your bio, this can work especially well if they tie in with your branding. Having a look at some popular brands and personalities on Instagram can really help to inspire you, you can do this by searching on Instagram or on Google.

You can then connect your account with Facebook, Twitter, Flickr, Tumblr and Foursquare by going to the gear icon on the top right and then 'Share Settings' under preferences which helps you to share your photos to other services and also allows your friends on Facebook to find you. It will also create a news story for anyone who follows you on Facebook and has their Facebook and Instagram account connected. You will then be offered the option to find your Facebook friends and invite any contacts from your phone and then you will be given the opportunity to follow some people on Instagram. Make sure you set your account to public. Your profile is also available now on the web and will show a selection of your recently uploaded photos above your profile photo and bio. To have a look at what some of the big brands have done simply type in www.instagram/username

Starter Images

Even though your Bio is important the images you upload are even more important and this is what is really going to be the deciding factor between whether users follow you or not. The best thing you can do for your business on Instagram is show people why they should get to know you. Before you start building your audience you will need to have uploaded at least 21 images to create some interest and attract users to follow you. The next chapter is dedicated to tips about how and what to post on Instagram.

INSTAGRAM BASICS

Now you have set up your profile you need to familiarise yourself with the app. Here is a quick guide to finding your way around Instagram:

The Instagram menu

The Instagram menu is situated along the bottom and is made up of the profile tab, the camera tab, the explore tab, the home tab and news.

- **The profile tab** The profile tab is the last icon on the bottom menu and is where you can edit your profile and also shows the images you have uploaded, you can either view these in a grid by clicking the grid icon above the images or in a vertical feed by clicking the icon with 3 horizontal lines. Above the images you can also navigate to the 'photo map' which lets others explore where you have taken your photos. This is an option and the 'adding your location' function is turned off by default.

- **The Camera tab** The camera tab is where you can take photos with the Instagram app or share photos from your library.

- **The Explore tab** The Explore tab is where you can find new and interesting people to follow. You can either search by username or by hashtag. You can also view a gallery of images that have been selected by Instagram who have based their selection on the things that the people you follow have liked as well as content that is trending on Instagram.

- **The Home tab** The Home tab shows your feed of images posted by you and your followers. This is where you can like, comment and mention others in the text area under the images.

Like To like an image simply click the heart icon under the image, or double tap the image and your user name will be added to the likers under the image.

Comment To comment simply add your comment to the text space under the image. You can also add emoji icons to comments which can really draw attention to your comments.

To delete a comment you have made on a post simply tap on the comment under the image and then swipe from right to left on your comment and choose to delete.

@Mention The @mention can be used in the comments section on Instagram for replying to comments and thanking. Thanking your followers for commenting is a common and good practice on Instagram, simply add the @ sign before the username. You can also use the @mention to tag or mention users in the caption area of your photo.

Instagram Direct Instagram allows you send images up to 15 users privately which will not appear in the News feed. You can access Instagram Direct by tapping the icon on top right of your home feed.

TAKING PHOTOS ON INSTAGRAM

When using Instagram you can take photos using the Instagram app or select an image from your image library from your iphone or android device.

- To take a picture simply tap the screen to focus and then tap the big blue button.

- To zoom in and crop your image simply move and pinch the photo to whichever scale you want within the frame and then press 'crop' on the top right.

- Click 'next' on the top right and you can then jazz up your photo with any of the 20 filters available.

- When you add a filter you can also add a border (Amaro, Rise and Valencia filters do not have borders.) Simply tap the square above the image to add the border and tap again to take away the border.

- You can also add blur, tear drop and tilt effects to your image and if you want to make your image more vibrant and to bring out details simply tap the sun icon on the right.

- You can add more interest to your image if you like by rotating it, simply tap on the tilted square image on the left.

- Click next and then add your caption and hashtags. You can tag people in the photo if you like by using the @ symbol followed by the username and you can add your photo to the photo map if you wish. If you want to draw someones attention to the image you can @mention them in the caption. In the caption you can add a URL but it will not be clickable.

- You can then select which other networks you want to share with, Facebook, Twitter, Tumblr and/or Flickr. To share with Foursquare you need to add your photo to the map.

- Finally when you are ready click 'Share' and your image will be published to the feed and all the networks you chose to share it with.

CREATING VIDEOS FOR INSTAGRAM

Instagram gives you another way to share your moments with video. You can either create videos using the Instagram video function or upload videos from your phone and then like photos you can add filters which have been created especially for video. The 15 second videos are a great way to show your followers how to do things and also a great way of bringing your brand to life. This is yet another opportunity for brands to reach their audiences and build a connection at minimal cost.

CHAPTER TWO

CREATING THE BEST VISUAL EXPERIENCE FOR YOUR FOLLOWERS

IN ORDER TO build a thriving community of brand advocates and customers who want to interact with your content, sign up to your newsletter and buy your products you are going to need to build trust, loyalty and likeability. The only way to do this is by communicating with them on regular basis in the right way and by consistently delivering the highest possible quality content which will grab their attention, appeal to their interests and add real value to their lives. Once your followers start engaging with your content, you will start building trust and start converting them into customers.

So that you can build a real connection with your followers you will need to think of ideas for images or videos which will appeal to your audience emotionally and get them to make friends with your brand. Your goal here needs to be to inspire and interest your followers, let them have fun and above all make them smile. Your audience want to see the personality of your business and your human side. Even businesses that are considered to be quite dull have been successful in driving interaction with humorous images or videos.

As with any social media you need to have a deep understanding of your audience. Hopefully by the time you have created your profile you will already have a clear idea of who your ideal customer is and what subjects and topics they are interested in. This whole topic about your target audience will be covered in more detail in the chapter about planning, later one.

With the help of sites like Instagram and Pinterest you can find out exactly what makes your audience tick. Never has there been so much opportunity to research what your customers are interested in than with a site like Instagram. You can gain huge insight into what your target audience's interests are and what they like by simply looking at their profiles and seeing what sort of images they are posting and what they are liking and commenting on. Instagram lets you dig even deeper into peoples personalities as users tend to share much more, they share their lives, creativity and feelings, probably more than on any other social network. By visiting the profiles of your target audience you will be able to see what types of images they are uploading, liking and sharing. This information is like gold and will not only help you with marketing and your building brand on Instagram but also on other social media platforms as well.

In this chapter you are going to learn about the different types of post, different types of content and tips on how help you create the best experience for your connections and followers so you can receive the highest engagement. Before you start posting here is a list of questions you should ask yourself about your audience when planning your content:

Who are the audiences you need to connect with?
Are these audiences using Instagram?
Are they following your competition on Instagram?
What are they interested in? What are they posting?
What are they looking for ?
What sort of topics would appeal to them?
What are the problems they have that they need solving?

Your competition on Instagram
You can find out a great deal of information about your target audience

from your competition as well. See what images they are uploading and see what their followers are liking and posting. It maybe they are not doing a great job and you maybe you will see ways you can do it better. It's definitely worthwhile spending as much time as possible researching your competitors.

IDEAS FOR DIFFERENT IMAGES & VIDEOS

You may be wondering how you are going to consistently produce and deliver a stream of compelling images to your audience on a regular basis for the foreseeable future. However once you have picked your topic of interest you will surprised how one idea will lead to another and you will be able to produce numerous images. When you post your images your followers will see these updates on their homepage feed and they can like and comment on your images.

Unless you are an artist or a fashion brand it is unlikely that your followers are going to want to see a constant stream of product pictures, this would be incredibly boring and will not help you to promote your brand or get the following you need for success on this platform. In order to build a real connection with your followers you will need to think of ideas for images or videos which will appeal to your audience emotionally and get them to make friends with your brand. Your goal here needs to be to inspire and interest your followers, let them have fun and above all make them smile. Your audience want to see the personality of your business and your human side. Even businesses that are considered to be quite dull have been successful in driving interaction with humorous images or videos. With Instagram your uploads need to offer a variety of images to spark interaction and keep your followers interested and engaged. It really is advisable to follow some top brands who are doing it right on Instagram simply go to http://50.nitrogr.am/ and you can see the top 50 brands. Here are some ideas for the types of images you can upload:

461

Relatable images

Relatable images are one of the most popular types of images and drive likes and comments. Relatable content is anything that your target audience can relate to and identify with, it's when your audience sees a piece of content and immediately think, "Yes, I know exactly what they mean and that is exactly how I feel when this happens." It's incredibly powerful because this content is immediately communicating to your audience that you understand them and you feel their pain or joy and you can empathise with them. With relatable content you are communicating with them on quite a deep level which all helps to build relationships and trust. This is why Someecards is so successful, most of their content is relatable.

Emotive images

Evoking an emotional response is an essential ingredient for success on Instagram. If you create content that evokes a strong positive emotional response it will help your audience associate that emotion with your brand. Content like this is very memorable and if you can make people feel something by posting an image, text or a video this can really help in building your brand and creating powerful associations. Evoking any of the primary emotions be it surprise, joy, or fear, sadness, anger or disgust is a certain way to get people sharing your content. Pictures that tug your heartstrings are great and images of cute animals and children are a real winner on Instagram, people also love pictures of food and beautiful places.

Educational images

Posting images about your subject is invaluable, this will help you to stand out as a thought leader and expert in your field. If your content is valuable and useful then your followers are likely to keep coming back for more and are likely to share your content too.

Informative images

This could be about letting your followers know about something that is happening, like a Webinar, a book launch, trade show or event in the area, or a special offer, or any information that will be of use or value to them.

Entertaining/amusing images

Social media is all about being social and having fun and people love seeing funny stuff. Posting funny images that appeal to the sense of humor of your target audience will always be a winner and will drive likes and comments.

Seasonal Images

Posting images relating to important holidays and annual celebrations is a really good way to stay connected with your audience. If you have an international audience then being aware of their holidays and religious celebrations will go a long way in building relationships.

Inspiring and motivational content

The truth is everyone has a bad day sometimes and needs a little bit of motivation or cheering up. A motivational quote will help to lift your audience and can really help to connect with them. If you know what your audience wants, what they aspire to and what their frustrations are then it is likely that you will be able to motivate them by posting content which inspires them. These types of post are also very shareable especially if put together with a colorful and inspiring image like a cartoon or photo.

Employee and behind the scenes content

People love to see what is going on behind the scenes. Giving your audience a behind the scenes view of your business helps to keeps your business and brand looking real, authentic and adds human interest. If you have news about your employees and the great things they are doing then post it. Maybe they have been involved in a fundraiser or they have won an employee of the month award. You can show pictures of your office, your employees, the sandwich girl bringing your lunch or the CEO shaking their booty at the company bash. You can get really creative here and this is where you can really tell the story behind your brand. Daily events happening in your business may seem mundane to you but to your audience they may be incredibly interesting. For example, if you are a restaurant you could show the delivery of one of your ingredients or maybe show one of your signature dishes and give the ingredients or produce an Instagram video showing how it is made.

Statistics

People love statistics which relate to their niche. If your business is B2B then posting statistics can gain a great deal of interest especially if they are displayed in a visually appealing way like with an infographic or graph. They are often shared if they are translated into a useful tip for your followers.

Special offers

Social media is a great way to get the message out about the special offers you have running but you will need to be careful not to post them too often or they just appear like advertising and bad noise in your audience's news feed. You need to make sure that what you are offering is of real value, that it is exclusive to your followers and you are offering them a deadline to redeem the offer.

Contests and sweepstakes

Contests and sweepstakes are always a great way to gain popularity, grow your audience, build your brand and build your opt-in email list. With contests your audience can have great fun with your brand and they can also create high levels of engagement. Creating and running contests will be covered in more detail later on.

Caption this

Posting a photo and then asking your audience to caption it is a really effective and light hearted way to drive engagement and you could also turn this into a contest. You can use your own images or images from stock photo sites or sites like Flickr, make sure you check the terms of uses and choose images which are either interesting, humorous or inspiring.

Internet Memes

Meme comes from the greek word 'mimema' which means something imitated. An internet meme is a style, action or idea which spreads virally across the internet. They can take the form of images, videos or hashtags. There are plenty of tools and apps out there to help you create memes such as www.memegen.com and imgur.com which are popular ones.

Your blog

Posting an image which relates to your latest blog post can be a very effective way of getting your followers onto your website or Blog. Make sure you always include an image to provoke interest and asking a question can create intrigue and curiosity.

Greetings

Simply posting an attractive image or a wishing your followers good morning, good night or enjoy your weekend will go a long way in breaking the ice and building relationships. These types of posts help to make positive associations with your brand.

Product photos

Unless you are really artistic or a fashion brand or have a creative collection of some sort then it is a good idea to follow the 80/20 rule, 20% product photos and 80% other photos relating and telling the story of your brand.

You really need to get creative with product photos and try and make them as interesting as possible. Taking pictures of your staff or your customers wearing or using your products can add interest and a personal touch rather than perhaps the product on its own. You could ask your followers to upload pictures of themselves using or wearing your product and have a follower of the day. This can be incredibly powerful and creates real buzz around your products and brand.

Event Photos

Photos before, during and after an event can create real hype around an event, exhibition or trade show. These type of photos make your followers feel part of the event and can help to draw them into a more personal connection with your business.

Charity events

If your business involves itself with charity then show your followers with your images as this is a great way to show the more human side of your business.

Customer focused photos

Photos of your customers using, wearing or eating your products is a great way to connect with your audience in a fun way. Some brands have really mastered this and have created high levels of interest and engagement and seen their follower numbers soar as a result. You can get your customers to post their photos with a certain hashtag so you can find them and also make this part of a contest.

Photos of your city/art/anything

People just love looking at interesting images and you may see lots of interesting and beautiful things in your day to day life. The sort of images you post will depend on your audience type and the image that you brand wants to promote but most people like beautiful things. It might be a beautiful sunset, flower or piece of art or architecture. If you think it's a great shot, chances are other people will too. Use Instagram as a window for people to look through and see you and your brand.

How to photos and videos

Instagram is a great way to visually show people how to do things, either by uploading a sequence of images or one image which has been split into 4. Restaurants can showcase their best dishes and then list the ingredients or create short videos. The possibilities are endless and can be incredibly inspiring for people.

Send sneak previews
Sending your new products to a group of people can make them feel they are in an elite group. People love to think they have the insider information or are the first to know about something.

Select a specific color or colors for you images
Some brands have been incredibly successful in creating galleries on Instagram that keep to one or a few specific colors. This can really help with branding and is very memorable for followers.

Introductory videos
Using short 15 second video feature on Instagram to post your own introduction video is a great way to reach your audience in the most personal way.

Teaser videos
It may be that you have some great content on YouTube and therefore you could create a teaser video on Instagram to promote your Channel.

TOP TIPS FOR POSTING ON INSTAGRAM
To make your Instagram marketing super successful here are a few tips on posting on Instagram:

Follow brands and your competition
If you start by following brands then you can see how they are using Instagram. You may be able to adopt different techniques and ideas. Also keep an eye on what your competition are doing. You can be pretty sure they will be doing the same. Using Nitrogram to find and follow brands can be really helpful, Nitrogram is an analytics and engagement platform that lists the top 50 brands on Instagram.

Create a location page

This is particularly useful if you have a bricks and mortar business. Just before uploading your photo you have the opportunity to tag that photo in the geotag field. That photo will then appear on a location page in Instagram and will help your business to get found by other instagrammers in your area, they will be able to view your images and hopefully as a result will either visit your business or start following you. Currently location search results are provided by Foursquare's location database so you will need to sign up for Foursquare in the app store or on Google Play. When you have done that go to the check-in tab and search for the place you want to add and then tap 'Add this place.' You should then be able to search for it on the location screen in Instagram. You can then add your photo, tap the place name above the photo and you can see the location you have created. This is where all your photos tagged with this location will appear.

Hashtags

Hashtags are big big big on Instagram. Hashtags help like minded people connect on Instagram and help people categorise and organize their photos. The purpose of hashtags is to help get your image found by connecting your photo with photos that other Instagram users have posted. When you put the hashtag sign before a word or phrase it becomes clickable and brings up all the content relating to that hashtag.

There are two ways of using hashtags on Instagram. Firstly for discoverability and secondly to find other follower made content and to extend your reach by appearing in search when people are searching for relevant topics. With hashtags you need to be as specific, relevant and descriptive as possible. To find out what is trending on Instagram check sites like Webstagram and then you can create content around popular hashtags.

Unlike other social sites, multiple hashtags do work on Instagram so you are safe to post more than just a few and many are successful posting up to ten to twelve.

When you have a sizeable audience you can create a hashtag specifically for your brand as well. Simply create a really amusing and unique hashtag and you may find people join in and then every time that hashtag is used it is associated with your brand.

Top Tip

If you use the same hashtags frequently then to save you having to type them out again and again it's a good idea to copy them onto a notes application on your mobile device so that they can be pasted into the caption area when you are posting.

Descriptions, URLS and product codes

Make sure to add descriptions to the caption area and if your are featuring products from a web page then include the URL to that specific product or a product code.

Add 'calls to action' to descriptions

One of the main advantages of social media is it gives consumers a voice and the opportunity to give you feedback about products which makes encouraging your followers to comment of paramount importance. Posting questions is a great way to encourage comments and engagement and makes your followers feel valued.

Add 'calls to action' to image

One of the main advantages of social media is it gives consumers a voice and the opportunity to give you feedback about products, so encouraging your followers to comment is of paramount importance. Posting questions is a great way to encourage comments and get your followers talking about your business. Asking questions also makes your followers feel their opinions are valued.

Adding a call to action to an image is a great way to get followers to interact and is a much more effective than adding them to your description. Obviously you cannot do this on every image but occasionally this can work very well.

Post regularly and consistently
Success is unlikely to come overnight with Instagram. It will take time to build your following, so you need to stay with it and post consistently but not madly, once a day is optimal and more if you have the content.

According to statistics videos gain seven times more engagement than photos. You can upload video for up to 15 seconds and it's a great way of building that emotional connection with your followers and stamping your personality on your brand.

Promos and discount Codes
A very effective way to get your followers over to your site is to offer promo codes and discounts. Don't forget to hashtag your special promotion images with #promocode. To find out what other businesses are doing simply search #promocode and have a look at some of the images.

Encourage followers to mention their friends
There is no share function on Instagram so getting your content to get seen by non followers is harder. However some brands have been successful in getting their followers to mention their friends in the comments with an @mention. You could do this by simply asking them to tell their friends about a certain promotion or competition or by asking if they know a friend who likes a certain thing.

Don't hog the feed
Constantly posting images is a sure way to get you unfollowed, as users want to see a variety of images from different users. Instagram is all about discovery, wonderment and inspiration so people do not want to

keep seeing more of the same.

Add logos to images
Adding logos to images can help with branding, however you need to make sure you keep it as small as possible so not to take over the image and ruin the experience.

ENHANCING YOUR IMAGES

You really don't have to be an expert photographer or graphic designer to create great images on Instagram and there are numerous applications for both Android and iPhone that can help you enhance your images.

Adobe Photoshop Express lets you add effects, add borders and alter exposure, saturation, tint, contrast and brightness. Other apps includeApple iPhoto, Aviary, Befunky, Morebeaute, Camera+, Camera awesome, Picfx and Lenslight to name but a few! 'Over' is a great app that lets you layer text over your images and use different fonts and sizes all from your mobile. Diptic, Photoshake and PicFrame let you combine multiple images into a single image, great for how to images, tutorial images and collages. Color Effects and ColorBlast let you grey out everything in an image except for a selected area that you choose to keep one vivid color.

If you are creating images with photo shop of any other photo editor then the image size requirement is 612 X 612 pixels.

INSTAGRAM DIRECT FOR BUSINESS

Instagram Direct for business Instagram now lets you send and share private images or videos with individuals and smaller groups of up to 15 people which will not appear in the feed. You can send a direct message to anyone even if they do not follow you. If you send it to someone who does not follow you your message will go in their requests queue and they can either accept your request or not. To do this simply take your photo as usual or select from your camera, add your favorite filter and then tap next and tap on 'direct' at the top of your screen. You then select the individual followers you want to send it to and then press 'send.' This definitely has advantages for businesses and can be used in the following ways for marketing:

Contests You can ask followers to send you their images via direct message rather than adding a hashtag for contest if you wish. This can make the contest easier to administer but may not get you the visibility you are looking for.

Sales Vouchers and Coupons You can use Instagram direct for rewarding your most loyal followers. Send a photo to a select few and thank them for being a great follower with details about a sales voucher or money off coupon.

Incentives interactions Post an image and ask a question and then state that the first 15 to comment will receive details by direct message about either a money off coupon or the details to enter a competition.

Send product photos Send photos of your product or a limited edition with a link where to buy, by direct message.

Ask permission to use your followers images You could use this feature to ask your followers to send you an image of them using your product which you can upload. This can be a win win for you and your followers. You get publicity as they will most probably upload the photo to their feed. This will be very appealing to your followers, suddenly they are promoted to all your followers using your product and they are more than likely to publicize the image that they are in to their friends.

Send sneak previews People love to think they have the insider information or are the first to know about something that is being launched. Sending your new products to a group of people can make them feel they are part of an elite group.

CHAPTER THREE

BUILDING YOUR AUDIENCE ON INSTAGRAM

BEFORE YOU START building your audience you will need to have uploaded some images to give your account some starter content and show off your brand's personality. Unless you are a very well known brand then users will be put off by an endless sequence of product images so you need to think very carefully about the story you want to tell and the images you are going to upload to tell that story. Once you are ready and have uploaded a good collection of images to show off your brand you can start building your audience.

Find your friends Instagram offers you the opportunity when you set up your account to invite your Facebook friends and contacts from your phone. Make sure you announce on the other platforms that you are on Instagram, this is crucial to getting you a head start.

Display Instagram badges You can find the code for Instagram badges here http://instagram.com/accounts/badges/ which can easily be embedded in your website or blog.

Display your Instagram handle Make sure you display your handle on your email signature and on all your marketing material.

Announce your profile on other social networks If you are active on other social networks then announce your presence on Instagram and invite your followers over to join you. It is likely that you will grow your reach through their followers and also you can often offer them a different and more personal experience on Instagram.

Use hashtags If you know your audience then you will know what hashtags they will be searching for. Hashtags are a great way to find your audience and also by adding hastags to your images you can help your audience find you. You can add up to thirty hashtags.

Follow Follow Follow Just like Twitter, the more people you follow the more will follow you back. If you engage by liking and commenting you will draw them back to you and also put you in front of other followers who may come and check out your profile. To find your target audience think about where they are now on Instagram and who they are likely to be already following, go to those profiles and then follow them and start to engage with their content.

Interact and engage Interacting and commenting is very important on Instagram. Liking and commenting on photos not only helps you to build relationships but also helps you to get seen by other followers and you will find this makes a big difference to the number of people who start following you.

Responding to comments One of the most important things you can do is to responding to your followers by replying to their comments.

Embed Instagram photos or video in your website or blog You can tempt your website visitors and embed your most popular images on your website or blog. Simply visit your profile on the web and click on your photo and then on the three dots icon on the right of the photo to get the embed code.

Following influencers in your niche Building relationships with key influencers in your niche is invaluable. Not only can you learn from their content but also these people can have literally 1000's of followers, imagine if they follow you back and then share your content.

Advertising on Instagram Instagram is slowly rolling out its advertising with sponsored posts in the newsfeed. Advertising is available to a small number of brands in the US and is being rolled out slowly to get it right for both partners and the Instagram community as a whole. You can see if a post is sponsored as it will have the word 'sponsored' on the top right.

HOSTING AN INSTAGRAM PHOTO CONTEST

Photo contests are a great way to promote your brand, gain new followers, build your opt-in list, promote a new product and overall increase your reach on Instagram. Once you have decided what exactly you want to achieve with your contest you can get started very easily. Here are the steps you need to take to create your contest:

Choose a really good prize
You need to make sure your prize is specific to your brand in order to attract your target audience. If you are launching a new product then offering this as a prize is a great way to promote it. Gift cards can work very well as prizes especially if you have a wide range of products. A gift card for your competition will tend to appeal to a wider segment of your target audience.

Decide on the type of contest and the duration
You will need to decide what type of contest you wish to run, this can be anything from a simple sweepstake to a photo or video contest. It's a good idea to check out other contests for ideas, to do this simply search contest and competition hashtags on Instagram. If you decide to go with a photo or video contest you will need to decide on a theme, what sort of image or video you want your followers to upload and what your conditions are for entering. Asking your entrants to snap a picture of them using, eating or drinking your product is great way to promote your product. Try to keep it simple and put as few constraints as possible in order to encourage more followers to submit their photos.

477

The duration of your contest will depend very much on the type of contest. If you are asking your audience to submit videos you will need to give them longer to prepare than a simple sweepstake.

Choose a unique #hashtag

Hashtags make it really easy for you to collect your entrants photos around a particular subject and also help you to build a community around that hashtag so everyone can view the images relating to that hashtag. You will need to choose a #hashtag which is simple but unique to your brand so that it is less likely to be chosen by anyone else.

Create a landing page with entry rules

Create a page for your contest where followers can view results and simple rules. Remember to include the following:

Rules

Here are some guidelines for your contest rules:

- The dates that your contest is running and how and when the winner will be picked.
- That they must follow you on Instagram.
- That they must upload a photo relevant to the topic.
- How many photos they are allowed to upload.
- How many times they are allowed to enter.
- Who can enter. Is your contest limited to a particular country only?
- Where, when and how the winner will be announces.

Entry form

If you want to build your opt-in list then you will need your entrants to enter their email and their Instagram user name. There are third parties like www.wishpond.com and www.woobox.com who can administer your competitions. Using third parties can also make your contests look extremely professional and can take away the admin headache.

Create a graphic

You will need to create a compelling graphic with an attention grabbing headline. An image of the prize you are offering with brief details on how to enter can work very well. Remember the images on Instagram are small so any text like Hashtags, username or URL's have to be large enough. If you are creating a separate landing page for your contest then using a URL shortener like bit.ly can make it much easier for your contestants to remember and type in your landing page URL.

Make sure you add your entry details to the caption area of your post and add hashtags like #instagramcontest, #contest, #win, #competition so you can get found by more people searching for contests.

Once you have created your graphic you can also post it on other networks like Facebook, Twitter, Pinterest.

Promoting your contest

To get the word out about your contest you can add a banner to your business website and post your contest graphic on other social networks. You can also mail details of your contest to your email subscribers and add your contest details to contest websites that will let you submit your contest for free.

Sharing photos which have been submitted on other platforms not only gets the words out about your contest but also makes your followers feel rewarded. You can monitor all the posts being uploaded with a tool called statigram.

Post Contest

After the contest make sure you announce the winner and share on your other platforms too. Also ask the winner if they can upload a picture of them using /eating /enjoying their prize or you could create a video of them receiving their prize.

Now is the time to mail your entrants and try and convert them into customers, offering them a discount voucher is also a very good idea to help them feel rewarded for entering.

Advertising on Instagram

Instagram is slowly rolling out its advertising with sponsored posts in the newsfeed. Advertising is available to a small number of brands in the US and is being started slowly to get it right for both partners and the Instagram community as a whole.

CHAPTER FOUR

DAY TO DAY ACTIVITY

THERE ARE CERTAIN things that you will need to do on a day to day basis to run your campaign on Instagram. It is a good idea to allot a specific amount of time and a particular time of the day to do this. Here are some of the things you will need to do:

Following your followers

This is important if you are customers are business owners themselves. Following your prospects and customers will go a long way in building relationships. By following you are showing them that you are interested in what they have to say and also helping them to achieve their goals by helping to build their audience.

Engaging, commenting and replying

When your followers start to engage with your content make sure you are listening and responding to them. Everyone is aiming for shares, likes and comments so if you are helping others out by commenting and liking their content it is going to draw attention to your brand and they are more likely to take interest in your content. This is one area where the reciprocation rule works very well on Instagram. Engaging with content will also draw attention to you and your brand and you will find that people will click on your page or profile to find out who you are and you may very well end up with another follower. Be friendly to your audience, be chatty, authentic, genuine and embrace the conversation. All this will all go a long well in building a positive image for your brand and will set you apart from your others who are continually ambushing their audience with self promotion.

Showing your audience you value and respect them

If you value and respect your audience they will most probably love, respect and value your business. Be kind, generous, offer as much help and value as possible, reply to their comments and make it obvious that you value your audience and are listening to them. Don't be afraid to be yourself rather than a stiff brand with no personality.

Dealing with negative comments

Every business at some time will have to deal with negativity from followers. Hopefully if you have a good product then this is not going to happen too often. There are 'trolls' out there who have nothing better to do than post negative comments, the best thing to do with them is just ignore them, delete their comments and block them if you have to.

However there will be real customers who have real concerns and complaints and may post negative comments publicly, there may also be people who really want to lash out to gain your attention as quickly as possible and spread the news to their friends too!

You need to deal with complaints as quickly as possible and be as transparent and authentic as possible. The best thing to do is to apologise and say how sorry you are to hear of the inconvenience they have been caused and offer to continue the conversation and deal with their concern by asking to call you or email you. You can then deal with this privately, give your customer the full attention they deserve and decide on your next course of action or compensation.

CHAPTER FIVE

MEASURING AND MONITORING YOUR RESULTS ON INSTAGRAM

TRACKING YOUR RESULTS on Instagram is the best way to find out if you are reaching the right audience and uploading the right content on Instagram.

Tracking your results is harder with Instagram since it is more difficult to drive traffic to particular web pages since you cannot add clickable links in captions. Brands can analyze their success by measuring the number of likes, comments and also their overall reach.

Having a large number of followers is important but engagement rates are more important. Once you see which images are creating the most engagement you can try to produce more of the same. Filters can make a difference to the engagement too so make sure your keep a track of which ones are working for you.

Measuring and monitoring your results and performance against your original goals and objectives on an ongoing basis is essential. This is where many businesses go wrong by carrying on aimlessly with what they are doing instead of checking to see what is working and what is not. Once you have this information you can steer your campaign in the right direction and achieve the results you are looking for.

Once you get started you will probably need to adjust your objectives according to how you are performing. For example, you may need to follow more people in order to grow the number of your followers or you may need to post images more often to drive more traffic to your blog or website.

GOOGLE ANALYTICS

The Overview Report

This report lets you see at a glance how much conversion value is generated from social channels. It compares all conversions with those resulting from social.

The Conversions Report

The Conversions Report helps you to quantify the value of social and shows conversion rates and the monetary value of conversions that occurred due to referrals from Instagram and any of the other social networks. Google Analytics can link visits from Instagram with the goals you have chosen and your E - commerce transactions. To do this you will need to configure your goals in Google Analytics which is found under 'Admin' and then 'Goals'. Goals in Google Analytics allow you to measure how often visitors take or complete a specific action and you can either create goals from the templates offered or create your own custom goals. The Conversions report can be found in the Standard Reporting tab under Traffic Sources > Social > Conversions.

The Networks Referral Report

The Networks Referral report tells you how many visitors the social networks have referred to your website and shows you how many page views, visits, the duration of the visits and the average number of pages viewed per visit. From this information you can determine which network referred the highest quality of traffic.

Data Hub Activity Report

The Data Hub activity report shows how people are engaging with your site on the social networks. You can see the most recent URLs that were shared, how they were shared and what was said.

The Social Visitors Flow Report
This report shows you the initial paths that your visitors took from social sites through your site and where they exited.

The Landing Pages Report
This report shows you engagement metrics for each URL. These include page views, average visit duration and pageviews and pages viewed per visit.

The Trackback Report The Trackback report shows you which sites are linking to your content and how many visits those sites are sending to you. This can help you to work out which sort of content is the most successful so you can create similar and also helps you to build relationships with those who are constantly linking to your content.

THIRD PARTY APLICATIONS
There are free tools that are available to help measure and analyze your campaigns such as:

Statigram
This is a tool solely for Instagram and provides statistics for the number of images you have, the number of likes, comments and followers.

It shows you which of your pages have the highest engagement, which of your followers are the most engaged and your growth or loss of followers. You can also manage contests with this tool.

Nitrogram
This tool shows engagement rates, statistics per photo, follower count and number of images shared. You can follow all the posts on #hashtags related to your brand and identify your biggest advocates. You can also view the top brands on Instagram.

Sumall

Sumall is definitely an analytics tool to keep an eye on as it can track all your campaigns on all your platforms. You can track sales, site visits and followers all in one place.

Latergrame.me

Latergrame.me lets you upload and schedule your Instagram posts from your computer or mobile phone. Instagram does not allow automatic posting but Latergrame helps you by letting you upload your image with caption to their library in advance. You simply drag and drop the image to your calendar in Latergrame and then you will receive a push notification when it is the time for the image to be posted, you simply swipe to open the notification and then post on Instagram.

Make Tumblr Work For Your Business

Alex Stearn

Table of Contents

CHAPTER ONE

GETTING STARTED ON TUMBLR

FOUNDED IN 2007 Tumblr is a microblogging platform and social networking site which was was sold to Yahoo in 2013 for approximately 1.1 billion. Tumblr got its name from the tumblelogs which were around at the time of its creation which tended to be shorter blogs accompanied by mixed media.

Tumblr offers an amazing platform for any business or brand to promote themselves within the Tumblr's huge and active community. Every user has a dashboard where they can view the posts from the blogs they follow and can interact by liking, commenting and reblogging. Tumblr also gives brands the freedom and flexibility to customize their own blogs in line with their branding and post their own content from their dashboard including: text, images, quotes, audio, video and links. Tumblr is different from other blogs in that it is more than acceptable to produce shorter blog posts and visual only posts but also absolutely fine to post longer blog posts as well.

Tumblr has millions of unique visitors per month and there are over 100 million active blogs. With regard to the audience it has a predominantly younger user base, statistics vary but it's safe to say that approximately half of its users are under 35 and about 30% are between 35 and 49. Gender wise Tumblr has a fairly equal split between women and men and the majority of its users reside in the USA with the remaining split between the UK, Canada , Brazil and Russia. The types drawn to Tumblr seem to be predominantly in the creative, artistic or fashion industries. If this is your target then it is probably a very good idea to have an active presence on Tumblr.

BENEFITS OF TUMBLR FOR BUSINESS

Tumblr has some seriously impressive features, however before you decide to build your presence on Tumblr you need to establish whether or not you will be able to find your target audience on Tumblr. If you are targeting a younger audience then this is a very good place to start. You can do this by using the search feature, simply create an account by signing up with your email, password and username and start searching. You can either search for keywords or go to www.Tumblr.com/explore or view some popular categories and selected blogs on www.tumble.com/spotlight . You can choose to follow individual blogs or a tag where you will see all the content relating to that tag. It may also be a good idea to establish whether your competition are on Tumblr and what sort of response they are getting which you can determine by the number of notes at the bottom of their posts.

Once you have established your audience are on Tumblr and you still can't decide whether this is the right platform to promote your business, then here is some more information to help you make that decision. Tumblr has some seriously impressive features and if you are thinking of using Tumblr as another way of building your brand and promoting your products then here is a run down of the main advantages it could offer your business:

It's Free You can have a presence on a site with its own source of traffic and all for free. If you are just starting out on your blogging journey, then what better way to showcase your content, create stories, start conversations and test the market? If you are just starting out in business then you can create your permanent website for free on Tumblr which can offer you the best of both worlds, you can create a few static pages with information about your business and then also offer your followers dynamic content by posting your announcements, news and blog posts as well. Tumblr gives you all the tools to help you build your brand, create a

492

lifestyle and tell the story about your brand and all for free. On Tumblr the possibilities are endless.

A new source of traffic If you are starting out in business then Tumblr can offer you the perfect platform with its built-in community of users. With literally millions of users Tumblr will offer you traffic that you would never have had without having a presence on the platform.

User friendly It is incredibly straightforward to set up a blog and you need absolutely no technical knowledge to do so, which means it's quick and easy to get going.

A new source of traffic Tumblr has its own community, therefore its own source of traffic. With literally millions of users on Tumblr your blog has more of a chance of being viewed by the community of users which already exists on the platform. Users can simply search for blogs they are interested in from their home page.

It's visual Tumblr is very visual in nature and therefore businesses that are creative tend to benefit the most, for example; photography, graphic design, fashion and jewellery design. However there are many categories that are still very successful on Tumblr and you only have to look on Tumblr's spotlight page to view the diversity of businesses and interests.

You can find new customers on Tumblr Tumblr like other social networks gives you the opportunity to find your customers and interact and engage with your audience. You can like and reblog posts (share posts) and likewise people can like or reblog your posts. Tumblr is renowned for a very engaged and active community of people who like to share. Tumblr does not support comments but if you want to add the function you can do so by adding either Disqus or Facebook comments. Facebook comments can be a little more complex to install but can offer you the best of both worlds and increase traffic to your blog from Facebook.

Very passionate users Tumblr is home to some of the most engaged communities and users are not only passionate about their niche but also about Tumblr and are completely hooked on the platform. It is therefore an excellent platform to become involved in and if you produce good content other users are very likely to either like or reblog.

Flexible The great thing about Tumblr is it is incredibly versatile, it's perfectly acceptable to produce long or short blog posts and posts can be just a few sentences long if you like. If you do not consider yourself a writer and writing long blog posts is not one of your strength then Tumblr is an ideal platform.

You can customize your blog You can customize your blog by using any of the free or premium designs and which is ideal if you want to keep your Tumblr in line with your branding.

You have full control You have absolute control of your site or blog on Tumblr. There are no character limitations, no file limitations and no advertising next to your content. You have full control to tell your story with whatever media you choose whether it's image, text, links, chat, video or audio. In addition the mobile app offers you the functionality to post anything from anywhere.

Choose your own domain You can choose a custom domain and therefore have a domain that will easily be remembered and associated with your brand.

Another way to get found through organic search Tumblr is available to anyone on the web, you do not have to have an account on Tumblr to view a blog on Tumblr and content is indexed by the search engines which makes it more likely to get your content found. Therefore you can use Tumblr and any of the available themes to build your own website if you like.

Long shelf life Online studies have shown that Tumblr posts have a long shelf life and things are still being reblogged long after they have been posted. In fact over one-third of reblogs on Tumblr are still occurring thirty days after the original post. This is a big advantage over some of the other platforms where posts are extremely time sensitive.

Works well with Instagram Instagram makes it very easy to share your images with Tumblr and because content on Tumblr is predominantly visual as well this is a great way of delivering similar content to two different audiences.

Use Tumblr for a particular campaign Tumblr is incredibly versatile. Many brands are using Tumblr to promote particular campaigns and then when that particular campaign is finished they can re-skin their Tumblr and use it to promote yet another campaign with a built in audience.

Backlinks Backlinks are incoming links to a website or blog coming from other sites. When people reblog your content on Tumblr then valuable backlinks are created which will help with your search engine optimization.

A central hub Businesses often use Tumblr as a central hub for social media activity. Each piece of content has its own URL and therefore you can post all your content to all your social media platforms. You can automatically post your content to Facebook and Twitter if you wish and you can post from Instagram, YouTube, Flickr and Vimeo.

A source of talented and creative people If you are looking for incredibly talented people to create content for you then you are going to find them on Tumblr with their ready made portfolios.

A source of information Tumblr offers a huge source of information which can curate and share with your own audience if you wish. You can be really successful on Tumblr by reblogging and using other users' content without ever having to create your own. As long as you know what your target audience are interested in, you are sure to find the kind of information and visual experience they are looking for on Tumblr.

Set up multiple blogs You can set up as many blogs as you want under one username which means you can post content to different audiences without having to login and out of different accounts.

In conclusion with Tumblr you really do get the best of both worlds, the opportunity to create your own website or blog for free which is visible on the web like any other website and also the opportunity to interact and engage with an enormous community of passionate, creative and active bloggers. It's hard to turn down a free opportunity like this.

SETTING UP YOUR TUMBLR

Once you have established that your audience are on Tumblr you will need to work out what exactly you want to achieve by using Tumblr and then work out and define exactly what your goals and objectives are.

Here are some possible goals you may want to achieve through using Tumblr:

- To use Tumblr as a blog
- To use Tumblr for a particular campaign you are planning
- To use Tumblr as your main website
- To find new customers
- To build and maintain relationships with current customers
- To generate leads by building an opt-in list
- To promote your products
- To increase sales
- To build your brand

Setting up your account
Setting up your account is very straight forward and all you need to do is

sign up with an email and password and then create a username. When creating your username try and create one which is as close as possible to your business or brand name and it's also a good idea to keep your brand consistent by using the same profile picture as you do on other platforms like Facebook and Twitter.

Your description is really important since this is how you will get found by the Tumblr community and also in web search. Make sure you include industry keywords while at the same time keeping it interesting for the reader.

Tumblr really does give you the opportunity to create something quite amazing to promote and build your brand. You can add your own custom theme or choose from numerous free or premium themes which can be installed within seconds, this is extremely effective for promoting your individual style or brand. You can literally make your Tumblr an extension of your brand and you have absolute freedom when it comes to the design of your blog, if you know HTML then you can even build your own custom theme.

When it comes to the design of your blog you need to think about a number of things, not only do you need to be consistent with your brand you need to somehow communicate clearly what it is exactly that you are offering. It maybe that a follower only visits your blog once and then receives your updates in their dashboard and never comes back again. You need to hit them with what you are offering early on so when they do see your updates in their dashboard they remember each time who you are and what you offer. There are many beautiful blogs out there but often it is not obvious what they actually offer in a business sense.

As well as letting you customize your Tumblr you can also have your own domain name. Having your own custom domain not only looks more professional but also lets you take your domain with you if you do decide at a later date to change your blogging platform. To set up a custom

497

domain simply purchase the name, for a two level domain, for example: website.com and then access your domain management centre and point the A record (ip address) to 66.6.44.4 or for three or more level domains, for example, blog.website.com, the CNAME record must point to domains.tumblr.com. This is really straightforward but if you are unclear about this simply call your domain provider's helpline, most providers are very helpful and will take you through the process with them.

Once you have done this you will need to go to your Tumblr account and click on the gear icon (Settings) and then click the pencil to the right of your 'username' section and enable 'Use a custom domain', enter your domain name and then click ' Test domain' and then 'Save.' Your domain may take up to 72 hours to take effect, up until then when you visit your domain or subdomain you will see a Tumblr error page. For more information you can visit this page http://www.tumblr.com/docs/en/custom_domains

Add comments to your blog

Tumblr does not support its own comments but having a comment system is really important if you wish to interact with your audience and start building relationships. To add comments to your blog then you can easily install Disqus comments. Simply sign up to Disqus.com and then follow the simple instructions to install which is a quick and simple procedure.

You can also add Facebook comments to Tumblr but this is a slightly more involved process and involves signing up as a Facebook developer, creating an app and adding code to your theme. Any programmer or website developer would find this straightforward or you can find numerous tutorials on the web if you want to try it yourself.

Ask me anything

This functionality offers you another way to interact with your audience and get feedback. When you have this function enabled users can ask you anything and you can choose whether you want to publish your answers publicly or answer that question privately.

Add pages to your Tumblr
Tumblr offers you the ability to add static pages to your blog. This is particularly good if you are going to use Tumblr as your main website. You can add text, links and links with anchor text and images.

To add pages simply go to your dashboard, click on the blog you would like to edit and then on 'Customize' and then scroll to the bottom of the 'Theme' section and click on '+Add a page'

You need to add your URL after the slash /. For example, your about page could be /about. Then add a title in the 'Page title' field and then click the toggle 'Show a link to this page' and then 'Save'

To create a page with a custom layout simply select the blog you want to add it to, click on 'Customize', then click on 'Add a page' and then select 'Custom Layout' from the drop down menu on the top left. Insert your custom code into the HTML editor, then add your URL after the slash /. For example, your about page could be /about. Then click the toggle 'Show a link to this page' and 'Save'

To delete or edit a page simply find the page you would like to delete or edit and click either edit or the X icon next to the page you wish to delete.

Redirecting pages
You can redirect pages to any URL outside Tumblr if you wish. You may want to redirect a page to your website, online store or an external blog. To do this simply select the blog and then click 'Customize' and then Click on '+ Add a page.' Next select 'Redirect' from the dropdown menu on the top left and type a page URL after the slash /. For example,

website or online shop. Then enter the domain URL you want to redirect to and then click the toggle 'Show a link to this page' and 'Save.'

You can also redirect pages to your posts with a specific tag. To do this simply select the blog and then click 'Customize' and then click on '+ Add a Page.' Next select 'Redirect' from the dropdown menu on the top left. Add the page ULR after the slash /, for example, www.mysite.com/ mytag (the tag you want to add) and then in the 'Redirect to' field add / tagged/mytag to the end of your blog URL and replace the 'mytag' with the tag you want to use.

Add your Email opt-in

You can easily add your email sign up button to your Tumblr blog. Simply retrieve your HTML code from your email provider and then paste it into your Tumblr theme. To do this click 'Customize' and then 'Edit HTML' and then paste the code after the body tag and click the 'Update Preview' button on the top right. If you are at all unclear about this or you want it even more customized then ask your web developer to do this for you.

Notes

There are two ways you can show your appreciation on Tumblr. The first is with a like which is represented by a heart icon and the second is a reblog on Tumblr which is represented by an icon with two arrows. Likes and reblogs are collectively called notes and are displayed under your post.

Download the mobile app

Tumblr makes sharing really easy from your mobile and you can share photos, animated Gifs, video, quotes, chat, links and text and engage with your audience from anywhere. The app can be downloaded for android, iOS and Windows.

CHAPTER TWO

CONTENT IS KING ON TUMBLR

'THE CONTENT THAT does best is the content that surprises you.'
David Karp. Founder, Tumblr.

Because there are no follower numbers displayed on Tumblr it really is all about the content. People are following others for the quality of their content and not just because they have a large follower count.

Reblogging is incredibly powerful on Tumblr and with Tumblr your biggest aim is to have your content reblogged, when this happens your content gets shared with the followers of the person who reblogged your post and their followers followers if they are reblogged and so on. About 90% of posts on Tumblr are reblogs which illustrates that there are a huge number of users who are looking for compelling content to pass on to their followers. In turn this means that there is huge potential to get your content out there on Tumblr and start building your brand. The big advantage about Tumblr is that people are actually going out of their way to find content and reblog that content so it can be associated with their brand.

To be successful on Tumblr you really need to focus on a particular niche and find or create content for one or two topics that not only relate to your brand but also that your audience will be keen to share with their audiences. The aim is that once you find your target audience and start posting or reblogging your valuable content you will reach even more of your target audience with your carefully crafted content.

As with all social media this is not just about plugging your product it is about helping others by producing useful and relevant content which is going to be of value to them by either inspiring them or solving a problem they have.

TUMBLR POSTING FORMATS

When it comes to posting content, Tumblr is one of the most flexible platforms and provides formats for you to post text, photos, quotes, links, chat, audio and video. You can add images and text to most types of post. Here are some ideas for the type of media you can post:

Images

Tumblr is very much a picture based blogging platform and images and animated GIFs are the most popular posts counting for over 80% of content. Tumblr is a great place to tell the story of your brand with images and in order to succeed in this platform you either need to get creative by uploading your own images or spend time curating so you can reblog other users' images.

If you are a photographer or you work in a creative industry then you are most likely to have all the images or resources you need to create whatever you want for your Tumblr. However, if not, you can easily either take your own photos or source images from sites like Flickr as long as you make sure you check the terms of use. There are also many apps and sites where you can add text and graphics to your images like www.picmonkey.com or www.canva.com . There are also numerous websites where you can create images for quotes and memes.

Animated GIF's

Tumblr is where the GIF action is taking place and GIFs have made a huge contribution to its popularity, the GIF tag is one of the most popular tags on Tumblr. An animated GIF (Graphics interchange format) is a graphic image that moves, it is made up of a series of images that are displayed in succession and then loop back to the beginning when the last frame has been displayed. Because GIFs are more immediate than a video and do not require you to press the play button, a GIF offers an instant experience for the viewer which makes them an incredibly effective media for quickly communicating a message.

GIF's have huge viral potential on Tumblr and can be used for all manner of things including humor, art and also they are very good way of showing how to do something quickly. Creating an animated GIF for a video can be a very effective way of promoting and getting that video found and viewed on Tumblr. Simply create your GIF and then tag it under GIF and post it with the URL to your full length video.

With the technology available on the web creating GIFs is no longer limited to those with expert graphic design skills and creating a GIF is actually very straightforward. There are numerous tutorials on how create to do this on this page, http://brands.tumblr.com/howtogif and there are also numerous free GIF generators available like www.imgflip.com/gifgenerator that also offer a pro version.

Quotes

If you want to win with quotes then you need to know your target audience and what their needs, desires and frustrations are. Equipped with this information you can either create or reblog quotes which either inspire, motivate or help make their day better in some way.

Tumblr lets you post quotes as text only but posting a quote over an image is often more effective and is more likely to get reblogged than text only. If you are not a whizz on Photoshop then you can use sites like www.picmonkey.com which let you add text to images, crop images, add effects and add frames. Other sites like www.imgflip.com create memes.

Text

If you are concentrating on using Tumblr for longer blog posts then it's a good idea to use a theme which is designed for this type of blog, you can find a number of designs in the 'Write a long thing' section at www.tumblr.com/themes . If you are reblogging long text posts and you want to avoid having your post truncated then simply click the reblog button and then the icon next to the gear icon and click on 'Text' which will format it for this type of post.

Audio

Tumblr lets you post audio and allows your followers to listen to music straight from your blog, it's also the perfect platform for podcasting. Tumblr offers you three different options to find the audio you want to upload in your post. You can find and upload songs with Spotify and Soundcloud who Tumblr have partnered with, or you can post the URL to a song or upload an MP3 file. Once posted a small black or white box will appear with a play and pause button.

Video

You can upload your video from your desktop or laptop or you can embed the code from a YouTube or Vimeo video. If you have your own YouTube channel then this is great way to reach a new audience and widen your reach. Even if you do not have your own contact you can still share other people's video as long as it is the sort of material that will appeal to your target audience. A short introductory video can go a long way to making that personal connection with your audience and putting a face behind your blog. Using Instagram with Tumblr can be very effective especially with Instagram's 15 second video function which is great for a quick introduction or how to video.

Chat

The purpose of the chat post is to copy and repost a chat you have had online or to re-tell a funny or interesting story. You can simply title your chat and then write the text from different characters and Tumblr will format it by separating the text and adding bold to the titles of the characters in the chat.

Link

Tumblr has its own category for link and automatically puts HTML when you add your title and URL. Once posted and a user clicks on your title in the post it will direct them straight to the URL.

IDEAS FOR CREATING CONTENT ON TUMBLR

You may be wondering how you are going to consistently produce and deliver a stream of compelling content to your audience on a regular basis for the foreseeable future. However once you have picked your topic of interest you will be surprised how one idea will lead to another and you will be able to produce a great variety of content.

Unless you are an artist or a fashion brand it is unlikely that your followers are going to want to see a constant stream of product pictures, this would be incredibly boring and will not help you to promote your brand or get the following you need for success on this platform. In order to build a real connection with your followers you will need to think of ideas for content which will appeal to your audience emotionally and get them to make friends with your brand. Your goal here needs to be to inspire and interest your followers, let them have fun and above all make them smile. Your audience want to see the personality of your business and your human side. Even businesses that are considered to be quite dull have been successful in driving interaction with humorous images or videos. With Tumblr you need to offer a variety of content to spark interaction and keep your followers interested and engaged.

Before you get started have a look at the popular tags and also at what your competitors are posting. When you look out for what is being liked and reblogged it is easy to see what's working and what's not and with all the incredible visuals on Tumblr it really isn't hard to get inspired. Here are some ideas for the type of content you should be creating or reblogging on Tumblr.

Relatable content

Relatable content is one of the most popular types of content and drives likes and reblogs and comments. Relatable content is anything that your target audience can relate to and identify with, it's when your audience sees a piece of content and immediately thinks, "Yes, I can relate to that and this is exactly the way I feel when this happens". It's incredibly powerful because this content is immediately communicating to your audience that you understand them and you feel their pain or joy and you can empathise with them. With relatable content you are communicating with them on quite a deep level which all helps to build relationships and trust. This is why Someecards is so successful, most of their content is relatable.

Emotive content

Creating content that is capable of generating emotion is going to go a long way in creating loyalty and a deeper connection with your audience. This type of content is most frequently reblogged on Tumblr. Once you know your audience and their typical wants and desires it can be easy to create this type of content. When your audience starts to idenitify emotionally with your content they will start to identify emotionally with your brand too. You can do this with all types of posts, images, GIFs videos, text and quotes.

Educational content

Posting informative content about your subject is invaluable, this will help you to stand out as a thought leader and expert in your field. If your content is valuable and useful then your followers are likely to keep coming back for more and are likely to share your content too. Remember your audience are looking to find and share valuable content with their audience too and will want to be associated with any compelling content you create.

Informative

This could be about letting your followers know about a something that is happening like a Webinar, a trade show or event in the area, or a special offer, or any information that will be of use or value to them.

Entertaining/amusing content

Humor is always a winner on Tumblr and one of the most popular tags, the #lol tag is usually at the top of the list on www.tumblr.com/explore. People just love sharing funny stuff. Even if you did not create it yourself but you think it is going to appeal to your target audience then share it. The aim here is to amuse and entertain your audience, humor is a winner all round and not only does humor break down barriers it is also more likely to be liked and reblogged.

Seasonal Content

Posting content relating to important holidays and annual celebrations is a really good way to stay connected with your audience and keep your content up to date and timely.

Inspiring and motivational content

The truth is everyone has a bad day sometimes and needs a little bit of motivation or cheering up. A motivational quote will help to lift your audience and can really help to connect with them. If you know what your audience wants, what they aspire to and what their frustrations are then it is likely that you will be able to motivate them by posting content which inspires them. These types of post are also very shareable especially if put together with a colorful and inspiring image like a cartoon or photo.

Employee and behind the scenes content

If you have news about your employees and the great things they are doing then post it. Maybe they have been involved in a fundraiser or they have won an employee of the month award. Giving your audience a behind the scenes view of your business helps to keeps your business and brand looking real, authentic and adds human interest.

Shared Content

Whilst it is great to post most of your own content, don't be afraid to share other peoples content as long as it is relevant. The more valuable content you share the more valuable you will become to your audience and the more likely they will keep coming back for more. Sharing content is also incredibly important in building relationships with your fans, they are going to be far more open to your brand if you are supporting theirs.

Statistics

People love statistics which relate to their niche and infographics do very well on Tumblr. Because most of us are visually wired, infographics can be one of the best ways to communicate information and numbers, they are easy to digest, fun to share and engaging. A picture really is worth a thousand words. To create infographics there are numerous sites online like www.piktochart.com and www.infogr.am

Questions

Asking questions about subjects that your audience may be interested in is a great way to encourage comments, interaction and community. People love to share their opinions and thoughts and love the opportunity to communicate, contribute and be heard. Even if you are posting an image or video it's really practice to ask a question.

Ask me a question post

Asking your followers to ask you a question is a great way to encourage interaction. You could also post a selection of questions and ask them to select one for you to answer.

Post about a book

Writing a post about a book you have read that may appeal to your target audience is a very effective way of delivering valuable content especially if it is going to help them in some way.

Top Ten lists

People love lists about who or what is top or best. Lists spark interest and this is most probably because people like to compare their choices and judgement with others. Some may like to see that their opinions match others and feel they are right in that choice or others may feel comforted by the fact their choices are not the same and they are unique.

Controversial

Posting a controversial statement can spark great conversation and interaction, remember people love to voice their opinions, have an input and be heard. It may be a good idea to stay out of the discussion here as you do not want to lose followers and you need to be sensitive to your audience in order not to upset them so be careful with what topics you pick.

Special offers

Tumblr is a great way to get the message out about the special offers you have running but you will need to be careful not to post them too often or they just appear like advertising and bad noise in your audience's news feed. You need to make sure that what you are offering is of real value, that it is exclusive to your followers and you are offering them a deadline to redeem the offer.

Contests and sweepstakes

Contests and sweepstakes are always a great way to gain popularity, grow your audience, build your brand and build your opt-in email list. With contests your audience can have great fun with your brand and they can also create high levels of engagement. Creating and running contests on Tumblr will be covered in more detail later on.

Voting polls & customer feedback

Creating a poll is a great way to encourage engagement on Tumblr. You can embed polls to Tumblr by using ww.polldaddy.com Polls can help give you a deeper understanding of your audience and also offers you valuable feedback about products or services.

Tips and tricks

Offering a weekly or daily 'Top Tip' can keep your audience hooked and returning again and again for the latest information and are a great way to increase loyalty and build relationships. Tips can be anything from instructions on how to do something to information about a useful app.

News and current events

Offering information about the latest news that relates to your niche is a certain way to keep people interested and sharing your content. Being current and up to date with local news is really useful to your audience and it keeps your business looking fresh and up to date. To keep up to date with news, subscribe to news feeds and blogs that offer news on your industry or your local area.

Negative content

People always like to hear about what not to do, for example: 10 Things not to do on a first date or 10 things not to say in a job interview, the list of possibilities for this type of post are endless and can create a great deal of amusement and interest.

Music if you are a musician

If you are a band and want to promote your music then there is no better way to promote your material than by posting links to your music and videos on Tumblr.

Fill in the blanks posts

Getting your audience involved with your content is a very powerful way of creating engagement. Fill in the blank posts can be way of creating engagement and conversation, for example:

- I love going to _____ on my holidays because…
- My monday morning must have this_____
- I always take _____ on holiday.

Caption this
Posting a photo and then asking your audience to caption it is a really effective and light hearted way to drive engagement and you could also turn this into a contest. You can use images from stock photo sites or sites like Flickr as long as you check the terms of use. When using images make sure you choose images which are either very interesting, humorous or inspiring.

Case studies
Case studies are a really effective way to demonstrate how something works with real examples. You can use case studies to show how your customers have used your products or services to benefit them in some way. You can also use them to demonstrate a principle or method of doing something by using other businesses as examples.

Internet Memes
Meme comes from the greek word 'mimema' which means something imitated. An internet meme is a style, action or idea which spreads virally across the internet. They can take the form of images, videos or hashtags. There are plenty of tools and apps out there to help you create memes such as www.memegen.com and imgur.com which are popular ones.

Like versus share votes
This involves combining two competing images in one post and then asking your audience to vote for which image they choose by liking or sharing. This is a really quick way to expand your reach and get your brand out there. To be successful at this you really need to have good subject and one that most people identify with.

Your blog
Creating regular blog posts is a very effective way of getting your followers onto your website. Make sure you always include an image to

provoke interest and asking a question can create intrigue and curiosity.

Greetings

Simply posting an attractive image or a wishing your followers good morning, good night or to enjoy their weekend will go a long way in breaking the ice and building relationships. These types of posts help to make positive associations with your brand.

Testimonials

You may have received a review on Google Places or Foursquare or simply a message from someone. Posting about good things that people write or say about you contributes to your social proof and builds trust. Remember people will believe more in what others say about your business than what you, as the owner, say about it.

Behind the scenes

Behind the scenes photos may seem uninteresting to you but to others they can bring your business to life and show an authenticity to your brand. You can show how a product is made or just show a glimpse of yourWednesday employees at work.

GPOYW This stands for Gratuitis picture of yourself Wednesday. This has been a tradition on Tumblr since about 2008 and is a fun way to show a photo of yourself from time to time.

TOP TIPS FOR POSTING CONTENT ON TUMBLR

Create a content calendar

Creating a content calendar will help you not only stay on topic but will also help you to pace yourself. If you do not have one then you may find you are frequently posting at the beginning and then suddenly run out of ideas later on. Once you start mapping your ideas out you will be able to work out just how frequently you will be able to post. There are many calendars online that can help you with this task including Google Calendar which offers you the opportunity to color code your entries.

Mix it up

Tumblr gives you so much opportunity to keep your feed interesting and varied. Offering a variety of content will keep your audience interested and wondering what your next post will be.

Tag your posts

Tags are big on Tumblr and if you want to get found then you need to tag your posts. Tagging is important because people not only search for tags they also follow tags. To add tags simply create your post and then add the keywords relevant to your blog post in the tag space below your post. When you start typing in the tag field you will find Tumblr will offer you various words relating to your letters you are typing in which you can choose as if you wish. Make sure you only tag your post with the relevant tags and try to be as specific as possible. On the right of your dashboard you will see that you can actually track tags.

Reblog

When you reblog content it not only appears on your Tumblr but also in the dashboard of your followers. Reblogging is a great way to offer great content to your audience without having to create it all yourself and if you choose wisely you can associate yourself with some great blogs and great content which will help towards building your brand. When you do reblog it's a really good idea to add your own comment and let your followers know why you have reblogged and why that particular piece of content may be relevant to them.

Post frequently

Tumblr is quite fast moving and as long as you have content that is relevant and interesting and not too much of the same you can really post as much as you like. To make sure you show up in the feed of people you are following you need to post content frequently.

Use the Queue

If you want to publish a string of posts while you are offline you can do so with the queue. The queue lets you stagger posts over time and you can queue between one and fifty posts a day. When you go to publish your post simply click the down arrow next to where it says 'Post' and then click on 'Add to Queue.'

Optimize your posts for search engine optimization

Make sure you add keywords to your title and if you are posting an image add important keywords to your description in the space for your caption. When you are adding a link to a post make sure you add a description of the content of the post and the content of the link you are pointing it to.

Add anchor text

Tumblr allows you to add anchor text to your links. You can direct your audience to your website with a link and create anchor text with popular keywords from your industry which also helps with search engine optimization.

Schedule your posts

Tumblr allows you to schedule your posts for particular dates and times in the future. This is really handy for keeping your account active while you are away from the office. Simply click on the down arrow when you go to post your update and click on 'schedule'. You can either enter the date like this 'Next Tuesday, 4pm' or 'mm/dd/yy 12:34am' then click 'Schedule'.

The personal touch

As with all social media it's about being social, being unique and authentic. To help your audience identify with you and become friends with your brand you need to add your personality. You can do this by adding a personal touch to your comments by explaining why you are posting, what you are posting and how it will help your audience in some way.

Watermark your posts

There are two schools of thought on this subject but it is often a good idea for marketing to watermark your images or brand them in some way. Often images will get copied and if people want to find the original source of an image a discreet watermark with your web address or Tumblr URL can help. Watermarks are not going to protect your images totally but they will help you get found and make people think twice before they decide to copy them.

Chapter Three

Building your Audience on Tumblr

THE MORE FOLLOWERS you gain on Tumblr the more chance you have of your posts being reblogged. Unlike other social networks the number of followers is not published, but what is visible is the number of notes on your posts. This makes Tumblr refreshingly different from other networks because your credibility is no longer based on your follower count. Even though building up a sizeable following is important, you can really devote your time to finding the right audience and creating high quality content without having to worry about how your follower count looks. Statistics show that the majority of reblogs on Tumblr are from followers of your followers so the more followers you have the more opportunity you have of increasing your reach.

Here are some tips and strategies on how to build a targeted audience on Tumblr:

Post quality content

The best way to build your audience is to create quality content. When you post quality content you are likely to get reblogged and shared on other platforms too. A post that is reblogged will be seen by your followers followers and so it is very powerful and you can reach out to a wide area on Tumblr.

Find Friends

Tumblr offers you the opportunity to find your friends via Facebook and your email. Simply click on 'Find blogs' from your dashboard or go straight to www.tumblr.com/lookup

Follow other users

When you follow other Tumblrs it brings attention to your Tumblr. It's really important to follow back anyone who follows you and really helps to build relationships on Tumblr. On Tumblr your follower count is not displayed so nobody knows how many people you are following, or how many people are following you!

Be the face of your blog

Tumblrs with faces are more likely to get followed than those without so it is a good idea if you are a personal brand to have a picture of yourself on your Tumblr so you can make that personal connection with your followers.

Use hashtags to find your target audience

By searching for hashtags about the subjects you think are important to your target audience you will be able to find them.

Use tags in your posts

You want to make sure you appear in as many Tumblr searches as possible. Tumblr search relies on tags so you need to make sure that all your posts are tagged properly with the relevant tags that relate to your content and are in line with your target audience's interest. Adding between 7 and 11 tags is probably the right number without over using tags

Reblog, like and comment

Liking, reblogging and commenting (if users have this function installed) is a great way to build relationships. Reblogging is incredibly powerful on Tumblr and whether you reblog from the original source or not, the action of reblogging will appear on the original tumblr account, the post will also display all the people who reblogged which will offer you even more exposure. There is an art to reblogging. Any text or images that are added to the reblog will be seen by your followers and by your followers

followers if they reblog. It is therefore a good idea to personalize your reblog by adding an interesting comment and by telling your followers why you have reblogged this, however make sure you don't remove any of the content that was posted by the original source.

Send fan mail

Fan mail is just that and should only be used to compliment someone on their blog or on a particular post. You can send unlimited fan mail, up to 500 per day to the blogs you follow but you will have to wait at least 48 hours after following them before you can send a mail. Fan mail is a great way of drawing attention to your blog and can be accessed at the top of your dashboard.

And now @mention

Tumblr has recently introduced the @mention. So now if you want to get somebody's attention in a post you can now @mention their username.

Encourage interaction

The more interaction you allow the better, so make sure you allow replies from the people you follow and the users who are following you and let people ask you questions. You can turn on all these features in your settings.

Add Tumblr buttons

You can add your Tumblr buttons to your website or blog here http://www.tumblr.com/buttons

Announce your presence

Announcing your presence on other networks like Facebook, Twitter and Google + is a great way to build your following. The more people that share your content on Tumblr the more you will widen your reach. You can choose to automatically share your posts with Facebook and Twitter or you can selectively post the updates you want to promote on those platforms. If you are going to be posting frequently on Tumblr then it's probably not such a good idea to link your Tumblr to Facebook, as fans on Facebook are less tolerant of frequent posting.

Allow submissions

Allowing others to submit posts to your Tumblr is a great way to get others to contribute and provide content while at the same time building relationships. You can enable this feature in your settings, simply click the gear icon and 'Let people submit posts'. Nothing will get posted to your blog without your approval.

Add the Facebook like button and Twitter buttons to your Tumblr and your posts

You can add your Facebook like button to your Tumblr. Simply visit this page https://developers.facebook.com/docs/plugins/like-button/ and get the code by entering your Tumblr URL where it says 'URL to like.' When you have the code, click ' Customize' then 'Edit HTML' and pick the place where you want to add the code, add and then click 'Update Preview' and save.

To add a like button to your post you can simply add this code next to your post. Again you need to visit 'Customize' and 'Edit HTML' and then place it where you want to in the body. The best place is just before where it says "{/block:Posts}"

<iframe src="http://www.facebook.com/plugins/like.php?href={Permalink}&layout=standard&show-faces=true&width=450&action=like&colorscheme=light" scrolling="no" frameborder="0" allowTransparency="true" style="border:none; overflow:hidden; width:300px; height:75px"></iframe>

To do the same with Twitter simply visit this page,https://about.twitter.com/resources/buttons

To add more sharing buttons go to www.sharethis.com and get the code and add it in the same way. Once you had added it will appear under each of your blog posts.

Tumblr train

www.tumbletrain is an imaginery train where the passengers are actually Tumblr users and are looking for followers. You simply get on the train (sign up) and then get exposed to the other passengers who will hopefully start following you. It definitely cannot harm joining the train but at the same time you cannot expect to get the most targeted followers however if these followers are going to share your content and widen your reach then it has got to be good thing. There are similar schemes available like www.tumblrfollowers.com. Joining as many as possible is good idea to kick start your following and getting the ball rolling with your content being shared.

Follow for follow

If you add this phrase into Tumblr search you will come up with all the users who want to be followed and will hopefully follow you back in return. You do not have to follow them all and it is probably advisable to be selective.

Get featured in Tumblr Spotlight

When you click on 'Find blogs' on the right hand side of your dashboard you will be taken to a page where you can search by category and also see blogs which have already been included in Spotlight. These blogs have been singled out for their original and unique creative content.

If you want to get featured in Spotlight and you feel your blog has enough content to show off your creativity then simply send a note to editors@tumblr including your URL and the category you would like to be featured in.

Guest blogging

Guest blogging on other people blogs is a good way to get some attention while you are building your audience. Find other blogs with similar topics and offer complimentary products and be on the look out for Tumblrs that allow you to post your content.

CREATING A CONTEST ON TUMBLR

Contests are always a great way to increase your reach and help increase your following on Tumblr. With Tumblr's flexibility and functionality it allows you to create great contests easily. Before going ahead you need to work out what it is you want to achieve from running a contest, is it to increase your following, build your opt-in or to promote a particular product? Once you have decided on this, here are the steps you need to take to set up a contest on Tumblr.

Check out Tumblr terms and conditions

Make sure you familiarise yourself with Tumblr's guidelines at http://www.tumblr.com/policy/en/contest_guidelines , for example, you are only allowed to offer prizes of up to $1000 without their permission and you are also not allowed to ask users to follow, reblog or like as a prerequisite for entering. The other thing you need to check are the rules for sweepstakes and contests in your particular country or state.

Pick your prize carefully

In order to gain the attention of your target audience it is really important to pick a prize that is relevant to your business and that your target audience will value. This way you can be sure that the majority of entrants will actually be interested in your product rather than offering a more generic type of prize that may get you a wider audience but will not necessarily be the right audience. Offering a gift card to purchase your products is a great way to appeal to the right audience and also a wider audience who will then have a choice of the products you are offering.

Decide on the type of contest

Are you going to run a simple sweepstake or ask your contestants to submit something like an image or video. Visual contests run very well on Tumblr and you can ask your entrants to submit their entries using the submit functionality which can be found in your settings. You can monitor all your entries and make sure the content is appropriate before displaying it on your Tumblr. If you are going to be asking your audience to submit artwork or images and then use them in some way you need to make sure you cover yourself legally and mention this in your terms and conditions.

Ask your contestants to tag their entry

This is particularly important if you are going to promote your contest on other platforms like Twitter and Instagram. When you pick your tag make sure it is unique and specific to your contest or business. This way you can search for your # hashtag.

Decide on the duration of the contest Decide on the duration of the competition. With photo and video competitions you will need to offer a longer time as entrants will require more time to take their photos or video. With sweepstakes the duration of the competition can be much shorter.

Set your rules and publish Tumblr allows you to create pages on your Tumblr so you can easily create a specific page for your contest outlining the rules and how to enter. Make sure you include details like who your contest is open to. Tumblr is global so you may not want to ship outside your country. Tumblr states that users under the age of 18 are not allowed to enter so make sure you include this rule. You also need to include the closing date for entries.

Create a landing page Tumblr gives you the functionality to easily add a page to your Tumblr so you can set up a page with images to promote your contest, add your rules and also ask them to submit their entry with their email address, contests are a great way to build your opt-in list. If you are promoting your contest on other networks you could also send them to an external webpage.

Create a compelling graphic You need to create an interesting graphic with an attention grabbing headline, for example; ' Enter to win a $50 Gift Card from 'your business name'.

Promoting your contest To promote you contest you will need to have built up a following already so you have followers to share your contest with. Even though you cannot ask them to share to enter they will most probably upload their own entry to their own dashboard and reblog it anyway. Make sure you add a banner to your website, you can also send out emails to your list announcing your contest and promote it on your other social networks as well.

Choosing the winner You will need to decide how you are going to choose the winner. Many contest organizers use random.org to generate a random number from the number of contestants. If you have a photo contest then you will need to decide how they are going to be judged.

Post Contest

Once you have picked or chosen your winners you can post your winners on your Tumblr and share your plans for any future contests. To keep your unsuccessful entrants happy it's a good idea to email them with a money off voucher or coupon and hopefully you will convert some into customers.

Advertising on Tumblr

Advertising on Tumblr comes in the way of sponsored posts for mobile, sponsored web posts, sponsored radar and sponsored spotlight. To advertise you need to contact the advertising team at Tumblr.

CHAPTER FOUR

DAY TO DAY ACTIVITY

THERE ARE CERTAIN things that you will need to do on a day to day basis to run your campaign on Tumblr. It is a good idea to allot a specific amount of time and a particular time of the day to do this. Here are some of the things you will need to do:

Following your customer's Tumblr's

This is important if your customers are business owners themselves. Following their Tumblr or following your customers will go a long way in building relationships. By following you are showing them that you are interested in what they have to say and also helping them to achieve their goals by helping to build their audience.

Showing your audience you value and respect them

If you value and respect your audience they will most probably love, respect and value your business. Be kind, generous, offer as much help and value as possible, reply to their comments and make it obvious that you value them and are listening to them. Don't be afraid to be yourself rather than a stiff brand with no personality.

Everyone is aiming for likes, shares and comments so if you are helping others out by commenting and liking their content it is going to draw attention to your brand and they are more likely to take interest in your content. This is one area where the reciprocation rule works very well on Tumblr. Engaging with content will also draw attention to you and your brand and you will find that people will click on your name to find out who you are and they may very well follow you. Be friendly to your

audience, be chatty, authentic, genuine and embrace the conversation. All this will all go a long well in building a positive image for your brand and will set you apart from your others who are continually ambushing their audience with self promotion.

Following influencers in your niche
Building relationships with key influencers in your niche is invaluable. Not only can you learn from their content but also these people can have literally thousands of followers, imagine if they follow you back and then share your content!

Dealing with negative comments
Every business at some time will have to deal with negativity from followers. Hopefully if you have a good product then this is not going to happen too often. There are ' trolls' out there who have nothing better to do than post negative comments, the best thing to do with them is just ignore them, delete their comments and block them.

However there will be real customers who have real concerns and complaints and may post negative comments publicly, there may also be people who really want to lash out to gain your attention as quickly as possible and spread the news to their friends too!

You need to deal with complaints as quickly as possible and be as transparent and authentic as possible. The best thing to do is to apologise and say how sorry you are to hear of the inconvenience they have been caused and offer to continue the conversation and deal with their concern by either private message or telephone. You can then deal with this privately, give your customer the full attention they deserve and decide on your next course of action or compensation.

Chapter Five

Measuring and Monitoring your Results

MEASURING AND MONITORING your results and performance against your original goals and objectives on a continual basis is essential. This is where many businesses go wrong, they carry on aimlessly posting content without checking to see what is working and what is not. Then after six months or a year they wonder why their campaign is making no positive difference at all.

When you measure your results you will discover so much information about your campaign which will allow you to steer your campaign in the right direction to achieve those SMART goals and objectives and stop anything that is not working.

When you originally work out your strategies and tactics for your campaign you will be estimating what you need to do to achieve your goals and objectives. However as you campaign runs you will see exactly what you need to do to achieve what you originally set out to do. For example, you may need to increase the number of people you follow to attract new followers or you may need to change the types of posts you make to increase engagement and reach. You may need to increase your number of posts in order to get more likes or reblogs. Perhaps you need to increase the number of competitions you run to increase the number of opt-in subscribers. This is what it is all about, making your campaign work for you by constantly measuring your success against the goals set and then adjusting those objectives accordingly in order to achieve the results.

There are many tools to available to help you measure your campaign on Tumblr including Google Analytics and other third party sites.

GOOGLE ANALYTICS

Google Analytics can provide a huge amount of information to measure the effectiveness of your campaign including the following:

How many visitors are visiting your Tumblr.
How often are they visiting your Tumblr.
Which are you most popular posts.
Which search terms your visitors found you through. (This is incredibly important for future tagging.)
Where your visitors are coming from.

Adding Google Analytics to your Tumblr

The first thing you need to do is install Google Analytics to your Tumblr and also make sure you have set up Google Analytics for any other websites or blogs so you can see how much traffic Tumblr is creating for your other sites.

Some themes are already set up to let you add your Analytics code straight into the appearance box. Simply select your particular blog and then click on 'Customize' and then scroll down to see if there is a field where you can add your Google Analytics code and add the code.

If your theme does not support that here is what to do in Google Analytics and Tumblr:

Google Analytics

- Simply login or create a new Google account if you do not already have one
- Once you are in, click on 'Admin' and then click on 'Create new account' and add your account name, for example Tumblr my blog

- Then choose 'http://' in the drop down menu and add either your Tumblr URL or your custom domain.
- Then select your business category, country, time zone, read and accept the terms and conditions and then click on ' Get tracking code'
- Copy your tracking code and 'Save'

In Tumblr

- On your Tumblr dashboard select the blog you want to update and then click on 'Customize'
- You can either paste your Google Analytics tracking code into the description section or click on 'Edit HTML' and paste before "</ head>"

To view your Tumblr metrics simply login to Google Analytics and select your blog

Google Analytics provides advanced reports that will let you track the effectiveness of your campaign and see how much traffic Tumblr is sending to your website or other blogs you may have.

The Overview Report This report lets you see at a glance how much conversion value is generated from social channels. It compares all conversions with those resulting from social.

The Conversions Report The conversions report helps you to quantify the value of social and shows conversion rates and the monetary value of conversions that occurred due to referrals from Tumblr and any of the other social networks. Google Analytics can link visits from Tumblr with the goals you have chosen and your E - commerce transactions. To do this you will need to configure your goals in Google Analytics which is found under 'Admin' and then 'Goals'. Goals in Google Analytics let you measure how often visitors take or complete a specific action and you can either create goals from the templates offered or create your own custom goals.

The Conversions report can be found in the Standard Reporting tab under Traffic Sources > Social > Conversions.

The Networks Referral Report The Networks Referral report tells you how many visitors the social networks have referred to your website and shows you how many pageviews, visits, the duration of the visits and the average number of pages viewed per visit. From this information you can determine which network referred the highest quality of traffic.

Data Hub Activity Report The Data Hub activity report shows how people are engaging with your site on the social networks . You can see the most recent URLSs that were shared, how they were shared and what was said.

The Social Visitors Flow Report This report shows you the initial paths that your visitors took from social sites through your site and where they exited.

The Landing Pages Report This report shows you engagement metrics for each URL. These include page views, average visit duration and pageviews and pages viewed per visit.

The Trackbacks Report The Trackback report shows you which sites are linking to your content and how many visits those sites are sending to you. This can help you to work out which sort of content is the most successful so you can create similar and also helps you to build relationships with those who are constantly linking to your content.

Tracking Custom Campaigns with Google Analytics

Google Analytics lets you create URL's for custom campaigns for website tracking. This helps you to identify which content is the most effective in driving visitors to your website and landing pages. For instance you may want to see which particular posts on Tumblr are sending you the most traffic, or you may want to see which links in an email or particular banners on your website are sending you the most traffic. Custom Campaigns let you measure this and see what is and what is not working by letting you add parameters to the end of your URL. You can either add you own or use the URL Builder.

To do this simply type 'URL builder" into Google and click on the first result. The URL builder form will only appear if you are signed into Google. You then need to add the URL, that you want to track, to the form provided and then complete the fields and click 'Submit.' You will then need to shorten the URL with bit.ly or goo.gl/ . Once you have set these up you can track the results within Google Analytics.

THIRD PARTY TOOLS FOR MEASURING

Union Metrics
Unionmetrics is the official analytical platform for Tumblr. Union Metrics focuses on delivering simple social metrics that enable marketers and agencies to measure and improve their social media campaigns.

They offer a free service and a mini service for bloggers and plans for brands and agencies. All plans offer information on blog engagement, follower and content analysis and paid plans offer Google Analytics integration and plans for brands offer competitor blog tracking and keyword based topic analysis as well.

Numblr
Numblr offers a free analysis for key metrics for Tumblr blogs. You can track your note to post ratio , type of post breakdown and percentage of original content. Numblr also allows you to analyze any other Tumblr blog so it's great for checking out the competition.

Make YouTube Work For Your Business

Alex Stearn

Table of Contents

CHAPTER ONE

GETTING STARTED ON YOUTUBE

YOUTUBE IS NOT only the worlds largest video sharing site and the second largest search engine, it is also a social network, a vibrant community of people who want to learn, be entertained, interact with each other and share content, and an advertising platform. The growth in the number of people with smart phones, together with increased availability and speed of the internet has fuelled an explosion in the number of videos viewed. YouTube is now seeing over four billion video views per day with over one billion unique users per month. These people are not necessarily going to YouTube to buy products and services, but they are going there to watch videos, be entertained, to find out about things they are interested in, or to find out how to do things. Any business that understands this and can produce interesting and compelling content aimed at the interests of their target audience has the opportunity to reap the marketing benefits that YouTube has to offer.

However, even though YouTube is the second largest search engine, many businesses are still ignoring it as a serious platform for finding new customers and building their brand. The fact is video and YouTube offer huge potential for businesses to generate leads, gain exposure and build their brand, particularly since businesses are far more likely to get video content ranked in Google search than any text article.

The main reasons why many businesses are frightened off, is because they think it's either too complicated, too expensive, too time consuming or they fear standing in front of a camera. But the truth is, producing videos no longer needs to be expensive or time consuming. Investing in high quality camera equipment is not always necessary and with today's smart phone technology creating quality videos is now relatively easy and inexpensive. Many of the most popular viral videos have been created on a phone or webcam. With regard to editing and production the availability of applications like 'iMovie' and 'Final Cut' have made uploading and editing videos incredibly straight forward and now YouTube has free editing features as well. Videos can now be easily embedded into websites, blogs and other social media with little or no technical expertise.

The very fact that YouTube is being under utilized by so many businesses means there is huge potential for those businesses who want to use it properly. Before you make any decision about whether YouTube is a viable platform to market your business, here are some reasons why deciding to use video and YouTube may be one of the smartest decisions you make:

A powerful platform to generate leads for your business

This has got to be the most important benefit for any business. As the second largest search engine YouTube is a very powerful platform for generating leads and driving traffic to a website by helping consumers find answers to their questions and search queries. Any business that realizes the huge potential available on YouTube to find new customers and then puts in a system to capture leads and convert them into paying customers is going to be onto a winner.

Fact, video sells stuff!

It just does. Viewers are three times more likely to purchase an item after watching a video.

Video levels the playing field

Video lets you compete with large companies and allows you to reach and communicate with your audience relatively inexpensively.

Creates a deeper relationship with your audience

People like to connect with people and face to face video content can create the deepest possible connection with any audience. If you or one of your colleagues become the face of your brand the relationship with your target audience will become much deeper, more powerful and more lasting. Video also creates a lasting impression and is well remembered which is powerful for any brand.

Video is mobile

With the increase in mobile devices businesses have even more opportunity to communicate with their target audience. Since people carry their mobiles on them most of time it is even more likely that a video will be viewed, as consumers can choose to watch in their own time and at their leisure. They are often more receptive, because if they do watch a video it's because they actually want to and not because they are forced too. People will also often read their mail on their phone in their leisure time so any video attached to that mail is also more likely to get watched, than if they are at their desk.

People love video

YouTube videos are appearing very high in search engine results and also consumers are going straight to YouTube with their questions, they are looking for businesses like yours to answer those questions in the most concise and straight forward way, which is often by video. Videos can deliver information in the most easy to understand form and videos can inspire, educate and entertain all at the same time. Most people would much rather watch a video than read a lengthy time consuming and complex instructional document, also 90% of information transmitted to the brain is visual and processed faster in the brain than text. According to a study performed by Forbes in association with Google, 75% of business executives watch a work-related video weekly and more than half of them watch a video on YouTube.

Drives traffic to websites

Videos drive traffic to websites. In the same study, Forbes discovered that 65% of executives visited a vendor's website after viewing a video and the younger executives particularly were more engaged and likely to make a purchase or call the vendor and share the video with other colleagues.

Increases sales conversions

Having a video on your site is like having a sales person active 24/7 and website visitors are more likely to buy a product on an online retail site after watching a video. Viewers spend more time on pages with videos and increase click through rates too.

Increases your email open rates

Videos increase email open rates and can decrease the number of opt-outs from your subscribers. The fact is, a good proportion of people would much rather watch a quick video than read an email and people like to connect with people.

Powerful for building your personal brand

There is no better way of creating a personal connection and building trust with your audience than with video. If you are your own personal brand then video is almost essential. It is incredibly powerful and offers you the opportunity to reach people in locations that you would never have had the opportunity of reaching before. If you produce good video, then you will be streets ahead of anyone who is just creating a blog and video will definitely give you the edge. There are numerous types of video you can use to help all areas of your business including regular Vlogs, instructional videos, coaching sessions and Webinars, you can also utilize Google 'Hangouts on Air'.

Videos get shared

YouTube videos are the number one type of content to get shared on social media, 700 videos a minute are shared on Twitter alone! Visual content also drives engagement which means it gets liked and commented on and therefore can help you to grow your reach and amplify your message.

Powerful for search engine optimization
YouTube is owned by Google and therefore YouTube videos get highly ranked within Google. Recent statistics show that a video is far more likely to get ranked in Google than a text page and far more likely to get viewed than any blog post. YouTube thumbnails often appear in Google search results which also increases click through and videos also help with your SEO by attracting more back links than plain text posts.

Makes your business stand out
Videos are almost always unique in their creation and are a great way to make your mark and stand out from the crowd. Consumers are far more likely to purchase from someone they have built a relationship with and video is the best way to deliver your message personally to a large number of people.

Video is continually working for you
Once your video is on the internet it can be continually working for you and it's like having a sales team working 24/7 for you which makes it an incredibly inexpensive method of promotion.

How YouTube can Benefit your Business
Quite simply YouTube means traffic, leads and sales. People love to watch video for all sorts of reasons and video executed properly can create the deepest possible connection with any audience and more than any other type of media.

There are four possible ways that you can make money through YouTube and these are:

- By creating video content to promote your own business and your own products by using YouTube as a traffic source, improving your search engine optimization, generating leads and building your brand.

- Making money from advertising on your videos with Google's Adsense.

- Affiliate marketing.

- Sponsorship.

The aim of this book is to outline how you can use YouTube as a traffic source, how to create compelling video content and outline the strategies and tactics you will need to implement to generate and capture leads, increase your sales and build your brand.

In order to make YouTube work for your business you will need to define and create clear goals, objectives and strategies. Here are some goals that you may wish to achieve for your business through using YouTube:

To use YouTube as a traffic and lead generator

To find new customers by creating compelling content, capturing leads and converting them into new customers with the use of your opt in list or by creating a sales funnel.

Example objectives:
- To create X Number of new leads per day.
- To add X number of new subscribers to email opt in
- To create X number of sales through sales funnel each day.

To inform your customers

Keep existing customers interested in products and keep them talking about and sharing your content.

Example objective: To create 1 Video per week/month

To become a thought leader in your industry and build your brand
Example Objective: To create consistently create video and at least 1 new video per week on a new subject relating to the industry.

To build a loyal following of subscribers and a community
Example Objective: To have X number of subscribers on channel in 1/6/12 months

To support your PR by adding a video with your PR releases
Example Objective: To add a video to every press release that is sent out.

To improve your sites search engine optimization through adding video to your site
It is thought that you should have self hosted videos on your site for selling your products, but this does not stop you from uploading them to YouTube as well and you may make some sales from your YouTube channel.
Example Objective: To add 1 Video demonstrating each product on website.

To enhance your blog posts with video
Example objective: To produce a video for every blog post to encourage more traffic from YouTube and to support the blog with video content as well to increase reach through YouTube.

To support your social media goals
Example objective: To support your social media goals by providing video content for your other social media platforms.

To capture leads from other channels to convert to sales
Example Objective: To create X number of videos per week/month to share on other social media platforms.

To support your PPC Advertising by remarketing

With ads on YouTube and across the Google display network you can remarket and advertise to people who have already watched any of your YouTube videos or subscribed or unsubscibed to your channel.

SETTING UP YOUR YOUTUBE CHANNEL FOR SUCCESS

This chapter will outline how to best set up your account on YouTube, how to optimize it for search and how to set up a system to maximize traffic, generate leads and then capture leads for conversion.

YouTube is now integrated with Google + and if you want to set up a channel on YouTube, or even if you just want to comment or subscribe to any other channels, or create playlists then you will need a Google + account. One of the benefits of the integration for you as a business owner, is that whenever someone comments on a video, the video will show up in their news feed. (If they have chosen that option.)

Setting up your YouTube account is straight forward and is your first step towards building your channel. If you do not have a YouTube account or a Google + account this is what you need to do. Go to YouTube and click 'Sign in' then click 'Create an account' which is situated under the sign in box. This will create a Google + account for you. Simply go ahead and fill in the form with your email, password, gender, birth date and mobile number and then agree to the terms and conditions. You will then need to verify your account which will later allow you to create videos longer than 15 minutes. Once you have added your photo you can then click back to YouTube.

You then need to click on 'YouTube settings' and then 'Create a Channel.' You can then set up your channel as either yourself, or click on 'To use a business or another name click here'. Now you can add your channel name, select your company type from the drop down menu, choose who can view your channel and agree to terms and conditions. You will then need to verify your account again.

You are now ready to create a custom URL for your business, simply click on the image icon on the top right of your account, click on 'YouTube settings', click on 'Advanced' and then click 'Create custom URL.' On the right of your account you will see 'Popular Channels' you may want to disable this so you are not drawing attention away from your videos.

The new 'One Channel Design' is called that because you can design it once to look good on all devices, PC's, Macs, Tablets, smart phones and smart TV's. The design also lets you have more control over what shows up on your channel and you can also arrange the layout of your channel with multiple layouts for videos and playlists.

Completing and uploading images for your channel icon and channel art (the image at the top of the channel) is easy, just follow the on screen instructions. You are now ready to brand your channel. To help with the set up YouTube has created a **'channel set up check list'** which can be found on the top right.

Set your channel icon
This is like your profile picture. Make sure it is consistent with your branding on other platforms so you are easily recognisable. This needs to be a square image 800 X 800 pixels

Add channel art
You can be consistent with your brand as your channel art will scale up and down to fit any devices, plus your social links will be available on any device and your subscribers will recognise your channel from wherever they are viewing. You have the option to upload from YouTube's gallery but it's better to upload an image which is consistent with your brand across your other platforms. If you are a personal brand then this is where you can really put your personality across. The recommended image size to upload is 2560 X1440 pixels. The image size is large

because it is designed to display on television screens as well. At the minimum width the channel art is 546 X 423 pixels, this is called the 'logo safe area' where your image and text will not be cut off and will always be visible, whatever the device. Make sure your most important information is in the 'logo safe area'. The areas to the right and left may or may not be visible depending on the device. YouTube provides a template you can download which allows you to see what will be visible on each type of device.

The About Section

The about section contains your channel description, links, featured channels and subscriptions:

- **Channel Description.** The first few words of your channel description will not only appear on your profile but they will be found in search and also in suggested categories on YouTube. Even though you have up to 5000 words to describe your channel it is important to write your most compelling sentence at the beginning. After the first sentence make sure your description is as interesting as possible at the same time including as many keywords from your industry as possible without losing the quality of the content. URL's do not work here, but you can add them in the next section.

- **Add Web links** At the top right of your channel art you can add your links, simply click 'Edit Links'. The top part is for custom links, one of which you can choose to display on your channel art and the bottom part is for up to four social links and one custom link which could be your website or blog or a link to subscribe to your YouTube channel. Your links will be displayed on the bottom right hand corner of your channel art.

- **Feature other channels** This is another section in the about section. Featured channels appear under the about tab but at the top right hand side of your channel. You may want to add other channels if you are in a network and this way you can cross promote. However, you can also choose not to display this which may be a good idea as it can draw people away from your channel.

• **Subscriptions** You can choose whether or not you want to display the channels you subscribe to and all you need to do to hide them is put a tick in the box where it says, 'Make my subscriptions private'.

Add your channel tags

To make your channel even more likely to be found in search you need to add tags to your channel. These are not easy to find. To do this simply go to the down arrow on the top right of your channel and click 'YouTube Settings', then under the heading 'Additional features' at the bottom click 'View Additional features' , then click 'Advanced' on the left. You will then see 'Channel Keywords' and this is where you need to add relevant keywords for your channel.

FINDING YOUR WAY AROUND YOUTUBE

Once you have created your account on YouTube it's a really good idea to have a look around and familiarise yourself with your account and your channel. Once you get to know YouTube you will find just how much it has to offer and just how straightforward it is to use. This section will give you a quick introduction to finding your way around YouTube and an explanation of the terms which will be mentioned throughout this book. If you are new to YouTube then this section will be really helpful.

By clicking on your channel icon on the top right of your screen you will display the following : My Channel, Video Manager, Subscriptions, Settings, Switch Account and Sign out.

My Channel

Home. When you click on 'My channel' you will arrive on your channel home page where you will be able to view your channel art with your channel icon and links to your website and social platforms, if you have added them.

Underneath your channel art you will be able to upload your trailer video. This video will be displayed alongside a description which is taken from the video description. You need to make this your welcome message. Your channel trailer is available if you have your 'Channel browse view' enabled. To enable, simply click on the pencil icon and then click on 'Edit channel navigation' and then click on 'Enable' in the 'Browse section' The 'Browse' view of your channel allows visitors to see the customized content (the channel trailer sections) you are displaying. Disabling the 'Browse' view will display your channel feed to all users.

Under your trailer video your viewers will be able to view the videos you have uploaded. You can organize your videos into sections. Sections let you feature sets of videos, such as your latest uploads or likes, or you can feature a custom set by using a playlist or tag. You can display your sections either as a horizontal row or a vertical list.

On the right you will see 'Popular channels' which have been selected by YouTube and also 'Featured Channels' which are the favorite channels you have chosen to display. You can choose to disable your 'Popular channels' but in doing so you will stop your channel from being recommended across YouTube on other channels.

You can see how the public view your channel by clicking 'View as public' on the top right of you channel art.

Videos

Your videos page shows all the videos you have uploaded in chronological order and also displays other videos that you have liked.

You can choose whether you want to display the videos you have liked to the public or not.

Playlists

Playlists make it possible for your viewers to watch multiple videos with minimal effort. Playlists are proven to increase view time and they also appear in search results and suggested videos so it is a very good idea to create them. You can create your own playlists and organize your videos into different sets or groups that relate to each other in some way. When you create your playlist you need to add a title and create a description for your playlist, this is your metadata which YouTube uses to index your videos and therefore you need to optimize your title, description and tags with specific keywords from your niche which also relate to your content. In your description you can include links to subscribe to your channel and other related videos and playlists.

You can use playlist to do the following:

- To group videos together that you want your viewers to watch in one session.
- To group videos around a subject or theme.
- To combine your most popular content for your more recent uploads.
- To group your most viewed videos to tempt your viewer to watch your best content.

Discussions

Discussions are where your viewers can leave comments about your channel and you can reply to them. This is a real opportunity to build relationships. If people are leaving positive comments then they are interested and it's only courteous to thank them and reply.

About

Your about section is where you add your channel description, your links and add your featured channels. It is also where you can display the channel which you are subscribed to and you can make this public or not.

The Dashboard

The dashboard is like the back office of your YouTube account and it is here you can find all the following, Video Manager, Community, Channel settings, Analytics and Creation Tools. You find your dashboard by clicking on the gear icon on the top right.

Video Manager

Your video manager is just that, it is where you upload and manage your videos and you will find the following:

- **Uploads** This is where you upload and edit your videos, add annotations, enhancements, add audio, add captions and add all your descriptions, titles and tags. You can also add your videos to playlists here.

- **Live Events** You can stream live events on YouTube. To do this you will need to go to 'Channel Settings' and enable 'live events'. If your account is in good order and you have more than 100 subscriber you will able to stream live events. With the right planning, testing and promotion you can use this functionality to broadcast live events like news, cultural or music events. There are full instruction on YouTube how to do this. You can also create 'Hangouts on Air' which encourage subscriber engagement and require less technical knowledge. More about Hangouts on Air later.

- **Playlists** This shows all your play lists.

- **Tags** This shows all the tags you have used.

- **Search history** Your search history is really useful and lets you see what you have previously searched for on YouTube which may help you find a particular video.

- **Favorites** This shows all the videos that you have favorited. To favourite a video simply click 'Add to' under the video you are watching and then you can choose where you want to add it to, either a playlist or your favorites.

- **Likes** This show all the videos you have liked.

Community

Community is where you can manage your comment settings and where you can manage your inbox.

Channel Settings

- **Features** This tells you how your account stands and what your account has been enabled to do, for example, whether your account has been enabled for monetization, longer videos , live events and whether you can upload custom thumbnails.

- **Defaults** This is where you can set your defaults for future video uploads. You can override these settings on individual videos.

- **In video Programming** This is a feature that lets you embed a chosen video or logo across all of your videos on your channel. By adding your channel avatar as an annotation you can lead viewers to your channel page and by adding a thumbnail annotation you can lead viewers to the video watch page.

- **Fan Finder** Fan finder helps to find and connect your channel to new fans at no cost to you . YouTube uses the information they have about what their viewers are watching and tries to match your channel with people they think may enjoy your videos. When you create your channel advert make sure it is as short and engaging as possible, after five seconds your viewer can skip, so your aim here is to make it so engaging that they do not do that. Make sure you show your viewers what your channel is about, make it clear why they should subscribe to your channel and include a call to action and an annotation.

- **Advanced** This is where you can choose whether or not you want to allow adverts to be displayed, where you can link your Adwords account and add an associated website URL . You can also specify here whether you want to display the number of subscribers you have and also if you want your channel to appear in other channels' recommendations.

Analytics

Analytics lets you measure and analyze your organic and paid traffic and view all your reports. This is explained in more detail in the chapter about measuring your campaign results.

Creation Tools

- **Audio Library** This is where you can download royalty free audio for your videos.
- Video Editor This is where you can edit your videos and add images, audio, transitions and titles.

SETTING UP YOUR SYSTEM TO GENERATE AND CAPTURE LEADS

Before we go into how you are going to get tons of subscribers and traffic to your channel you will need to have a system in place so that you can capture leads and convert them into sales. Without some kind of strategy you are just wasting time and money. Inspiring videos are great to build your brand and stand out from the crowd but in order to let them really work for your business they need to help you to generate and capture leads so you can convert them into paying customers.

The one time that most people are going to be interested in you is when they have found and watched your video. This is when they need your information, they may not be ready to buy your product yet but this is when they are most likely to subscribe and opt into your list.

Basically your videos are your tool to generate and capture new leads and channel then into your sales funnel. You simply create compelling video content that your audience will love with the sole intention of getting them onto your list by offering them something of value for free. Once they are on your list you have the opportunity to convert these leads into customers.

Here is a quick step by step process showing how to do it:

1. Create your special free offer

Firstly you need to think of something that your target audience really want and it needs to be something they would consider really valuable, this could be a free ebook, a short video course or a Webinar about a really hot topic or a special money offer coupon. Webinars and videos can be incredibly effective as they help to create an immediate personal connection with your audience from the start which can be extremely powerful as people generally like to buy from people they like and trust. When choosing your offer you need to ask yourself this one question: is this valuable enough that it is my ideal customer would pay for it? If your answer to this question is yes, then this is probably the right offer and you are likely to persuade them to volunteer their email. If your answer is no then you will need to think again. This really is one of the most important parts of this lead generation system and in order to create a really positive first experience with your prospect you need to really wow them with your offer.

2. Create your landing page

You will then need to create a special landing page with your offer and your email opt-in capture form. You can either ask a web developer to create this for you or use a landing page generator service like, www.leadpages.net, www.launcheffect.com or www.instapage.com or www.unbounce.com . For a monthly fee these websites offer an incredibly user friendly service with numerous templates, design examples and tutorials to help you put your landing page together. Your landing page needs to be specific to the one goal you want to achieve which is to visually promote your offer and then capture the email addresses of your prospects. Make sure you set up your opt-in email list with your email service provider first. Providers include www.aweber.com www.constantcontact.com or www.mailchimp.com

3. Create your video
Create a video which is aimed at the interests of your target audience.

4. Include a call to action and send them to your landing page
Include a strong call to action at the end of the video to sign up for a free offer, making sure you give the viewer enough time to take that action

5. Send them to a thank you page
By this time you will have their email and you will need to:

- Thank them for purchasing.
- Deliver the free gift.
- Offer them another gift or bonus gift for sharing you on other social networks.

Chapter Two

Content Is King on YouTube

WHETHER YOU ARE creating your own videos or employing a production company you will need to create consistently exceptional video content which is going to be of value to your target audience. There are definitely certain factors that will enhance your viewers experience and contribute to making your videos a success, but the most important elements are your subject and its content.

When it comes to your content simply standing in front of a camera advertising your product is not going to work. You will need to produce content that is going to either interest, entertain or help your audience in some way. This is not saying you should not produce the occasional product video, but in order to win new viewers and build an audience you will need to get creative and produce compelling content around subjects that your audience are searching for. By offering this information you will have more chance of capturing the right audience through YouTube and Google and converting them into customers by building a relationship and trust with your audience.

To start you need to research your target audience, find out who they are and what they are interested in and what they want. Once you have this information you can think about the sort of content that you can create around these subjects. Google's Keyword Planner is a very effective way of finding out what particular keywords people are searching for around your products or services. The Keyword Planner will also help by offering you information on the average number of times a word is searched for and the amount of competition for that word. You can even view a graph which displays seasonal trends to help you to decide when the best time is to promote your video in order to receive the maximum possible number of views.

IDEAS FOR DIFFERENT TYPES OF VIDEO CONTENT

Once you are clear about your subject or topic you can decide which type of video you want to create. Here are some ideas for the different types of video that you can create on YouTube.

Your YouTube trailer video

The first video you need to create is you Your Tube trailer video. Your channel trailer is the introduction video to your channel and is the first video that your unsubscribed visitors will see when they view your channel. Before creating this video you need to ask yourself these questions:

What do my audience really want to hear?
What value can I offer my subscribers?
How can I best convince first time unsubscribed visitors to subscribe to my channel?
How can I make this compelling enough and interesting enough?
How can I deliver this in the most unique way?

Make sure when creating it you keep it short and straight to the point, describe your channel, add a call to action and at the end of the video ask viewers to subscribe. Do make sure the viewer has time to take action before the video finishes. Clicking the edit pencil lets you add or remove or trailer

Video blogging

Vlogging or video blogging is a form of blogging using video. Video blogging opens up a whole new world to smaller businesses who otherwise would not be able to afford the high cost of television advertising. If you are a personal brand then vlogging can be a very effective way of creating a successful channel on YouTube and building your brand.

By putting a face to your business you instantly create a connection with your audience like no other media and is even better because your audience can actually interact with you and your content by writing comments, asking questions and sharing your content.

Video Blogging is the single most powerful and inexpensive way to build a lasting connection and relationship with your audience. Delivering content on a regular basis helps to draw attention to your brand, promotes interaction and helps to build trust with your audience. It keeps your current customers interested and engaged and gives potential customers a fast introduction to what your business is all about. Vlogging also helps to make you stand out as an authority on your subject, so when it comes to your prospects making a purchasing decision, they will be more likely to buy from you.

How you produce your videos will depend very much on your budget, you can either produce your own videos with very little expense using a webcam, iphone or video camera, or you can employ a production company to produce them. If you do decide to use a production company then most companies will be willing to produce videos for you on a regular contractual basis.

Here are some tips for Vlogging:

- Aim to publish regularly, once a week if you can.
- Release videos on a set day of the week and let your audience know in the video which day you broadcast.
- Plan a schedule but be flexible too so you can include content about current trends and news.
- Create enough video content that you can still deliver when you are on vacation.

- If you know what your audience like, you can also publish quality content from other channels to your subscribers.
- Create content around calendar events which are relevant to your audience.

Industry Statistics

For B2B businesses using statistics as a subject for a video can be very effective. People love statistics especially when they are dressed up to look interesting, they also love to share them too! Statistics provide knowledge and certainty about facts, they also provide a foundation for people to base their business ideas and models around. Putting a video together with interesting statistics can be as easy as putting a power point presentation together and adding narration and some royalty free music. If you don't want to stand in front of the camera then these types of video are perfect and can go viral too!

Q & A videos

Providing the answers to questions that your audience have asked can be an invaluable way of building trust and uploading this type of video on a regular basis can create quite a loyal following. Done well can this type of video can help to position you as an expert and build authority around your subject. Once you start posting your videos you may find that other questions arise from your subscribers and you can then use these as subject material for your next video.

Tutorials & how to videos

More and more people are coming to YouTube to learn how to do certain tasks and if you put a query into Google then you will find numerous YouTube videos appearing in the search results. These types of videos are incredibly useful when building your brand and very helpful in generating and capturing new leads for your business.

Product demonstration videos

Product demonstration videos are a great way to capture your product's best features while also entertaining your audience especially if your video manages to capture your enthusiasm about your products. When creating your video you need to remember you are first selling yourself so you need to be professional, clear, brief and to the point about what you want to say.

New product videos/promotional videos

Product videos definitely belong on your website however even though you do not want to keep shouting about your product, keeping your subscribers updated occasionally on your new products is a good idea especially if they are done in an entertaining way.

Entertaining/fun viral videos

Entertaining videos help to build your brand's personality and if you are lucky enough to produce a viral video you can increase your visibility massively.

Employee videos

Introducing your staff helps to give an insider view of your business and build a connection with your audience. It's a great way to create an emotional connection with your business and makes your business more transparent, approachable and friendly.

Event videos

If you are producing an event or exhibiting at a trade show or exhibition then an inspiring video about the event is a great way to show your event to those people who could not attend and is also a very effective form of promotion for your next event. Telling a story with your video is very effective way of adding interest and can help to create an emotional connection with your audience.

Customer Testimonials

What better way to promote your business than having people saying nice things about your product or service!

Explainer Videos

Explainer videos are just that and they explain what your business is about and can be either animated or live action. Explainer videos should be about 1 – 2 minutes long and belong on your website but there is no harm in adding it to your channel for your subscribers to view if they wish. You can now create inexpensive animated videos with user friendly services like www.goanimate.com which you can use to create very professional videos.

TIPS FOR CREATING EXCEPTIONAL VIDEOS

The subject and the content of your video is going to be a major contribution to making your video compelling enough for your audience to watch. However there are still certain things you can do to help create exceptional videos from pre-production stage through to uploading your video. As a general rule 80% of the work involved in creating your video needs to go into the pre-production/planning stage. Here are some of the things you need to do and think about when creating your videos:

Study other videos for inspiration and ideas

The point of this is not to copy but to inspire and get you thinking how you can use certain techniques and adapt them to your videos. Try and watch as many videos as possible which are similar to the ones you are planning and take note of the ones which have been particularly good at gaining your attention and how they have done that.

What is your goal

Your goal is the first thing you need to think about . What is the point of the video, what do you want to gain from the video and what action do you want your audience to take at the end of the video.

Figure out your story

Every video needs to tell a story so you will need to figure out what your story is going to be about, who or what will be the focus of the story and where it is going to take place. Like any story it needs to have a beginning, middle and end. The beginning is the most important and if you do not grab your audience's attention in the first couple of seconds or they will simply switch off. YouTube statistics show that the first fifteen seconds is where your viewers are most likely to drop off. So before you go any further you need to ask your yourself these questions:

- What does my audience want most?
- What do they want to know?
- What do they need?
- How can I emotionally connect with my audience?

To hook your audience you need to make your first shot intriguing, you need to address your audience and introduce them to what they are about to watch. Asking a question at the beginning of your video can be a really effective way of igniting your audience's curiosity.

Choose your location

Shooting outdoors not only adds interest to your video but also allows you to benefit from natural light. If you are shooting inside then make sure you have a clean uncluttered background, that you or the area is well lit and you have either a good source of natural light or a light source behind your camera or webcam. If you are going to be creating video content regularly then it is definitely worth investing in some proper lighting and a back drop which will really help to make your videos look professional.

Plan it out

Even if your video is just thirty seconds long it is a good idea to create a storyboard. A story board helps you to map out the order of events and who and what is going to be on camera. There are storyboard apps that you can download for android and iphone which can help you with this process. If you are employing a production team then a storyboard will help you to communicate and convey your ideas to them.

Write your script

Make a script, or at least create a list of points you need to remember and make sure you include your keywords in the script in order to optimize your video for search. Make sure you keep your script interesting throughout, your main aim is to engage, interest and entertain your audience.

Keep it short and simple

There are exceptions to this rule but for the most part it's best to keep your message short and simple and try not to cram too much information into one video by keeping to one subject, you can always make another video if you have more content. You need to get to the point quickly and deliver your message without wasting any time. Your viewers are hungry for information, so make sure you give them what they want without too much fluff. If you take too long to get to the point your viewer will simply switch off and go elsewhere. Your video length needs to be as long as it keeps your viewers interested so do not try to stretch it out just to make it longer.

Prepare and practice

Preparation and practicing in front of the camera are important. You can purchase inexpensive teleprompters which work with ipads and there are also apps available to download on iphone and android devices that let you read off a script whilst looking directly at the camera.

Use a microphone

If you are creating your own video with either your webcam or a camera it is worthwhile investing in a microphone. People are very unforgiving when it comes to bad sound.

Filming

To make your video as interesting as possible use different camera angles.

Editing

When it comes to editing it is a good idea to map it out on paper first and then pick only the most necessary and best clips. YouTube's own video editor offers you tools to combine multiple videos and images to create new videos, trim your uploads to customizable lengths, add audio and customize clips with special tools and effects. You can also add transitions and other graphics to make your video more interesting.

Add a call to action

In order to succeed on YouTube you need to get your viewers to take an action and to do this you need to prompt them by adding a strong, clear and specific call to action at the end of your video. You can ask them go to a specific landing page with your special offer to capture their email address, ask them to like, share or comment or ask them to subscribe with clear instructions on how to subscribe. In order to get your audience to take action it helps to deliver your call to action by talking directly to the camera. You can also add graphics to encourage people to subscribe and by using spotlight annotations you can make these graphics clickable. If you want to encourage your audience to comment then asking them a question and asking them to comment is a very effective way of encouraging engagement.

Add YouTube annotations to your video

Annotations are a way of adding interactive content to your videos. YouTube have made it incredibly easy to overlay text, add clickable links and they also allow you to add background information to your videos. Simply click the down arrow next to 'Upload' at the top of your account and then click on 'Video Manager,' then next to the thumbnail of your video click 'Edit' and then 'Annotations.' There are five types of annotations to choose from, speech bubble, spotlight, note, title, and label.

Use keywords in your filename

To help optimize your video for search you need to include the keywords in your filename when uploading, this tells YouTube and Google what the video is all about and will increase the chances of getting found.

Add your keywords to your title and description

Make sure the title of your video begins with your keywords and then add a secondary keyword to expand on the title. For example, Video Marketing - A guide to video marketing on YouTube. When it comes to adding your description the more text the better, between 200 – 400 words is optimal, make sure you write a useful and interesting description, while at the same time including all your possible keyword variations without obvious keyword stuffing which Google doesn't like.

Add your website link or landing page link

Make sure your website link, link to your email capture page, or a link to your special offer is on the first line of your video description. You can also add the link to your video and your channel to the bottom of the description.

Tags

Add your main keywords and your channel name too. Adding your channel name means that all of your videos will get grouped together in the related videos field. When adding tags try to be as specific as possible and don't go overboard, you want your content to be found by the right audience who are searching for your particular content.

Upload a transcript of your video

This transcript is a word for word description of what you say in your video, this is incredibly important as it communicates to Google and YouTube exactly what your video is about and will help you get your video ranked favourably. You can upload a transcript under the 'Captions' tab of your video in the 'Video Manager'. You will be offered two choices, one to transcribe and sync and one to upload a file. You can add your own transcript but it can save time if you outsource this job and then upload a .txt file. You can find people who can do this on sites like

Fiverr.com or simply type 'video transcription services' into Google search. When you have uploaded your file YouTube will sync your transcript file with your video.

Use custom thumbnails for your videos

YouTube will either choose a thumbnail, or for some users in some areas they can choose their own. YouTube are slowly rolling out this feature to everyone. One very good way of attracting viewers is to overlay title text to a desirable shot from your video. This way your potential viewers will see exactly what they are going to get and will be more likely to watch. To upload your own thumbnail simply go to the down arrow next to 'Upload' at the top of the page then click on 'Video Manager' and then click on the 'Edit' button next to your video. Under your three thumbnails images click custom thumbnail. If you do not have that option then it just means that YouTube have not introduced this is your area yet but you will have it in time.

Add a standard introduction to your videos

If you are going to be regularly uploading videos then branding every video with a standard introduction (no more than about five seconds) can be a very effective way of helping your audience identify with your brand and gives your channel a feel of professionalism and consistency. However there are two schools of thought about this and some people just see introductions as a waste of their time especially if they are regularly watching your videos. As an alternative to a standard introduction you can give a quick introduction of yourself with each video and give a brief introduction to the topic. Keeping to a fairly standard introduction script will in itself help to offer a consistent and professional experience for your viewers and will help with your branding. Another way of keeping your viewers interested with an introduction is to start with a quick introduction to your subject before your standard introduction. Starting with a question can be a great way to hook your audience. There are many ways you can get an introduction created for your video, either through a video production company or inexpensively through sites like like Fiverr.com or Splasheo.com .

CREATING HANGOUTS ON AIR

YouTube Live lets users livestream any event to their YouTube channel. This type of live streaming is for advanced creators and is ideal for large music, news and cultural events. To do this you will need to go to 'Channel Settings' and enable live events. However, there is another type of live event which is ideal for business use and this is with Google + Hangouts on Air. Google + 'Hangouts on Air' and 'YouTube Live' are two separate features.

Hangouts on Air enable you to live stream your Google + Hangout on your YouTube channel and your Google + homepage. If you have a Google + profile and a verified YouTube channel you will be able to use Hangouts on Air as long as your account is in good standing.

Google + Hangouts have made everything possible in terms of connecting and broadcasting live to both individuals and groups of people on video. Anyone with a verified Google + account who has installed the plugin and has a webcam can stream Hangouts on Air live to YouTube, their Google+ profile and their website. This amazing technology has opened up numerous of opportunities for businesses to connect with their customers and prospects.

Google + Hangouts

Hangouts are found on the top right of your Google + profile and are found in green text in quotes. Google + Hangouts can be used for private video chats or video conferencing with up to 9 other people or just text chat with another person or a group of people. Hangouts are only visible to the people who are invited and are useful for groups of friends who want to communicate or for companies who want to run private meetings. They are not recorded or streamed to YouTube or your profile.

Hangouts on Air (HOA)

HOA' s are found in the drop down menu on the left of your Google + profile and you can also create a Hangout on Air from the 'Events' tab. With HOA's you can have up to 10 people participating but the difference is they are publicly viewable to an unlimited audience and they are automatically streamed to your YouTube account and your Google + profile. Having an HOA is like having your very own TV programme with the added advantage that you can actually interact with your audience, plus it's free! HOA's automatically get ranked in Google and offer you yet another way of getting found in search.

There are great benefits to using HOA's, you can run your own Webinar without incurring the high costs which are usually involved in running one and without the restrictions on audience numbers, also there is no need for viewers to download any special software to watch and listen.

One of the best things about HOA's is that they are incredibly straightforward and you need no technical knowledge to run a very professional looking meet up or presentation. You can share your screen and upload your slides from SlideShare by simply selecting the SlideShare option and you can also install a Q & A app which allows viewers to ask questions during the HOA. When you turn the Q & A app on you will see an area to the right of the HOA where your viewers can post their questions and you can answer them.

When you start your hangout and before you start broadcasting, you can take the URL and embed it on your website, blog or Facebook for live streaming. After your HOA is over it will be visible for anyone to watch, unless you choose for it not to be.

The opportunities for marketing are limitless, you don't even have to be live on camera to do an HOA, you can do a slide presentation and then stream it to YouTube. Here are a few other ideas for using HOA's:

- Run a Webinar. A huge money saving when compared to the well known online meeting services and your audience do not have to download any software either and they can ask questions if the Q & A app is installed.
- Run a press conference.
- Customer service session.
- Customer meeting especially useful for overseas customers.
- Q & A sessions.
- Product launch.
- Product demonstrations.
- Consulting sessions.
- How to videos.
- Teaching videos/ language teaching.
- Private coaching sessions.
- Give presentations / Slide shows.

Creating Google + Hangouts on Air

To create an HOA you need to make sure your computer has the supported browser (Chrome) and the minimum processing and bandwidth requirements. Most PC's and Macs will have this but it is a good idea to check in Google + Help for more information about 'Hangout system requirements'. These are the steps involved in starting and broadcasting an HOA.

- **Install Link with YouTube and verify.** When you originally click the 'Create Hangout on Air' button you will need to install the latest version of the Google + voice and video plugin. Simply follow the simple on screen instructions. In order to stream your HOA to YouTube and so that your Hangout on Air can be recorded, you will need to link your Google + page or profile to your YouTube channel. Both your Google + and YouTube account must be linked to the same Gmail account. You will then need to verify your YouTube channel which will allow you to have unlimited length videos. If you do not verify it you are limited to fifteen minutes of video. To verify your channel go to your YouTube settings and click verify and they will send you a text message with a verification code. You can start an HOA from either your Google+ page or your profile. Also when you use your page your HOA will be connected with your own personal YouTube account unless you have linked your page to a separate YouTube account.

- **Click 'Start a Hangout on Air'**

- **Name your Hangout on Air** Try to use a name that will grab your audience's attention and inspire them.

- **Now invite people from the drop down options** These can include your Google Circles, friends and family. You can't invite public (non Google+ users) to participate but they will be able to watch the Hangout broadcasting.

- **Click 'Start the Hangout'.** Your HOA will begin but you will not be broadcasting and your HOA will not be recording. You can check to see if your camera angle and lighting is all ok before you start broadcasting. This is when you can stream your HOA live on another website by embedding your Hangout link. This is found on the bottom right of the screen along with your YouTube event page and this is where people can watch your HOA. If you want to send your participants a link so they can directly link to the Hangout, then you can get this from the top of the screen and then send this out by email or text.

- **Press 'Start Broadcasting'** Your broadcast will be posted live on your Google + homepage and your HOA will also run on your YouTube channel.

- **Control your Hangout on Air** When you create a Hangout then you are in control of what people hear and see. You can mute people if they are noisy or you can click on a persons video to make that person appear on the main screen.

- **Open Chat** You can open up a chat window where your participants can communicate. If you want people who are just viewing to be able to communicate or chat then you can let them do that either on YouTube, the comments on your blog, or on Google +.

- **Edit your recording** You can edit your recording on YouTube when it is finished and the post will be updated on Google+ automatically.

TIPS FOR HANGOUTS ON AIR

- **Get familiar** Watch some other HOA's to get an idea of what can be achieved and what does and doesn't work.

- **Know what you want to achieve** Be clear about your marketing goals and how your audience are going to benefit as a result of hosting your HOA .

- **PLAN PLAN PLAN** Make sure you plan and know exactly what you are going to say and how you are going to present your HOA. If you are going to use slides then practice sharing your screen and using the slides. Also plan how you are going to involve and draw your participants into the HOA.

- **TEST TEST TEST** Before you start broadcasting you will need to practice and test the various features available to make yourself familiar with audio and video settings. Make sure all the screens you want to show are open and ready to share. To practice simply choose a group with no one in it, or select yourself when you select your invites and don't press 'Start Broadcast'.

- **Get hardwired** Make sure you are hardwired with your internet connection and use an ethernet cable. Wifi is just not good enough and you may experience screen freezing or other bad quality issues.

- **Screen share** If you have interesting visuals that you think your audience will benefit from then share them. You can share your screen with your audience by clicking the screen share option on the left menu and then clicking the screen you wish to share. You can also upload slides to SlideShare and share them with your audience. When you select the SlideShare option your face will appear in a small screen at the bottom of the screen while your slides show at the top. You can also share your documents on screen with Google Drive.

- **Avoid audio feedback** To avoid audio feedback (a terrible ringing or screeching noise) use a headset microphone, this will also block out noise from the tapping of a keyboard which can be very distracting for the end user. To control audio settings click on the gear icon on the top right.

- **Make sure you light up your area** Natural light is good but if you do have a light source make sure it is behind the webcam and facing you.

- **Install Google Chrome** For optimal performance it may be a good idea to install Chrome browser since it is a Google product .

- **Brand your HOA** You can brand your HOAand add your name and business name to the lower third of your screen so it is visible to your audience. You can do this with the 'Lower third app', a third party app, which is part of the 'Hangout Toolbox' and can be found on the left toolbar. If you do not see this you just go to 'View more apps' and search for 'Hangout toolbox'. You can then add your lower third text or upload a custom branded image. You can also ask your participants to do this so your audience are clear about who everyone is.

- **Be ready** Make sure you are ready and looking professional. Remember this is a live representation of your brand, so make sure your background area is tidy and bright as possible and practice your presentation skills.

- **Check your position** Make sure you are centred on the screen and that while broadcasting you need to look at the camera above your screen so it looks like you are looking at your audience and not at your screen.

- **Use Hangout chat** This is found on the left menu and is used for chat within the Hangout with your participants. This is not seen by the public and is not recorded. If you would like to offer the opportunity for your audience to interact and ask questions during the HOA then simply turn on the Q&A app which is found in the left column.

- **Control who is on air** Use the cameraman app to control who is on air. This is the video icon which is found when you hover over someone's thumbnail in the film strip. Participants will see anyone who has been hidden but the public will not.

- **Manage your HOA** If someone behaves inappropriately at your Hangout you can simply hover over their thumbnail and eject them.

- **Mute yourself when you are not talking** Before the HOA

starts ask all participants to mute their microphones when they are not speaking. As the creator of the Hangout you can mute a participant if they are being noisy.

- **Edit your HOA** You can edit your video after broadcasting with the YouTube video editor. You can combine videos, trim your videos to custom lengths, add approved music and customize with special tools and effects. http://www.youtube.com/editor

- **Connect with your participants before your HOA starts** Arrange for your participants to attend twenty minutes before broadcast so you can prepare them and answer any questions before hand.

- **Leave time for Q&A's** Make sure you leave enough time at the end of the event for Q&A's.

- **Deleting your HOA** If you do not want your HOA to be watched you can simply delete it from your Google + profile and then make it private on your YouTube account.

PROMOTING YOUR HANGOUT ON AIR

Build your audience
Before you start creating events make sure you have built up your subscribers on YouTube. If you have a good following on Google + this is a great way to promote your HOA as well.

Promote with your embed Code
When you start your HOA you will find an embed code at the top of the Hangout which you can shorten. You can embed this link into your website or blog and Facebook make sure you embed it before you hit the broadcast button!

Promote on all your social networks

Promote your HOA on your other social media networks by creating and posting a compelling image. You could use a promoted post on Facebook to make sure as many people hear about you HOA on Facebook.

Create a publicity video on YouTube

Create a sort teaser video about what the HOA is going to be about to create some buzz about the event. You can create a short 'Hype' Video at http://www.hypemyhangout.com/

Optimize on YouTube for after event views

Make sure you optimize your video on YouTube. Simply visit your video manager and make sure you fill in your description and use all your keywords so this broadcast keeps getting found long after it has been broadcasted.

Send out emails

Send out invitations to your email contacts and you opt-in list and your LinkedIn connections if you are on LinkedIn.

Advertise it on your website or blog

Add an image or text to your blog advertising your online event .

Advertise on Google Adwords

By advertising your event with Google Adwords and using keywords that will catch your target audience you can grow following on Google +.

Ask your participants to promote it

Ask your participants to invite their Circles and share your promotional images. You could also ask them to add any promotional images to their website or Blog and encourage them to write a blog post about the subject and HOA.

Schedule and publicize your Hangout on Air with an event on Google + .

If you have already got an audience on Google + then you can schedule your HOA and let your audience know about it well in advance, simply click on the 'Events' tab, then 'Event Options' and then 'Advanced' and then click on 'Make this an Event on Air' (this is usually used for offline public events) then click on 'Show more options' where you will be able to add more detailed information. Make sure you make it clear that the event is an online event. Google + does not give you the URL of your HOA until you have started it. However, there is a simple way around this, you can either add the URL for your Google + homepage or add your YouTube UR for the HOA, http://www.youtube.com/user/ *username*/live (Replace username with the name of your youtube account.) This way people will be directed to your YouTube account where the HOA will be streaming. Make sure you are specific about the time of your 'HOA' so that when your attendees arrive at the address, the 'HOA' is taking place, otherwise they will be directed to the homepage.

Add a good image promoting the HOA and complete the event form with all the information. You can then select who you want to invite and the Hangout will appear on Google Calendar for anyone who uses it.

Create some buzz

Start talking about your event or Hangout 4 −5 Days before the date and post an image.

Google + Communities

Sharing information about your HOA on any relevant Google + Communities that you are a member of will be a good way of getting people to watch your HOA.

Share on SlideShare

After your event has taken place you can upload it to SlideShare which will help to drive additional traffic.

Chapter Three

Building your Audience on YouTube

IN ORDER TO leverage the power of YouTube you will need subscribers. You will need to build an audience of loyal viewers who want to keep coming back for your compelling content. In addition to optimising your videos for search, having subscribers who regularly watch your videos is going to be a major contribution to getting your videos ranked highly in both Google and YouTube search. Having people viewing, favoriting, commenting and liking your videos is all going to help with your YouTube ranking. Here are some essential strategies for getting you more subscribers on YouTube:

Post content regularly

In order to create a successful channel and attract regular subscribers your will need to post video content regularly and keep to a regular schedule. Many businesses get discouraged when they don't immediately get hundreds of views on their channel but this is normal and it will take time to build your views unless of course, you have instantly managed to create viral content.

Ask for subscribers

At the end of each video you need to ask your viewers to subscribe, give them a reason why they should subscribe and let them know how to do it. You can also ask them to add a comment, or like your video. If you ask you usually get ! Don't forget you can use annotations and include a clickable subscribe link in your video itself but make sure you give your viewers enough time to complete the action before the video finishes.

Subscribe & interact with other channels

If you subscribe to other similar channels and interact with those channels you are likely to get reciprocal subscriptions and other subscribers are more likely to like, comment or share your content. Responding to comments and questions will help to build relationships and will show that you value your subscribers.

Cross promotion & collaboration

By working with other creators you can cross promote your content with other channels who have similar audiences, this is a great way to widen your reach and attract new audiences. Creating Hangouts on Air with other channel owners and recording video chats with other channels can also really help to increase your exposure to new audiences.

Add featured channels

Featured channels show on the right hand side of your channel. This is where you can add a link to other channels you like. This is a great way to build relationships with people who have similar audiences and hopefully they will reciprocate by adding your channel to their featured channels.

Optimize your videos

Make sure your title, descriptions and tags are completed and optimized properly, that you add a transcript and choose the best thumbnail image for your video.

Link your channel with Google+

Google + creates another place for your videos to be discovered. If you already have a YouTube channel then it is a very good idea to link it with Google +. You can engage your subscribers with Google Hangouts and broadcast them live on your YouTube channel with Hangouts on Air. When anyone comments on any of video of yours, it will appear in their feed in Google+ which will help to widen your reach on Google +

Please note if you already have a Google + account and a YouTube channel and you disconnect these, you will not be able to leave comments on other peoples videos.

Add YouTube subscribe button

You can choose which subscribe button you want to add to your website. The instructions how to do this are at this page https:// developers.google.com/youtube/youtube_subscribe_button.

Promote your channel

Promote your channel at every opportunity, on your blog, website and other social media platforms, use Facebook promoted posts, and add your videos to your blog posts and articles. Submitting your video to Stumbleupon has proved a powerful means of getting your site found.

Advertise on YouTube

With Adwords for video you only pay to have your video viewed and it's a great way to get the ball rolling and build a following. You can reach your targeted audience based on where they live, what they are interested in and their gender. Your ads can drive comments, likes, subscriptions and comments.

Send to your email list

Inviting your current opt-in subscribers to subscribe to your YouTube channel is another way to grow your reach and continue to build trust and rapport.

Promote your video on SlideShare

The ability to upload videos on SlideShare as well as presentations is still under utilized by it's users. Getting views and exposure on SlideShare for any business related video is quite likely to be viewed by more people on SlideShare than on YouTube. If you are uploading to YouTube then make sure you upload to SlideShare as well.

CHAPTER FOUR

DAY TO DAY ACTIVITY

THERE ARE CERTAIN things that you will need to do on a day to day basis to successfully run your campaign on YouTube. It is a good idea to allot a specific amount of time and a particular time of the day to do this. Here are some of the things you will need to do:

Subscribing to your customer channels

This is important if your customers are business owners themselves. Subscribing to their channels will go a long way in building relationships. By subscribing you are showing them that you are interested in what they have to say and also helping them to achieve their goals by helping them to build their audience.

Respond to comments

When your subscribers start to engage with your content, make sure you are listening and responding to them. There is nothing worse than going to a YouTube channel where subscribers have taken the time to ask questions and then have not been responded to by the channel owner. Answering and responding to comments not only helps to build relationships but also helps to build trust and authenticity for your business.

Showing your audience you value and respect them

If you value and respect your audience they will most probably love, respect and value your business. Be kind, generous, offer as much help and value as possible, reply to their comments and make it obvious that you value them and are listening to them. Don't be afraid to be yourself rather than a stiff brand with no personality. Be friendly to your audience, be chatty, authentic, genuine and embrace the conversation. All this will all go a long well in building a positive image for your brand and will set you apart from your others who are continually ambushing their audience with self promotion.

Everyone is aiming for shares, likes and comments so if you are helping others out by commenting and liking their content it is going to draw attention to your brand and they are more likely to take an interest in your content. This is one area where the reciprocation rule works very well on YouTube. Engaging with content will also draw attention to you and your brand and you will find that people will click on your name to find out who you are and they may very well subscribe to your channel.

Following influencers in your niche

Building relationships with key influencers in your niche is invaluable. Not only can you learn from their content but also these people can have literally thousands of subscribers, imagine if they subscribe to your channel and then share your content!

Dealing with negative comments

Every business at some time will have to deal with negativity from followers. Hopefully if you have a good product then this is not going to happen too often. There are the 'trolls' out there who have nothing better to do than post negative comments, the best thing to do with them is just ignore them, delete their comments and block them if they really become a problem. However there will be real customers who have real concerns and complaints and may post negative comments publicly, there may also be people who really want to lash out to gain your attention as quickly as possible and spread the news to their friends too! You need to deal with these complaints as quickly as possible and be as transparent and authentic as possible. The best thing to do is to apologise and say how sorry you are to hear of the inconvenience they have been caused and offer to continue the conversation and deal with their concern by either private message or telephone. You can then deal with this privately, give your customer the full attention they deserve and decide on your next course of action or compensation.

Chapter Five

Measuring and Monitoring your Results

MEASURING AND MONITORING your results and performance against your original goals and objectives on a continual basis is essential. This is where many businesses go wrong, they carry on aimlessly posting content without checking to see what is working and what is not. Then after 6 months or a year they wonder why their campaign is making no positive difference at all.

When you measure your results you will discover so much information about your campaign which will allow you to steer your campaign in the right direction to achieve those SMART goals and objectives and stop anything that is not working.

When you originally plan your content and work out your strategies and tactics for your campaign you will be estimating what you need to do to achieve your goals and objectives. However, as you campaign develops will have a better idea of what you need to do to achieve your goals and objectives. For example, you may need to increase the amount you spend on advertising to attract new subscribers, or you may need to create more content around a certain subject that you have found to be very popular.

This is what it is all about, making your campaign work for you by constantly measuring your success against the goals set and then adjusting your strategies accordingly in order to achieve the results.

YOUTUBE ANALYTICS

YouTube Analytics provides you with a wealth of information to measure your campaign and your performance and shows you data about your earning, engagement, traffic sources and more. Analytics provides filters which help you sort by content, geography and date. You can find out whether a video is popular in a certain region or look at its performance over a specific period of time. Analytics are found under the gear icon on the top right and you can view and download the following reports:

The Overview Report

The overview report shows you how your content is performing on YouTube and shows you the number of views and the estimated minutes watched for the channel and for individual videos. It shows engagement metrics including likes, comments and shares and your top ten most viewed videos. It shows demographic information about the gender and location of your viewers and also the top traffic sources for your videos.

The Views Report

The views report displays data about the views and estimated minutes watched.

The Devices Report

The devices report shows information about the different devices and operating systems that viewers use to watch your videos.

The demographics Report

Displays information about the gender and age of your audience. You can alter the date range and geographic location to see how the audience varies.

Audience Retention Reports

The Audience Retention report is a measure of your videos ability to keep its audience. It is a graph which displays data for both organic

586

traffic and paid traffic and shows the following:

- **Absolute Audience Retention:** The views of every moment of your video as a percentage of views. You can see for instance on the graph if viewers have rewatched a video, if they have started watching midway through the video or if the video has been abandoned or fast forwarded. If you discover that people have stopped watching at a particular point then you can make a change for the better. The first fifteen seconds is probably the most important part to keep an eye on for drop off.

- **Relative Audience Retention:** This shows your video's capacity to retain viewers during playback in comparison to all YouTube videos of similar length. The higher the graph at a given moment the more viewers kept watching your video over the previous seconds of playback compared against other videos at the same moment in their playbacks.

The Engagement Report
Engagement reports are a great way to understand your audience's interest and show you how users are integrating with your channel by displaying the number of likes, dislikes, favorites, comments and shares.

Traffic Sources Reports
The traffic resources report shows you the various sources through which your content was found. There are numerous ways your videos could be found, through YouTube or Google search, through other social networking websites like Google +,Twitter, LinkedIn and Facebook.

The Earnings Report
This is for partners who are using YouTube to earn money through Adsense and show your total number of views and estimated earnings.

GOOGLE ANALYTICS

Google Analytics will be able to give you detailed information about the impact YouTube is having on your business and provides advanced reports that will let you track the effectiveness of your campaign with the following social reports:

The Overview Report This report lets you see at a glance how much conversion value is generated from social channels. It compares all conversions with those conversions resulting from social.

The Conversions Report The conversions report helps you to quantify the value of social and shows conversion rates and the monetary value of conversions that occurred due to referrals from YouTube and any of the other social networks. Google Analytics can link visits from YouTube with the goals you have chosen and your E - commerce transactions. To do this you will need to configure your goals in Google Analytics which is found under 'Admin' and then 'Goals'. Goals in Google Analytics let you measure how often visitors take or complete a specific action and you can either create goals from the templates offered or create your own custom goals.

The Conversions report can be found in the Standard Reporting tab under Traffic Sources > Social > Conversions.

The Networks Referral Report The Networks Referral report tells you how many visitors the social networks have referred to your website and shows you how many page views, visits, the duration of the visits and the average number of pages viewed per visit. From this information you can determine which network referred the highest quality of traffic.

Data Hub Activity Report The Data Hub activity report shows how people are engaging with your site on the social networks . You can see the most recent URL's that were shared, how they were shared and what was said.

The Social Visitors Flow Report This report displays the initial paths that your visitors took from social sites through to your site and where they exited.

The Landing Pages Report This report displays engagement metrics for each URL. These include page views, average visit duration and pages viewed per visit.

The Trackbacks Report The Trackback report shows you which sites are linking to your content and how many visits those sites are sending to you. This can help you to work out which sort of content is the most successful so you can create similar and it also helps you to build relationships with those who are constantly linking to your content.

Make Foursquare, Vine and Snapchat Work For Your Business

Alex Stearn

Table of Contents

CHAPTER ONE

MAKE FOURSQUARE WORK FOR YOUR BUSINESS

'FOURSQUARE HELPS YOU to find the perfect places to go with friends'

Foursquare is a free mobile app with geo location capabilities which lets users post their location when they arrive at a certain place and then share it with their friends on Facebook and Twitter. This helps users to discover places which have been recommended by their friends and allows them to receive special offers and information from the places they have checked into. Foursquare users can simply check into the places that they are visiting using their smartphone, this could be a restaurant, bar, beauty parlour, hairdresser or any type of bricks and mortar business. There are literally millions of businesses on Foursquare and millions of check-ins per day.

Foursquare offers its users recommendations on places to visit based on the information they already have on these users and where they have visited before and where their friends have visited. Once a user has checked in they can start receiving updates from the business about special offers, promotions and organized events and they can also leave tips about that business for other Foursquare users to see.

When a user is in the area of the place they are planning to visit they will find the venue together with other businesses in the area on the Foursquare app. All they need to do is tap on the name of the place they want to check into and this action will unlock any special deals that are available at that place. Users can also mention their friends when they check in by simply typing in their name. If their friends have 'check-in by friends' turned on, they will automatically be checked in. If they have their 'check-in by friends' turned off it will only show up as a mention and they will receive a notification that they have been mentioned.

Foursquare has recently introduced a new app called 'Swarm' which makes it even easier for users to connect and meet up with friends by letting its users see who of their friends are close by. Foursquare users can simply download the app and they will e bale to find al their Foursquare friends on Swarm.

With Swarm, users can literally tap on the photo of a friend and see where they are, they can 'like' their check-in, or send a message. They can also tap one tab and Swarm will show them a feed with details of all their friend's recent check-ins. Users who choose to turn on neighbourhood sharing can also see which friends are in their neighbourhood. Neighbourhood sharing will not show a users specific location and this functionality can be easily turned off by users if they wish. The screen color turns from orange to grey when it is switched off.

Users can check-in anywhere by simply tapping on the top right corner to update their current location, they can also add or mention a friend, leave a comment, add a photo and add a sticker to their check in if they want. Stickers fall into two categories, mood or category.

The plans tab lets uses tell their friends what their plans are and users can simply tap on this tab and see where their friends are planning to go and what they are planning to do.

Swarm users can also compete with their friends for Mayorship of their favorite place rather than competing against the all Foursquare users. With so many users it became nearly impossible for users to become Mayor which ruined the game. The mayorship is awarded to users who visit a venue the most over a sixty day period and businesses can create special awards for the Mayor.

Benefits of Foursquare for Users

The biggest benefits for users using the Foursquare app are as follows:

It's very social Users can share where they are and what they are doing with their friends which makes it really easy for them to meet up. With Foursquare's new additional app for users called 'Swarm' it's even easier for users to meet up. With the new app you can see at a glance who is nearby. By tapping on a friends image users can see where they are, like their check-in and send them a message. Users can also check-in their friends or mention them when checking in. With the 'Plans' tab on Swarm users can also tell their friends that they are looking for something to do.

Saves them money Users often save money and benefit from special promotions and offers from venues they have previously checked into.

They can receive updates after their visit Users can continue to receive information about events, promotions and more from the places they have checked into long after they have visited.

Read tips Users can find out useful information about the venue by reading tips (information about about a venue left by other users) and they can also leave tips about a venue themselves once they have checked in. Tips are ranked by the number of likes that a tip gets and those with the most likes will appear at the top.

Create lists of Favorites Users can create lists of their favorite places which they can also share with their friends.

Customers feel valued The very fact that users can leave tips and advice for other users makes them feel their opinions are heard and that they actually matter. Also because users receive information about special offers from businesses through Foursquare means they are rewarded for being a customer.

It's Fun

Users can compete for Mayorship of a venue and stickers. This adds interest and fun to the app and users seem to love competing.

BENEFITS OF FOURSQUARE FOR BUSINESS

As well as building awareness, loyalty and driving traffic to businesses, Foursquare offers businesses a myriad of marketing benefits including:

Social Proof

Because users are actively checking into places with Foursquare and sharing this information with their Friends means that their friends are getting to hear about businesses in the most powerful way, word of mouth. When a user checks into a place this is as good as a recommendation and with the click of a mouse their friends can find out exactly where they are which is very likely to influence them to go and visit too. Businesses can leverage the power of social proof to build a loyal customer following on Foursquare by offering special offers, promotions and incentives for customers to visit again.

Free Advertising

Foursquare allows businesses to list their venue for free and just by doing so businesses can benefit from being in front of users who may be searching for places to visit in their area. Even if users are not searching for a particular business they may still see special offers from other businesses in an area which are listed on Foursquare. This is powerful for any business wishing to create awareness about their business and may very well encourage a future visit from any user who has been in the area and seen details of a special offer or promotion on Foursquare.

A desirable demographic

The people using the app are usually young, educated and employed with disposable incomes. This demographic is notorious for being incredibly

598

sociable and wanting to make their whereabouts and what they are doing known to all their friends. This is great word of mouth advertising for any business.

Communication
Businesses with a listing on Foursquare can continue to communicate special offers, promotions and events to Foursquare users long after they users have left their venue.

Benefit from a competitive game
Foursquare users love the competitive side to this app . Users can compete to be Mayor of a venue. If a user has checked into a venue on more days than any of their friends in the last 60 days,they will be crowned Mayor. Businesses can create special rewards for the Mayor. All these things help to create repeat custom and customer loyalty for any business.

Foursquare Tips
Foursquare allows users to leave tips which then turn into public notes or recommendations about a place from other users. This could be anything, for example, 'Try the Chocolate fudge cake, it's the best I ever tasted' or 'well worth coming for happy hour, cocktails are half price'. This not only creates buzz for a business but also tips or recommendations written by other customers are far more powerful and more likely to be read and believed than anything written by the owner themselves. For the customers who are leaving the tips this very action can help to make them feel their opinions actually matter and that they are being listened to and valued as a customer which encourages customer loyalty.

Customer Service
Customer feedback is incredibly important for any kind of business but especially for service based businesses. Many customers will leave a place without comment and even if something has been very wrong with the

service the owner doesn't get to hear about it . However with Foursquare, businesses can easily listen to what their customers are saying by reading the tips that are being left about their business. With this information businesses can pick up on both the good and the bad and quickly make changes where necessary.

Customer Loyalty
Businesses can offer customers rewards, incentives and special offers for returning which will help to encourage repeat custom and build customer loyalty.

Build a mailing list
Email marketing is still one of the most effective ways for businesses to communicate with their customers and prospects. As with marketing on all of the social media platforms one of the main priorities for any business should be to get users to sign up to their opt in. With Foursquare business pages, businesses not only have the opportunity to stay in contact thorough updates but can also capture user email addresses by offering a special promotion and sending them to a special page where they can claim their offer.

Track and measure
With Foursquare analytics businesses can discover who is coming to their venue and how often, they can see how many check ins they are getting, how many shares on Facebook and Twitter and who is the Mayor of their business. Foursquare also sends a weekly email to business users with details about activity on their account.

CLAIMING YOUR BUSINESS ON FOURSQUARE
So if you have decided that you would like to benefit from what Foursquare has to offer you as a business, here is how to claim your place and get listed on Foursquare.

It is more than likely that you will find your business has already been listed on Foursquare by one of your customers who has already checked in. To check to see if your business is already on Foursquare simply visit the website http://business.foursquare.com/listing/ or you can download the app 'Foursquare for businesses' and set up an account on your android or iphone device.

Claiming your business on Foursquare

To claim you business simply search for your business by name and area. If you see your business select it and if not then you need to scroll down to the bottom of the list and add it. You will then be asked to complete a form and claim and verify ownership of your business which you can do by either phone or email. Foursquare will automatically link your account with your twitter account, use your Twitter username and take your profile picture from Twitter, this you can change if you wish. If you are managing multiple businesses between 10 and 100 businesses you will need to complete another form.

Creating your Page on Foursquare

Creating a page is the best way to manage your business on Foursquare and reach and communicate with users who are on Foursquare. Your brand page offers users the inside scoop on your place. Once you have set up your page and are posting your special offers and updates anyone who has checked into your business will be able to see these updates on their phone or on your brand page on the web too. If you are promoting any special offers these will be displayed when any user is searching for offers in your area. This is an incredibly powerful way of maintaining contact and communicating offers, loyalty schemes ,incentives and upcoming events.

You can add your address, telephone number, page description, links to your website and social media links. Make sure your description is keyword rich so your listing is optimized for search and make sure you give users a good reason to follow you by listing the benefits they will receive for following you. You can then upload a banner image of

860x130pixels. Foursquare will automatically take your profile picture from your twitter account but you can change it if you like by clicking 'Edit' at the top of the page.

Adding 'Tips' to your own page gives you the opportunity to communicate important information to your customers about specialities or special services and also helps to encourage other users to start leaving tips too.

To add page managers to your account, simply click 'Manager Home' at the top and then 'Manage Listing'.

You can choose to share your updates on Facebook too. Simply visit your 'Listings' page to make sure you have connected your Facebook and Twitter pages. When you create your update you can decide if you want to share it with Facebook and Twitter, you will find this option to the left of the share button.

POSTING UPDATES ON FOURSQUARE

Once you have created your Foursquare page you can start posting updates and anyone who has checked into your business will be able to see those updates. You can either create text updates, for example, latest menus or specials you are offering, or you can post images of your products. If you have a number of venues then these updates can be shared with all of them or they can be location specific.

You can also use your page to post updates about any special offers or contests you are running on your website. This way you can send users to a page with a form so they can claim your offer and you can capture their email address.

CREATING FOURSQUARE SPECIALS

Foursquare specials are a great way to reward your customers and attract new ones, they give your customers a reason to check in and spread the word. Foursquare specials are easy to administer and manage but specials must offer something of particular value and be specific to Foursquare users if they are to be approved. When you create a special it is displayed as an orange pin on Foursquare so people searching for special offers can easily identify special offers available in a particular area. Specials are created in three steps; composing your 'Special', scheduling your 'Special' and posting an update about your special.

To create specials from the managers home page, select 'Specials' and then click on 'Create a new special'. When you have selected and completed all the details about the special simply click 'Create Special' You will then need to schedule your special and select your start and end date. Click 'Schedule Special' and the 'on' button will appear. You can then send an update to your customers with the 'Special' attached.

ADDING MENUS TO FOURSQUARE

You can add menus to Foursquare with www.Locu.com or www.SinglePlatform.com . Simply register and you can add and edit your menus and they will automatically be published to your Foursquare business page within just a few minutes.

CREATING LISTS ON FOURSQUARE

Foursquare allows users and venues to create lists of tips and recommended venues. Other users can follow these lists and also contribute to the lists if this feature is enabled by the list creator.

To create a list, click on 'To-Do List' from the home screen, then search for the first venue you would like to add. When you find it click on the name and then click 'Save' and you can create the name of the list you wish to add it to. You can then add an image to the list and either use the image of the first venue or pick your own. You can also add tips to any of the venues you add.

As a business if you create a list around a certain topic in your area can be a really valuable benefit for users and when they see your list they see your brand helping to find them the things you love. For example, if you own a restaurant you could create a list with the best tourist attractions in your city or town, don/t forget to add your business to the list.

FourSquare Events

Foursquare can help to drive attendance, traffic and engagement for any event and even B2B companies can encourage their delegates to check in at their event on Foursquare. By creating an event on Foursquare users can check into your business and your event and you can encourage users and attendees to share your event on other networks like Facebook and Twitter. This will help to bring even more traffic through your doors and can also help to create awareness for any future events. When a user checks into an event, Foursquare will give them the option to tag a friend, write a message or share a photo.

Creating an event on Foursquare is straightforward and free. You can create events for any of the listings you manage by selecting your brand page. When you are on your manager's home page click the drop down next to 'Edit profile for' and select the individual venue were you plan to host the event. Then select 'Manage your listing' and towards the bottom you will see a section called 'Events'. Simply select your date, add the title of your event and the start and end times and then 'Add event'. You will see your event displayed in the sections called 'Scheduled events' and if you want to see how it will look to users simply go up the page and click on 'View this location' and you will your event under 'Upcoming events'.

You can add tips to your event, for example; the first 10 people to check in at 'Event Name' will receive a free gift.

Once you have created your event make sure you check in on behalf of your company and make sure you remind people to check in by putting up some signs. You can also offer them an incentive to do so, for example, a small free gift at the event.

PROMOTING YOUR BUSINESS ON FOURSQUARE

The more people who check into your venue on Foursquare the more opportunities you will have to grow your business through word of mouth and recommendations. Here are some tips on how to grow your following:

Display Foursquare Check in stickers

You can order Foursquare window clings by mail and also find logos and check in artwork at this URL https://foursquare.com/about/logos Make sure you display these in the most prominent places like at the payment station, on entrance doors and at the table to remind your customers to check in. You can even offer a sign with an incentive to check in, for example, check in on Foursquare and receive a free cup of coffee. Once they have checked they may very well share with their friends on Facebook or Twitter.

Add Foursquare 'like' button to your website

You will find the various Foursquare button on this page too https://foursquare.com/about/logos. There is a ' Save' To Foursquare button A 'Like' button. People who click on these can then subscribe to your updates without even visiting.

Use signs at your venue

Make sure your remind users to check in at your venue with special check in signs. Check out logo and sign design here https://foursquare.com/about/logos

Create Specials

Offering specials will encourage new users to try your business.

Use events to attract new audiences

Make sure you encourage users to check in at your event .

Mail your customers

If you have a mailing list of customers or even your suppliers let them know you are on Foursquare and invite them to follow your business by embedding a like button into your mail.

Chapter Two

Make Snapchat Work For Your Business

SNAPCHAT IS A mobile app that allows its users to send videos and photos to the friends that they choose. Users can add captions and drawings and set the number of seconds their friends can view it for. Once received and viewed the image or video vanishes within seconds never to be seen again. This ephemerality is what makes Snapchat so unique, thrilling, exciting and exclusive. This app is not about beautiful pictures its about fun, authenticity and how you feel at a particular moment.

Top brands have quickly embraced the marketing possibilities and are already having success with sneak previews, coupons and competitions. Snapchat allows brands to have a personal connection with their audience and can encourage engagement with a brand like no other social media. The act of sending an image to a user grabs their attention while at the same time allows them to interact with users in a more personal way. On the users side it can make them feel like they are getting the inside scoop on a brand or they are privileged to be the first to know about an offer, new product or promotion.

At the moment it is predominantly used by the under 25's who are joining in their millions simply because it's fun to use and leaves no permanent record of their activity. If this is your target audience then Snapchat may be a great way to grab some attention for your brand.

Snapchat Basics

To sign up to Snapchat simply download the mobile app and then sign up with your email and password. You can then create a better and shorter username which is consistent with your brand. It will then allow you to import your contacts from your phone. Snapchat will then return with a list of contacts that it has identified as users of the service and then you can add then by clicking the icon with the person and plus button to the right of their names. You can remove or block any user by holding your finger down on their name until the menu pops up.

How to send snaps

Simply press the camera icon at the top left and then press the button at the bottom of the screen. You can add color drawings by clicking on the pencil icon. If you want to add text simply double tap on the screen and then add your message. If you want to save your shot then you can press the downward arrow which will send it to your camera. You can then set the number of seconds you wish your viewers to view by simply clicking on the circle on the left with number inside. When you are ready to send click the arrow on the bottom left, select your recipients and send. To send a video simply hold down the button and take the video and use the same process to send.

How to send a Snapchat story

Snapchat introduced stories in 2013. Stories let users take either pictures or videos throughout the day which can then be viewed by their friends as one continuous stream of snaps. The story is represented by a circle with segments, each segment representing a different part of the story. The story and can be viewed for an unlimited number of times by recipients over 24 hour period.

To send a story simply take the picture or video as usual and then press the button with the square and plus sign which adds your snap to the story.

SNAPCHAT FOR YOUR BUSINESS

So how can you Snapchat to promote your business?

Because of the short period of time that the recipient has to view a snap the simple act of sending a snap creates buzz, interest and urgency. This can work extremeley well for brands wanting to gain attention. Any interesting snap delivering the right message and call to action can create great results in terms of attention, engagement and an action taken by the recipient.

Contests.
Contests can be great fun on Snapchat and can create a sense of urgency and excitement. You can send snaps containing clues or tips that the user has to collect together to enter or claim a money off coupon and can work a bit like a scavenger hunt.

Coupons.
Snapchat works very effectively for quickly sending money off coupons or offers to users and can help you to both reward your customers and entice them to come back and buy more. Some brands have run successful campaigns where they have asked users to take a picture of themselves using or eating their product and then in return offer them a money off voucher.

Sneak previews.
Sending fleeting images of your new collection or product to users can create excitement and buzz, you can also included a money off token. The new Snapchat stories can work very well here as they allow you to send a series of snaps which are available for up to 24 hours and are set for the user to be viewed in the order they were sent. You could for instance tempt users by sending them a series of product images and then a money off code or voucher in the last snap.

The thing to remember with Snapchat is you need to make whatever you are offering or doing as fun as possible and refrain from posting unless you have something really valuable to say or offer. If your offerings are uninteresting and ruin the users experience it will not be long before they delete you.

BUILDING YOUR AUDIENCE ON SNAPCHAT

Before you can actually send any Snaps you need usernames and therefore you need to build your audience by building your friend list. To do this you will either need a very good presence on another social network or you will need to advertise so you can offer a very attractive incentive so users will voluntarily add you to their Snapchat account.

Offer an Incentive.

A really good way of doing this is to announce on another network like Facebook, Twitter or Instagram that you are going to offer them something special like a coupon. You could also create some buzz by offering a special prize to the first X number of people who send you a 'Selfie' and add you to their account. If you do this make sure you send some kind of consolation prize to the people who did not win or they will quickly become disinterested and delete you as their friend.

If you offer an incentive for users to take a picture of themselves wearing your product it is quite likely they will not only send that to you but also to their friends. If you ask them also to add your brand name to the Snap this could really spread the word about your brand and get others to join in. For example, 'Me eating a .... at......' Or 'Me wearing ....'

Point of sale.

Offer your customers a coupon or information on their receipt about a promotion you are doing on Snapchat to tempt them to add your account. You could also promote your contest at the checkout on a poster or tent card.

Promote your username.

Promote you username by adding it to your website or blog and offer users and incentive on your website to add you as a friend.

Announce on Email.
Announce your username in your newsletter with an incentive to add your account.

Facebook Advertising
Facebook advertising is another very effective way of finding Snapchat users. Most Snapchat users will have a Facebook account and if you can tempt them with an advert on Facebook to add you to their friend list you will have an incredibly powerful platform to gain their attention and stay in contact.

Google Adwords
Using Google Adwords to create a Snapchat campaign is a very effective way of promoting a competition or incentive with the main aim to get users to add you to their friend list. However you need to make sure you are very specific with the keywords you choose so you catch your target audience.

Magazine advertising
If you are running a contest or offer then a magazine which is popular with your target audience could be a very effective way of promoting your contest and getting users to add you to their Snapchat account.

MEASURING YOUR RESULTS
In terms of measuring results it is really down to monitoring the number of sales your campaign produces, how many coupons or codes you collect, how many entries you have for a competition and how many users have actually opened your Snap.

CHAPTER THREE

MAKE VINE WORK FOR YOUR BUSINESS
"THE BEST WAY to create and share short, looping videos."

Vine is a mobile app which allows you to create video clips with a maximum length of 6 seconds and then share them on your social networks or embed them in your blog or website. The app was founded in June 2012 and acquired by Twitter in September 2012.

Vine is an incredibly inexpensive and simple way of creating interesting visual content and then using it to promote your brand particularly to a younger audience. Literally you can put together a really effective piece of visual content without any editing or video production skills and because Vines are so easily shared on other social networks it makes it can make it incredibly easy to reach a target audience. For example, sharing a Vine advertising your product on your Twitter profile is an incredibly effective way of giving your audience a quick glimpse of your brand.

Like all visual content Vines can help to make your business look real, authentic and also help you make that valuable personal connection with your audience. One of the main benefits of Vines is that they are so short and with the competition today for peoples attention this can be a huge advantage as they are very much more likely to get viewed than a longer video.

With the introduction of web profiles Vine is now an even more viable platform for brands as they can now be viewed, liked, commented on and shared from your desktop or laptop and viewed in full screen TV mode.

GETTING STARTED

To use Vine you need to download the app and then add a profile image and a few words about yourself or business under 'Profile' and then 'Settings'. You can invite your friends and contacts by either text, email and you can connect your Facebook and Twitter accounts.

On the home screen you can see videos that your friends have uploaded and popular vines. You can also find Vines by category from the 'Explore' button found on the 'Home' menu

To upload your video simply click on the video icon on the top right and you will be taken to the video screen. To start recording simply tap the screen and hold, release your finger and then tap and hold again if you wish. When you have finished you can add your description, add a location, add to a channel (category) and then share with Vine, Facebook, Twitter or embed if you wish.

Vine has also recently introduced the functionality to upload actual videos which is great news for brands as they will have the opportunity to upload and share higher quality content is now available.

VINE FOR MARKETING

Here are some ideas for different types of vine you can create to promote your brand;

Quick introduction

What better way to introduce yourself to your audience than recording a six second introduction. When people find you through your Vines they may want to scroll back and find your more of your Vines and if you have a specific vine introducing yourself this will help you make that essential personal connection. You can also use Vine to quickly introduce your brand story by creating a vine with a series of images or drawings including your logo. Done well this can be incredibly effective in creating a memorable picture of your brand.

Brand beliefs, culture or ethos

Creating a Vine around your corporate beliefs or ethos is a great way to quickly communicate what you are all about and can help to demonstrate how you relate to your target audience.

Sneek previews

A Vine can be a great way to create buzz around a new product without giving too much away. You can really create intrigue to get your audience interested before your product launch or before it's available in store or on your website.

Behind the scenes

People love to get a peak of whats going on behind the scenes, to see your office, your place of work or to see how things are made. The aim here is to show off the personality of your brand and creating fun or light hearted Vines can be a very effective way of helping users make friends with your brand.

How to's

This type of vine is incredibly popular. If you search under the hashtag #howto you will find numerous Vines with ideas about how to do this.

Anything

The chances are that anything you find interesting or funny then others will too. Producing these types of general interest Vines can help to build your brand's personality. Having anything good or funny associated with your brand is extremely valuable and not only creates the feel good factor around your brand but also helps to leave a lasting memorable impression.

615

Coupons or codes
Vines are a great way of communicating special offers and are a fun way to promote a discount shopping code.

Unboxing
You can either create a vine of you unboxing one of your products or ask your followers to send you a Vine of them unboxing your product.

TIPS FOR CREATING GREAT VINES
Watch some Vines
Watching other Vines produced by other businesses or brands is a great way to get inspired and will give you heaps of ideas of what can be done. Once you start watching what other people have created you may be able to apply ideas to your business. To see some brands who are creating using some great Vines to help build their brand please visit https://vine.co/AlexStearn

Plan your Vine
Planning your Vine is essential and you can do this by creating a storyboard and sketching out your Vine frame by frame. This way you can work out how many shots you need and exactly what each shot needs to show.

Tell a story
You can do this by editing together totally different shots.

Use a tripod
There is nothing worse than a shaky Vine. Using A tripod is an essential piece of equipment which which will make all the difference to the quality of your Vine.

Use the Stop Motion technique
The Stop motion/stop frame is an animation technique to make an

object look like it is moving on its own. The object is moved slightly in each frame making it look like the object is moving. These stop motion Vines are incredibly popular on Vine and very effective.

Lighting

Make sure the area where you are filming is well lit and either has a good source of natural light or you have another source of light behind the camera.

Use lenses

There are lenses available for iPhone that allow you to shoot macro, wide angled or fisheye.

Sound

Using headphones with a built in microphone can really improve the sound quality of your Vine, obviously try and minimise sound from outside as much as possible.

Practice before you post

Vines can be incredibly effective if they include good content and are well made. It's worth practicing and practicing to get the best result before you upload. Small improvements can make a big difference even if it is only six seconds.

Use effects

By putting something in front of the camera and then taking it away quickly you can slowly bring and image into view. Putting a black piece of card in front of the camera can create a transition between shots.

Include your logo

Including your logo wherever possible is a great way to promote your brand and helps your audience to make that connection between your great content and your brand. You can do this by displaying your logo on anything like T shirts or other merchandise or displaying your logo on your office wall.

Add a title or description

Adding one or two words to your Vine's description can often be enough to communicate the right message or vibe.

Add an image on Facebook

Vines are given only a small space on Facebook so in order to gain attention and create maximum engagement it's a good idea to take the best possible photo of your Vine and then post the URL,title and description.

HOW TO BUILD YOUR AUDIENCE

Add hashtags.

Adding the relevant hashtags to your vine descriptions will help to get it found by people searching for particular content.

Comment, like and revine.

Commenting, liking and revining will draw attention to your profile and users will very often reciprocate by liking and revining yours.

Add your username.

Publicize your username on your website, blog and in your email signature.

Share and Embed your Vines.

Vines can be incredibly viral and sharing your Vines on Twitter, Facebook and on your website or blog will widen your reach. Vines can easily be embedded from your mobile and from the web. From Mobile simply click on the three dots under any Vine and you will be able to easily embed or share.

Chapter Four

Make Periscope Work for your Business

What is Periscope?

Periscope is Twitter's new live streaming app, it lets you stream video live to your followers, let's your followers interact with your broadcast and then offers playback for up to 24 hours after broadcast. It also offers you the opportunity to save your broadcast for later so you can distribute after that initial 24 hour playback period.

Periscope is not only proving to be great fun but is also offering brands an even better opportunity to connect and interact with their audience in a more personal way and build invaluable relationships and trust. This genius little app lets you either broadcast yourself to your followers or watch broadcasts in a fun, informal and totally unique way. The unique part is that you can interact with the broadcast while you are watching by posting comments which are seen by the broadcaster and all the viewers. You can also show your love and approval for the broadcast or the broadcaster by tapping your screen which produces a flurry of really pretty colored love hearts. The broadcaster can see all this action, they can see who joins the broadcast, see the comments which then offers them the opportunity to respond to comments and questions. This functionality is making Periscope a complete hit and totally addictive, users are absolutely loving it.

With over 7 million users signing up in the first 3 months, Periscope is growing fast. It's early success is most probably down to the fact that

Periscope has the power of Twitter driving traffic to the app. It is also extremely easy to use and requires no technical knowledge. You simply sign up, press a few buttons and you are up and broadcasting. Your followers will be automatically notified that you are broadcasting and if you have signed up with Twitter then your periscope link will be automatically tweeted to your followers as well. It's no wonder this app is sky rocketing to success.

THE BENEFITS OF USING PERISCOPE FOR BUSINESS

Periscope lets viewers experience what is going on around the globe, meaning you could switch form watching a beautiful sunset in Egypt to a buzzing event in New York. It's not wonder Periscope is so addictive. But how can this new app be good for Brands and how can you maximize this app to help you grow your business?

Live streaming on Periscope has a multitude of benefits for business and brands . The benefits are endless and even more powerful because the opportunity for relationship building is maximized by the fact that your audience can interact with you and each other while you are broadcasting . We all know that one of the best ways to reach your audience and build a connection with your audience is through video but this goes one step further. Periscope is like social media on steroids, it really is awesome! However like all social media it is all about relationship building, trust and giving value. It's not a place to just try push your products all the time, this is just going to bore people and put them off. This is a place to start getting yourself and your brand known by offering great content and building influence.

Here are a list of benefits for using this app and then further down this page you will find a list of ideas about how to use Periscope to build your business and your brand.

1. It's really easy to use, you can press a few buttons and go, no need for fancy equipment and you do not require any technical knowledge at all.

2. Followers and Twitter users are automatically notified when you are broadcasting which makes it easier to gain viewers and build an audience.

3. It's live and people love that, even though there is always a replay the attraction seems to be the live interaction.

4. When you broadcast you can interact with your audience live and demonstrate your real passion. This offers your audience a level of transparency that can not be achieved through other forms of social media.

5. Your audience can interact and network with each other. They are having a real conversation with you and others on the 'Scope' .

6. You can build personal connections and make you and your brand more memorable.

7. Your audience can get to know you.

8. Your presentation can be as long or as short as you want.

9. You can reach people all over the world.

10. Like other social networks you can find your ideal customers by working out where they will be hanging out and following them.

11. You can target individual users or a small group and have a private session or you can target all your followers and have a public session.

12. Offers you the opportunity to offer info in a bite size format on a regular basis.

13. Provides another way to listen to your audience and find out what

they want.

14. Offers numerous ways for you to promote your business without being pushy.

HOW YOU CAN USE PERISCOPE FOR BUSINESS

Literally there are endless ways you can use Periscope.

1. To connect with you audience in the most personal way and increase your 'likeabilty'.

2. Run Q & A Sessions.

3. Interview your customers or other experts in your field.

4. Show behind the scenes content from Trade Shows or Events.

5. Demonstrate your products.

6. Use it to create Buzz about your next webinar.

7. Share your promotions, deals and competitions.

8. Help build relationships with you staff and customers by introducing your staff on your 'Scopes'.

9. Share your latest news about new products.

10. Offer Sneak previews of your products.

11. Market Research. Periscope is a great place to communicate with your customers and prospects and find out what they want.

12. Offer regular scopes to inspire your followers.

13 Offer bite size business tips.

14. Offers your audience a glimpse of any events you are running. This is especially useful for those that can not attend and can help to promote your next event.

15. Promote your YouTube Channel. This is such a great way to promote your Channel. You can do a teaser on Periscope for your video on YouTube and you can upload your 'scopes' to YouTube too.

16. Introduce your latest blog post by offering a teaser of information and then sending them to your blog or website for the rest.

17. Broadcast your next book launch or signing or use a broadcast to invite them.

How to Start Broadcasting on Periscope

1. First download the free app from Google play or iTunes.

2. You can now either register with your Twitter credentials or without and register with your phone number.

3. When you sign up with Twitter it will automatically take your Twitter username, however you don't have to keep this and you can change this if you want to. At present you only have this opportunity to change your username and after that you can not. So if you want to grab that one special name (like your own) THEN DO IT NOW . Even if you don't necessarily want to start using Periscope right away ,its a good idea to grab your name now as when it gets more popular it will much harder to get the name you want. Also REMEMBER once you have created your account it is currently NOT possible to change your username so think

very carefully before you press the 'Create your account'.

4. If you don't have a Twitter account then you can sign up with your phone number, Its really easy. Simply add your phone number and your confirmation number will be sent to your mobile and then you add it and away you go.

5. Once you have created your account by pressing 'Create Account ' you can now create your Bio and add your photo. If you signed up with Twitter then Periscope will import your bio and profile picture. These can be changed. To edit your bio, simply double tap the bio and you can add whatever you want. Even though Periscope does not support website links by offering clickable links, you can still add it (the simpler the URL the better).

6. To upload your profile photo simply tap on the profile photo and you can choose from your camera roll or take a new one.

How to find Followers and Grow your Audience on Periscope

As the app matures it will get easier to find who you want to follow. Here are a few ways how to build your audience

1. Announce your presence on your other social media platforms

Your existing customers are by far your most important audience for Periscope. Not only can you build on your existing relationships but also these people are far more likely to be supportive, interact and share your on Periscope . Maybe your followers have not met you in person (via video) before. This is an excellent way of letting your audience get to know you. Simply write a post telling your followers on Facebook or any platform that you now have an account on Periscope and ask them to follow you. You can continue promoting your account by announcing your broadcasts on other platforms too.

2. Search users in your niche

For starters I would follow some familiar people. Here's is one you can follow for starters AlexStearnCom ツ

The best way to find followers is to find people in your niche. Find them through search and then click on their followers and then follow people you want to follow. You can follower a handful of your broadcaster's followers while they are broadcasting and they will be notified. If they see you present they may well follow you back. You can easily follow users who are commenting on a broadcast by tapping on their name and it won't take you away from the broadcast.

3. Follow your Twitter Followers

When someone you follow on Twitter joins Periscope you will be notified and you can choose whether to follow them. You can also follow any of your Twitter followers. However be discerning here , you don't really want to follow for follow as you will be inundated with notifications about Scopes you are not really interested in.

4. You can follow Periscope most loved

These are the people with the most hearts. Following people with large follower numbers may give you exposure but you still may not necessarily attract the right followers. Whether you want to follow these people is up to you.

5. Follow users watching Broadcasts

A great way to find people you resonate with is by following people while you are watching a broadcast. Already a huge amount of networking is going on and you can follow people by clicking on their comment and view their profile. If you think they are a good fit then you can follow and you may find they follow you back. If you are on iOS , click the icon of the three people in the bottom right corner of the navigation menu. If you are on Android press the icon is at the top of the screen on the navigation menu.

Here you will be able to see your Twitter followers and below them Periscope's most loved.

6. How to get on the Periscope 'Most Loved' List

The people who are at the top of the most loved list are those with the most hearts. Each user has a limit of 500 hearts per broadcast. You can use your hearts on broadcasts and on replays. There are ways to get more hearts and broadcasters are already offering incentives for giving all your hearts away.

TOP TIPS FOR BROADCASTING ON PERISCOPE

1. Plan your Scope before you broadcast

You do not need a script but you do need to have a good idea of what you are going to talk about .

2. Set up your location and use a Tripod for your Smartphone

It's definitely a good idea to invest in a tripod, only a few dollars. This will stop all the shake and arm ache! Make sure you decide on a location which has good light and where you are comfortable.

3. Use a microphone especially if you are outside.

Actually the standard of sound is pretty good using just your smartphone but with a microphone it is even better. If you are outside then a microphone is essential to help your voice stand out against any background noise.

4. Set up your image for your introduction

Make sure have an attractive and interesting 'cover image' at the start of your broadcast. Your 'thumbnail' is taken at the beginning of your scope. One idea is to create a topic /title on your laptop. An intro image like this is great wen people are joining.

5. Promote your Scope

You can promote your broadcast before you get started by either Tweeting or posting on Facebook or other social media platforms.

6. Cut out all interruptions
Before you broadcast make sure you switch on Airplane Mode and switch your wifi on, this way you will not get interrupted with calls. Also it's a really good idea to put your phone on Do Not Disturb mode so you will not get notifications which can be distracting when you are broadcasting. You will find this in your settings.

7. To broadcast simply click on the broadcast icon at the bottom.

8. Add your compelling Broadcast Title
Your Title is really important way to gain the attention of your followers. Try and choose a compelling title which will stimulate your audience's curiosity without being misleading. Including emojis will add color and interest and using #Hashtags in your title can also help to increase your reach on Periscope. Hashtags help people to find what they are looking for on Twitter which will open you up to a much wider audience. You can see what is trending on Twitter search too and use sites like Hashtagify.me to find relevant hashtags. Make sure only you use Hashtags which are appropriate for your content.

9. Choose whether you want to share your location or not
You can choose if you want to share your location or not . Periscope does not offer your exact location anymore so you are safe to add it without giving away your address!

10. Choose to Broadcast Private or Public
If you want to have a private broadcast and broadcast to only a few selected users then click on the padlock icon. This is really handy for testing and practising on Periscope.

11. Choose who can comment

If you choose to click on that icon (the chat icon above) only people whom you follow will be able to comment on the broadcast.

12 Twitter Icon

If you want your followers on Twitter to be notified then click the bird icon (shown on image above) and a tweet like this one will be created automatically for your followers.

13. Block Trolls

Unfortunately you may get some unwanted comments , you can easily block these users just by tapping on their username, you have the option to follow or block. BLOCK BLOCK them.

14. How to Save your broadcast

Periscope will automatically save your broadcast so it can be replayed for up to 24 hours after the broadcast but if you want to save it for yourself you can turn that function on in your settings and you will be offered the option to save it to your camera roll once the broadcast is over.

15. How to end your broadcast?

At the end of your broadcast you can simply swipe down from the top.

16. How to flip the camera

During the broadcast you can flip the camera so you can go from filming yourself to filming what ever is around you, simply double tap on the screen.

17. Don't want a replay?

No worries you can find the option to delete the replay after the broadcast.

TIPS ON HOW TO GET THE MOST OUT OF PERISCOPE

1. Announce your scope in advance
Even though Twitter posts your link when you broadcast, make sure you send a tweet out before make sure you send a text out before so people can plan to join before.

2. Engage with your followers
Try and welcome and thank individuals as they join. As your Scopes become more popular this may be difficult but until then this adds a great vibe to the Scope.

3. Introduce yourself every so often
This way new viewers who join late can find out who you are and what the subject of the Scope is.

4. Ask your followers to share your broadcast with their followers
This is very simple for users. There is a people icon on the bottom right of the screen, when this is clicked viewers can share the broadcast.

5. Get to the point and give value quickly
I have watched some broadcasts and seen viewers eave quickly when the broadcaster is not getting to the point. Try and keep your broadcast as upbeat and interesting as possible.

6. Thank people for sending you hearts
If people are sending hearts then be sure to thank them. I don't think there is anything wrong with asking people to tap on the screen if they like the scope. Some 'Scopers' offer incentives offering a prize for the most hearts. An example would be if you had a large Twitter following and offered the person who gave the most hearts a shoutout. There are other incentives like money off coupons etc. The platform is so new but I am sure some very inventive ways of getting people to send hearts you will emerge :)

7. Ask viewers where they are from

This is great to get people interacting and it's wonderful to see where everyone is from and demonstrates the power of this little app.

8. Ask if your viewers have any questions
Before you close ask your viewers if they have any questions. It's all about engagement and offing value.

9. Promote your offering clearly
Remind your viewers them to follow you or hold up a piece of card with your URL written.

10. Watch the replay
After the broadcast you can watch the replay and follow people who have watched your broadcast by simply clicking on the comments. This really helps you as it's not easy doing this while broadcasting.

GETTING THE MOST OUT OF BEING A VIEWER ON PERISCOPE
If you are not quite ready to dive in yourself and broadcast on Periscope you can just enjoy watching and learning until you are ready to take the leap. Watching Scopes is where half the fun is and you can network and gain news contacts too .

1. First of all you will need to download the app from either iTunes or Google Play

2. You can either sign up with Twitter or with your phone number as explained previously

3. Find some users by pressing the People icon at the bottom right and then you can search for people by name or subject. If you signed up with Twitter then you can follow people you are following on Twitter.

4. When you arrive on the app you will be taken to the viewing section (TV icon) and this will show if anyone is live and will give you a list of

most recent broadcasts from the people you are following. To watch simply tap on the broadcast and away you go.

5. You will also be notified with a push notification every time someone you follow is broadcasting so you can hop straight onto the broadcast from the notification. This will also happen while you are watching a broadcast as well. This is where you need to be really discerning about who you follow and make sure you only follow people you are interested in, otherwise you are going to get loads of notifications. This may get quite annoying and you are then more likely to miss the ones you are actually interested in. You can turn Push Notifications off altogether but that may not be the best idea as you may miss some great broadcasts. You can do this in Settings- Periscope-Notifications .

6. So once you are on the broadcast this is where the fun starts . Assuming that the broadcaster is allowing all users to chat (the broadcaster can choose to only let this who they follow chat) You can comment and ask questions throughout the broadcast.
To Comment click inside the 'Say Something' box and type your comment. If you want to reply to someone else's comment, just tap on their comment and press 'Reply.'

7. You can click on the username of anyone who is commenting and view their profile and then 'Follow' them if you wish.

8. You can see who is viewing the broadcast by tapping on the number of viewers in the bottom right or by swiping from left to right and you you can also see the title of the broadcast here too.

9. If you like the broadcast and think it will help your Followers you can share with them and with Twitter and you can choose to share with specific people as well . Simply swipe the screen from left to right and you will see the share icon.

So that's it a complete guide on how to use Periscope and what the benefits and the uses are for business. It's still early on so there will be lots more to find out and learn but this will definitely help you to get started.

My best piece of advice is to do a couple of practice runs to a private audience just to get used to using the app. Even though it is straight forward, preparation is everything. When you ready to go with your first scope don't get too hung up on how many viewers and followers you have , everyone has to start somewhere, right!

The more you scope the better you will get at multi tasking and learning how to best engage your audience, it can be a challenge keeping up with the comments, engaging with your audience and keeping on subject.

Building your Brand through Social Media

YOUR MAIN AIM through this whole process is going to be to connect, capture, and convert your prospects through your website or blog and through social media . This involves the following:

- **Connect:** Your product needs to be the connection between your prospect and what they need so the first thing you need to do is connect those two things. In order to do this you need to identify who they are, find them out of all the millions of people on the Internet, and then connect with them by offering them something they want or need.
- **Capture:** Once you have found them you need to capture them on your website, blog, or social. This is so you can continue your relationship with them either by email or through social media and communicate your brand message. To do this you need to offer them some sort of incentive so you can capture their name and email address.
- **Convert:** When you have captured your prospect you need to convert them into a paying customer by nurturing them and continuing to build a relationship by offering them the content they want through email and social media and then moving them toward signing up for a special or exclusive offer.

To achieve this successfully you are going to need to have a well-defined brand, and that brand needs to be communicated through everything you do through social media, your website, blog, and your email campaign.

Whether you are a one person small business, a large corporation, or an organization, your brand is one of the most important attributes of your business. Your brand is what you want your prospects and customers to respect, trust, and fall in love with so they will buy and continue to buy your products and services. Your brand is what is going to set you apart from any other business and what will give your business the competitive edge.

Never has there been a better time for your business to build your brand and communicate your brand message to your target audience than through social media. Your brand is the main ingredient for success, and social media is giving you the channels to communicate your brand. You can literally communicate with your audience every day. If you get it right and connect the right brand experience with the right target audience, you are onto an all-around winner.

It may be that you have a well-established brand already or maybe you have not created your brand yet or it just needs some tweaking or fine tuning. Maybe you are not exactly sure what your brand is, or you feel it needs a complete overhaul. Whatever your situation is, you need to know that your brand is going to underpin your whole social media campaign, and it needs to be strong, clear, well-defined, and consistent. Once defined, your business is going to create it, be it, communicate it, display it, picture it, speak it, promote it, and most of all, be true to it. This chapter is going to take you through everything you need know and do to define and create your brand so you can get into the hearts and minds of your target audience by communicating the right message and brand experience.

There are many definitions of the word brand but this is the one I like best because it incorporates pretty much all the necessary information you will need to help you to define your own brand.

Brand, the definition
Your brand is more than a name, symbol, or logo. It is your commitment

and your promise to your customer. Your brand is the defined personality of either yourself as an individual brand or your product, service, company, or organization. It's what sets you apart and differentiates your business from your competition and any other business. Your brand is created and influenced by your vision and everything you stand for, including people, visuals, culture, style, perception, words, messages, PR, opinions, news media, and, especially, social media.

Why is your brand so important to your business?

Branding is important because it helps you and your business build and create powerful and lasting relationships by communicating everything you want to say about your product or service to your prospects and customers. A strong brand encourages loyalty and will ultimately create a strong customer base and increase your sales by doing the following:

- Demonstrating to your prospects and customers that you are professional and committed to offering them what you promise
- Making your business easily recognizable
- Creating a clear distinction from your competition
- Making your business memorable
- Creating an emotional attachment with your audience
- Helping to create trust
- Helping to build customer loyalty and repeat custom
- Creating a valuable asset which will be financially beneficial if you sell your business
- Creating a competitive advantage

To do all the above you are going to have to find a way to get into the hearts and minds of your customers so they will ultimately buy and continue to buy your products or services. Before launching your campaign and setting up profiles, posting content, and engaging, you will need to have a clear picture of exactly what your brand is or what you want your brand to be. You will need to define exactly how your brand is perceived now, how you want your brand to be perceived, where your business fits into the market, who your target audience is, and how you want your business to develop in the future.

To do this you need a deep understanding of your business and the people who are going to be most interested in your products and how you are going to serve them. When it comes to defining your ideal target audience, you need to work out which of your products are the most popular and the most profitable so you can focus your efforts in finding and connecting with the right audience and then creating the right brand experience for them.

YOUR VISION/YOUR STORY

If you want to create a strong brand, one of the first things you need to do is create a clear visual picture of how you see your business now and in the future. This is about daring to see what your business could be without constraints or limitations.

This exercise will not only help you work out what you want to achieve financially and creatively, but it also makes you focus on what really matters and will help you create your own unique voice and story. This is incredibly important when it comes to your branding as this is what is going to make your business stand out from others and give you that edge.

To do this, you need to get away from all distractions and think about how you would like to see your business grow and develop in the next three years. This is more than just putting a mission statement together. This is about your core business beliefs, why you are doing it, what you want your business to be, and how you want to be perceived in your market. To help you do this you will need to ask yourself the following questions and record your answers:

- Why did you originally start your business or why are you starting a business?
- How did your original business idea come about?
- What changes are you looking to make in peoples' lives?

636

- What are you hoping to achieve?
- What aspects of your business are really important to you?
- What are your hopes and dreams?
- What is your definition of success?
- What sort of turnover and income defines that success?
- How many employees does your business have?
- Why are you in business?
- What are your core values in your business?
- What impact do you want to have?
- What influence do you want to have?
- What sort of things do you want the media to be saying about you?
- What do you want your customers to be saying about you?
- How you want to be portrayed on social media?
- How many social media followers/fans do you want?
- What markets are you in? Are you local, national, or international?

Once you have completed this exercise, you will have all the material you need so that you can create the unique experience required to make your business stand out from all the others in your niche. This is the first step toward creating a brand for your business. This is the beginning of your story.

DEFINING YOUR BRAND

Whether you are responsible for defining, creating, and developing your brand in-house or you are employing a local branding and marketing agency, you will need to carry out an analysis of your business to define your brand. Completing the following exercise will help you define and clarify your brand:

- A factual description of what your business is and the purpose of your business
- Describe your product or service in one sentence
- List all your products and/or services.
- What are the benefits and features of all of your products?

- Which are your most profitable products/services?
- Which are your most popular products/services?
- Who are your ideal customers for each of your products or services? (Consumer or business, age, gender, income, occupation, education, stage in family life cycle.)
- Out of these customers, which ones who are most likely to buy your most profitable products?
- Is the market and demand large enough to provide you with the number of customers you need to buy your most profitable products and achieve your financial goals?
- If your answer to the previous question is no then ask yourself the same question for each of your other products.
- Who are your three main competitors? (Have a look at their social media accounts.)
- What distinguishes your business from your competition? What special thing are you bringing to the market that is of real value? What is your unique selling point? What solutions are your products offering your customers that will meet their needs or solve their problems?
- If you are already in business, write down what your customers are already saying about your business. What do you think they would say about how your product or service makes them feel emotionally? (You may need to ask your customers if you do not already know.) What qualities and words would you use to describe the personality of your business as it is now? Here are some examples of words you may wish to use: high cost, low cost, high quality, value for money, expensive, cheap, excellent customer service, friendly, professional, happy, serious, innovative, eccentric, quiet, loud, beautiful, relaxing, motivating, sincere, adventurous, amusing, charming, decisive, kind, imaginative, proactive, intuitive, loving, trustworthy, extrovert, vibrant, transparent, intelligent, creative, dynamic, resourceful.
- Now, whether you are already in business or starting out, write down all the words to describe how you want and need your

brand to be perceived and what qualities you want to be associated with your brand in order to match the needs and expectations of your ideal customers. If you are already in business, hopefully this will be exactly the same as how you perceive you are at the current time.

- What is the evidence that backs up what you have said about your brand? This could be customer testimonials or any evidence about product or service quality.
- What is the biggest opportunity for your business right now?
- What products are you thinking of introducing in the near future?

How to get into the Minds and Hearts of your Target Audience

Your target audience is your most important commodity, as they are the future customers and ambassadors of your business. Every single one of them is valuable, and every single one of them can make a difference to your business. This can be because they are actually going to buy your products or simply spread the word by interacting with you on Facebook.

However, it's a big social world out there. The possibilities of finding new people are limitless, but targeting everyone is not the solution. The biggest mistake you can make is trying to reach everyone and then not appealing to anyone. Your first step is to identify exactly who the people are who are going to be interested in your products or services, and then you need to find out everything about them. You need to get inside their heads and work out what motivates these people, what their needs, hopes, aspirations, fears, and dreams are. Your product or service is the link between them and what they want. When you know this you can tailor every single message or piece of content toward them.

When you know exactly who your ideal customers are, social media offers you the opportunity to go find and reach them. It's then up to you to capture them so you can continue to communicate. When you know everything about your customers you are more likely to speak the right language to be able to communicate with them and build trust to the point where the next natural progression is for them to buy your product.

It's only when you truly understand your audience that you can start converting them into customers. Once you know you are targeting the right audience, you can confidently focus every ounce of your effort creating exactly the right content, nurturing them, engaging with them, and looking after them. It's only a matter of time before they will buy your product.

Creating your ideal customer persona or avatar

The following exercise is absolutely essential. Your answers to the questions will be the very information that is going to help you communicate with your customer in the right way, by providing them with the right content and the correct brand experience. Once you have done this exercise you are going to own some very powerful information. If you do not do this exercise it is very unlikely that you are going to be able to truly connect with your target audience in the way that is necessary to build trust so that you can ultimately convert them into your customers.

Your answers to the questions in the previous section will have given you a clear idea of which types of customers you need to target to give you the best chance of achieving your financial goals. You now need to find out everything about them so you can get your brand into their hearts and minds. The best way to do this is to create an imaginary persona or avatar of your ideal customer and you can build this picture by finding out the following:

- Describe your ideal customer and include the following details: are they a consumer or in business, their age, gender, income, occupation, education, and stage in family life cycle.
- Where do they live?
- What do they want most of all?

- What are their core values?
- What is their preferred lifestyle?
- What do they do on a day-to-day basis?
- What are their hopes and aspirations?
- What important truth matters to them?
- What motivates and inspires them?
- What sort of routines do they have?
- What are their day-to-day priorities?
- How do they have fun?
- What do they do in their spare time?
- What subjects are they interested in?
- Which books do they read?
- Which TV programs do they watch?
- What magazines do they read?
- Who do they follow on social media?
- Who are their role models?
- What really makes them tick?
- What are their fears and frustrations?
- What are their suspicions?
- What are their insecurities?
- What are their typical worries?
- What is the perfect solution to their worries?
- What are their dreams?
- What do they need to make them feel happy and fulfilled?

Big Questions

To answer the following questions you will need to step inside your ideal customer's mind and imagine you are them.

- How do you feel when you find your product or service? What is your initial emotional reaction?
- What are the words that go through your head?
- How can I justify buying this product for myself?
- Are you ready to buy immediately?
- Do you have any suspicions that the product may not be what it

says?

- What are those suspicions? Why do you have them?
- Do you need more convincing?
- What do you need to convince you that the product is right for you?
- What do you feel when you have the product in your hand?

The reason why these are such big questions is because your answers to them will establish whether or not you have correctly defined your ideal customer and whether you have really understood their needs, desires, and fears. If you are imagining yourself as your ideal customer and you are saying "woo-hoo", ecstatically jumping up and down with glee, immediately buying the product, or relieved that you have at long last found the solution to your problem, then you have created the right avatar. If not, then you need to think again.

It's only when you have imagined yourself in the hearts and minds of your target audience that you are going to be able to connect with them on any emotional level. With the information from the above exercise, you will have everything you need to produce exactly the right content to match the needs, desires, and expectations of your ideal customer so that you can create the right brand experience and sell your products. This information is like gold.

COMMUNICATING YOUR BRAND

Once you have gone through all the processes outlined in this chapter you will have a clear idea about what your brand is, what is stands for, and how you stand out from similar businesses. You now have to work out how to best communicate this to your ideal customer so that when they hear or see your brand name they immediately make that essential emotional connection. This is what is going to make them eventually love your brand above all others.

When you are clear about what your brand is, what it stands for, and how you are going to stand out from other similar businesses, you then need to work out how you can communicate this message in the best possible way. Your main aim here is to create an emotional connection with your target audience that is going to help them grow to love your brand, remember your brand, and remain loyal to it. To do this you need to communicate your brand story through every aspect of your business, including your social media campaign.

With the information you now have you are armed with everything you need to create a consistent brand. If you have not already done so, you can either hand all this information over to a marketing agency or use it yourself to create all the following:

- **Your logo:** Your logo will give a clear guideline for all your promotional material, including your website or blog, stationery, templates, or any marketing material that needs to be created for online or offline promotion.
- **Your brand message: This is** the main message you want to communicate about your brand.
- **Your tagline:** A short, memorable statement about your brand that captures the personality of your brand and communicates how you or your product will benefit your customer.
- **All your 'about' descriptions:** You can communicate your brand story through all your 'about' sections on all your social media platforms you are using.
- **The content you create for your business:** Every piece of content you create for your business needs to be tailor-made for your target audience. You will need to pick who and what subjects or topics you want to be associated with your brand, as anything you pick to write about will be a representation of your brand.
- **Your website and/or blog:** The 'about' page of your website is probably the most visited page on any website and there is a reason for this. People want to find out about your business and

what is different or special about it. This is a great place to introduce and expand on the story of your brand. This is where you can really go to town and communicate your beliefs and uniqueness.. Also, the visual style of your website or blog and your individual voice should be evident throughout your site and be consistent with your brand.

- **Video content:** Videos are an incredibly powerful way of creating a personal connection with your audience. Make sure that whatever video content you produce and whatever you say is always consistent with your brand.

THE ESSENTIAL SOCIAL MEDIA MARKETING PLAN

BEFORE LAUNCHING INTO your campaign you will need to know exactly what you want your business to achieve and what achieve and what you hope to gain through marketing on social media. Without the necessary planning and preparation, your campaign is very unlikely to succeed.

The next few chapters take you through everything you need to do to plan your campaign before actually posting content. In this chapter you will learn how to create your mission statement, set goals and objectives, and plan the strategies and tactics you need to implement to achieve those goals. In the following chapter you will learn exactly how to prepare your business, your website and blog, and your email campaign so you can capture and convert customers.

CREATING YOUR MISSION STATEMENT

Many campaigns fail at the first hurdle simply because they do not have a clear idea about why they are undertaking a campaign or what they want to achieve. They set up a profile on Facebook or Twitter and have little or no idea why exactly they are doing it. "Everyone else is doing it ... we probably should too." Then they launch in without first articulating the purpose of their social media campaign and aimlessly start posting content. Before long, they realize that this is having no positive effect on their business, and they either give up or continue half-heartedly.

Once you have defined your brand and your target audience you will need to produce your mission statement for your social media campaign. Your mission statement is vital for your business as a whole and for your

645

prospects and customers, and it should clearly state your commitment and promise to them as well as communicate your brand message. You will be able to include this in your social media bio's and on your business page. To create your mission statement, simply follow these for four easy steps:

- **Describe what your business does:** Describe exactly what you do, what you offer, and the purpose of your business.
- **Describe the way you operate:** Include your core values, your level of customer service, and your commitment to your customers. You can include how your core values contribute to the quality of your product or service.
- **Who are you doing it for?:** Who are your customers? Business owners, entrepreneurs, working women, gardeners, shop owners, etc.
- **The value you are bringing:** What benefit are you offering your customers ? What value are you bringing them?

Once you have created your statement, everyone will know exactly what you are about. You will know what you need to deliver to your customers. Your employees will know what is expected of them. Your customers and prospects will know what your promise is and what they can expect when buying your products and services.

SETTING YOUR GOALS AND OBJECTIVE FOR YOUR CAMPAIGN

Setting goals and objectives is the key to your success on social media. Once they are set, you will be ready to plan and create the strategies and tactics to achieve those goals and objectives. You will be able to review and measure the success of your campaign.

Definition of a goal

A goal is a statement rooted in your business's mission, and it will define what you want to accomplish and offer a broad direction for your business to follow. The three main goals of any business will ultimately be to increase sales, to reduce costs, and to improve customer service. Each goal will have a direct effect on the others. Here are some examples within those three main goals:

1. To increase revenue and generate sales
- To increase website traffic
- To increase brand awareness through social media
- To build a reputation as an expert within the industry
- To build a loyal and engaged community on social media
- To increase the number of customers from word-of-mouth and referrals
- To increase the number of sales
- To increase average spending per customer
- To increase the number of leads generated
- To introduce new products
- To increase online visibility
- To promote an event
- To build a highly targeted list of email subscribers
- To connect with new customers
- To build trust and build relationships with prospects and customers
- To put a content marketing strategy in place
- To increase business in 'X' country/state
- To become a thought leader in your industry
- To develop new markets by introducing product into 'X' country/state
- To decrease spending on traditional forms of advertising and invest 'X' amount in social media marketing
- To build relationships with key influencers on social media

2. To reduce Costs
- To decrease spending on traditional forms of advertising and invest in social media marketing

3. To deliver customer satisfaction and retain customers

- To answer customer questions promptly
- To respond to customer complaints promptly, politely, and helpfully
- To provide online help/technical support
- To respond to customer feedback
- To listen to your customers

Setting measurable objectives

Once you set your broader goals, you need to get more specific and create SMART objectives (specific, measurable, attainable, relevant, and timely). Here is an explanation of exactly what each of those terms means:

- **Specific:** You need to target particular areas for improvement.
- **Measurable:** Your progress needs to be quantifiable, and putting concrete figures on your goals is essential for success and is the only way to measure the effectiveness of your campaign.
- **Attainable/Realistic:** You need to be realistic with the resources you have available, and the results you are expecting need to be realistic.
- **Relevant:** Your goals need to be relevant to the business climate you are in.
- **Time Bound:** Make sure you set a realistic time period to achieve your goals. If a time is not set then things tend not to get done.

Here are some examples of the sort of SMART objectives you should be setting:

- Increase sales of product X by X%
- To build an audience of X number fans on Facebook within one year.
- To increase number of followers by X per week

- To increase website traffic from Facebook by X times
- To increase opt-in list subscribers by X per week
- Increase conversions from Facebook by X per week
- To increase the number of leads generated from Facebook by X per week
- To increase the number of new customers by X per month
- To increase the average spending per customer by X
- Introduce X number of new products every 6 months
- To increase sales from X country/state by X%
- To decrease spending on traditional forms of advertising by X and invest X amount in Twitter marketing
- To achieve a X% reach (number of people who see posts) on Facebook
- Utilize Facebook to increase attendants at X event by X people
- Utilize Facebook to increase YouTube views by X people per week

Choosing your Strategies and Tactics

Once you have set your quantifiable goals and objectives, you are going to have to work out how you are going to accomplish them though social media. You will need to think about the strategies and tactics you are going to use, and they need to be quantifiable as well. Here are some examples of the strategies you may want to implement:

- To create a free offer with built-in subscriber opt-in form
- To post content on Facebook X times per day
- To make X% of posts photo/posts
- To spend X on promoted posts per month
- To create X number of highlighted posts per month
- To spend X on social media advertising
- To increase spend on social media advertising in X country/state by X%
- To create X number of blog posts per week/month and post them on Facebook with images

- To post X offers per month/6 months on Facebook
- To run X competitions/contests per year on Facebook
- To create X events on Facebook
- To create X videos on YouTube per month
- To spend X minutes per day liking customers pages (B2B only)
- To spend X minutes per day 'liking', commenting, and sharing customer posts
- To follow X influencers on Twitter per week
- To create X number of online events per year

Of course, at the beginning, you are going to need to make an educated guess at the number of times you need to do one thing to achieve another. As your campaign runs, you will need to adjust certain aspects to achieve your goals. For example, you may need to spend more on promoted posts to increase your reach, spend more advertising to increase the number of fans, or you may need to change the type of content you are posting to increase the amount of engagement.

The only way you can do this is by constantly monitoring and measuring your results against the original goals and objectives you set and adjusting your campaign accordingly.

The only way you can do this is by constantly monitoring and measuring your results against the original goals and objectives you set and adjusting your campaign accordingly.

CREATING YOUR SOCIAL MEDIA POSTING CALENDAR

Now that you have your strategies in place, you will have a good idea of the amount and type of content you need to post to achieve those objectives. One of the most challenging tasks of your social media campaign is going to be to consistently deliver a high standard of content to your fans on a daily basis. You are going to need to post between one to four times a day. This does not mean you need to create numerous blog articles each day, but you are going to need to communicate in some way and find unique ways for your audience to interact with your brand and offer some kind of value on a regular basis. This may seem daunting to begin with, but you will be surprised just how one idea leads to another.

To help you map out your content for the next six months or the year ahead, you need to create a social media posting calendar which is going to be your key to consistent posting. There are many online tools and apps that can help you with this. Google Calendar is a very good calendar to use, and it lets you color code the different types of posts. You can also use Hootsuite, the social media dashboard, to plot out your calendar or use a spreadsheet in Excel. There are also other online applications, like www.trello.com, which has easy to use drag-and-drop features. Using mind-mapping applications like 'Simplemind' can really help when brainstorming for content ideas.

To get started you will simply need to map out and schedule the days of the week for each week of the year and decide what types of post you are going to create for certain days. You will need to balance the type of content in order to create variety and interest for your audience. You then need to create topics or themes and break the year down into weeks/months and make a schedule. You can add all the things that you are planning within your business, like offers, contests, product launches, and webinars, and then add all the things going on outside your business, like public holidays and special events. You need to incorporate all that information into your daily action plan.

It may seem daunting to look at a blank calendar, but you will be surprised how it comes together when you start breaking it down into months, weeks, and days. A posting calendar will help you keep your campaign focused, on track, and in line with your brand and your marketing goals and also keep it balanced in terms of the subject and type of media you use. A calendar will help you look ahead and help you to incorporate your marketing plan into your social media campaign. It may be that you are launching a new product, or maybe certain products tie in with specific holidays. You may have certain industry events you need to attend or are perhaps creating your own. Maybe you are going to run a competition at a certain time of the year. Whatever it is you are planning throughout the year, you need to include it on your calendar.

Preparing your Business For Success

WHETHER YOUR SITE is being found through an organic search, an advertising campaign, or social media, all your hard work is going to be wasted unless you have put a system in place to capture leads and convert them into customers. This system has to start from the moment your prospect either hits your website, your blog, or your social media, and your ultimate goal is to convert your browsers into buyers.

Firstly, the unfortunate fact is that the majority of your website visitors are unlikely to buy from you on their first visit. If you do not have a website that grabs their attention within the first couple of seconds, they will move very quickly onto another site. Secondly, even if your site does catch their eye, they are still likely to check out other sites and still may not return. To make any kind of impact at all your site needs to grab their attention and then capture their email address so you can continue your relationship with them through email. This chapter is going to take you through steps you will need to take, from getting your website or blog ready to setting up and creating your email campaign.

Email is still one of the most powerful ways to convert prospects into customers and has a conversion rate three times higher than social media conversion rates. That is not to say that your social media campaign is any less important, as this is where you are going to find and nurture your leads and transfer them to your opt-in by either capturing them on social media or on your website or blog. This chapter is going to take you through steps you will need to take from getting your website or blog ready to setting up and creating your email campaign.

PREPARING YOUR WEBSITE FOR SUCCESS

Whether you already have a website or blog or you are creating a new site from scratch, you need to make sure it has the necessary features to grab the attention of your target audience and capture their email addresses. Capturing the email addresses of your target audience has to be one of your most important goals when creating your website. Once your prospects have voluntarily submitted their email address, you have the opportunity to build a relationship, communicate your message, and promote your products and services on an ongoing and regular basis. A well thought-out and crafted email campaign can immediately establish trust and favor with your subscribers. Don't forget that it is you who owns your opt-in list and nobody can take it away from you. As long as you are providing your subscribers value with great content, they are likely to want to keep hearing from you. Remember you cannot rely on social media to continue your relationship as these platforms are changing all the time. You need to build your email list.

Once you have completed the exercise in the branding section and have your ideal customer persona or avatar, you will have a clear picture of what your target audience's pain point or problem is and how your product can help solve it or make their life better in some way. If you have a blog, and most businesses today need a blog, you will also have all the tools you need to create the right content to attract your target audience. Armed with this information you are halfway ready to putting a system in place, so your products sell themselves and your website is working like an extra sales person selling your products 24/7.

When your visitor arrives at your site, you have only three seconds to grab their attention. You need to connect emotionally with them and let them know immediately that they have arrived at the right place by communicating exactly how you are going to help them and what it is you are offering them.

Once they are on your site, you then need to win their interest and confidence so that they will voluntarily submit their email address. To do this you will need to create a lead magnet and offer your audience something which is incredibly valuable to them for free. There are numerous ways you can do this and which one you use will depend very much on what type of business you are and what your goals are. If you are a business offering technical solutions, you could offer them a free trial. If you are offering information, you could offer them a free report, a short video training series, or an ebook. If you are selling some kind of product or service, you could offer them a money-off voucher. These work particularly well for restaurants and the service industry as a whole. Whatever you are offering, it needs to be really good to attract your audience and get them to volunteer their email.

Here are the features you need to have on your website or blog or any landing page with a special offer.

- **Keep your design simple:** Your site needs to have a clean and simple design, and you need to communicate your most important message clearly and concisely to your target audience. Your most important content with any call-to-action needs to be placed above the fold, where they will be easily seen, and your call-to-action should have an easily seen button link rather than just a text link.

- **Make your site easy to navigate:** Really this is so important. Try to use the minimum number of pages you can and make your menu titles as easy to understand as possible.

- **Clearly communicate your message:** You want your visitors to subscribe to your opt-in, so you need to place your compelling offer with an image and title of the offer someplace where it is visible. The message and benefit of your offer needs be descriptive and specific.

- **Add a clear call-to-action:** In order for your visitors to sign up, they will need to be told what to do. Make sure you have a direct call-to-action, for example, "Download your free ebook now" or

"Sign up for your discount voucher now." Your call-to-action needs to be clearly visible with an eye-catching button link which is much more effective than a text link.

- **Add clear contact information:** Make it easy for your prospects to contact you by placing your contact details where they will be easily seen. With the technology available, you can even add chat features so that as soon as your prospect arrives on your site a chat form appears asking if you can be of any assistance. Obviously you need the resources to be able to man this, but it is an incredibly powerful way of quickly building trust and showing how much you value your website visitors by being available to answer any of their questions.

- **Email capture form:** Your email capture form needs to be as simple as possible, preferably just asking for their name and email. You need to state on the form that their email address is safe with you and will not be shared with anyone. Make sure your form is in a prominent position and consider using a pop-up form that appears 20 seconds after your prospect has arrived on your site. Your email sign-up form needs to go at the top, side, and bottom of your webpage and also on your 'about page,' which is often the most popular page on your site.

- **Privacy policy:** You need a clear privacy policy on your website to make it clear that you will not be spamming them or selling their information.

- **Thank you page:** Once your visitor has completed the form, you will have them as a lead, but before you let them go you can send them to a thank you page where you can offer them the opportunity to share your offer with their friends by including social sharing buttons.

- **Mobile Friendly:** You need to make sure your offer is easily visible and easy to complete on a cellphone. This is incredibly important, as more and more people are purchasing from their cellphone. There is nothing more annoying for the user than if the site is hard to navigate from their cellphone.

- Don't add external links to other sites. Be careful not to fall into the trap of wanting to make your site more interesting by adding lots of content and links to other external sites, as this will only detract from your main goals and you'll end up sending traffic away from your site.

Landing pages

Landing pages are incredibly effective if you want to promote specific offers for specific products to specific audiences. A landing page is a page that is designed to give information about an offer and then capture a lead with a form for your visitor to complete so that they can download or claim that offer. Landing pages are highly effective in capturing leads because they are designed to be specific in their goal, which is to capture the contact information of your visitor.

The landing page should have a clear, uncluttered design and not have any links or navigation menus that could take your visitor away from the landing page. It should contain the following:

- A headline (The title of the offer)
- A description of the offer, clearly detailing the benefits to your visitor
- A compelling image of the offer
- A clear call-to-action. This can be in the form of an image or text.
- A form to capture contact information (The fewer fields required to be completed, the more leads you will receive.)
- A clear privacy policy on your website that makes it clear that you will not be spamming them or selling their information
- A thank you page leading them to another offer or social sharing

You can either ask your web developer to create landing pages or there are numerous tools available on the Internet where you can easily create one, for example: www.leadpages.net, www.unbounce.com, www.launcheffect.com, and www.instapage.com

SETTING UP AND CREATING YOUR EMAIL CAMPAIGN

Once you have created your lead capture system on your website, blog, or separate landing page and have your subscribers' permission to send them your email, you are going to need a really good email campaign to convert those leads into sales.

Email is still one of the most effective forms of converting leads into sales, and email is more powerful than ever. Not only is it cost effective but it also provides one of the most direct and personal lines of communication with your customer. Once subscribed, they have invited you into their inbox on a regular basis and producing valuable content for your subscribers will develop trust and deepen your relationship with them. Your email will also work hand in hand with your social media campaign. As you build your relationship with your fans on social media, they are more likely to deem your emails valuable and open them.

The first thing you need to do is set yourself up with a good email marketing provider and there are many you can choose from: www.aweber.com, www.constantcontact.com, and www.mailchimp.com to name a few. It's important to use a system where you have a confirmed opt-in. This is when the subscriber is sent an email to confirm their email address. This verifies that you are gaining consent and legally protects you. It also helps you to keep a clean list, and it protects you from sending emails to incorrect addresses. You can then automate your emails with an auto responder and send out emails automatically over time.

Your next task is to plan and create your email campaign. Here are a few tips for doing so:

- **Be clear about your goals:** You need to be absolutely clear from day one what you want to achieve through email. Are you using it to introduce a new product at some time? Are you launching an event? Whatever you do, make sure you know exactly what it is that you want to achieve.

- **Keep it simple and in line with your branding:** Make sure your email design ties in with your branding. Most email providers offer templates which you can add your own branding to, or you can get a designer to create a particular design. Keep it really simple. Sometimes if things are too fancy they become impersonal.

- **Send a regular newsletter:** Plan to send a regular newsletter email at least once a month and once a week if you can. You can also plan to send off information about offers which tie in with special holidays and occasions throughout the year or competitions or events that you may be planning.

- **Plan your topics:** You need to plan the topics you want to cover in each email, and this should tie in nicely with the plan for your blog articles. You then need to deliver high quality content which is tailor-made to fit with your subscribers' interests, and it needs to be so good that they are looking forward to the next email from you. If you are sending emails about offers then you need to show them clearly how these offers are going to benefit their lives.

- **Attention-grabbing titles:** This is where you need to get really creative. Your main goal here is to get your subscriber to open your email, and you need to create a headline that is going to make your subscriber curious and inquisitive and eager to open your mail. Questions work really well as titles, and you will often see your open rates increase. This is because people find questions intriguing and they feel like you are directly addressing them. Try and avoid the words that will trigger spam filters. Simply search Google for a list of these words to avoid.

- **Be authentic and true to your brand:** Write your emails in a style that your audience will grow to recognize, 'like,' and identify with your brand. Write so your subscriber feels like you are just writing to them. You need to establish yourself as a likeable expert for your subscribers. Try and create a personal relationship with them by addressing them by name and giving them a warm friendly introduction. Offering them the opportunity to connect with you and answer any of their questions by simply replying to your mail is a great way to create a connection and trust.

- **Keep it simple** Make sure your emails are simply constructed and straight to the point so you keep your subscribers' interest and get them quickly to the place you want them to go, like your blog or offer.

- **Include social sharing buttons:** Include all your social sharing icons and links in your mail.

- **Make them feel safe:** Make sure your subscribers are clear that their email will not be shared and that they can unsubscribe anytime.

- **Analyze your open rates:** Most email service providers include statistics in their packages so you can analyze open rates, bounce rates, click through rates, unsubscribers, and social sharing statistics. These results give you the opportunity to find out what is and what is not working.

Blog Blog Blog

THIS CHAPTER IS for anyone who does not have a blog. The word blog has been mentioned numerous times throughout the book and has become an essential part of any online business today.

What is a Blog?

A blog (short for web log) is a term used to describe a website that provides an ongoing journal of individual news stories which are based around a certain subject or subjects (blog posts.) Blogs have given people the power of the media. Anyone can now create a personal type of news that appeals to a high number of small niche audiences.

Bloggers simply complete a simple online form with a title and body and then post it. The Blog post then appears at the top of the website as the most recent article. Over time the posts build up to become a collection of posts which are then archived chronologically for easy reference. Each blog post can then become a discussion with space for comments below the post, readers can leave comments and questions. This is where bloggers start to build relationships and a community with their readers and other bloggers who may have similar interests. Blogs were one of the earliest forms of social media and started growing in the late 1990s. The number of blogs has exploded in recent years and blogs now underpin the majority of successful social media campaigns.

Why Blog for Business?

Blogging is one of the most beneficial tools that a business has to communicate it's expertise and ideas to its prospects and customers and to engage with them. Businesses can share information about their business and about any subject that may be of interest to their niche. It is a fact that businesses with blogs benefit from an increase in the number of visitors to their website, increased leads, increase in inbound links and increased sales. Here are some of the reasons why and the benefits that come with blogging:

- **Underpins your whole social media campaign** Your blog is the focus of all your social media efforts and the centre of all your content marketing efforts. One of the main goals of any business today will be to get people to their blog to read their valuable and targeted content and social media will be one of the main tools they can use to drive traffic to their blog.

- **Increased website traffic** A well optimized blog will increase your chances of being found in search. Google loves unique fresh content and if this is created regularly, this will boost your traffic.

- Builds brand awareness A Blog offers a business the opportunity to build a community and build awareness for their products or services. The more people who see your blog, the more people see your brand.

- **Provides valuable information for your niche** Creating a Blog gives your business a voice and provides your niche with valuable information in relation to the subjects that they are interested in. This may include information about market trends, industry news and insight into your products and services and what is behind them.

- **Thought leadership** Sharing your expertise with valuable information will make you stand out as a thought leader in your particular field and will help you to build a professional online reputation.

- **Builds trust & creates warm leads** When you are providing valuable content for your niche on a regular basis, answering their questions and addressing their concerns, this in turn creates trust between you and your prospective customers. This trust leads to more leads and will result in sales. When your audience become regular readers of your blog they become warm rather than cold leads, the ice has been broken and they are half way there in terms of buying your product.

- **You gain more knowledge** While writing your blog you will be continually researching your subject, learning about new technology, products and new trends. In turn, this keeps you ahead of the game and in the eyes of your customers it makes you an expert. As time goes by you become more and more knowledgable and can steer your business in line with market trends and keep your products and services up to the minute. You will also find that blogging is inspiring and your ideas will snowball, as you learn more material you will find more material to blog about.

- **Interaction and feedback** When your blog has room for comments and discussion it will give you the opportunity to hear what people are saying, the questions they are asking and insight into what they want out of your products. Feedback like this is invaluable to your business and also leads to more ideas for more blog posts. This kind of feedback also encourages a conversation and you actually get the opportunity to communicate with prospective customers.

HOW TO CREATE A BLOG?

Creating your blog is incredibly straight forward. There are a number of free blogging platforms that are available, however, if you read the terms and conditions of most of these platforms you will find that at the end of the day you do not actually own the content and you will not have full control of your blog. You will have no control of the advertising displayed, you are unlikely to be able to include an email capture form, you will not be able to have you own domain name and you will not be able to install plugins. With a free platform your domain name will look something like http://mybusinessblog.theirblogplatformname.com and overall it is not going to look that professional.

The best and safest way of creating a blog and running with your own domain name is to create one with wordpress.org or you can use website creators like www.wix.com or www.squarespace.com who both offer blogs with their product and you can add your own domain. Using any of these will give you full control over your site.

Wordpress.org is a free open source platform which means it can be modified and customized and by anyone. You can use custom themes or you can choose from hundreds of free themes and plugins. The wordpress.org blogging platform is free but you will need to purchase a domain name and host your site on your own server, however most hosting companies offer inexpensive monthly plans and a one click installation solutions. You will also need to make sure you back up your blog and you may very well find this is included in your hosting package.

WHAT MAKES A SUCCESSFUL BLOG?

For those businesses that are doing it right blogging can be hugely beneficial and they will often see an increase of over 50% of website visitors and leads. However, many blogs also fail to make any positive difference to a business, so it is essential that before you waste time and resources you understand what you need to do to create a successful blog:

Set Goals and objectives

First of all you will need to be about clear what your marketing goals are and set clear objectives for what you want to achieve from your blog.

Example Goal 1

Increase brand awareness through Facebook.
Objective:
Achieve X number of shares per month on Facebook.

Example Goal 2

Increase Traffic to website from blog.
Objective: To achieve an increase of X Traffic from blog.

Example Goal 3
Increase the number of leads for product A.
Objective: To gain X number of new opt-ins per week.

Example Goal 4
To create interaction and engagement.
Objective: To have at least X number of comments on each blog post.

Example Goal 5
To become a thought leader in the industry.
Objective: To write X number of guest posts per month/year.

Example Goal 6
To increase the ranking of blog in Google and Bing.
Objective: To achieve X number of backlinks from other websites in 6 months.

Create top content for your audience
Again it's all about your audience and what they want, what they are interested in, what makes them tick and what problems they need solving. If you can identify these things then you are half way to finding the valuable content that is going to keep your audience interested and engaged. When you create your content it needs to be either inspiring, educational, informative or entertaining. If you can create content that people really value, they are more likely to share your content, more likely to sign up for your updates and more likely to come back looking for more. Creating content around your product or services is not going to provide enough interest to your readers and it is unlikely to get shared. Of course the occasional post is ok but try and keep away from this unless you can tie it in with something which is of real value to your audience.

Create a content plan

Your content plan is the backbone to your blog. You will need to decide what topics you are going to build your blog around so that you can stay consistent. There may be certain keywords that you want to target and need to incorporate into your content. Once you know your topics or subjects then you can decide which types of posts you are going to create. There are numerous types of blog posts you can use, for example; tutorials, how to's , interviews, reviews, book reviews, advice, Q and A's, case studies, trend reports and the latest news in your industry. When you have decided on all this you then write a schedule and if you have certain events that happen every year in your industry make sure you include these in your plan.

Newsworthy posts

Make sure you are blogging about whats new in your industry and keep an eye on trending topics relating to your industry so you can create blog posts that are really up to date. You can do this by checking out what is trending on the social sites and also signing up for Google alerts which will keep you up to date on new info relating to your interests and queries.

Frequent and consistent blogging

It is proven that the more high quality content you produce, the more views your blog will get. You will need to post at least once a week if not more. Google loves fresh content so the more posts you have, the more opportunities you are going to have to be found.

Optimize your blog for search

Look for keywords and phrases that people are looking for. There are tools available to do this like word tracker, Google trends and Google keyword planner. You can find out the amount of competition by typing a phrase into Google search and seeing how many results it brings up. In order to get found you will need to concentrate your efforts on low competition keywords and phrases and the more specific your words and phrases are the better. You can then create your content around your chosen keyword or phrase as long as the content is highly relevant. When creating your blog post make sure you put the word/phrase in the page title, the header and the body. If you put the phrase in your meta tag it will be displayed in bold font in the search results which will make it stand out even more.

Attention grabbing headline
To catch your readers attention you need a good headline, a headline that will need to intrigue your audience enough to make them feel that they absolutely have to read this post. It needs to be simple and to the point as well as containing valuable keywords. Here are some example headlines that really work:
How to ....
7 ways to successfully ....
Why you should do ..... to ....
Secrets that every ...... should know.
The secret formula for success in ......
5 quick and easy ways to ....
What every serious ...... should know about......
7 things every ..... should avoid to ......

A great design
Your blog needs to be inviting and although the content is what people are looking for the blog still needs to be visually appealing and reflect your brand. If your blog is just text based it's going to look cold and uninviting and lack interest, so you need to include compelling images to engage your audience. It is definitely a good idea to spend time researching different themes. Another thing to watch with your design is your side bar, make sure you have only what is absolutely necessary so you do not pull your readers attention away from the action you want them to take.

Formatting

You need to make it as easy as possible for your reader to read and digest your blog. If you format your blog with headings, bold subtitles and bullet points it will be a much more enjoyable to read than one long paragraph.

Ask a question at the end of your post

Asking a question at the end of your post is likely to provoke discussion. People like to think their opinions matter and it's a great way for your readers to interact and network with each other too. Make sure you answer any questions your readers ask, there is nothing worse than seeing bloggers ignoring their readers.

Tags

Tags help people to find your content within your blog and with the search engines, they also help to group related posts together.

11 THINGS EVERY BLOG SHOULD HAVE

An incentive to join your opt-in

One of the main goals of your blog is to captures leads. The majority of your readers will probably only read one of your blog posts so it's really important to try and get them on your opt-in list so they will keep reading your blog. You will need to make sure you give them some kind of incentive to complete the email capture form, like a free report, free ebook, or simply email updates.

An engaging image

A blog needs at least one image to make it look interesting and inviting. Blogs without images are simply boring. You can use your own images, stock photos, or images from photo sharing sites like Flickr.

Clear call-to-actions

You need to make it very clear both within and outside of your text. what you want your readers to do. This could be anything from signing up for email updates, a free trial, a free offer, a request for a quote, or more information on a product.

Email capture form

You can either include a prominent form on your blog or install a pop-up mail capture form. If you do install a pop-up then make sure the reader has a good few seconds to read the heading and start reading the article before the form pops up. It is also a good practice to put at least three email sign-up forms on the page, one below the article, one in the footer, and one on the top beside the article or right above it.

About section

Your "about" section is the introduction to you and your blog. It's probably the most viewed page of any blog. People like to know who is writing the blog and feel acquainted with that person, so you need to get your personality over in this section. Make sure you include your name and a picture of yourself. This will help your readers make a personal connection with you. A video of yourself is also a great a way of getting your readers acquainted too. Above all, focus on how you are going to help your readers, what problems you are going to solve for them, and introduce some of the topics you are going to talk about. Remember, your blog is about your audience's needs and not yours.

Contact page

A simple contact form works best but also make it really easy for people to reach out to you. Make sure you include all your social sharing buttons and an email capture form.

Easy to search archives

If the content of your blog posts is interesting your readers are going to want to read more so you need to make the previous blog posts easily accessible. On many sites it really is incredibly difficult to find content, so you need to get yourself a custom archive page. A search box at the top of your blog is a great idea for helping your readers find content.

Social sharing plug-ins

You need to include buttons or links to all the social networks where you have a presence. There are hundreds of plug-ins you can use to do this. Also make sure you have sharing buttons next to your articles as well.

RSS Feed

RSS (Rich Site Summary) is a format for delivering regularly changing content on the Internet. It saves you from checking the sites you are interested in for new content. Instead, it retrieves the content from sites you are interested in. Make sure you have the RSS feed and then have a clear call-to-action making it clear why they should subscribe to your feed. If you want to keep up-to-date with your favorite bloggers you can sign up to either My Yahoo, www.bloglines.com, or www.newsgator.com.

Comments section

Your blog needs a comment section which will encourage interaction and help you to build relationships with your readers. You can install Facebook comments easily with a WordPress plug-in. Disqus is another favorite comment provider.

A guest bloggers welcome page

Guest posting is becoming more and more important in the blogging community and making it obvious that you will accept guest posts is going to go a long way to building relationships with other bloggers. The benefits of having other people contributing to your blog are that you will have more valuable content on your site and more exposure if your guest blogger promotes their posts on their site. You may also gain from the opportunity to produce a guest post on their blog at a later date. Guest blogging is a top method of getting back links to your blog, which is essential for search engine optimization.

Privacy policy & terms of service pages

Make it clear your email readers are safe with you and you are not going to share their information with any other parties.

PROMOTING YOUR BLOG

If you want to run a successful blog, you cannot just rely on search to get it out into the blogosphere. You need to find other ways of promoting your content and getting found.

- **Promote on your social sites:** Posting your blog content on social sites is essential. You can connect your blog to Twitter and Facebook so your content is automatically shared. Or you can use Hootsuite or Tweetdec to share your content to multiple sites, which will save you time. When posting, use an image to grab your audience's attention and make sure you use popular hashtags for your topic which will open up more opportunities to being found by new people.

- **Guest blogging:** Guest blogging is a great way of gaining a larger following. It will also give your blog more exposure, credibility, and increase your inbound links, which is essential for SEO. Most bloggers allow guest bloggers to post their bio, including their social profiles and blog URL, on their site.

- **Social sharing buttons:** As mentioned previously, it is essential to have social sharing buttons next to your blog articles.

- **Comment on other blogs:** There is so much opportunity for you to promote yourself today with the number of blogs and social sites. If you comment on other peoples' blogs you can often leave a URL, but only if it is relevant to the article being commented on and you are adding some value to the article.

- **Website and email:** If you have a website then try and point people to your blog. You can do this by adding visual links on your "about" page and other pages. Also make sure you have a link to your blog in your email and send an email to your current contacts telling them about your blog.

- **Create a Google Adwords campaign:** If you are serious about driving traffic to your site and generating leads and you have your blog set up to catch leads and subscribers, an Adwords campaign may kick start your traffic while you are waiting for your blog to get found naturally in search results. Getting quick results like this will also allow you to see if your blog design and format is working and whether any incentives you are offering are enough to generate subscribers and leads.

- **Submit your blog to Reddit and Stumbleupon:** Both of these websites allow their users to rate web content. Reddit is a collection of webpages which have been submitted by its users. Stumbleupon is a collection of web pages that has been given the thumbs up. You can submit pages directly on its submit page or by installing the Firefox add-on or the Chrome extension. It is best not add too many of your own pages to Stumbleupon but make sure you add both the Reddit and Stumbleupon buttons to your blog so other people can.

THE ESSENTIAL WORDPRESS PLUGINS FOR YOUR BLOG

One of the best things about WordPress for your blog is that it is easy to customize and you need little or no technical or design knowledge to create a great blog. There are a ton of plug-ins you can install to make your site even better, but there are so many it is difficult to choose which ones are really important. To help you, here are some plug-ins that are essential for your blog:

- **The Facebook comments plug-in:** Installing Facebook comments into your blog can be tricky, but with this easy to use plug-in you can easily administer and customize Facebook comments from your WordPress site. Another plug-in, **Facebook comments SEO,** will insert a Facebook comment form, Open Graph tags, and insert all Facebook comments into your WordPress database for better search engine optimization. When it comes to spammers, Facebook with Open Graph is managing to weed out spammers and trolls with great effectiveness. Facebook allows you to login with Facebook,

Yahoo, and Microsoft Live.

- **Disqus comment system:** The other popular comment system Disqus replaces your WordPress comment system with comments hosted and powered by Disqus. It features threaded comments and replies, notifications and replies by email, aggregated comments and social mentions, full spam filtering, and black-and-white lists. Disqus allows you to login with Facebook, Twitter, and Google.

- **Facebook Chat:** This is great if you want to chat with your visitors in real time. When installed, Facebook Chat will display on the bottom right. This is great for supplying support on your site.

- **Broken Link Checker:** This essential plug-in scans your site and notifies you if it finds any broken links or missing images and then lets you replace the link with one that works.

- **RB Internal Links:** This plug-in assists you with internal links and cuts the risk of error pages and broken links.

- **Social Sharing Plugins:** There are numerous social sharing plugins available for WordPress. **Flare** is a simple yet eye-catching sharing bar that you can customize depending on which buttons you want to display. It helps to get you followed or 'liked' and helps get your content shared via posts, pages, and media types. The other great feature Flare has is that you can display your Flare at the top, bottom, or right of your post content. When Flare is displayed on the left and right of your posts, it follows your visitors down the page and conveniently hides when not needed. Other social sharing plug-ins include: **Floating Social Media Icon, Social Stickers,** and **Shareaholic,** to name but a few.

- **All-In-One Schema Rich Snippets:** Rich snippets are markup tags that webmasters can put in their sites in order to tell Google what type of content they have on their site so that Google can better display it in search results. It is basically a short summary of your page. Rich snippets are very interactive, let you stand out from your competition, and help with your search engine ranking. Unless you are a techie then implementing them can be tricky. However, this plug-in makes it really simple by giving you a meta box to fill in every time you create a new blog post.

- **Contact Form Plug-ins:** It is very important to make it easy for your visitors to contact you, and a form really does help with this. There are numerous plug-ins available for you to easily install, and here are a few: **Contact 7, Fast Secure Contact form, Contact form, and Contactme.**

- **Simple Pull Quote:** The Simple Pull Quote WordPpress plug-in provides an easy way for you to insert and pull quotes into your blog posts. This is great for bringing attention to important pieces of information and adding interest to a post.

- **Backup Plug-ins:** Backing up your files and database is essential. It may be that your hosting service provides this, but there are very good plug-ins that do this: Vaultpress, BackWPup, Backup buddy, and Backup.

- **Related Posts Plug-ins:** Related post plug-ins help your visitors to stay on your site by analyzing the content on your site and pulling in similar articles from your site for them to read. One of the most popular ones is **nrelate related** content which is simple to install and activate. **WordPress related posts** is another one.

- **Search Everything Plug-in:** This plug-in increases the ability of the WordPress search, and you can configure it to search for anything you choose.

- **Google Analytics Plugin:** The Google Analytics plug-in allows you to easily integrate Google Analytics using Google Analytics tracking code.

- **Google XML Sitemaps:** It is essential that the search engines can index your site and this plug-in will generate a special XML sitemap.

- **SEO Friendly images:** This plug-in automatically adds alt and title attributes to all your images, which helps to improve traffic from search engines.

- **Akismet (Comments and Spam):** The more traffic you receive, the more likely it is for you to receive spam and fake comments. Akismet checks your comments against Akismet web services to see if they look like spam or not and then lets you review it under your comments admin screen.
- **Social Author Bio:** Social Author Bio automatically adds an author box along with Gravatar and social icons on posts.
- **Thank Me Later:** This great little plug-in automatically sends a thank you note by email to anyone who has commented on your blog. You can personalize your email and set up exactly when you want to send it, and you can set it up to only send it out once or as a chain of emails. This plug-in is great for engaging people who comment on your blog, and you could use it to encourage people to join your opt-in.

MEASURING YOUR RESULTS

Measuring the success of your blog is crucial in order to steer your blog in the right direction so that your business can benefit from all the rewards a top blog can offer. Here are a number of ways you can measure your success:

Google Analytics

You can easily measure the number of social media shares, number of leads, subscribers, and comments on your blog. For more detailed information on your blog performance, setting up a Google Analytics account is essential and will offer you a wealth of detailed information so you can measure results, including the following:

- **The number of back links:** In the left side bar under **Standard Reports** you will find a section **Traffic Sources,** and then under **Social,** you will find **Trackbacks**. You will find here any web pages that have linked to any page of your site with the number of visits.
- **The number of visits:** Obviously this is one of the most

675

important statistics, and you will be able to easily see how many visits you have and information about where your traffic is coming from.

- **Page views:** You will be able to see which pages are generating the most interest, and therefore, you will be able to plan more content similar to this.

- **Keywords:** You can keep track of your success with how your traffic is being generated by keywords. You will be able to see if your optimization for certain keywords are working and whether your blog is being found by keywords that you had not considered. When you identify which keywords are the most popular, you can try and work them into other blog posts.

- **Conversions:** In Google Analytics you will also be able to track conversions, which is an action on your site that is important to your business. This could be a download, sign up, or purchase. You will need to define your goals in analytics in order to track the conversion. You will be able to see conversion rates and also the value of conversions if you set a monetary value. There are detailed instructions available in Google Analytics on how to set this up, or you can employ a web developer or specialist to do it.

THE ICING ON THE CAKE

FOLLOWING ALL THE steps, instructions, and strategies is going to go a long way to making your campaign succeed, but what does it take to make you really good? If you have ever followed or are following certain brands on social media, you will probably have discovered that there are certain brands or businesses that stand out from the crowd. These are the brands and businesses that seem bigger than their products. These are the ones who usually have a sizeable and highly targeted audience, the best quality content, the greatest amount of interaction and engagement, and often post viral content. They literally have their audience hanging on their every word and get the highest open rates for their emails. They appear to understand their audience and relate to them by going out of their way by either helping them to achieve their dreams, calm their fears or confirm their suspicions, and offer them incredible value. It is obvious by the interaction that they have built a loving and respecting community, and you can be almost sure that all this is transferring to their balance sheets. These businesses are what I call 'The Social Media Superstars.' They are the game changers and they truly know how to leverage the power of social media to work for their business.

These 'Social Media Superstars' can often be compared to those party animals who always seem to be the most popular at any party and are more often than not surrounded by an audience of engaged and happy people having a great time. These people also always seem to be the most interesting, the most interested, the most charismatic, and the most engaged. They almost always tend to be good listeners as well. So how can you emulate this scenario, and what does it take to stand out from the crowd in social media marketing?

It's all about your audience and a few other things!

The reasons these individuals, businesses, and brands are good at social media marketing is not because they have particular powers. It's not by chance or coincidence. It's because they know that it's all about the audience and a few other things!

Of course your aim is to ultimately benefit your business, but in order to do this you need to make it all about your audience and what they want. If you give them what they want by either making their life better or easier in some way or solving a problem they may have, then you are going to build a valuable base of fans who trust you, open your emails, and are ready to go to the next step and buy your product. You will find that your fans will become ambassadors and advocates and will then be doing the work for you by sharing your content and promoting your brand in the most powerful way, word-of-mouth. To achieve this and stand out from the crowd, you need to go the extra mile by doing the following:

- Being fully committed and positive about your campaign and in it for the long term
- Totally believing in what you are offering. This could be your product, your service, or yourself, if you are a personal brand.
- Making it all about your audience, knowing exactly who they are, what makes them tick, what they need, and how to connect with them
- Putting your audience's needs above your own and demonstrating the rich content and service you provide
- Putting the relationship with your audience first, by listening to them, understanding them, and embracing conversation where you can
- Offering your audience incredible value with free information and advice
- Being authentic and true to your brand

So if there is one piece of insight I want to leave you with, it is this:

IT'S ALL ABOUT YOUR AUDIENCE and WHAT THEY WANT

I really hope you have enjoyed the book, have found it of great value, and that you will continue using it as your manual for your success on social media. The world of social media is continually changing, and it is my commitment to keep updating the books when these changes happen. If you would like to continue receiving these social media updates by email, please sign up at www.alexstearn.com

I will also be continually posting helpful and inspirational tips, building a community on all the major social media platforms and look forward to connecting with you on any of your preferred social networks.

Lastly I would love your feedback about the book and would be very grateful if you could take just a moment to leave a review on Amazon and of course please feel fee to contact me if you have any questions at alex@alexstearn.com

Website: www.alexstearn.com

www.facebook.com/alexandrastearn
www.instagram.com/alexstearn
www.twitter.com/alexstearncom
www.pinterest.com/alexstearn
www.google.com/+/alexstearn
www.alexstearn.tumblr.com
www.youtube.com/alexstearn
www.linkedin.com/in/alexstearn

We'd love to hear from you

Thank you for your recent purchase of 'Make Social Media Work for your Business' I really hope you have enjoyed the book and your business will benefit greatly.

If you have any questions about the book or about social media marketing in general, please do not hesitate to contact me by email at **alex@alexstearn.com** or Facebook at **www.facebook.com/alexandrastearn** and I will do my best to reply as soon as possible. I also offer regular updates, ebooks and social media tips in my newsletter at www.alexstearn.com and a group on Facebook which is all about supporting each other in our social media efforts and networking. Would love you to come and join us at this link
http://bit.ly/yourgroup

Lastly, if you have enjoyed the book I would be so grateful if you could leave a review on Amazon, your feedback is so valuable and also helps others benefit from your experience.

Looking forward to seeing you soon in the group

Printed in Great Britain
by Amazon